THAT TIME I GOT REINCARNATED AS A

SLIME

11

Author: **FUSE**

Artist: **TAIKI KAWAKAMI**

Character design: **MITZ VAH**

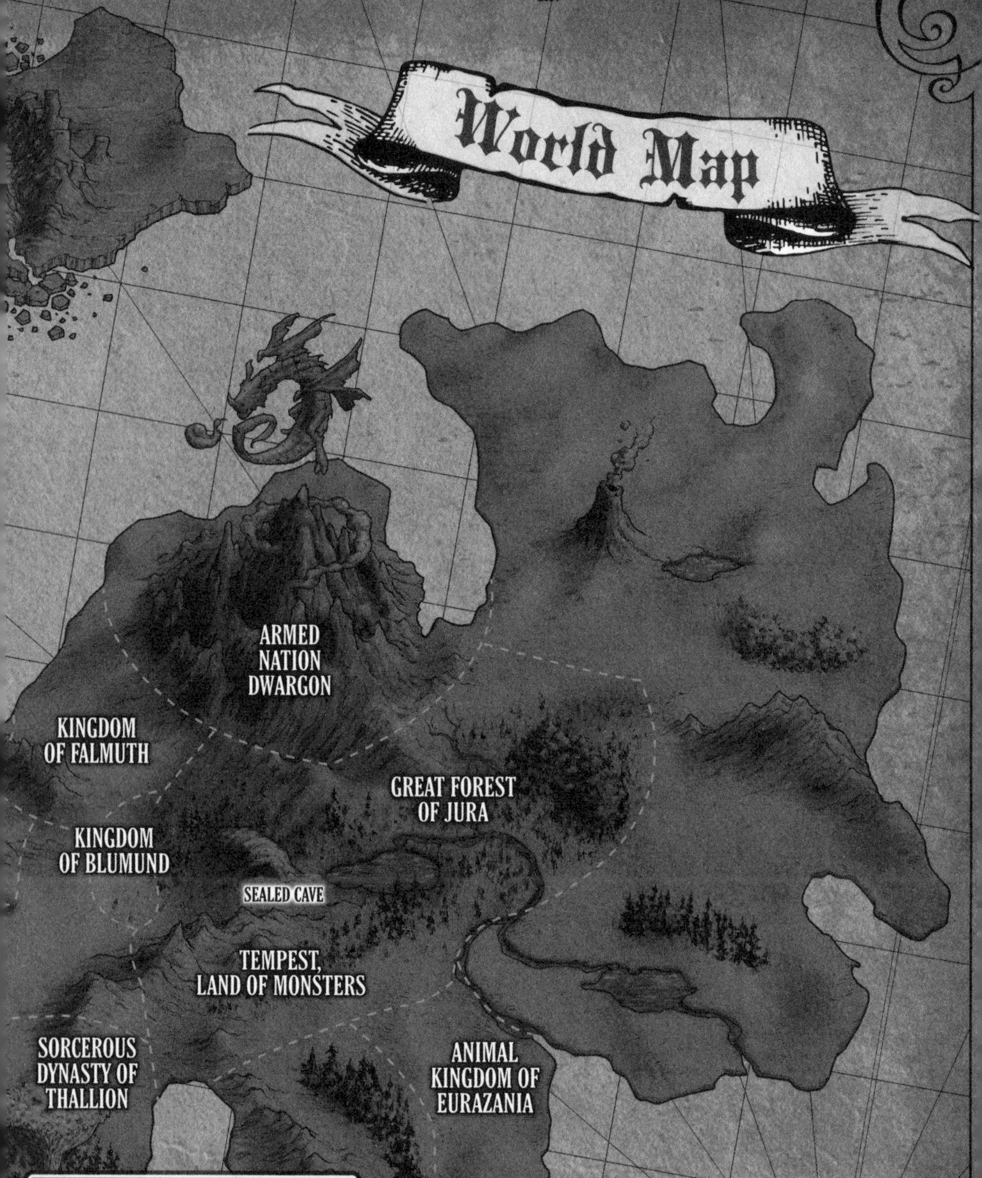
World Map
ARMED NATION DWARGON
KINGDOM OF FALMUTH
GREAT FOREST OF JURA
KINGDOM OF BLUMUND
SEALED CAVE
TEMPEST, LAND OF MONSTERS
SORCEROUS DYNASTY OF THALLION
ANIMAL KINGDOM OF EURAZANIA

PLOT SUMMARY

Rimuru headed to the human Kingdom of Engrassia to find the children left behind by the late Shizu. Along the way, between registering as an adventurer in Blumund and engaging in top-secret negotiations with the King, he learned about the challenges in dealing with humans. Then, when he reached Engrassia, he met another transplant from Japan, Yuuki Kagurazaka, and was able to meet Shizu's five orphaned foster children, who were students at Yuuki's school. But because they were other-worlders brought here by incomplete summoning, they had little time left to live. Rimuru then becomes their teacher with the aim of saving their lives... ▼

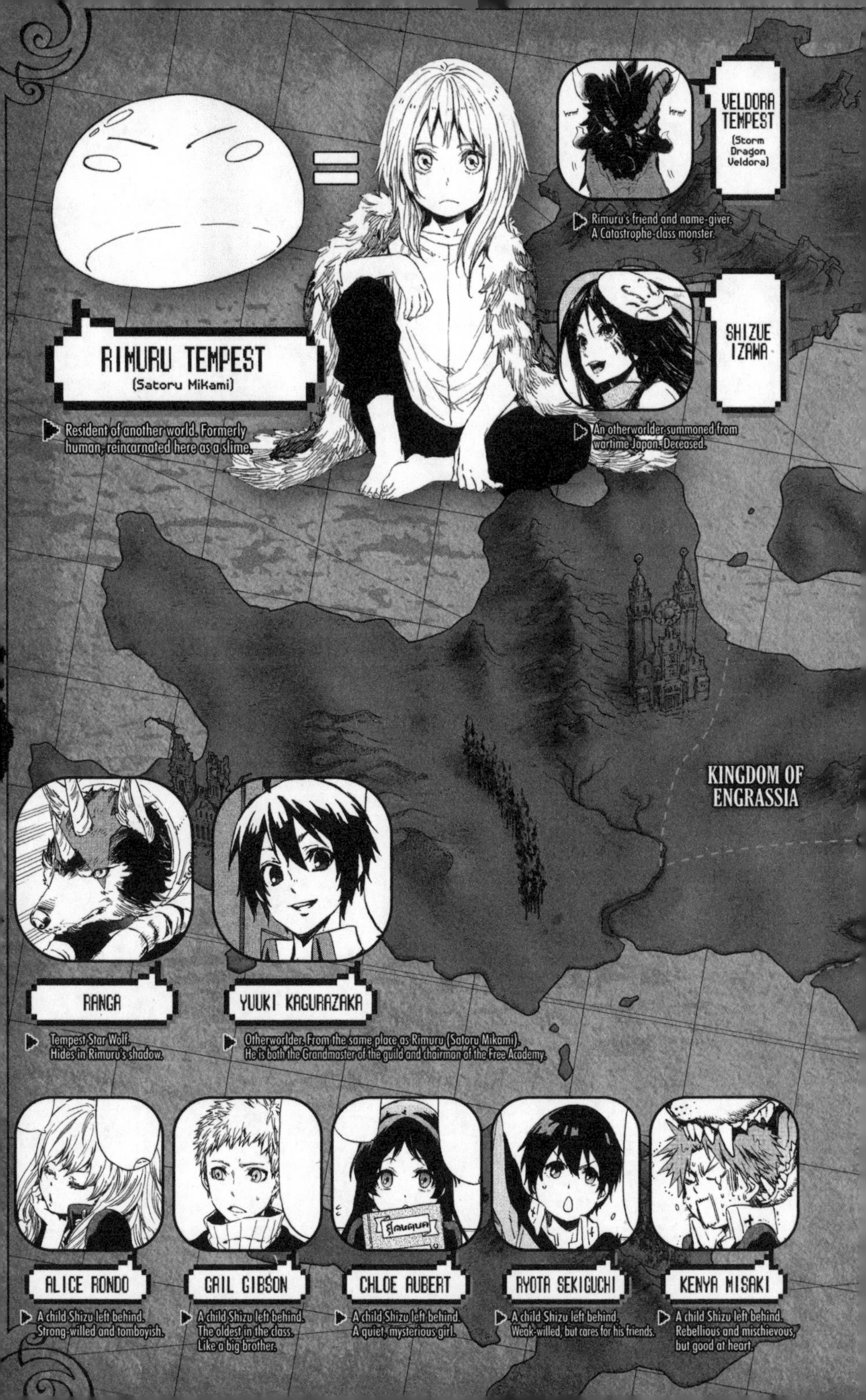

RIMURU TEMPEST
(Satoru Mikami)
Resident of another world. Formerly human, reincarnated here as a slime.
VELDORA TEMPEST
(Storm Dragon Veldora)
Rimuru's friend and name-giver. A Catastrophe-class monster.
SHIZUE IZAWA
An otherworlder summoned from wartime Japan. Deceased.
KINGDOM OF ENGRASSIA
RANGA
Tempest Star Wolf. Hides in Rimuru's shadow.
YUUKI KAGURAZAKA
Otherworlder. From the same place as Rimuru (Satoru Mikami). He is both the Grandmaster of the guild and chairman of the Free Academy.
ALICE RONDO
A child Shizu left behind. Strong-willed and tomboyish.
GAIL GIBSON
A child Shizu left behind. The oldest in the class. Like a big brother.
CHLOE AUBERT
A child Shizu left behind. A quiet, mysterious girl.
RYOTA SEKIGUCHI
A child Shizu left behind. Weak-willed, but cares for his friends.
KENYA MISAKI
A child Shizu left behind. Rebellious and mischievous, but good at heart.

CONTENTS

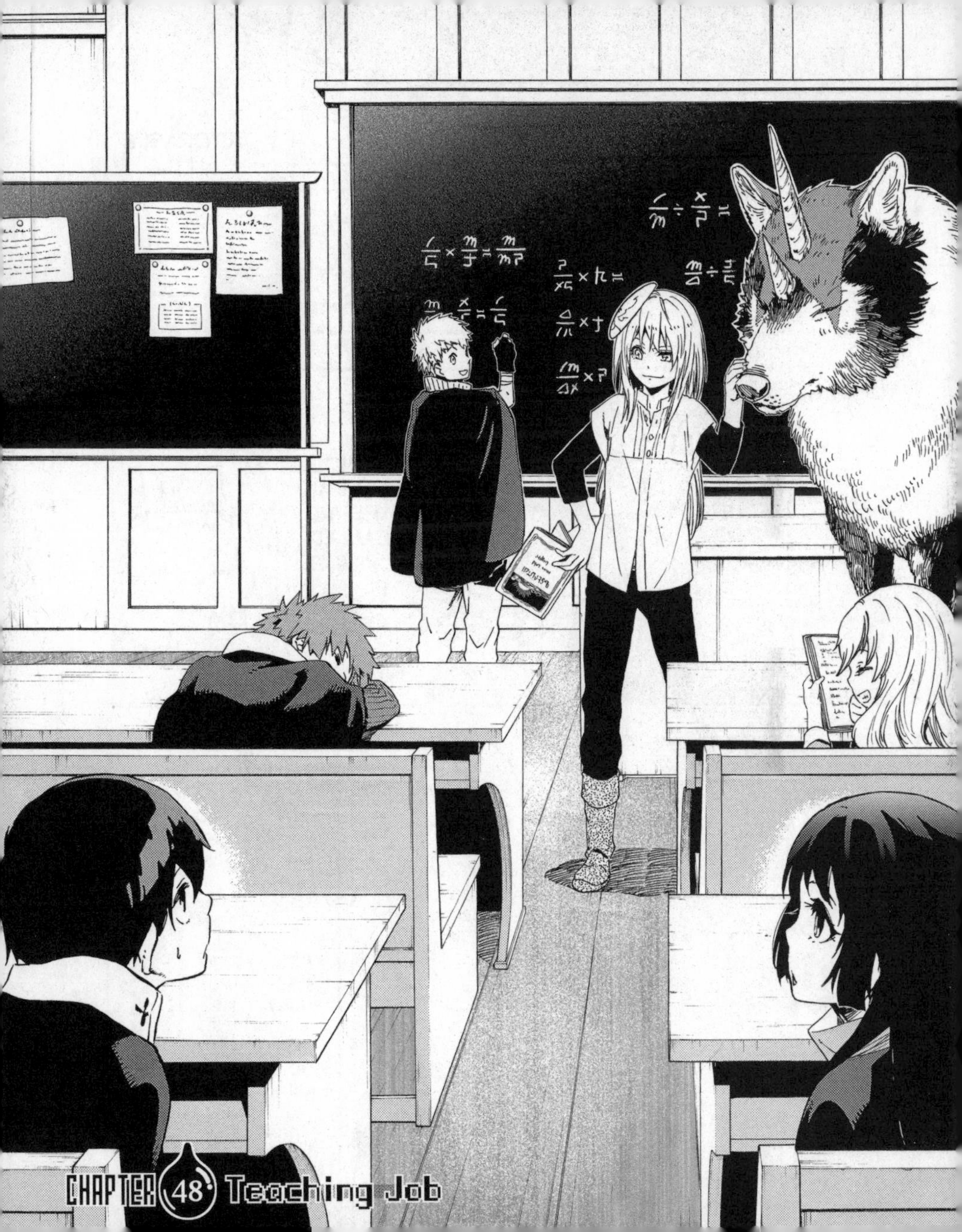

CHAPTER 48 Teaching Job

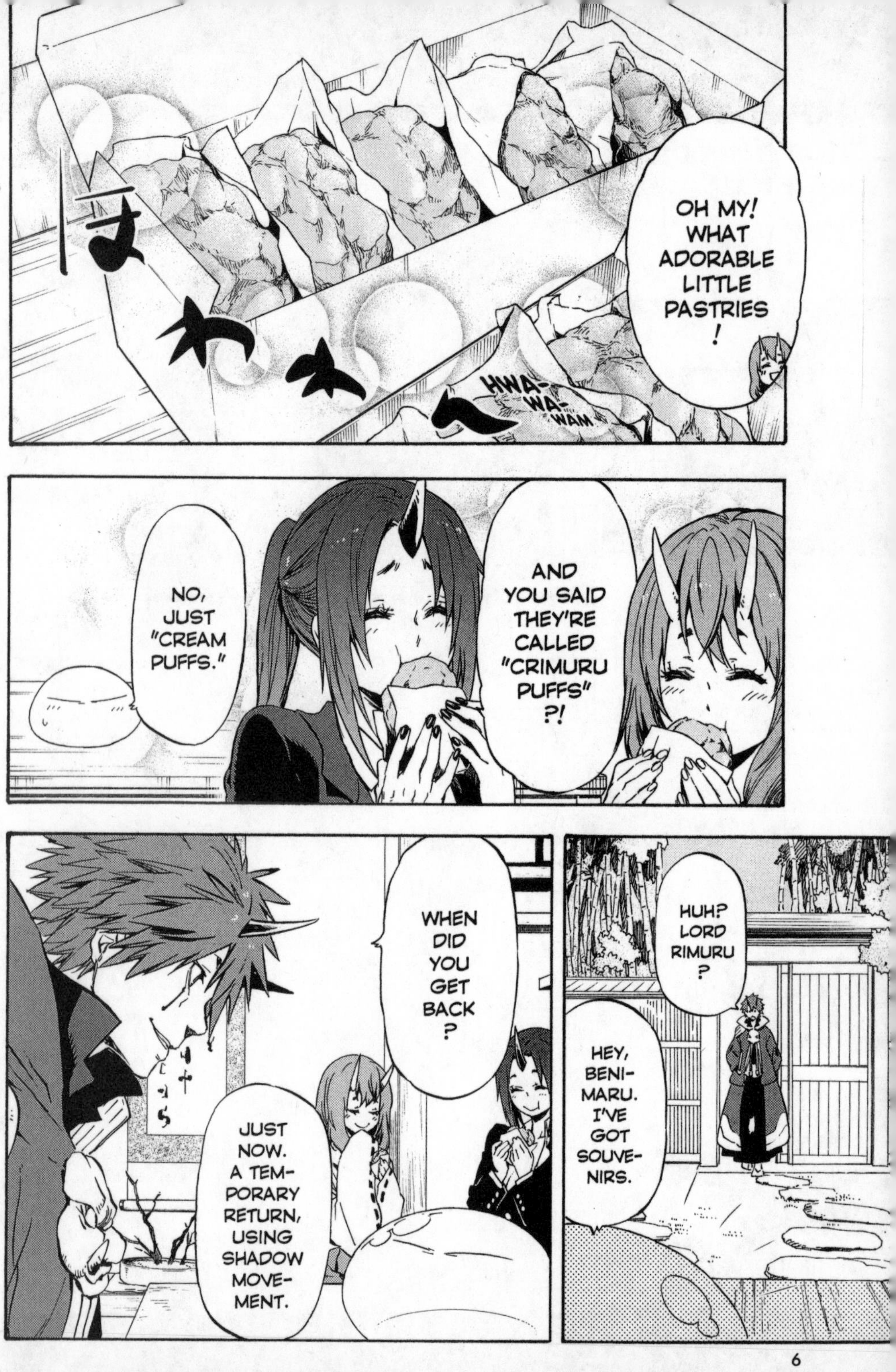
OH MY! WHAT ADORABLE LITTLE PASTRIES!
HWA-WA-WAM
AND YOU SAID THEY'RE CALLED "CRIMURU PUFFS"?!
NO, JUST "CREAM PUFFS."
HUH? LORD RIMURU?
HEY, BENI-MARU. I'VE GOT SOUVE-NIRS.
WHEN DID YOU GET BACK?
JUST NOW. A TEM-PORARY RETURN, USING SHADOW MOVE-MENT.

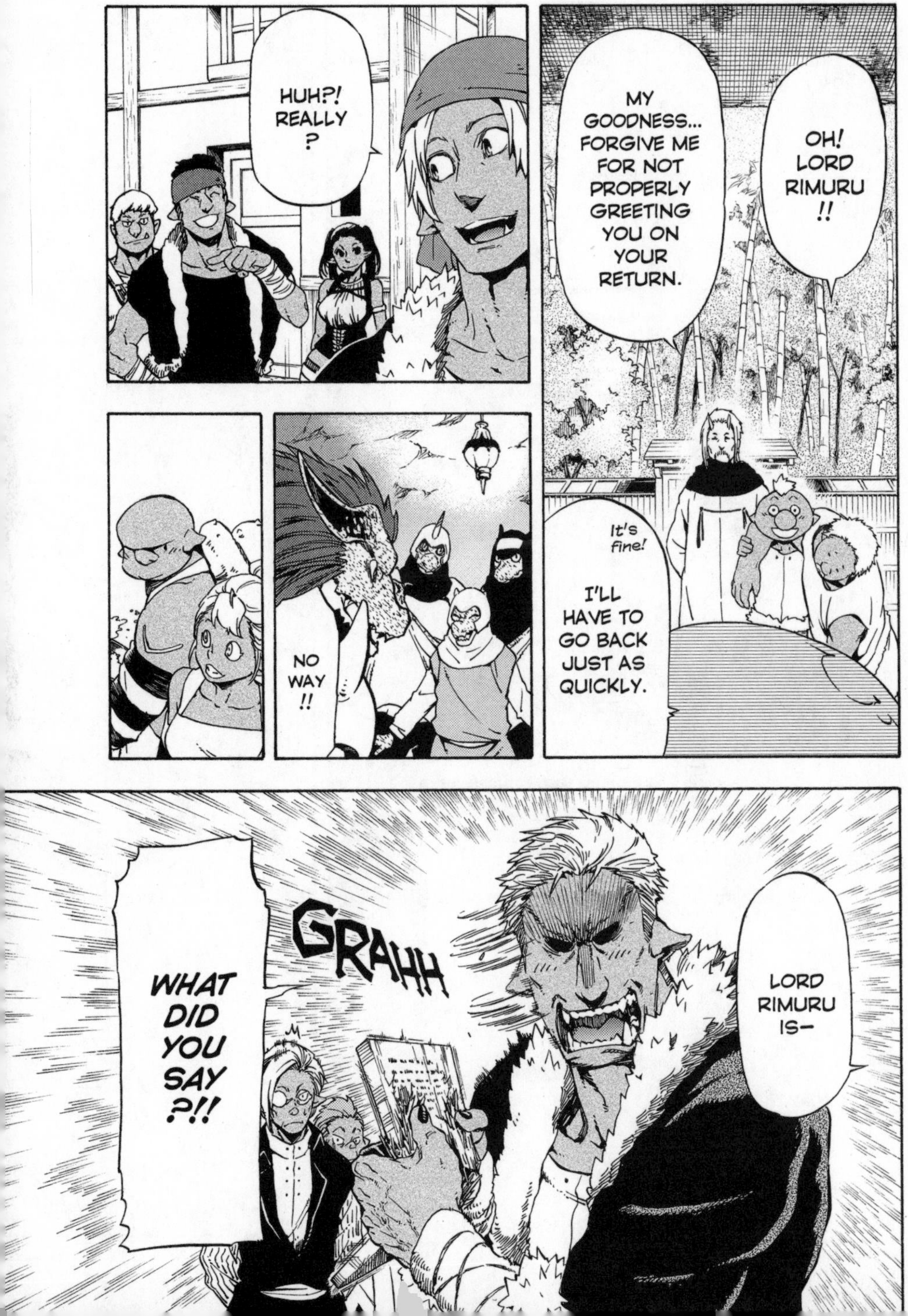
OH! LORD RIMURU!!
MY GOODNESS... FORGIVE ME FOR NOT PROPERLY GREETING YOU ON YOUR RETURN.
It's fine!
I'LL HAVE TO GO BACK JUST AS QUICKLY.
HUH?! REALLY?
NO WAY!!
LORD RIMURU IS—
GRAHH
WHAT DID YOU SAY?!!

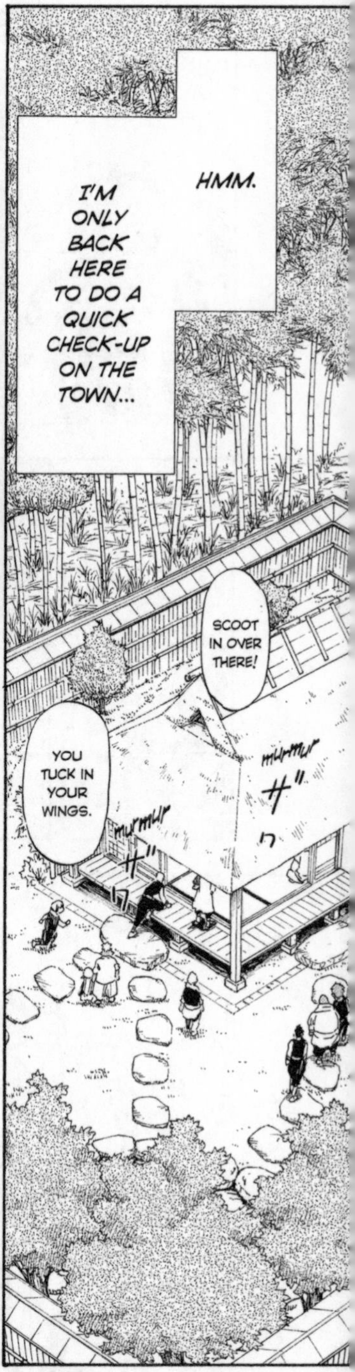
HMM.
I'M ONLY BACK HERE TO DO A QUICK CHECK-UP ON THE TOWN...
SCOOT IN OVER THERE!
murmur
YOU TUCK IN YOUR WINGS.
murmur

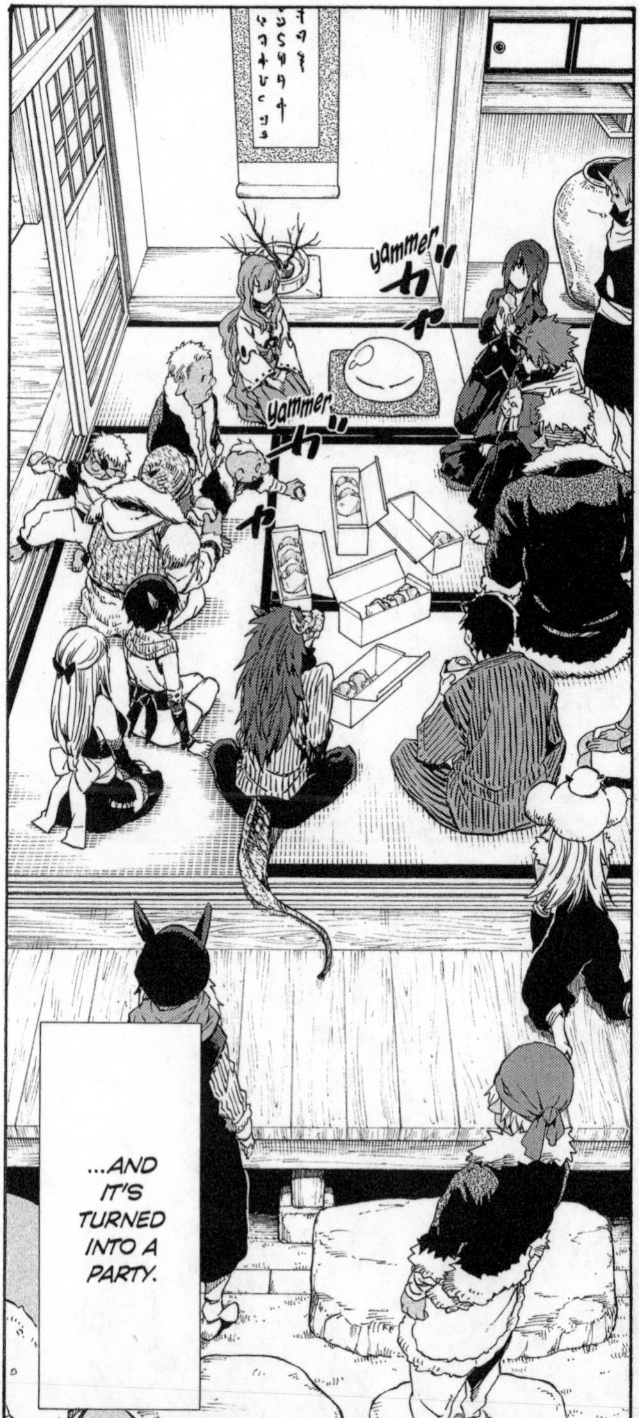
yammer
yammer
...AND IT'S TURNED INTO A PARTY.

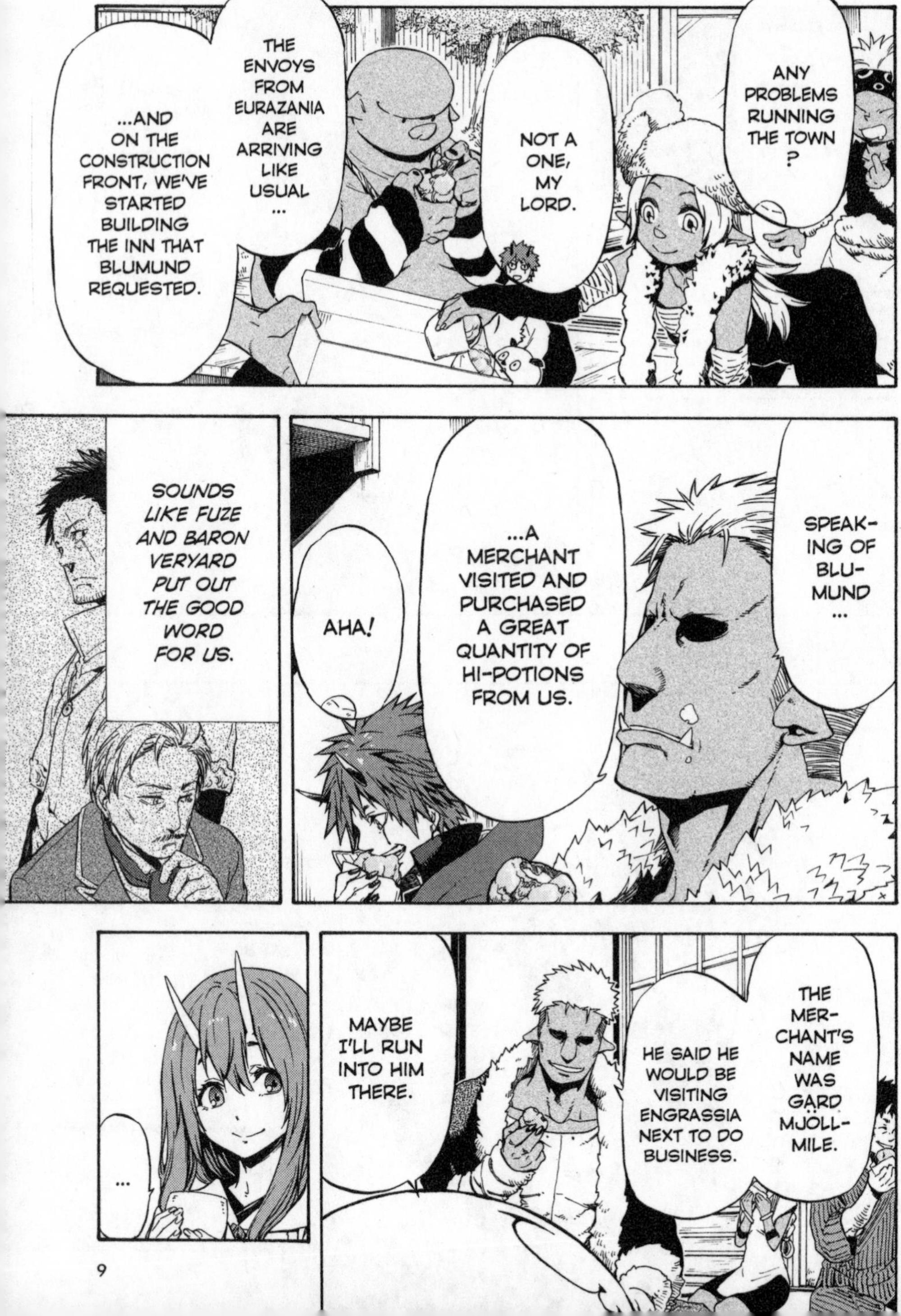
ANY PROBLEMS RUNNING THE TOWN?
NOT A ONE, MY LORD.
THE ENVOYS FROM EURAZANIA ARE ARRIVING LIKE USUAL...
...AND ON THE CONSTRUCTION FRONT, WE'VE STARTED BUILDING THE INN THAT BLUMUND REQUESTED.
SPEAKING OF BLUMUND...
...A MERCHANT VISITED AND PURCHASED A GREAT QUANTITY OF HI-POTIONS FROM US.
AHA!
SOUNDS LIKE FUZE AND BARON VERYARD PUT OUT THE GOOD WORD FOR US.
THE MERCHANT'S NAME WAS GARD MJÖLLMILE.
HE SAID HE WOULD BE VISITING ENGRASSIA NEXT TO DO BUSINESS.
MAYBE I'LL RUN INTO HIM THERE.
...

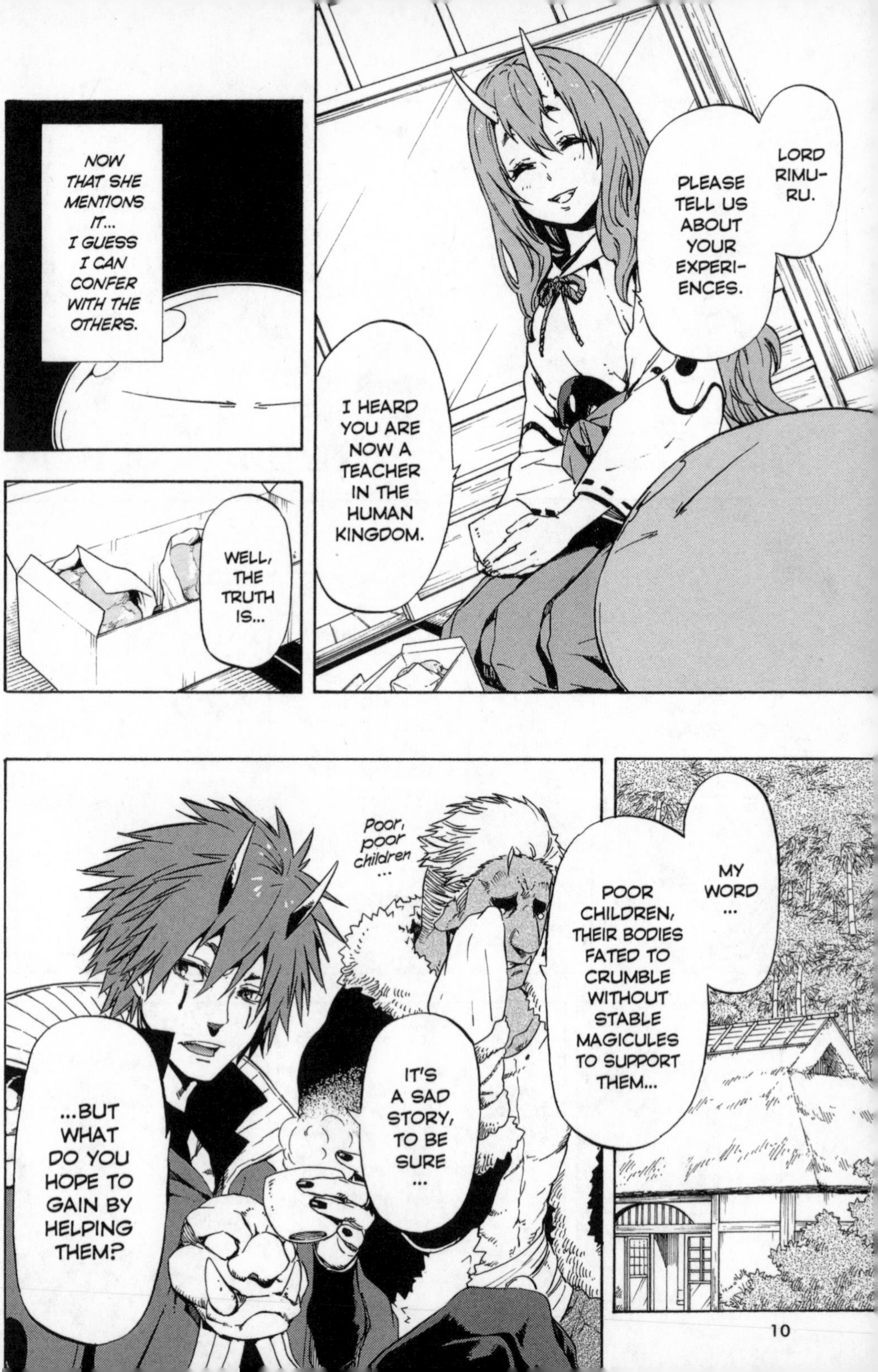
LORD RIMU-RU.
PLEASE TELL US ABOUT YOUR EXPERIENCES.
I HEARD YOU ARE NOW A TEACHER IN THE HUMAN KINGDOM.
NOW THAT SHE MENTIONS IT... I GUESS I CAN CONFER WITH THE OTHERS.
WELL, THE TRUTH IS...
MY WORD...
POOR CHILDREN, THEIR BODIES FATED TO CRUMBLE WITHOUT STABLE MAGICULES TO SUPPORT THEM...
Poor, poor children...
IT'S A SAD STORY, TO BE SURE...
...BUT WHAT DO YOU HOPE TO GAIN BY HELPING THEM?

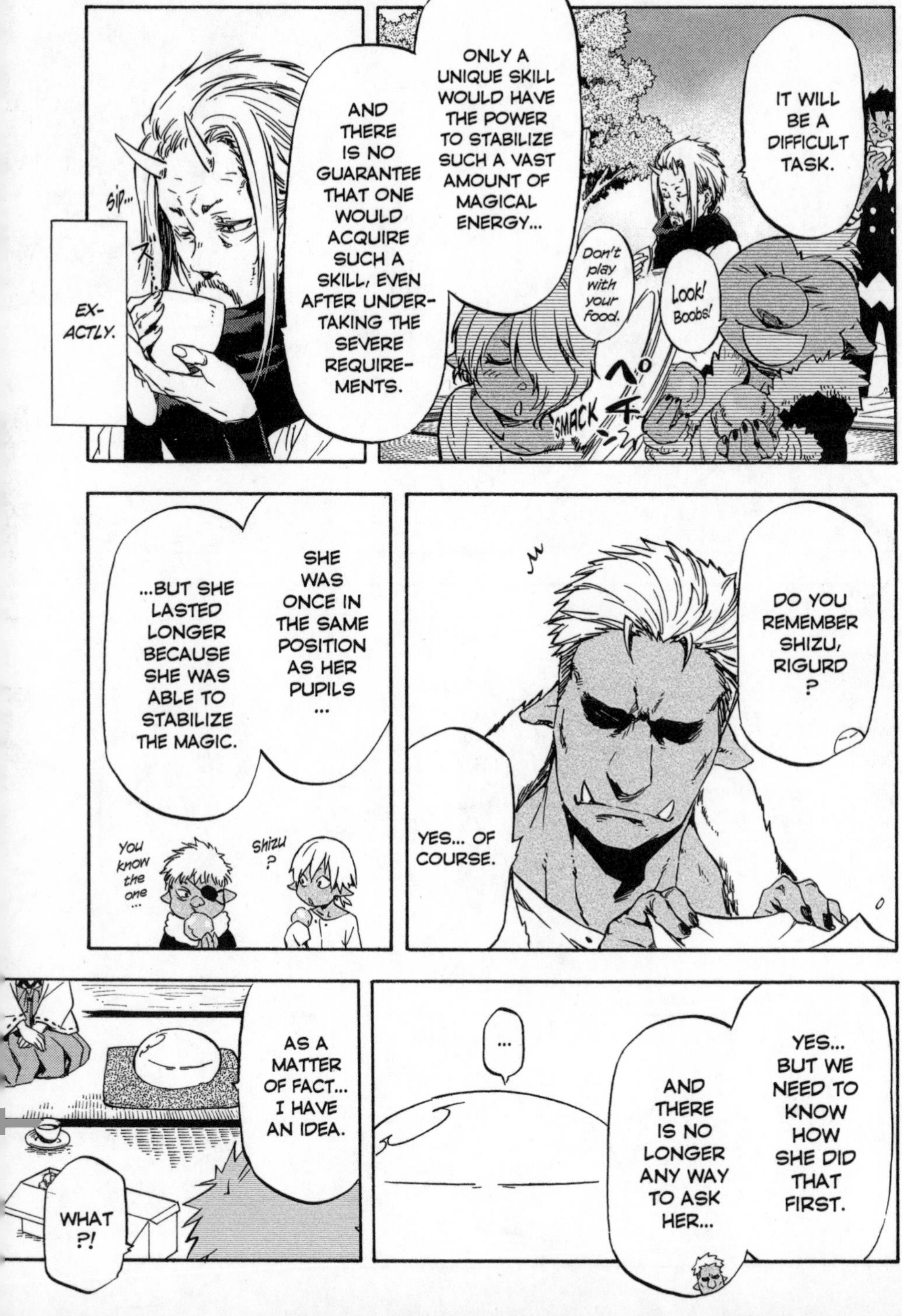
IT WILL BE A DIFFICULT TASK.
ONLY A UNIQUE SKILL WOULD HAVE THE POWER TO STABILIZE SUCH A VAST AMOUNT OF MAGICAL ENERGY...
AND THERE IS NO GUARANTEE THAT ONE WOULD ACQUIRE SUCH A SKILL, EVEN AFTER UNDER-TAKING THE SEVERE REQUIRE-MENTS.
Look! Boobs!
Don't play with your food.
SMACK
EX-ACTLY.
Sip...
DO YOU REMEMBER SHIZU, RIGURD?
YES... OF COURSE.
SHE WAS ONCE IN THE SAME POSITION AS HER PUPILS...
...BUT SHE LASTED LONGER BECAUSE SHE WAS ABLE TO STABILIZE THE MAGIC.
Shizu?
You know the one...
YES... BUT WE NEED TO KNOW HOW SHE DID THAT FIRST.
AND THERE IS NO LONGER ANY WAY TO ASK HER...
...
AS A MATTER OF FACT... I HAVE AN IDEA.
WHAT?!

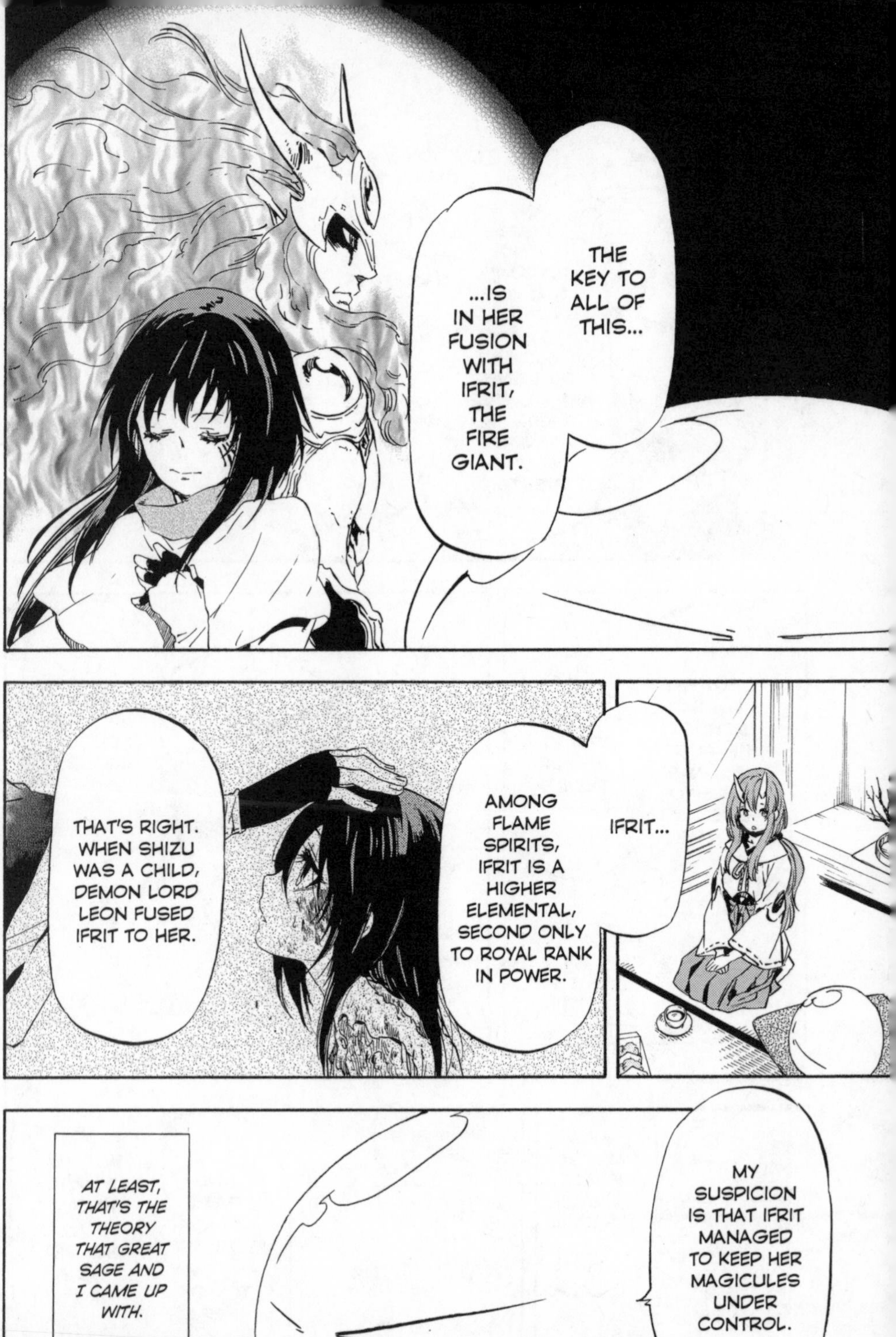
THE KEY TO ALL OF THIS...
...IS IN HER FUSION WITH IFRIT, THE FIRE GIANT.
IFRIT...
AMONG FLAME SPIRITS, IFRIT IS A HIGHER ELEMENTAL, SECOND ONLY TO ROYAL RANK IN POWER.
THAT'S RIGHT. WHEN SHIZU WAS A CHILD, DEMON LORD LEON FUSED IFRIT TO HER.
MY SUSPICION IS THAT IFRIT MANAGED TO KEEP HER MAGICULES UNDER CONTROL.
AT LEAST, THAT'S THE THEORY THAT GREAT SAGE AND I CAME UP WITH.

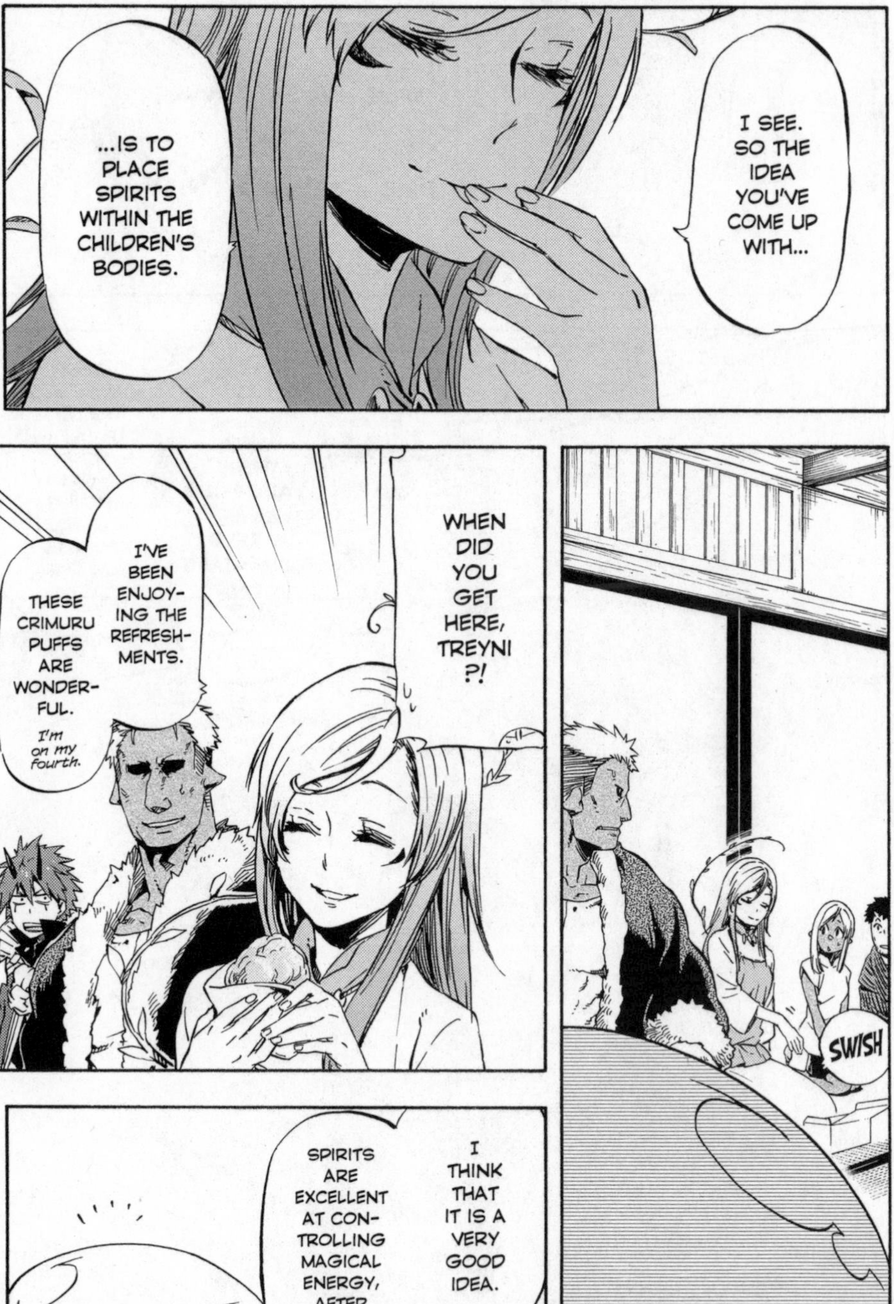
I SEE. SO THE IDEA YOU'VE COME UP WITH...
...IS TO PLACE SPIRITS WITHIN THE CHILDREN'S BODIES.
SWISH
WHEN DID YOU GET HERE, TREYNI?!
I'VE BEEN ENJOY-ING THE REFRESH-MENTS.
THESE CRIMURU PUFFS ARE WONDER-FUL.
I'm on my fourth.
FOURTH?!
I THINK THAT IT IS A VERY GOOD IDEA.
SPIRITS ARE EXCELLENT AT CON-TROLLING MAGICAL ENERGY, AFTER ALL.

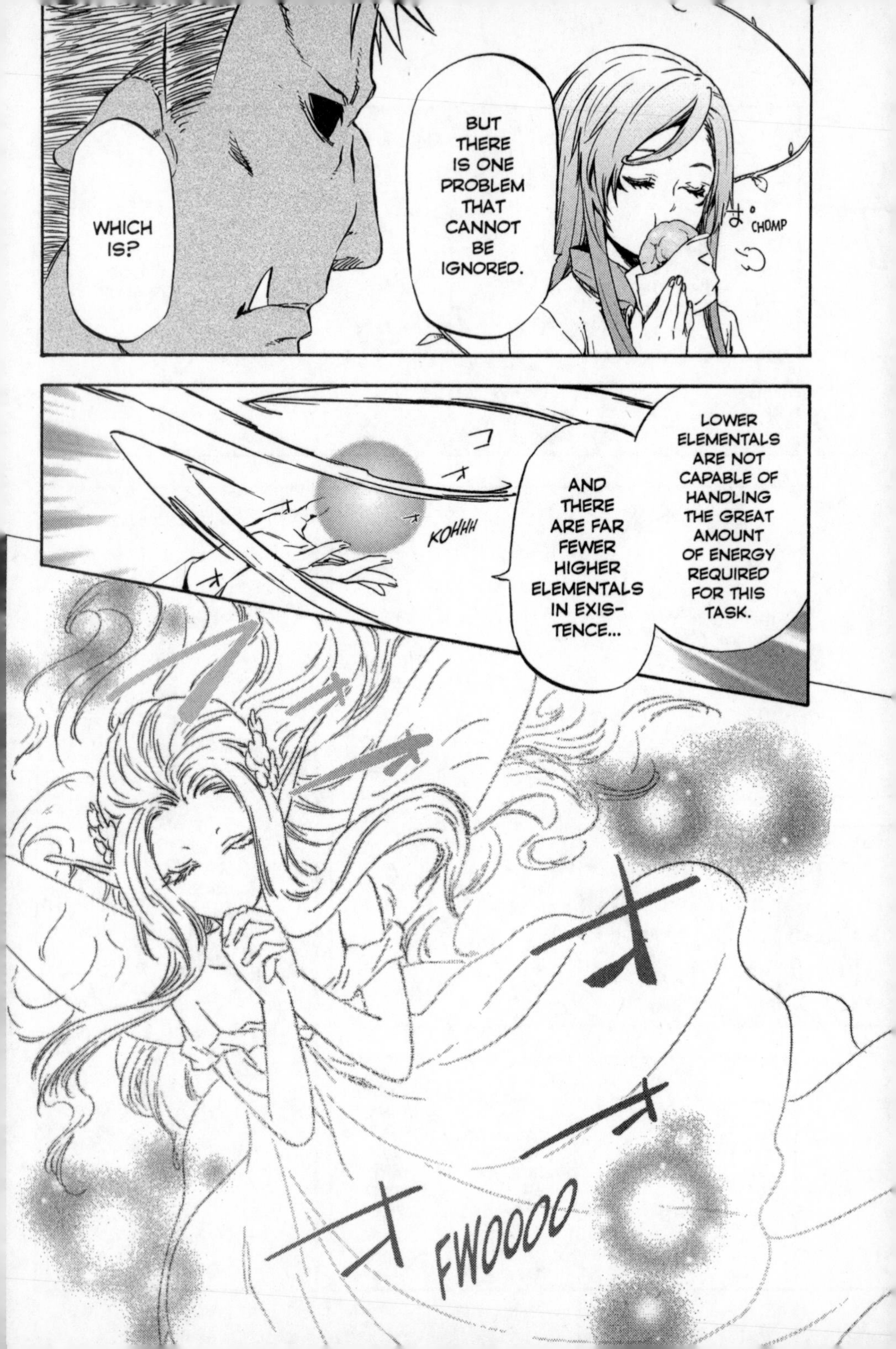
CHOMP
BUT THERE IS ONE PROBLEM THAT CANNOT BE IGNORED.
WHICH IS?
LOWER ELEMENTALS ARE NOT CAPABLE OF HANDLING THE GREAT AMOUNT OF ENERGY REQUIRED FOR THIS TASK.
AND THERE ARE FAR FEWER HIGHER ELEMENTALS IN EXIS-TENCE...
KOHHH
FWOOOO

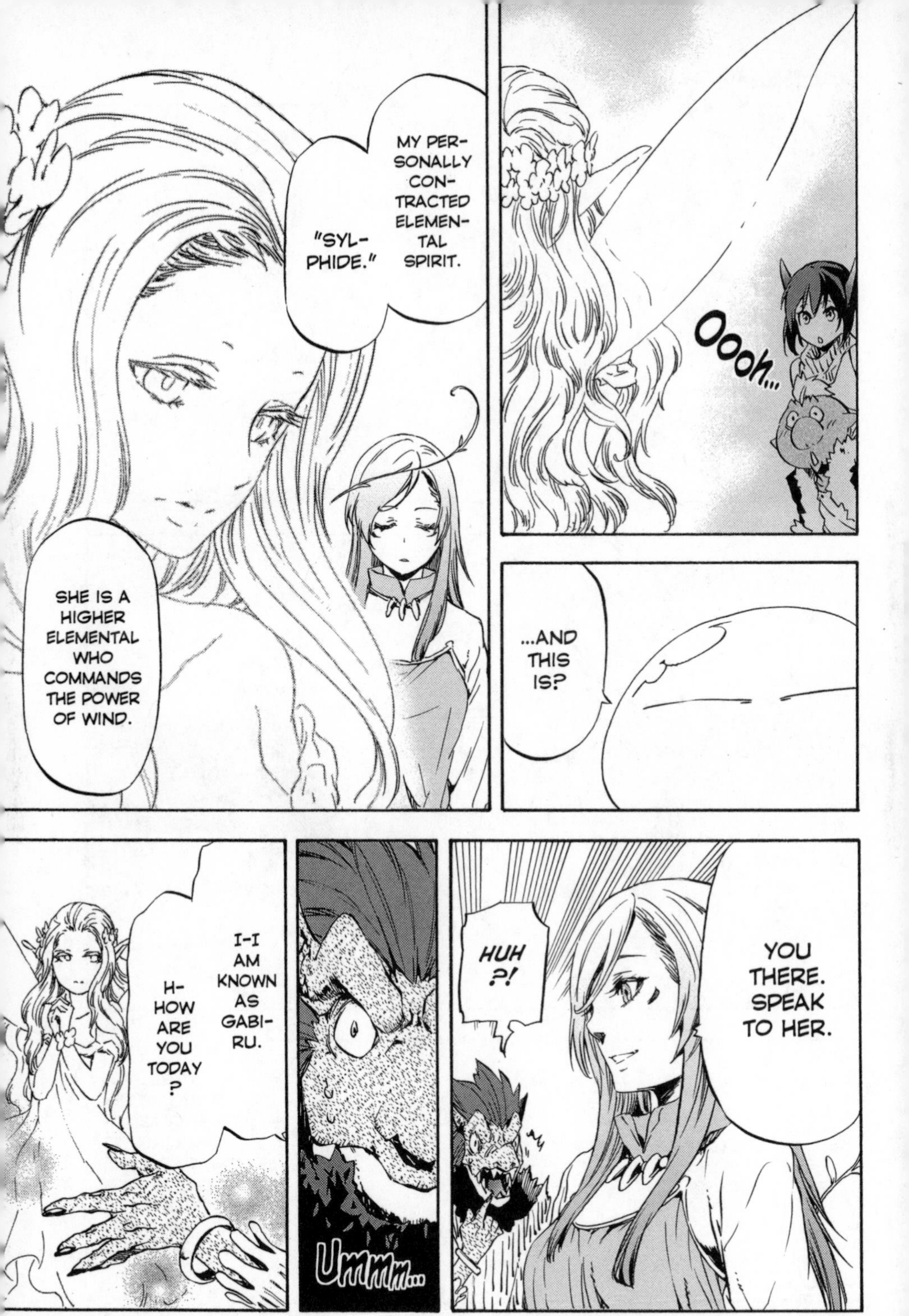
Oooh...
...AND THIS IS?
MY PERSONALLY CONTRACTED ELEMENTAL SPIRIT.
"SYLPHIDE."
SHE IS A HIGHER ELEMENTAL WHO COMMANDS THE POWER OF WIND.
YOU THERE. SPEAK TO HER.
HUH?!
Ummm...
I-I AM KNOWN AS GABIRU.
H-HOW ARE YOU TODAY?

GONNNG

Hmph!

STARE...

AS YOU CAN SEE, HIGHER ELEMENTALS ARE CAPRICIOUS.

IF THEY DO NOT LIKE YOU, THEY WILL NOT OFFER YOU THEIR HELP.

WOW, THAT WAS HARSH.

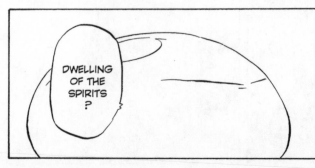

DWELLING OF THE SPIRITS ?

STILL... IF YOU WERE TO SUCCEED IN TRAVELING TO THE DWELLING OF THE SPIRITS, YOU MIGHT FIND A SPIRIT WITH AN AGREEABLE AFFINITY...

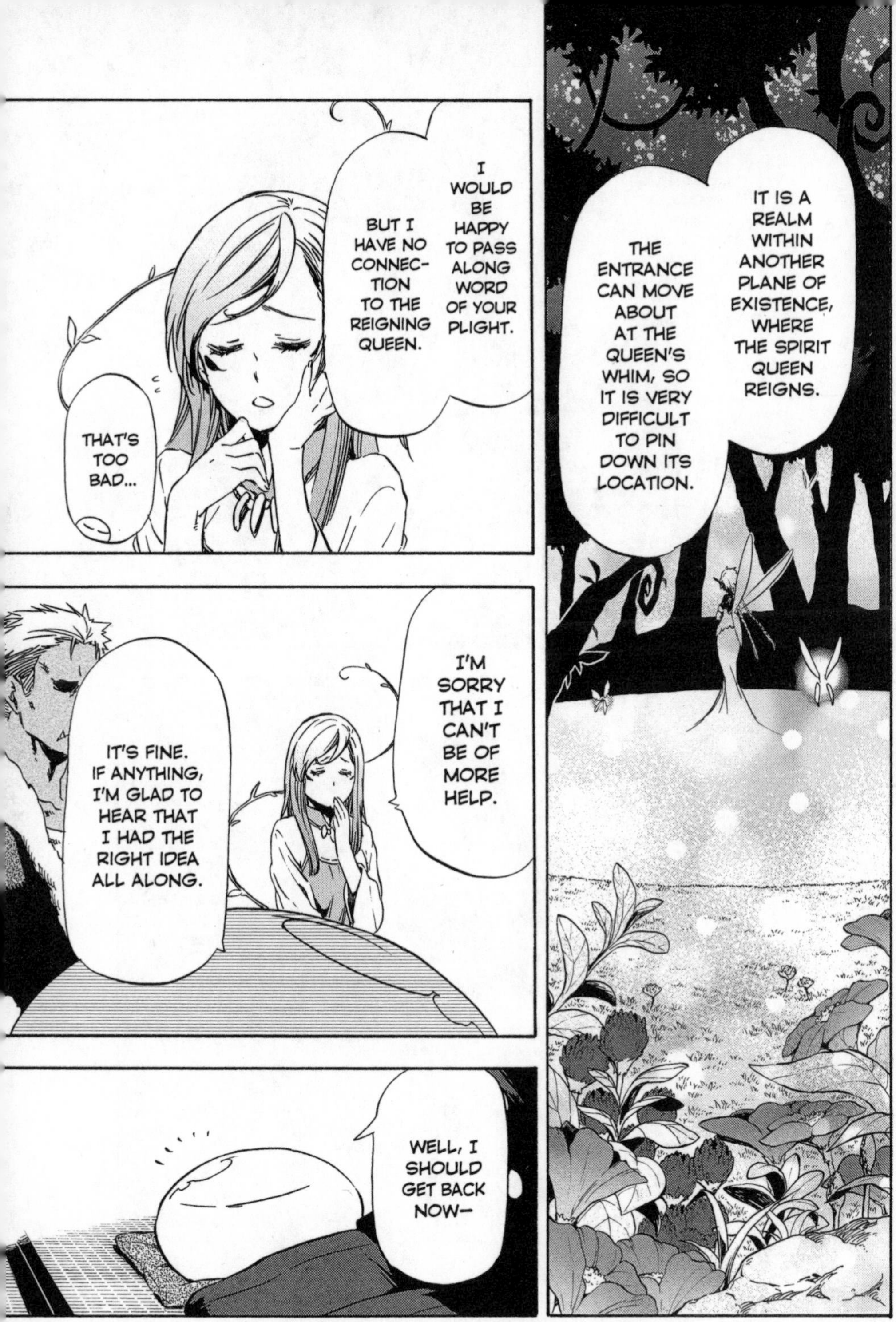
IT IS A REALM WITHIN ANOTHER PLANE OF EXISTENCE, WHERE THE SPIRIT QUEEN REIGNS.
THE ENTRANCE CAN MOVE ABOUT AT THE QUEEN'S WHIM, SO IT IS VERY DIFFICULT TO PIN DOWN ITS LOCATION.
I WOULD BE HAPPY TO PASS ALONG WORD OF YOUR PLIGHT.
BUT I HAVE NO CONNEC-TION TO THE REIGNING QUEEN.
THAT'S TOO BAD...
I'M SORRY THAT I CAN'T BE OF MORE HELP.
IT'S FINE. IF ANYTHING, I'M GLAD TO HEAR THAT I HAD THE RIGHT IDEA ALL ALONG.
WELL, I SHOULD GET BACK NOW—

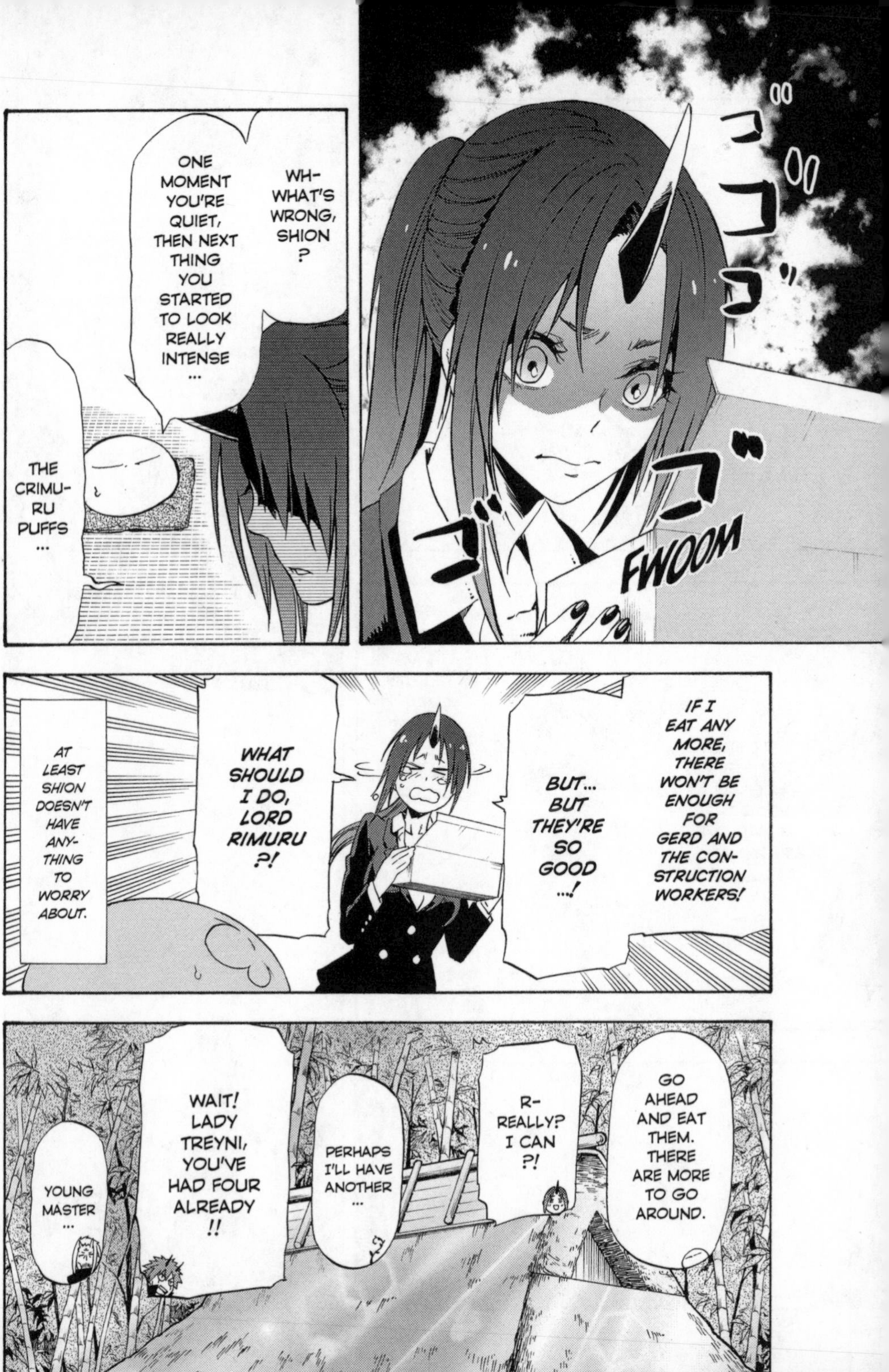

ゴゴゴ
ゴゴ
FWOOM
WH- WHAT'S WRONG, SHION?
ONE MOMENT YOU'RE QUIET, THEN NEXT THING YOU STARTED TO LOOK REALLY INTENSE...
THE CRIMU-RU PUFFS...
IF I EAT ANY MORE, THERE WON'T BE ENOUGH FOR GERD AND THE CON-STRUCTION WORKERS!
BUT... BUT THEY'RE SO GOOD...!
WHAT SHOULD I DO, LORD RIMURU?!
AT LEAST SHION DOESN'T HAVE ANY-THING TO WORRY ABOUT.
GO AHEAD AND EAT THEM. THERE ARE MORE TO GO AROUND.
R- REALLY? I CAN?!
PERHAPS I'LL HAVE ANOTHER...
WAIT! LADY TREYNI, YOU'VE HAD FOUR ALREADY!!
YOUNG MASTER...

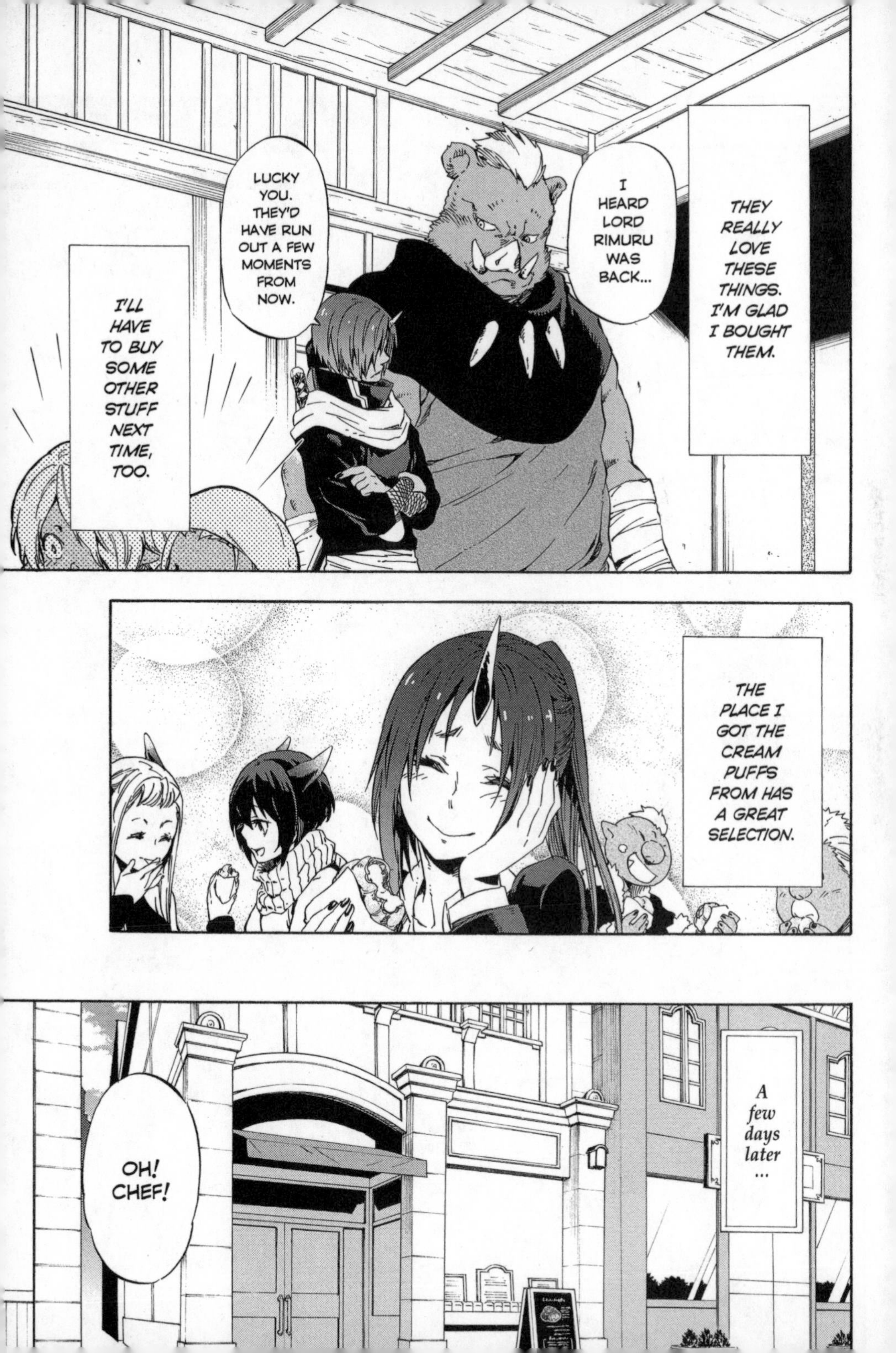
THEY REALLY LOVE THESE THINGS. I'M GLAD I BOUGHT THEM.
I HEARD LORD RIMURU WAS BACK...
LUCKY YOU. THEY'D HAVE RUN OUT A FEW MOMENTS FROM NOW.
I'LL HAVE TO BUY SOME OTHER STUFF NEXT TIME, TOO.
THE PLACE I GOT THE CREAM PUFFS FROM HAS A GREAT SELECTION.
A few days later...
OH! CHEF!

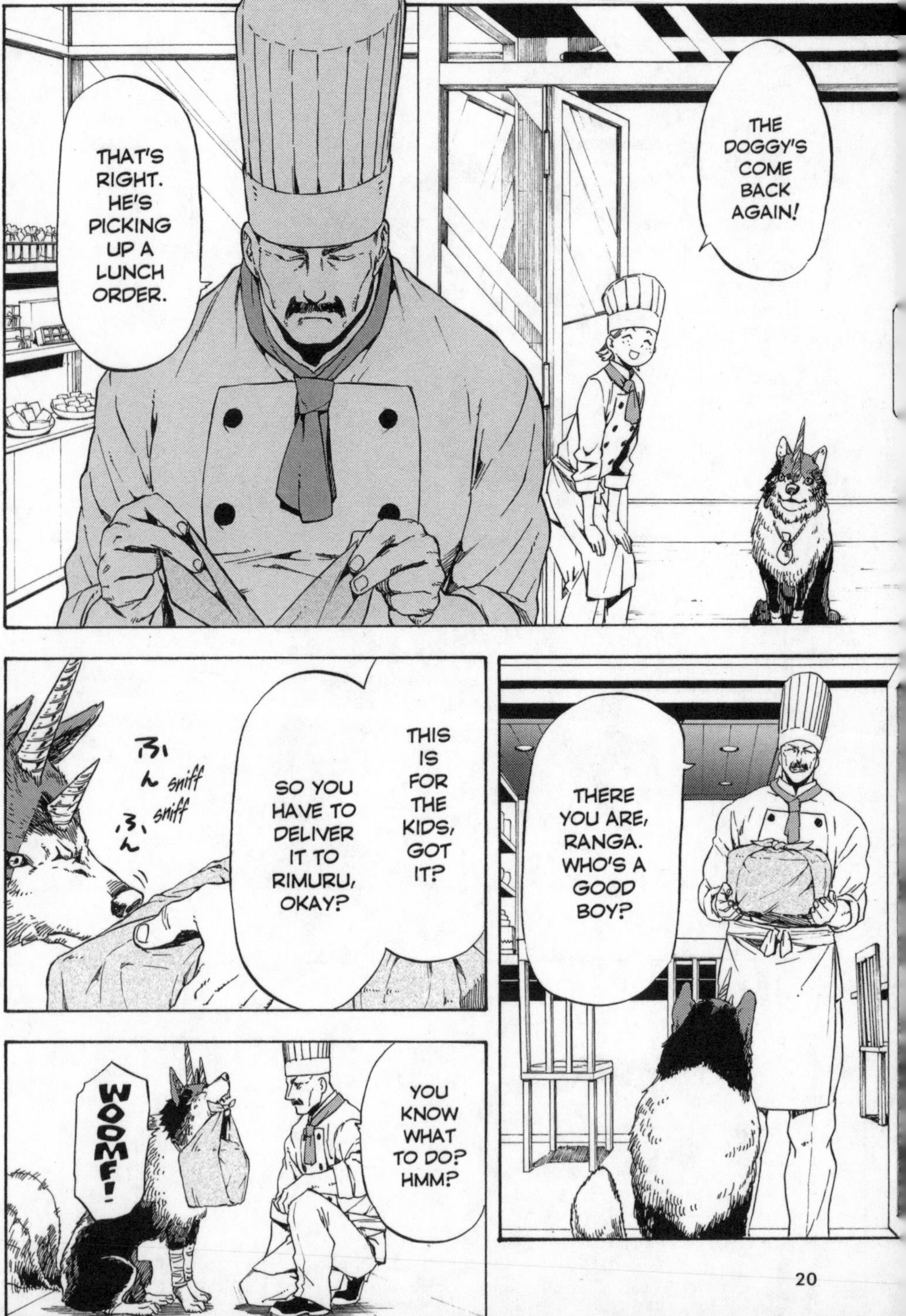
THE DOGGY'S COME BACK AGAIN!
THAT'S RIGHT. HE'S PICKING UP A LUNCH ORDER.
THERE YOU ARE, RANGA. WHO'S A GOOD BOY?
THIS IS FOR THE KIDS, GOT IT?
SO YOU HAVE TO DELIVER IT TO RIMURU, OKAY?
ふん sniff
ふん sniff
YOU KNOW WHAT TO DO? HMM?
WOOMF!

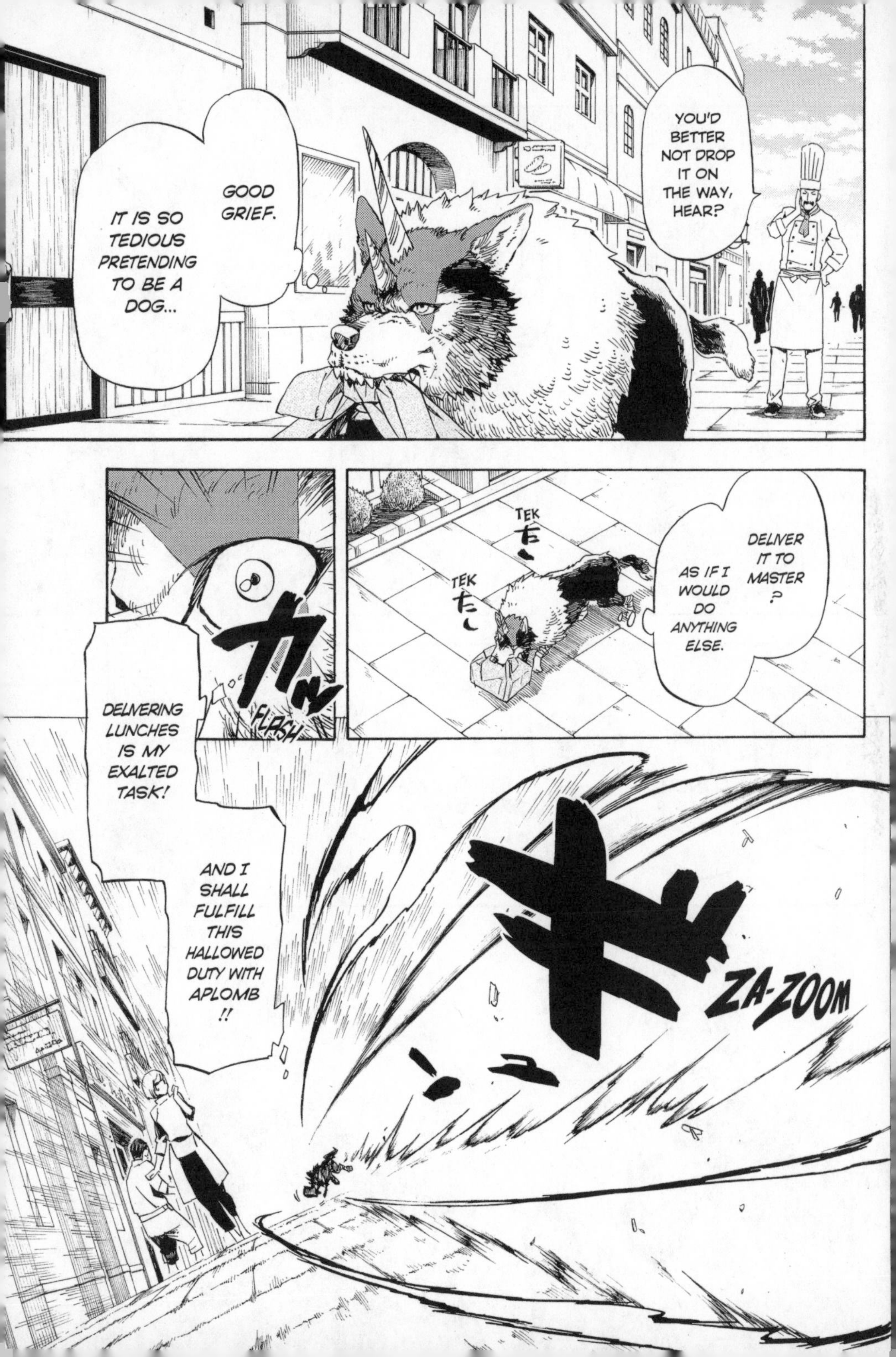
YOU'D BETTER NOT DROP IT ON THE WAY, HEAR?
GOOD GRIEF.
IT IS SO TEDIOUS PRETENDING TO BE A DOG...
TEK
TEK
DELIVER IT TO MASTER?
AS IF I WOULD DO ANYTHING ELSE.
FLASH
DELIVERING LUNCHES IS MY EXALTED TASK!
AND I SHALL FULFILL THIS HALLOWED DUTY WITH APLOMB!!
ZA-ZOOM

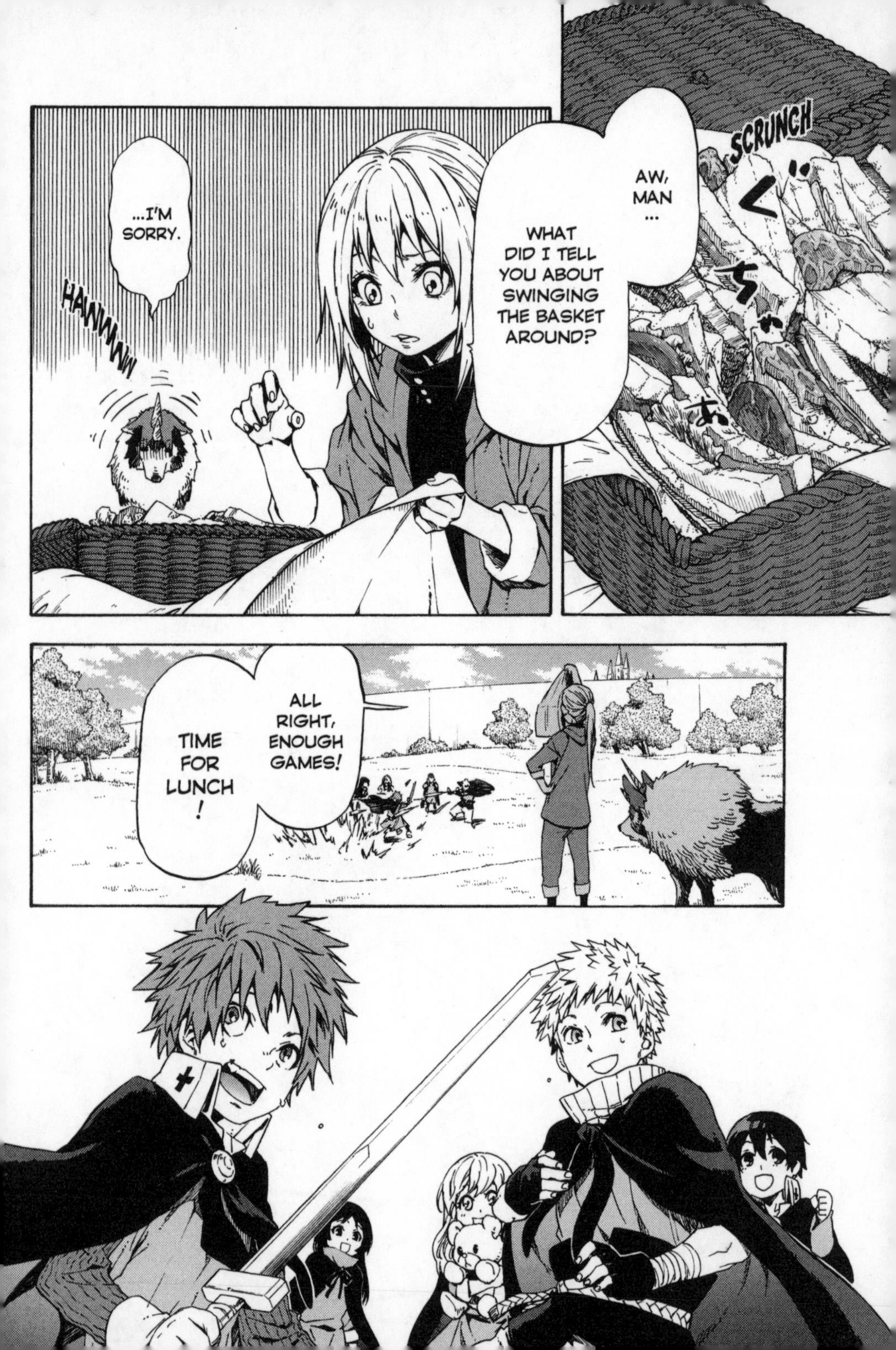
SCRUNCH
AW, MAN ...
WHAT DID I TELL YOU ABOUT SWINGING THE BASKET AROUND?
...I'M SORRY.
ALL RIGHT, ENOUGH GAMES!
TIME FOR LUNCH!

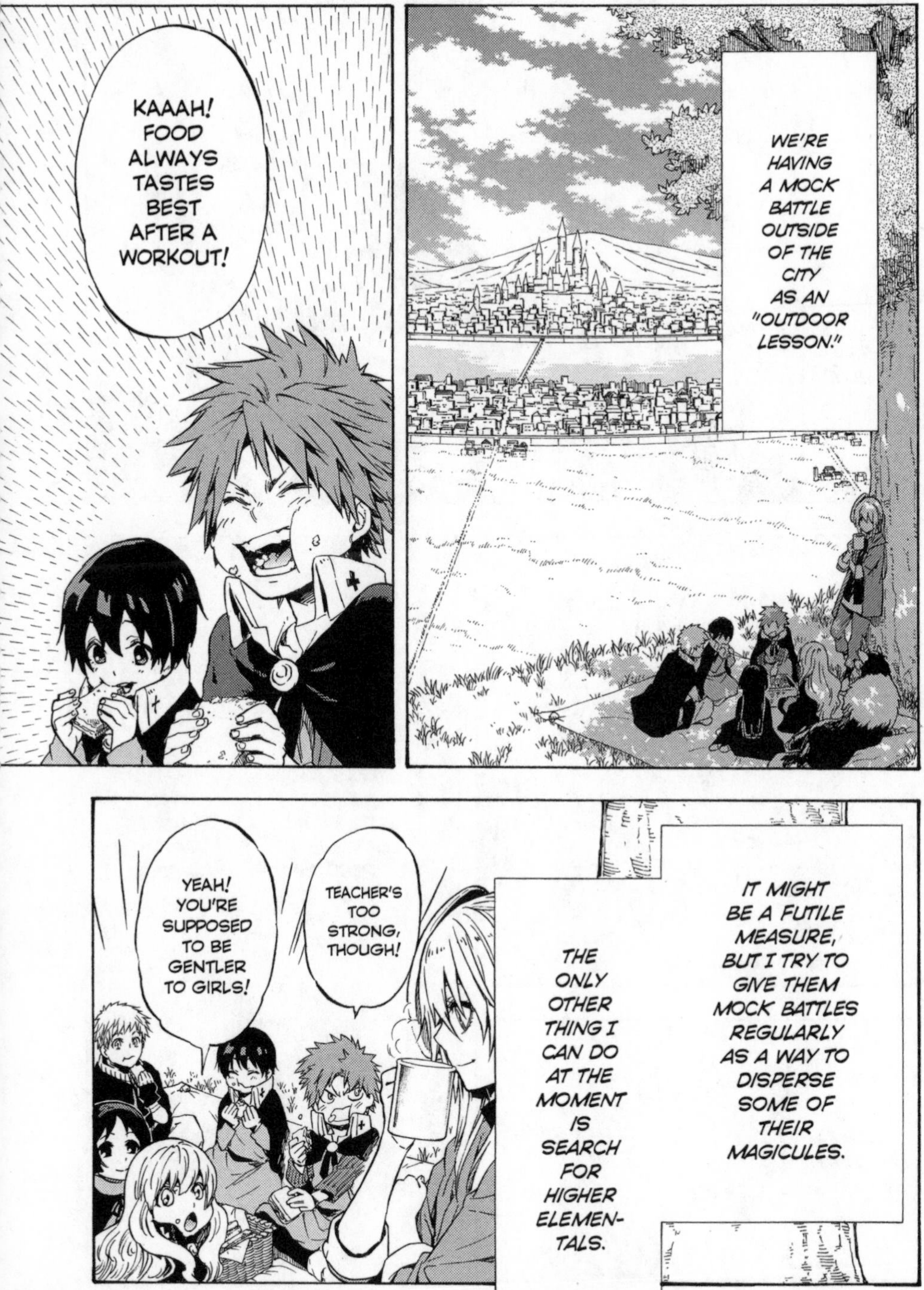
WE'RE HAVING A MOCK BATTLE OUTSIDE OF THE CITY AS AN "OUTDOOR LESSON."
KAAAH! FOOD ALWAYS TASTES BEST AFTER A WORKOUT!
IT MIGHT BE A FUTILE MEASURE, BUT I TRY TO GIVE THEM MOCK BATTLES REGULARLY AS A WAY TO DISPERSE SOME OF THEIR MAGICULES.
THE ONLY OTHER THING I CAN DO AT THE MOMENT IS SEARCH FOR HIGHER ELEMEN-TALS.
TEACHER'S TOO STRONG, THOUGH!
YEAH! YOU'RE SUPPOSED TO BE GENTLER TO GIRLS!

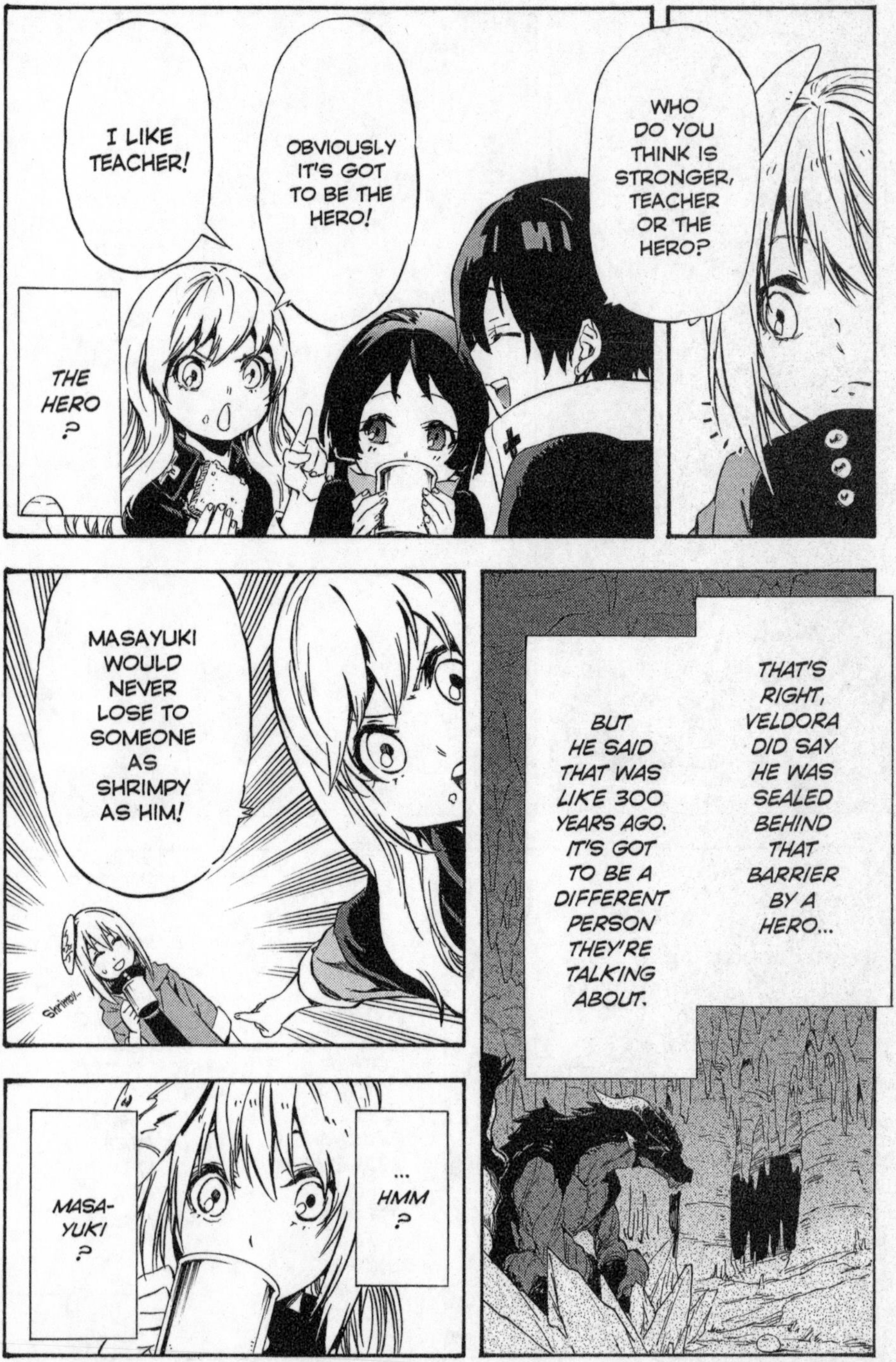
WHO DO YOU THINK IS STRONGER, TEACHER OR THE HERO?
OBVIOUSLY IT'S GOT TO BE THE HERO!
I LIKE TEACHER!
THE HERO?
THAT'S RIGHT, VELDORA DID SAY HE WAS SEALED BEHIND THAT BARRIER BY A HERO...
BUT HE SAID THAT WAS LIKE 300 YEARS AGO. IT'S GOT TO BE A DIFFERENT PERSON THEY'RE TALKING ABOUT.
MASAYUKI WOULD NEVER LOSE TO SOMEONE AS SHRIMPY AS HIM!
Shrimpy...
...HMM?
MASA-YUKI?

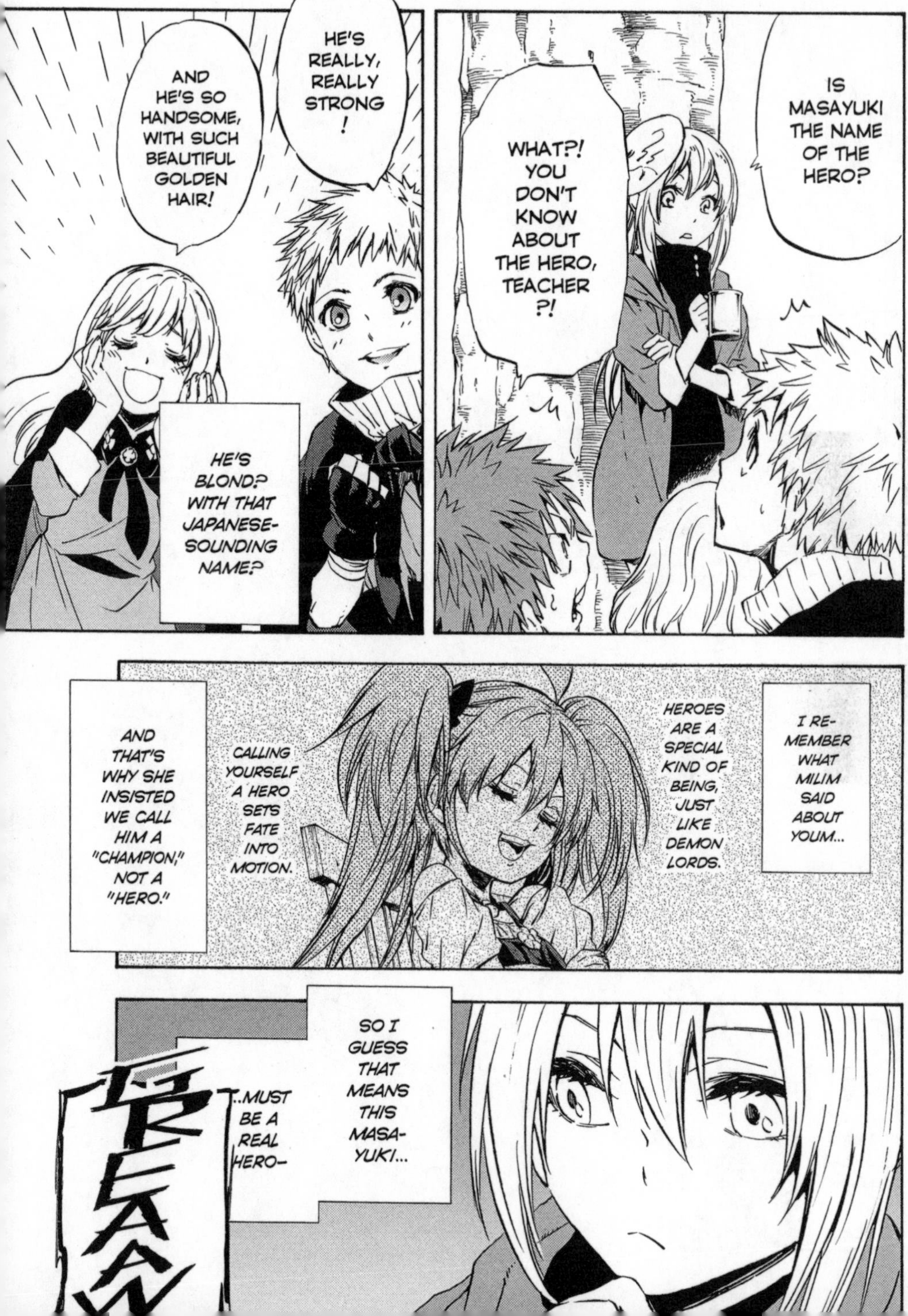

IS MASAYUKI THE NAME OF THE HERO?
WHAT?! YOU DON'T KNOW ABOUT THE HERO, TEACHER?!
HE'S REALLY, REALLY STRONG!
AND HE'S SO HANDSOME, WITH SUCH BEAUTIFUL GOLDEN HAIR!
HE'S BLOND? WITH THAT JAPANESE-SOUNDING NAME?
I REMEMBER WHAT MILIM SAID ABOUT YOUM...
HEROES ARE A SPECIAL KIND OF BEING, JUST LIKE DEMON LORDS.
CALLING YOURSELF A HERO SETS FATE INTO MOTION.
AND THAT'S WHY SHE INSISTED WE CALL HIM A "CHAMPION," NOT A "HERO."
SO I GUESS THAT MEANS THIS MASA-YUKI...
...MUST BE A REAL HERO—

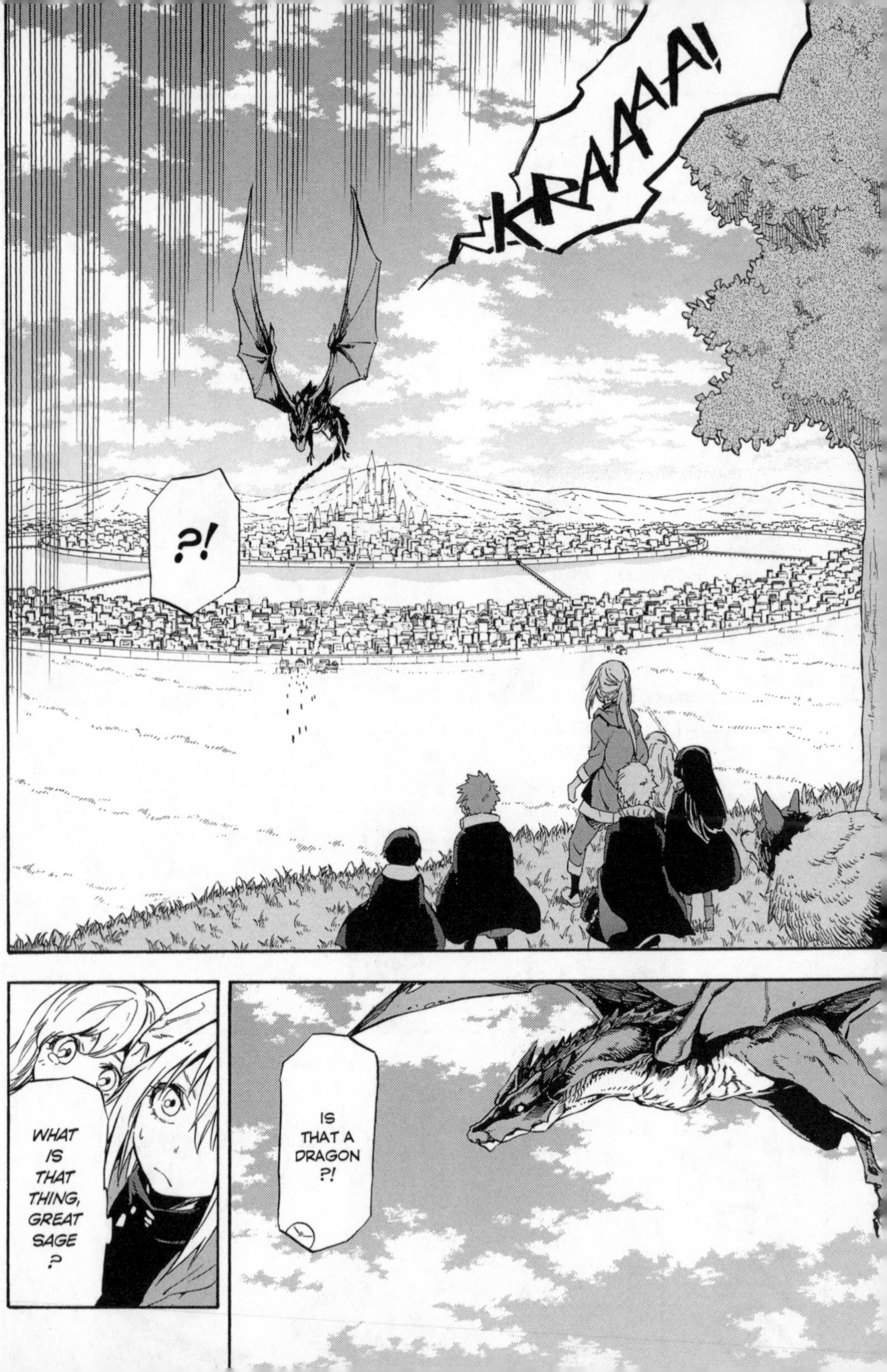
KRAAAAA!
?!
IS THAT A DRAGON ?!
WHAT IS THAT THING, GREAT SAGE ?

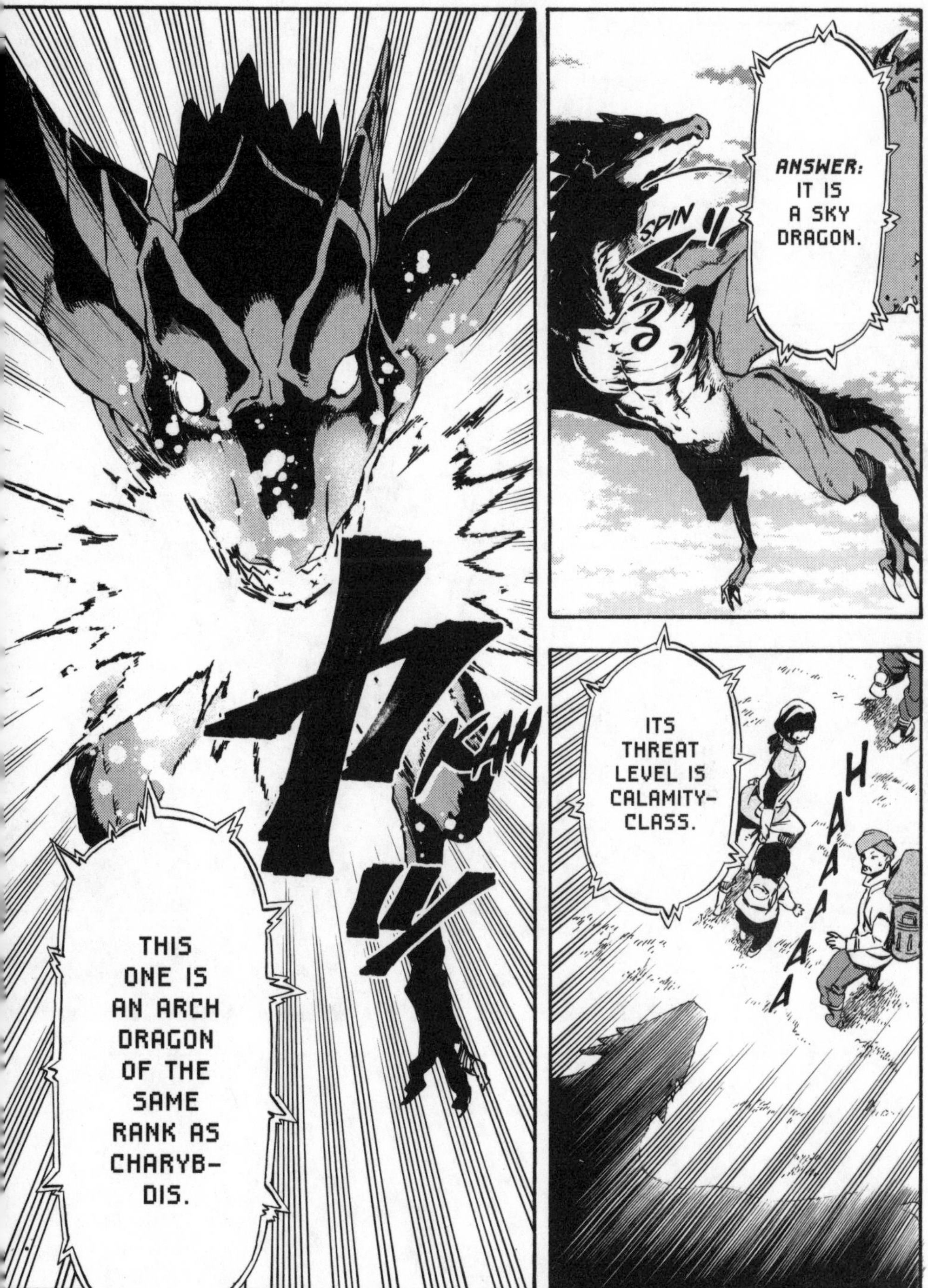
ANSWER: IT IS A SKY DRAGON.
SPIN
ITS THREAT LEVEL IS CALAMITY-CLASS.
HAAAAA
KAAH
THIS ONE IS AN ARCH DRAGON OF THE SAME RANK AS CHARYB-DIS.

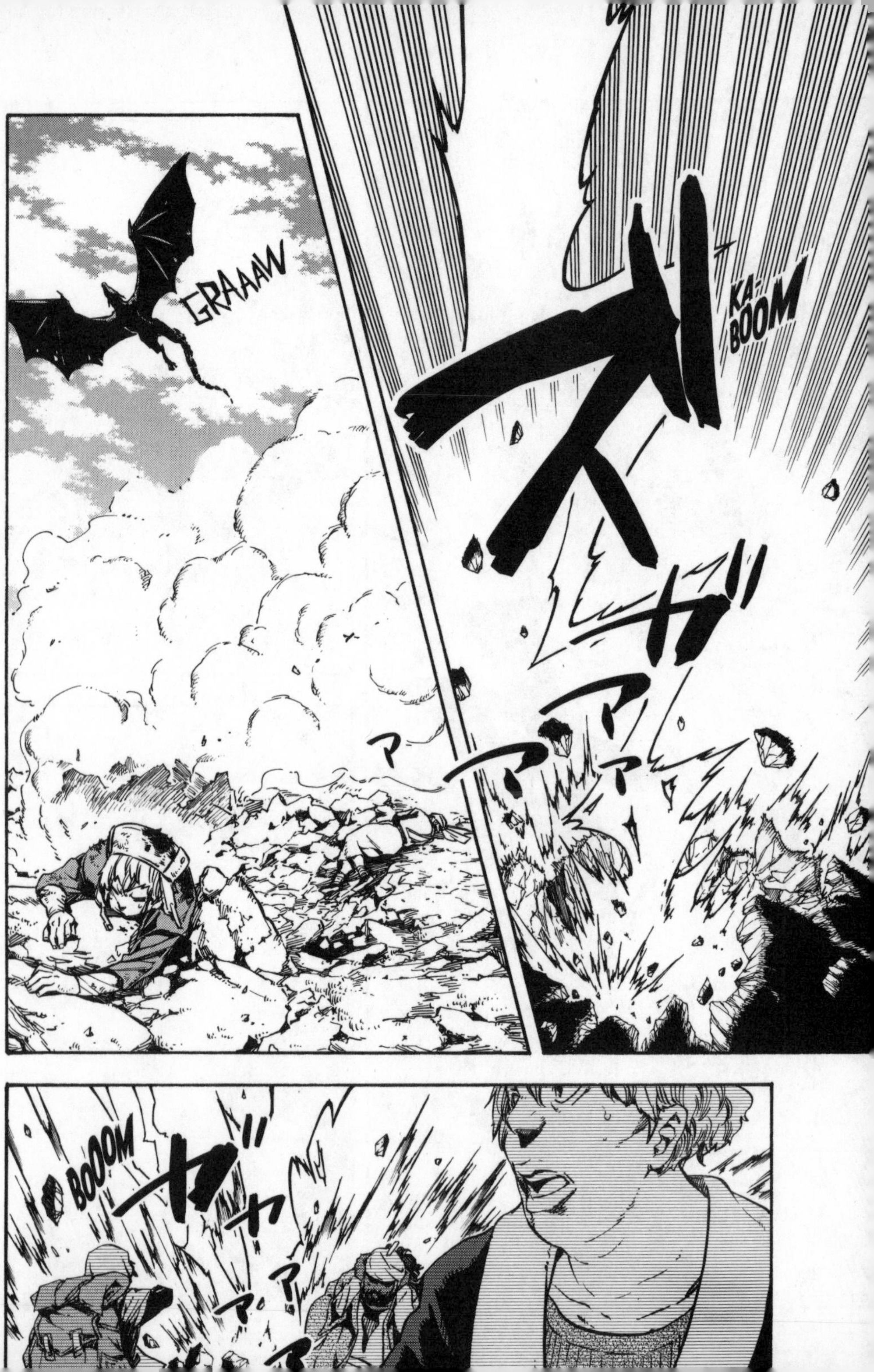
KA-BOOM
GRAAAW
BOOOM

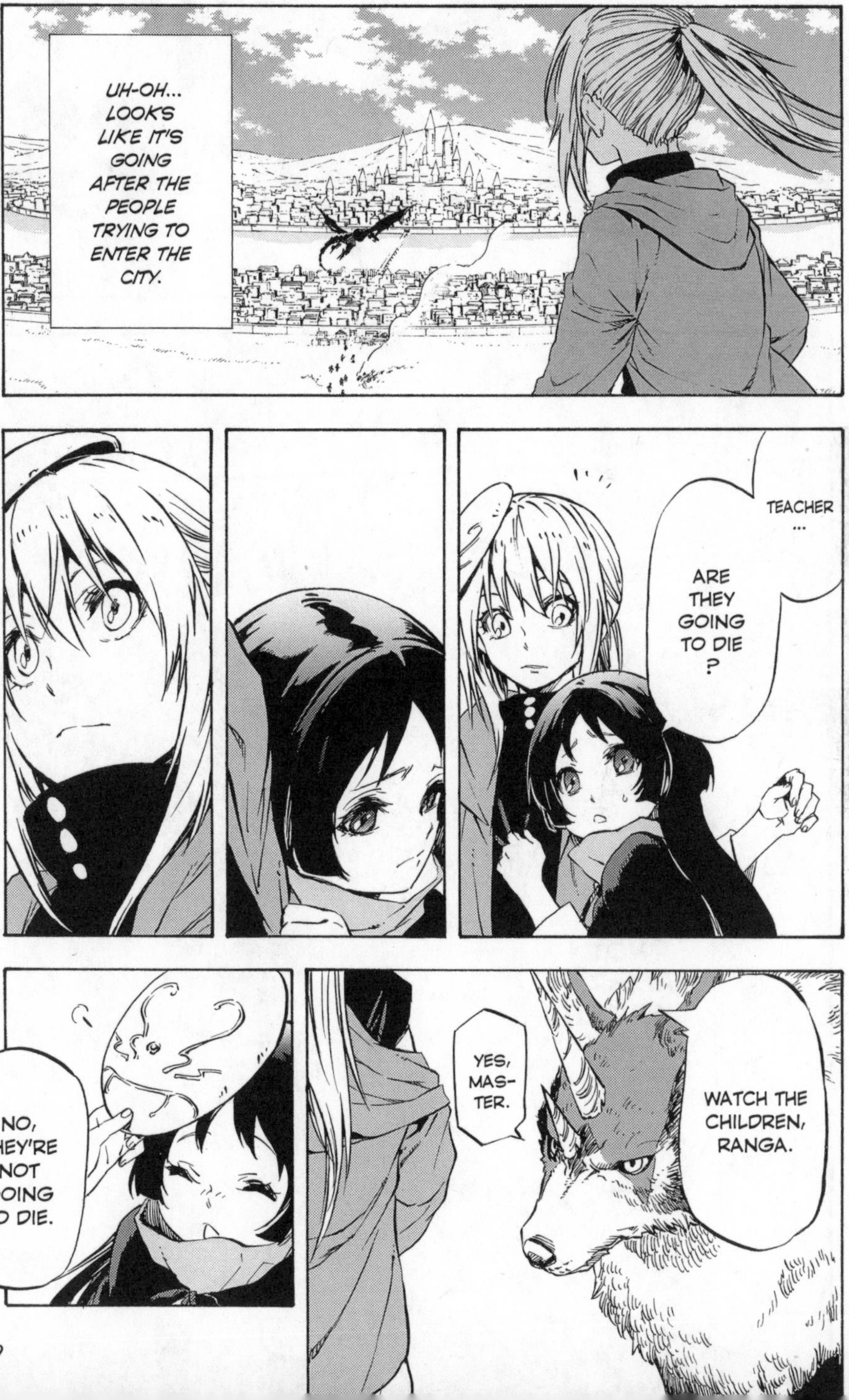
UH-OH... LOOKS LIKE IT'S GOING AFTER THE PEOPLE TRYING TO ENTER THE CITY.
TEACHER ... ARE THEY GOING TO DIE ?
WATCH THE CHILDREN, RANGA.
YES, MAS-TER.
NO, THEY'RE NOT GOING TO DIE.

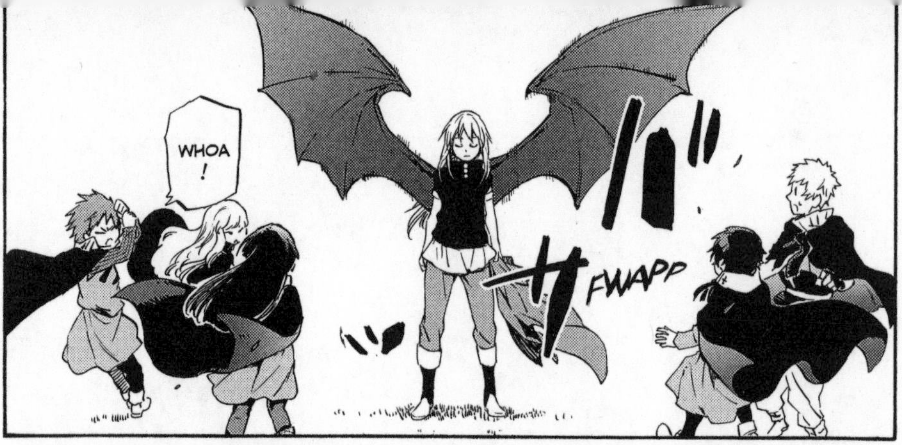
WHOA!
FWAPP

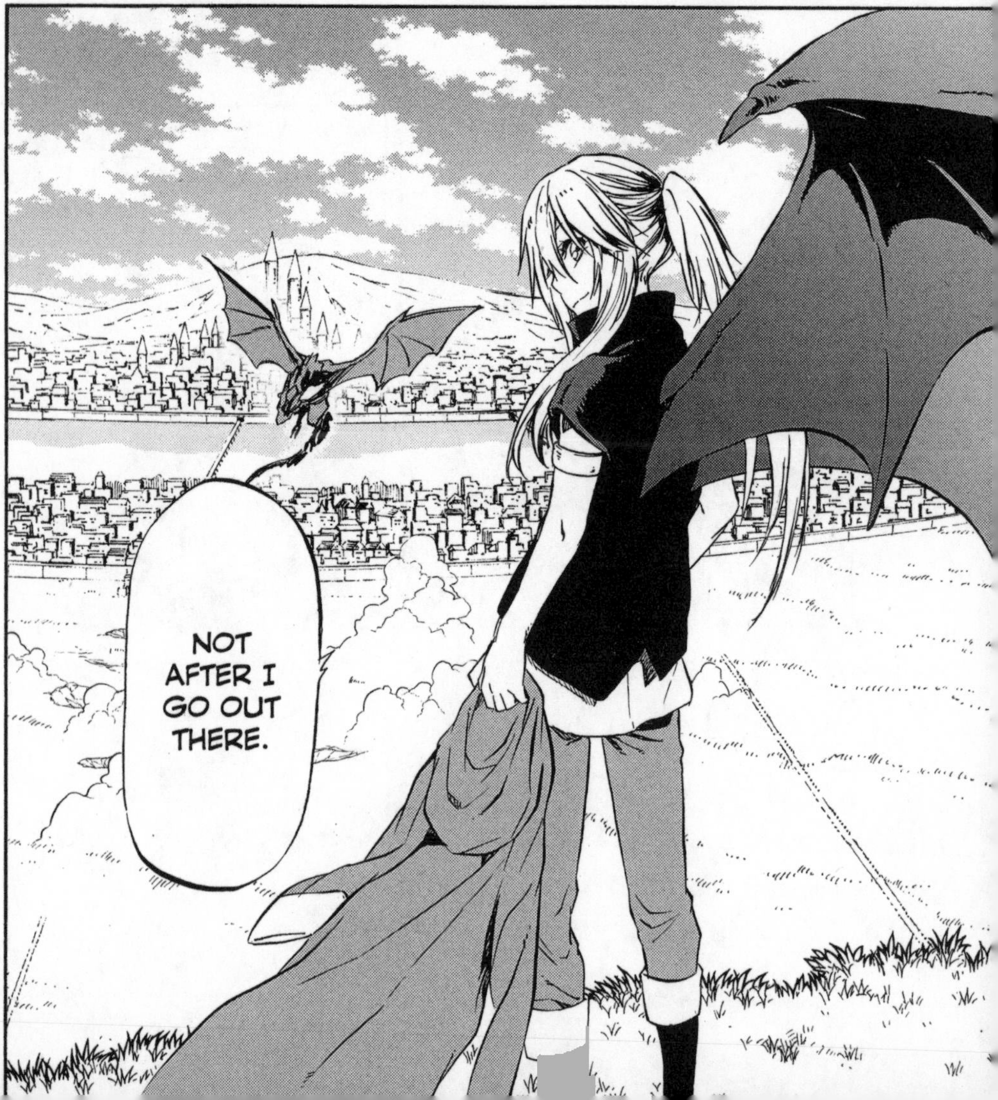
NOT AFTER I GO OUT THERE.

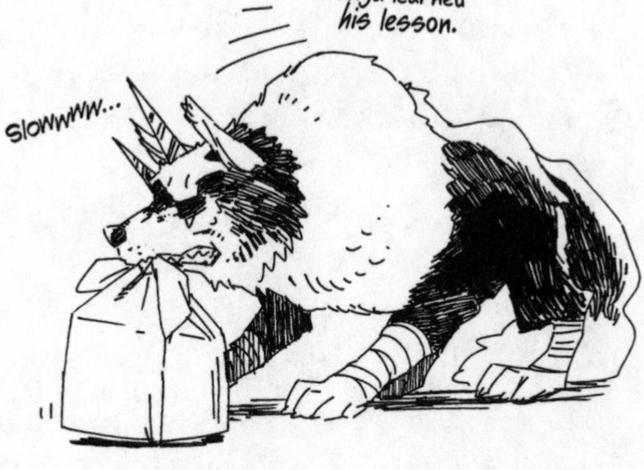
Ranga learned
his lesson.
SlowWWW...

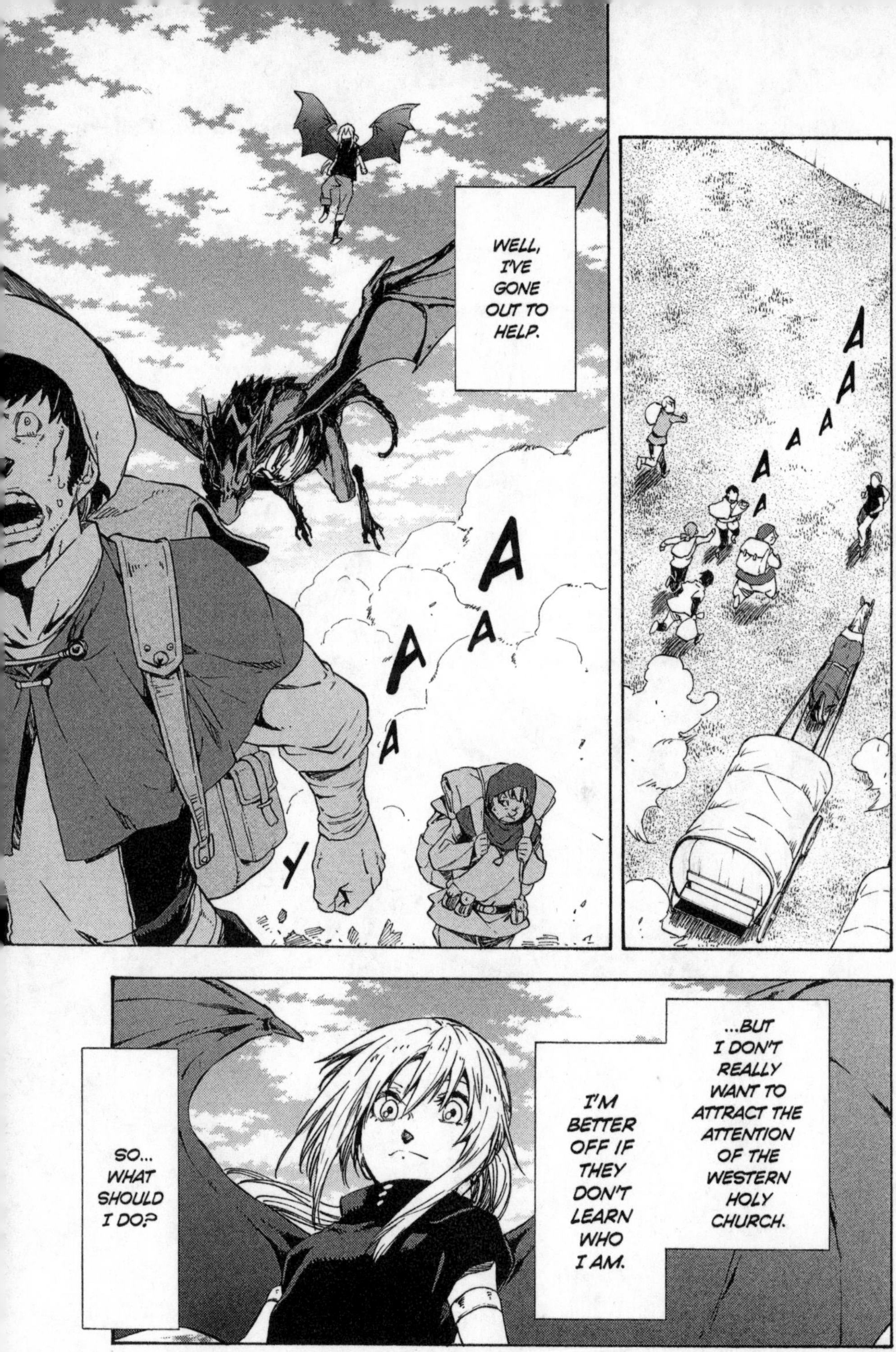
AAAAAA
WELL, I'VE GONE OUT TO HELP.
AAAAY
...BUT I DON'T REALLY WANT TO ATTRACT THE ATTENTION OF THE WESTERN HOLY CHURCH.
I'M BETTER OFF IF THEY DON'T LEARN WHO I AM.
SO... WHAT SHOULD I DO?

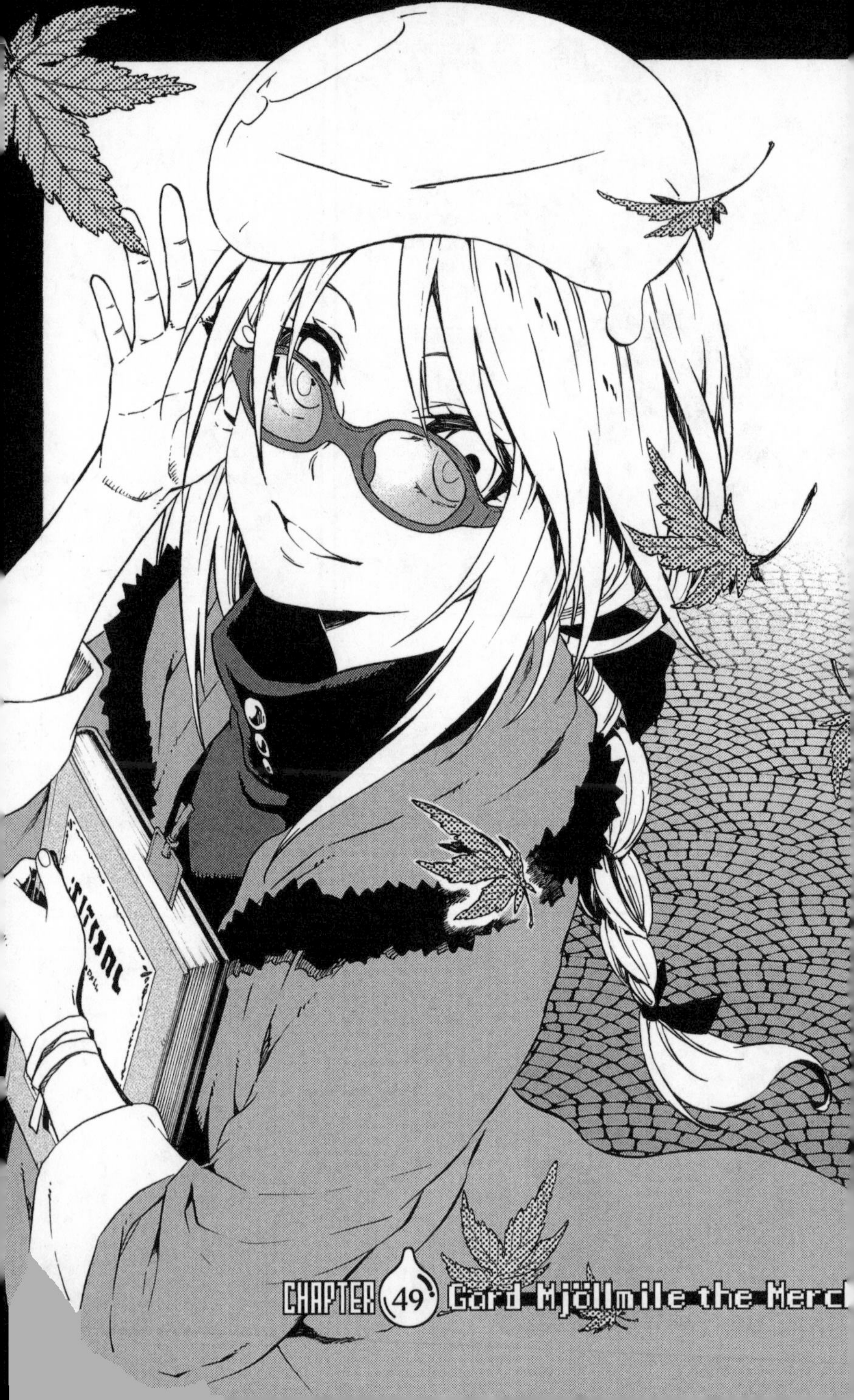

CHAPTER 49 Gard Mjöllmile the Merc

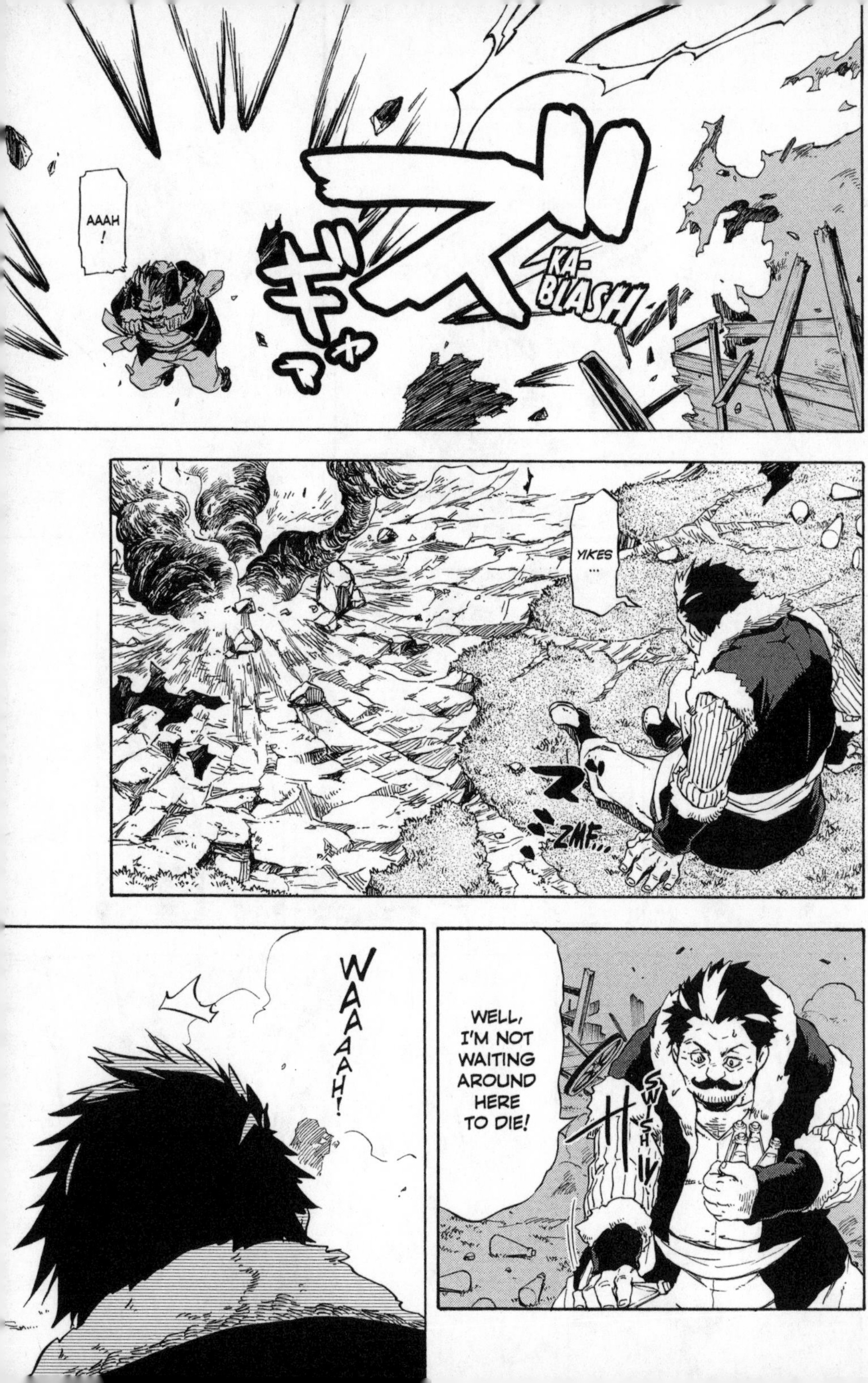
KA-BLASH
AAAH!
YIKES...
ZMF...
WELL, I'M NOT WAITING AROUND HERE TO DIE!
SWISH
WAAAAAH!

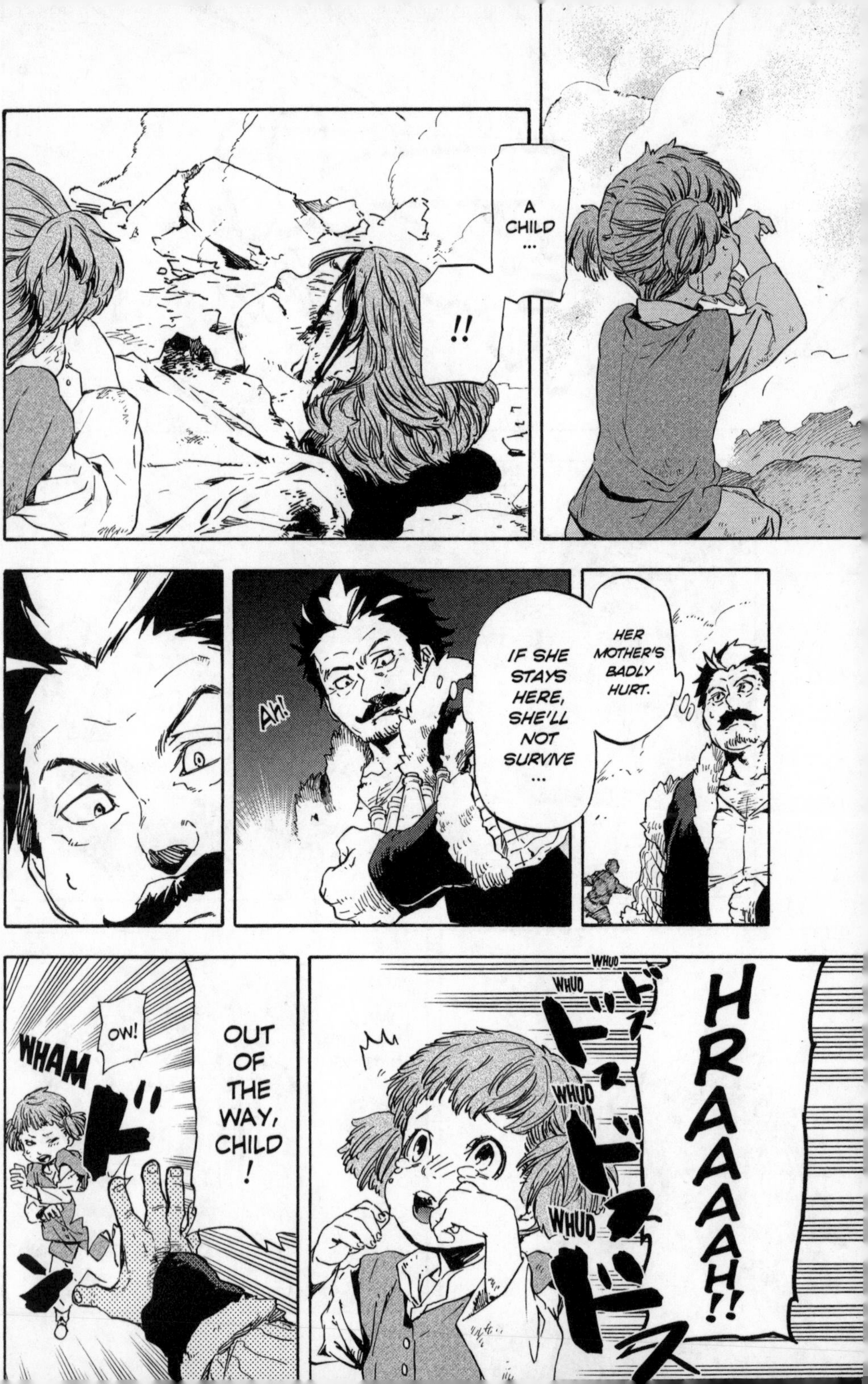
A CHILD ...
!!
HER MOTHER'S BADLY HURT.
IF SHE STAYS HERE, SHE'LL NOT SURVIVE ...
Ah!
HRAAAAH!!
WHUD
WHUD
WHUD
WHUD
OUT OF THE WAY, CHILD!
OW!
WHAM

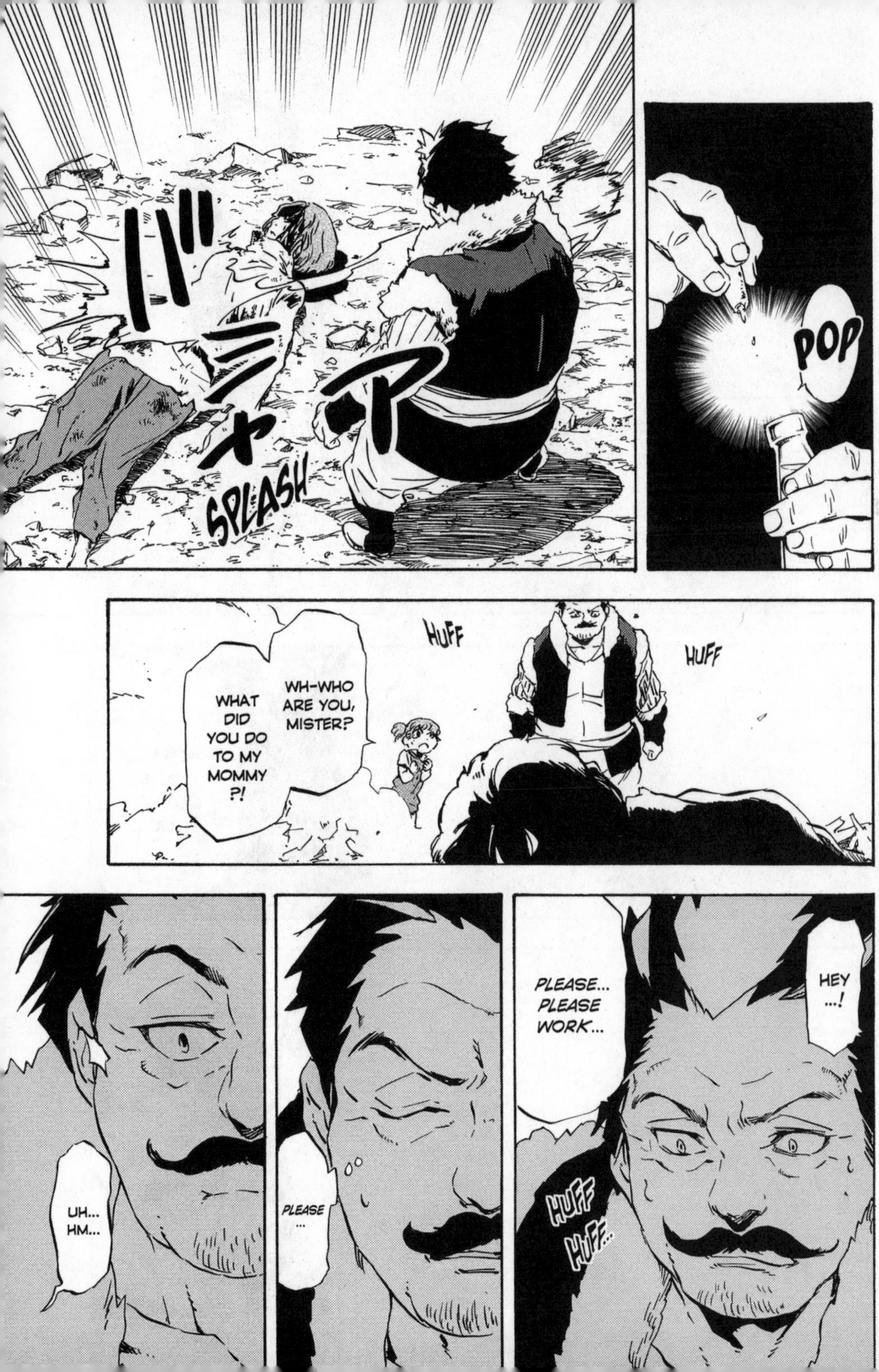
POP
バシャア
SPLASH
HUFF
HUFF
WH-WHO ARE YOU, MISTER? WHAT DID YOU DO TO MY MOMMY ?!
HEY ...!
PLEASE... PLEASE WORK...
HUFF HUFF...
PLEASE ...
UH... HM...

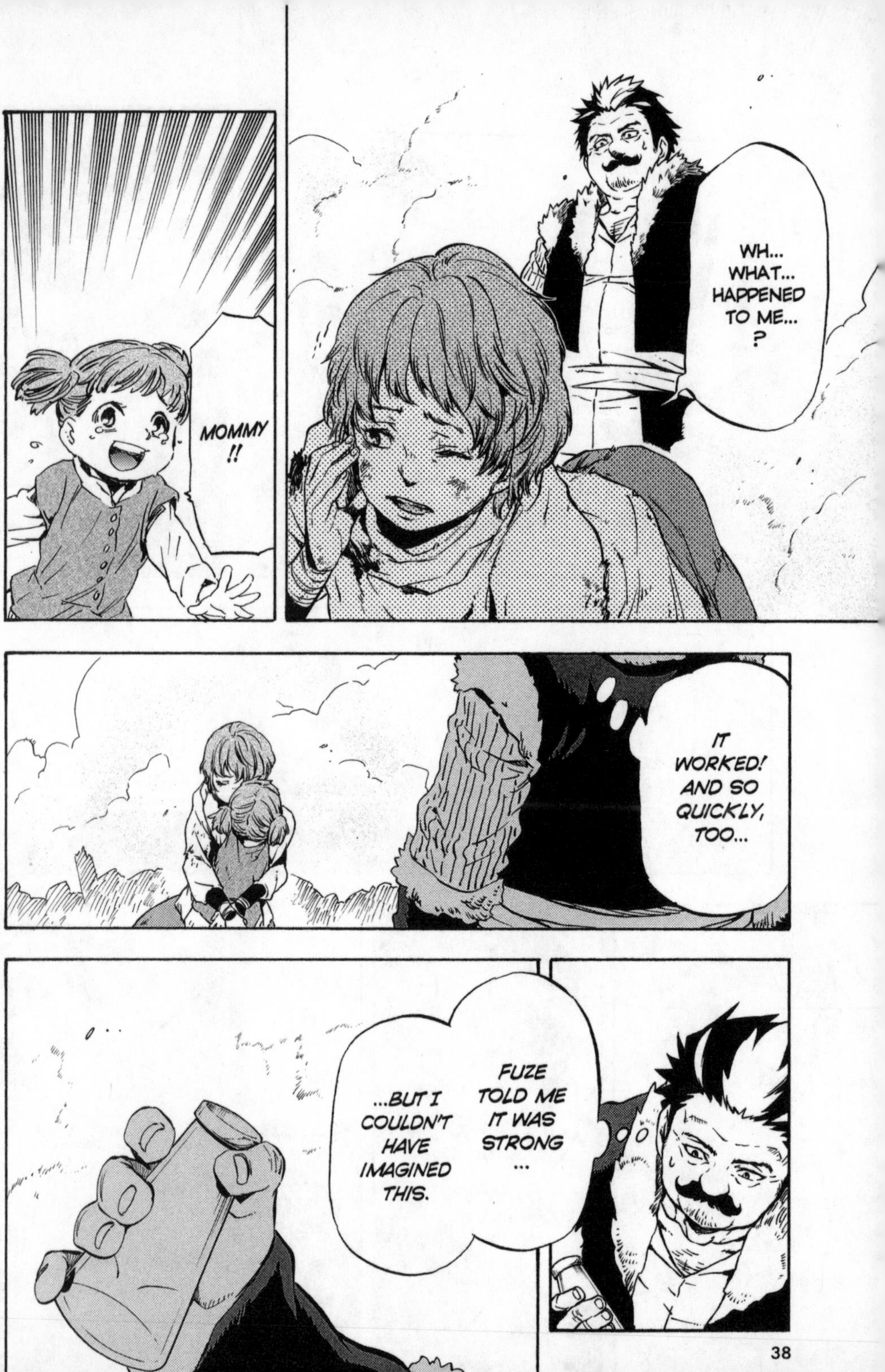
WH... WHAT... HAPPENED TO ME... ?
MOMMY !!
IT WORKED! AND SO QUICKLY, TOO...
FUZE TOLD ME IT WAS STRONG ...
...BUT I COULDN'T HAVE IMAGINED THIS.

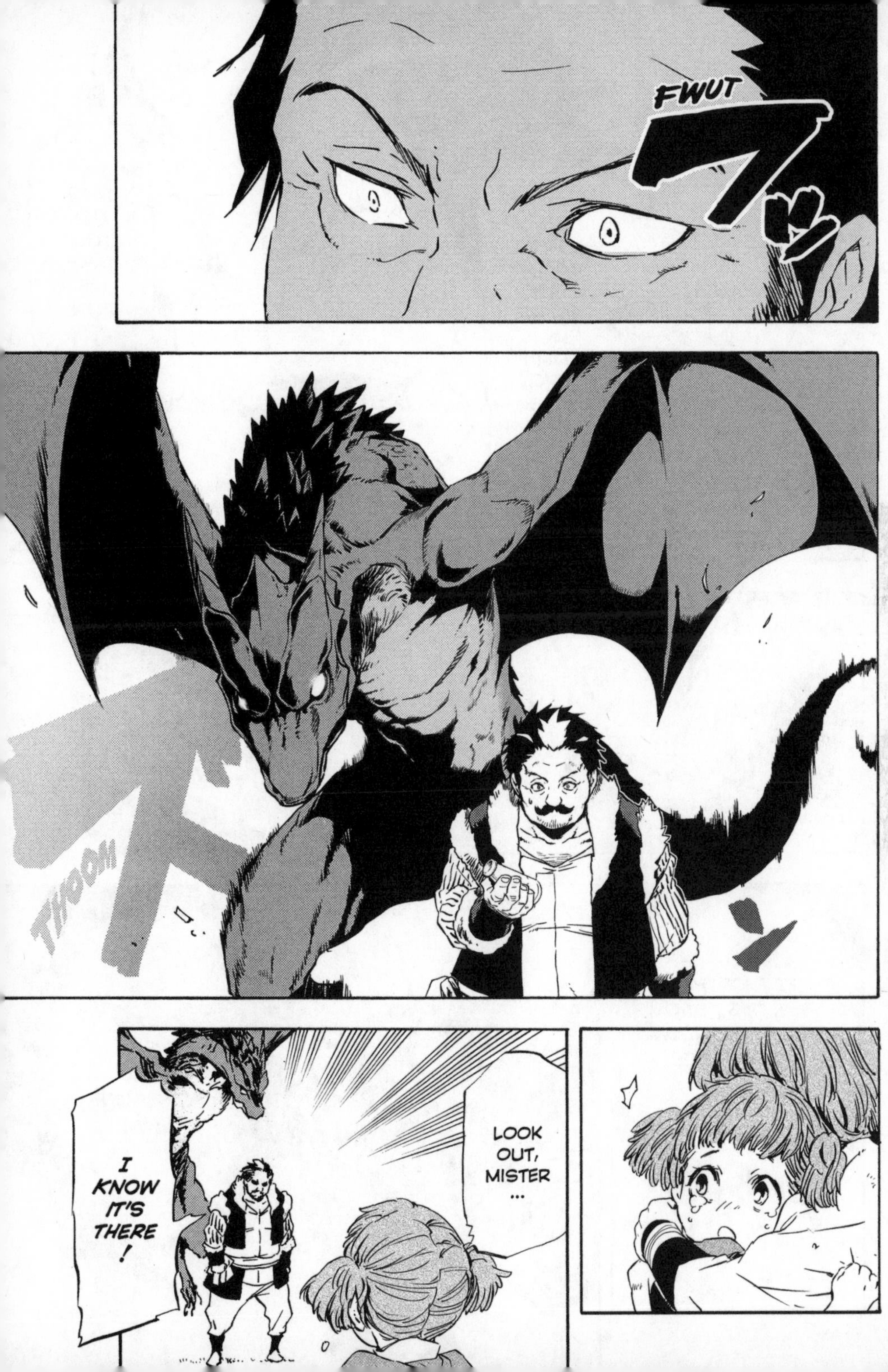
FWUT
THOOM
LOOK OUT, MISTER ...
I KNOW IT'S THERE!

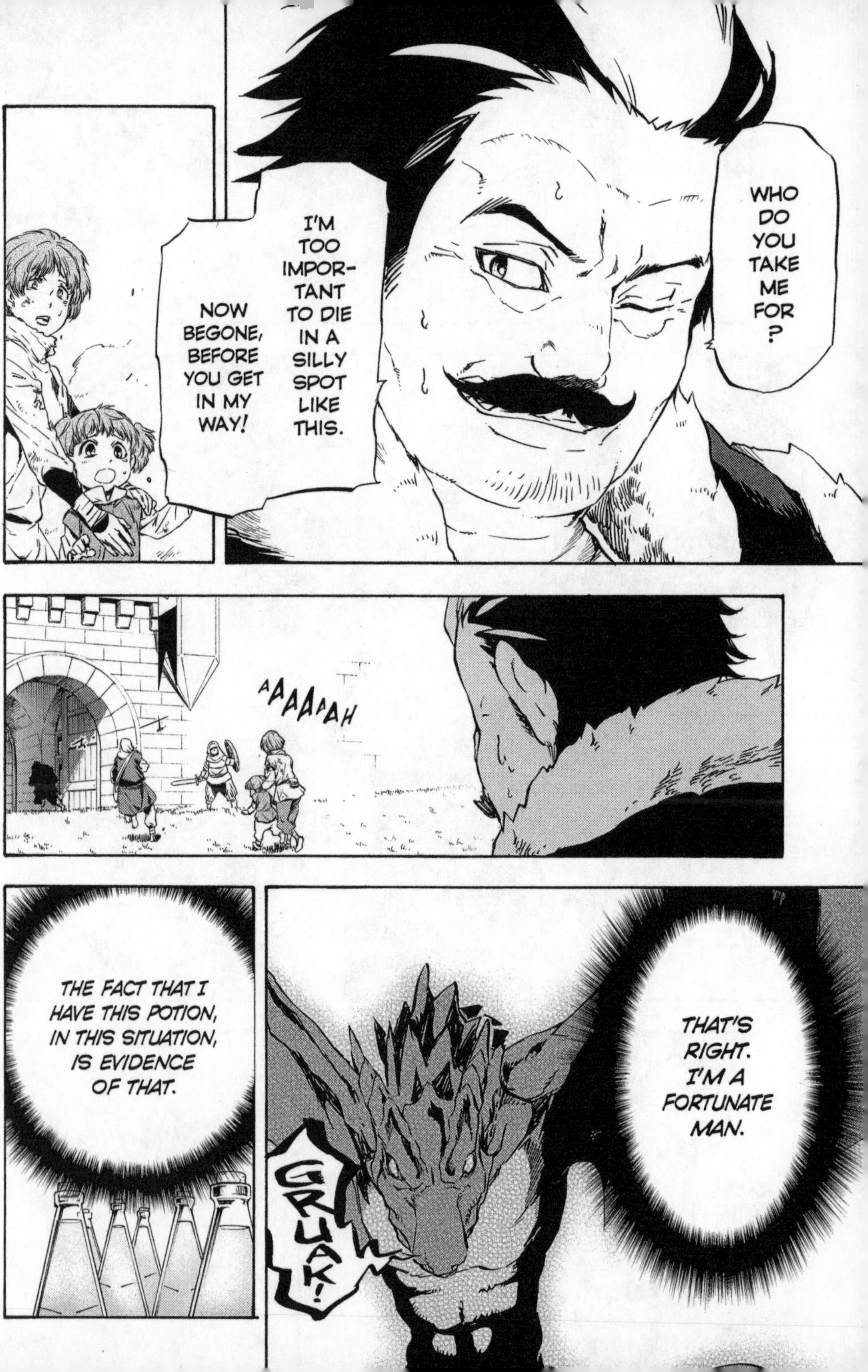
WHO DO YOU TAKE ME FOR?
I'M TOO IMPORTANT TO DIE IN A SILLY SPOT LIKE THIS.
NOW BEGONE, BEFORE YOU GET IN MY WAY!
AAAAAAH
THAT'S RIGHT. I'M A FORTUNATE MAN.
GRUAK!
THE FACT THAT I HAVE THIS POTION, IN THIS SITUATION, IS EVIDENCE OF THAT.

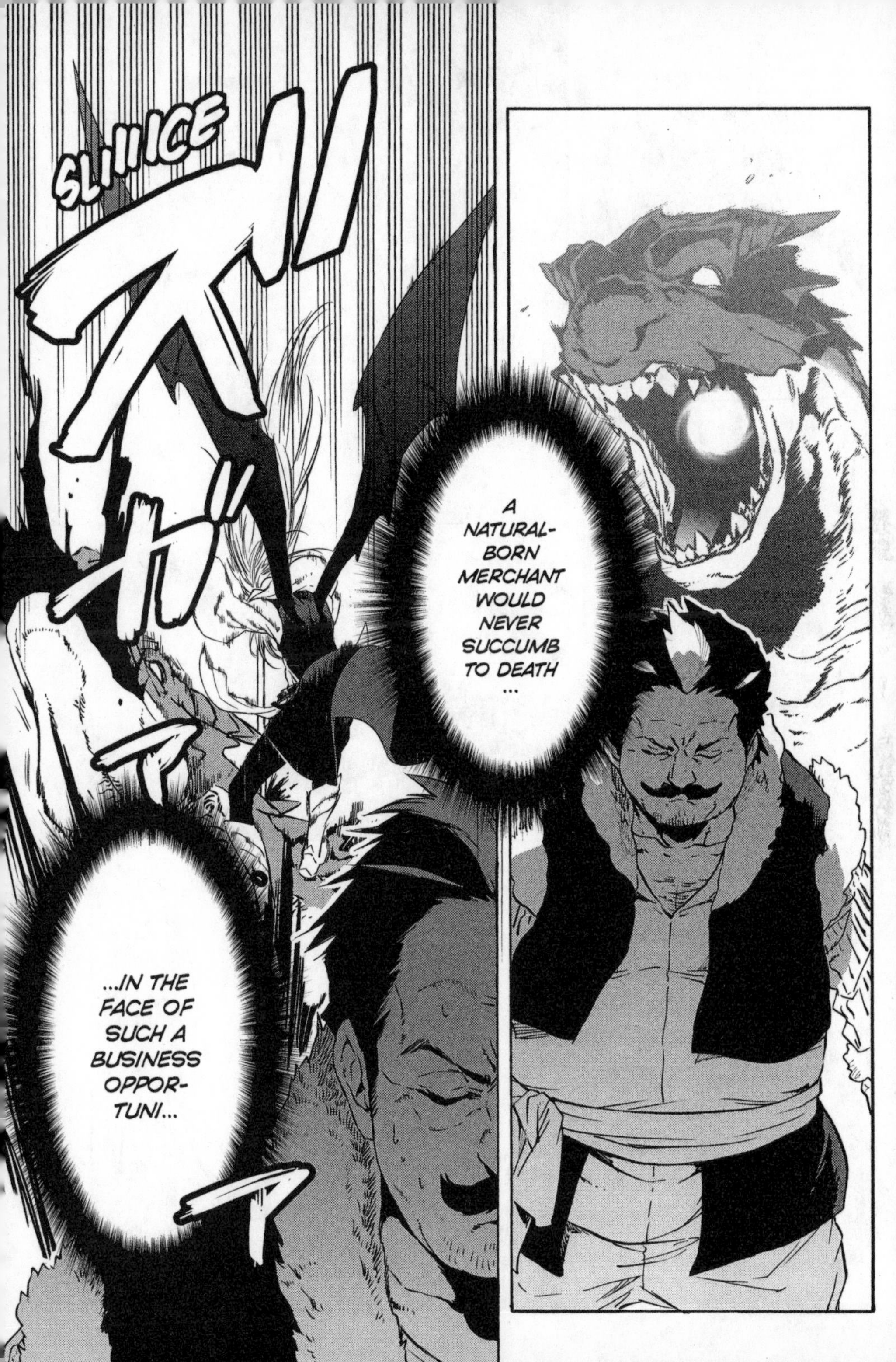
A NATURAL-BORN MERCHANT WOULD NEVER SUCCUMB TO DEATH...
SLIIICE
...IN THE FACE OF SUCH A BUSINESS OPPOR-TUNI...

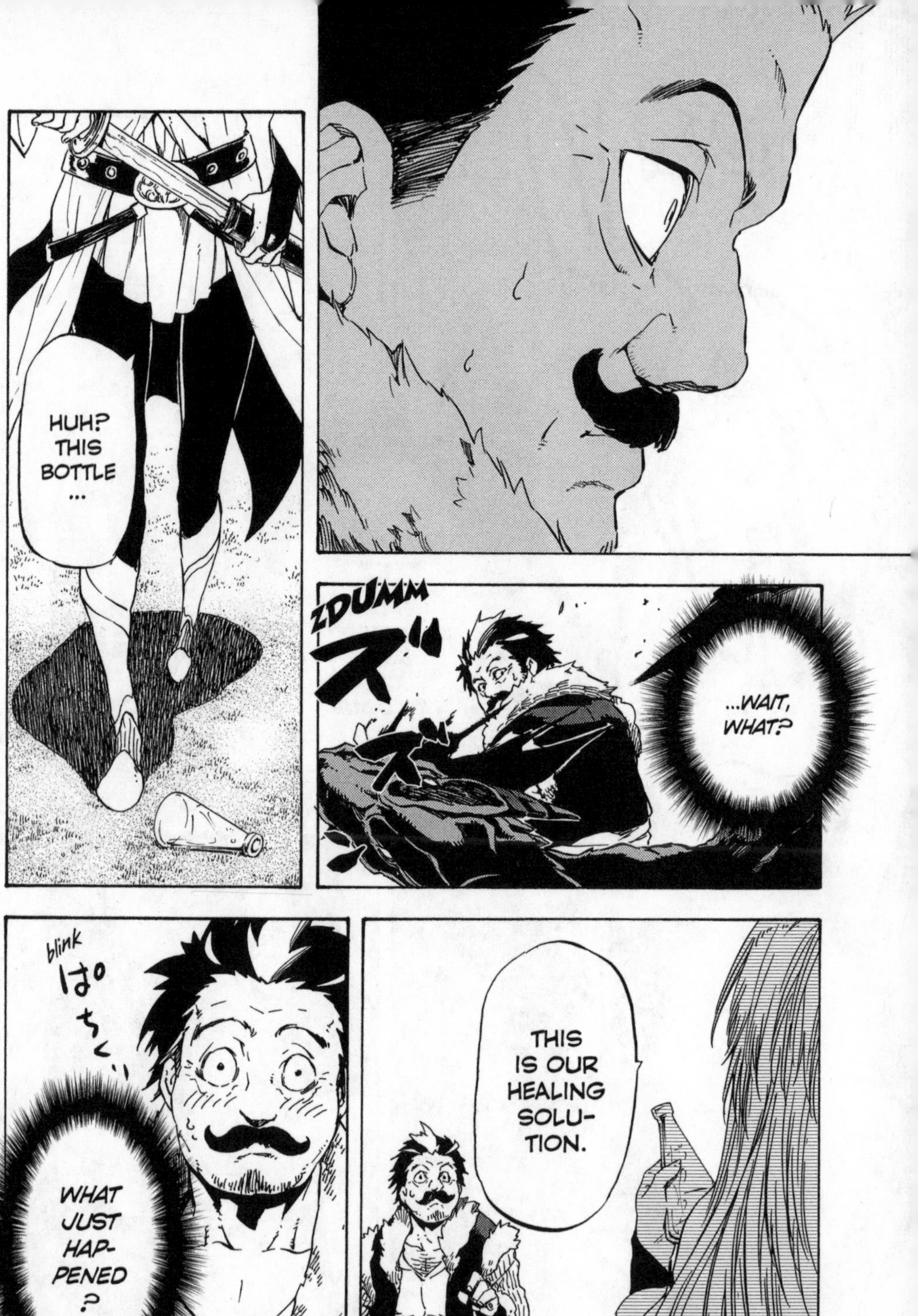
ZDUMM
ズ
...WAIT, WHAT?
HUH? THIS BOTTLE ...
THIS IS OUR HEALING SOLUTION.
blink
WHAT JUST HAPPENED?

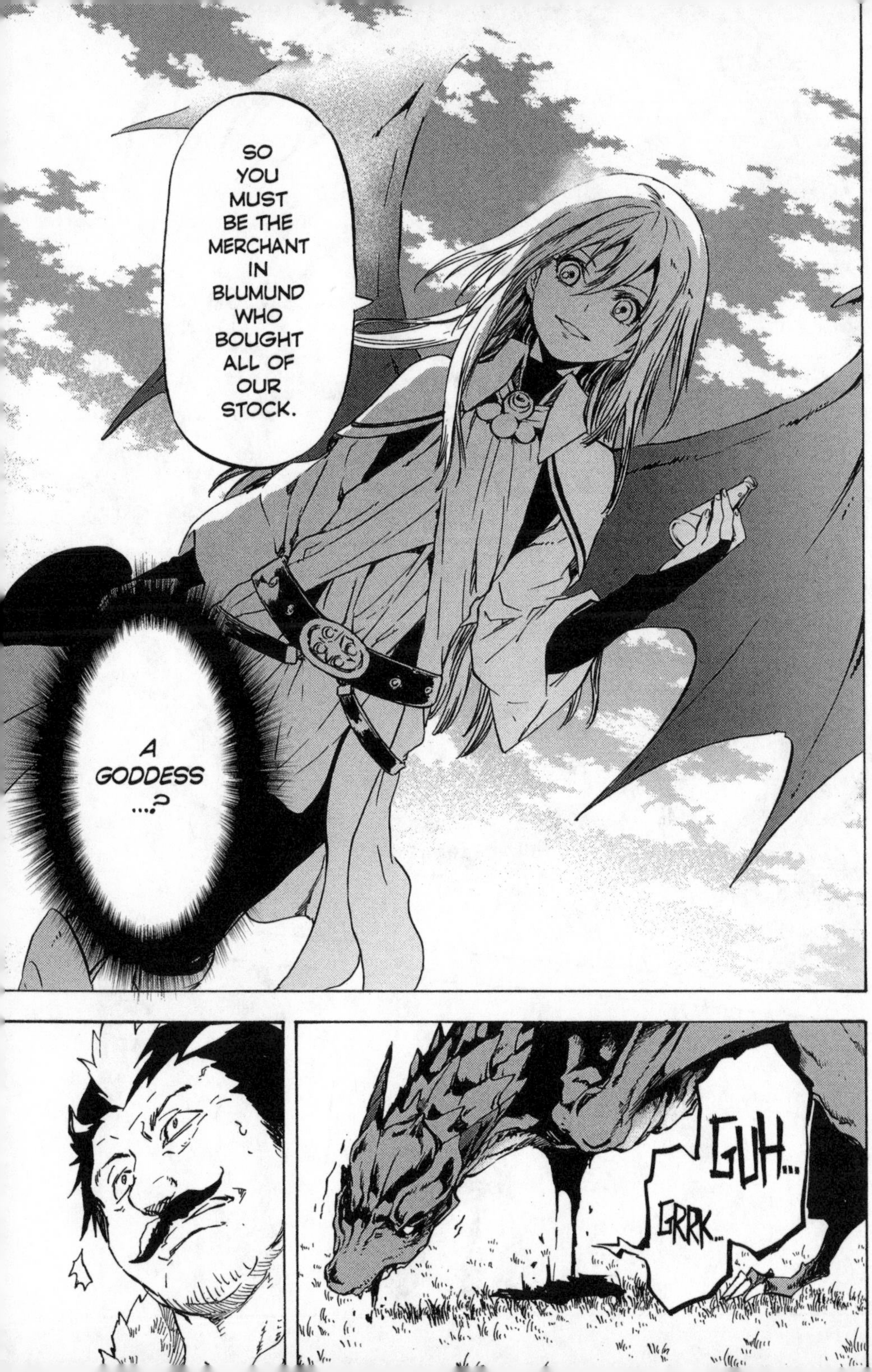
SO YOU MUST BE THE MERCHANT IN BLUMUND WHO BOUGHT ALL OF OUR STOCK.
A GODDESS ...?
GUH...
GRRK...

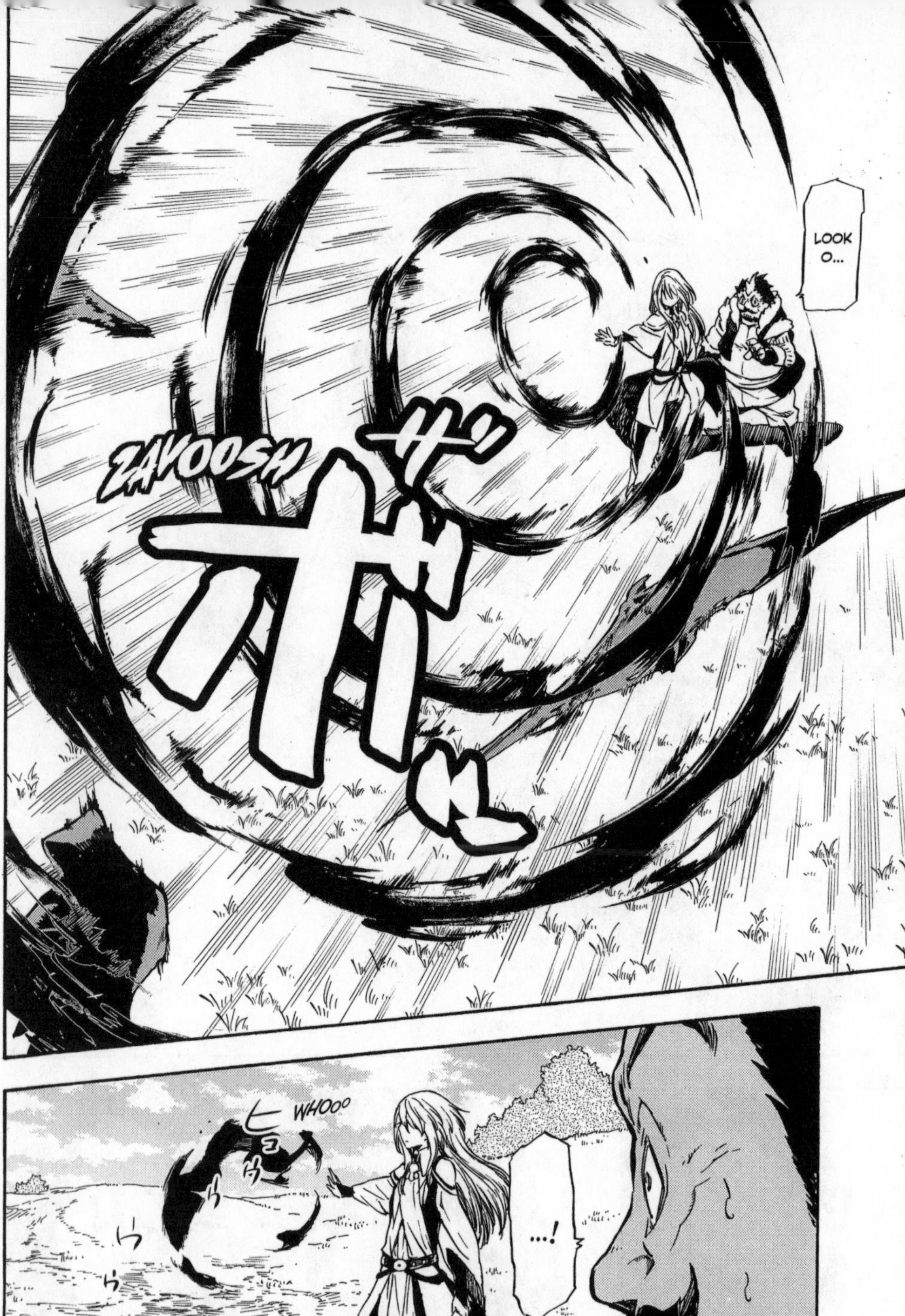
LOOK O...
ZAVOOSH
WHOOO
...!

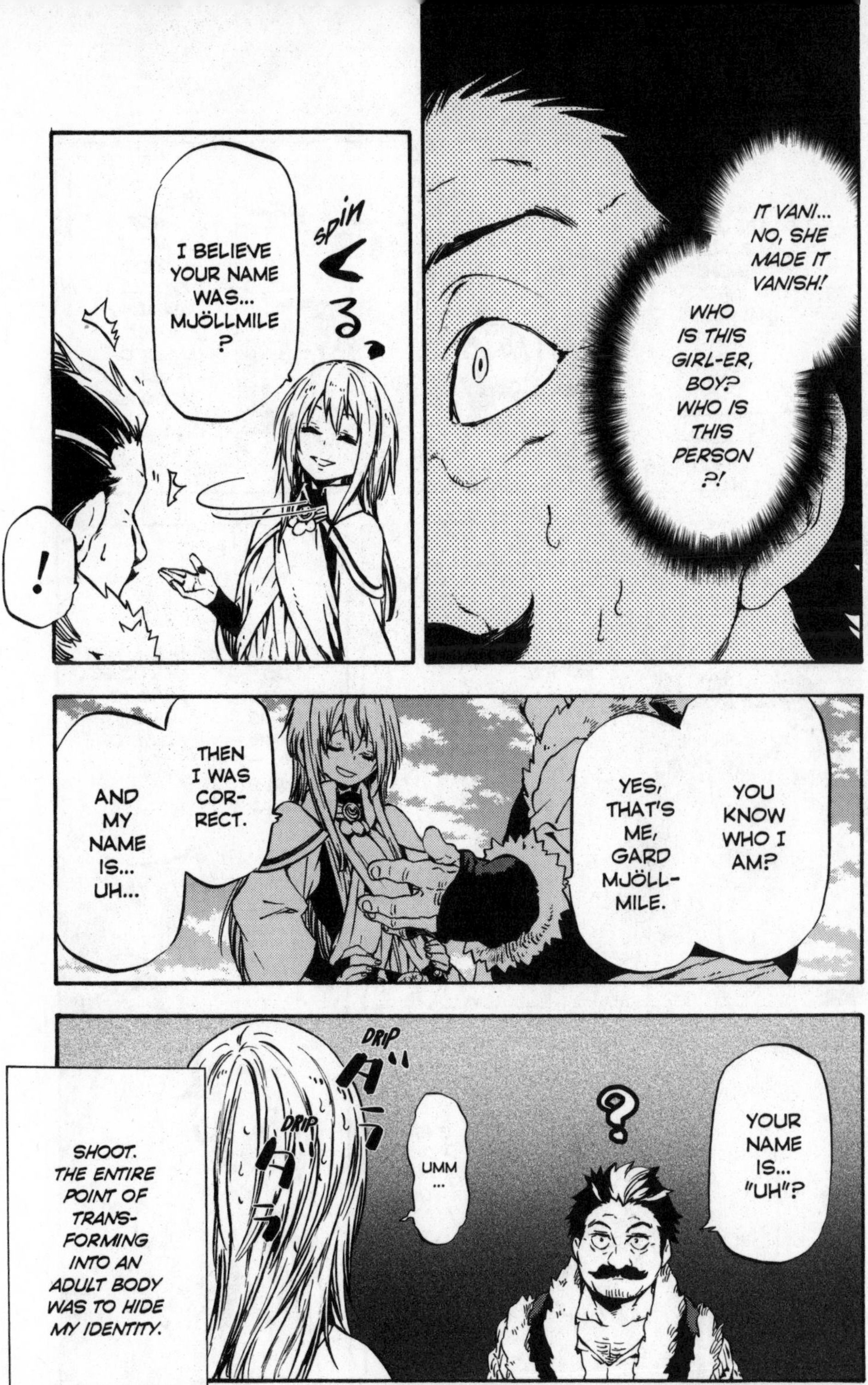
IT VANI... NO, SHE MADE IT VANISH!
WHO IS THIS GIRL-ER, BOY? WHO IS THIS PERSON?!
spin
I BELIEVE YOUR NAME WAS... MJÖLLMILE?
!
YOU KNOW WHO I AM?
YES, THAT'S ME, GARD MJÖLL-MILE.
THEN I WAS COR-RECT.
AND MY NAME IS... UH...
YOUR NAME IS... "UH"?
UMM...
DRIP
DRIP
SHOOT. THE ENTIRE POINT OF TRANS-FORMING INTO AN ADULT BODY WAS TO HIDE MY IDENTITY.

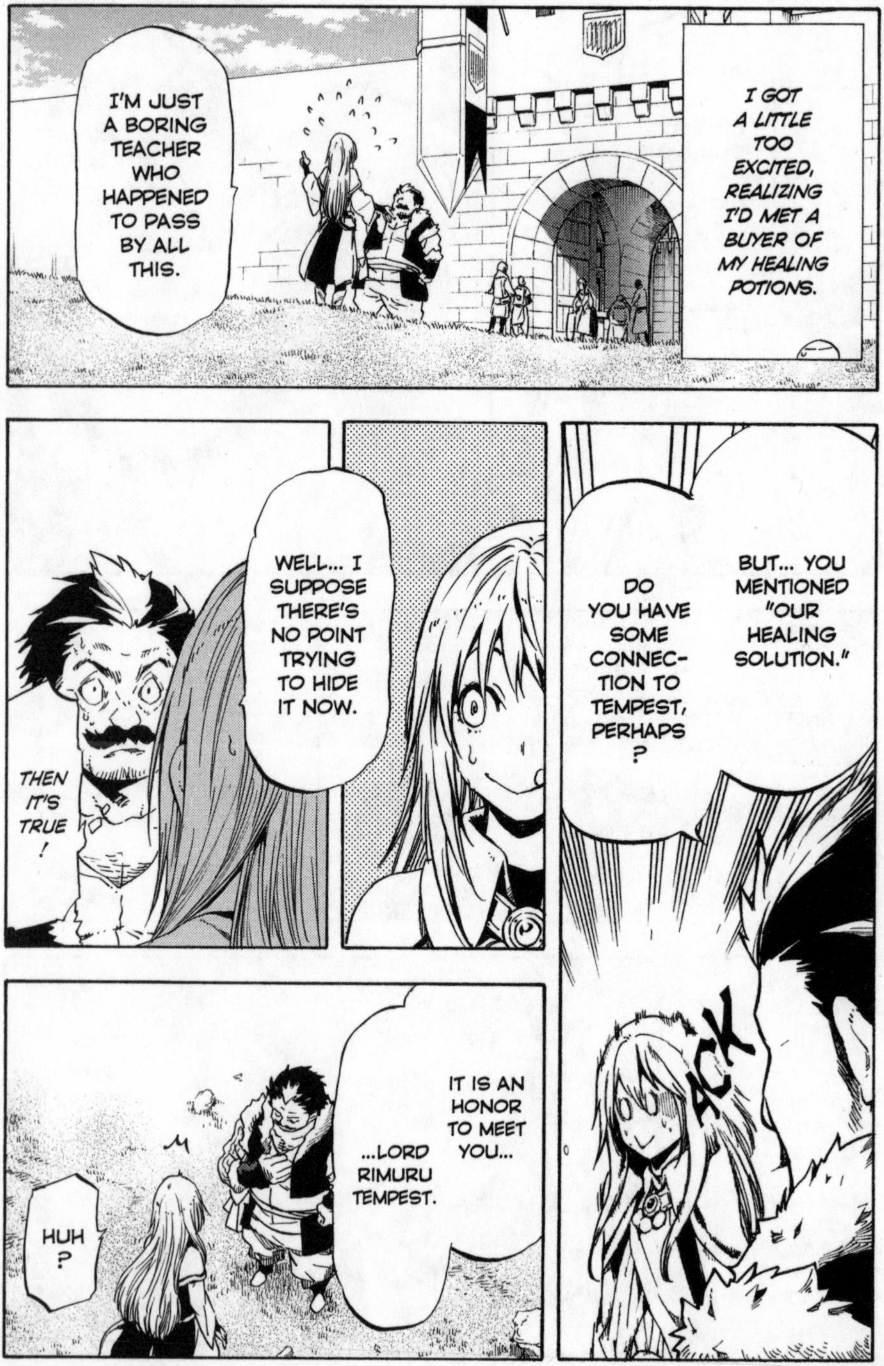
I GOT A LITTLE TOO EXCITED, REALIZING I'D MET A BUYER OF MY HEALING POTIONS.
I'M JUST A BORING TEACHER WHO HAPPENED TO PASS BY ALL THIS.
BUT... YOU MENTIONED "OUR HEALING SOLUTION."
DO YOU HAVE SOME CONNEC-TION TO TEMPEST, PERHAPS?
ACK
WELL... I SUPPOSE THERE'S NO POINT TRYING TO HIDE IT NOW.
THEN IT'S TRUE!
IT IS AN HONOR TO MEET YOU...
...LORD RIMURU TEMPEST.
HUH?

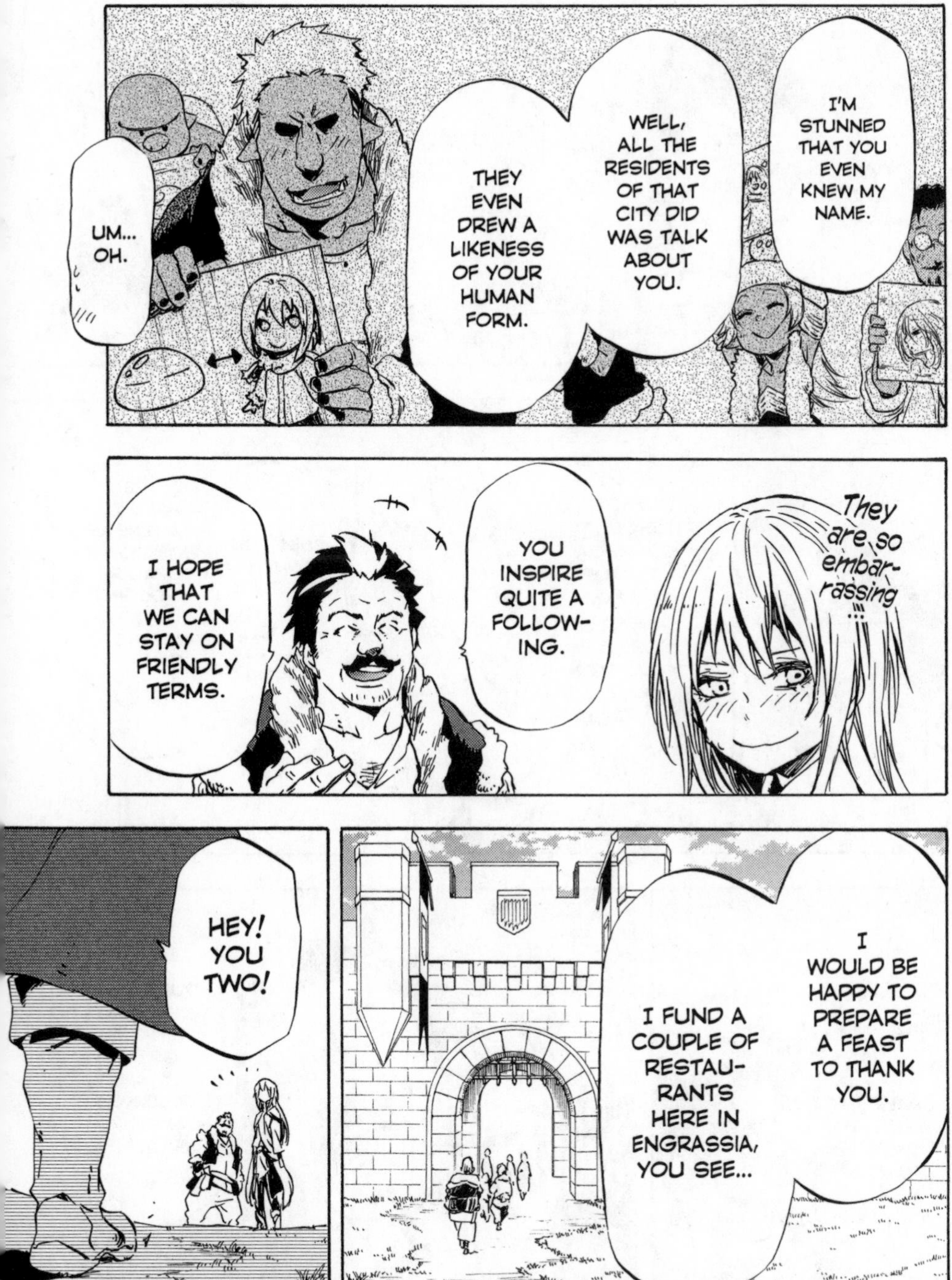
I'M STUNNED THAT YOU EVEN KNEW MY NAME.
WELL, ALL THE RESIDENTS OF THAT CITY DID WAS TALK ABOUT YOU.
THEY EVEN DREW A LIKENESS OF YOUR HUMAN FORM.
UM... OH.
They are so embar-rassing...
YOU INSPIRE QUITE A FOLLOW-ING.
I HOPE THAT WE CAN STAY ON FRIENDLY TERMS.
I WOULD BE HAPPY TO PREPARE A FEAST TO THANK YOU.
I FUND A COUPLE OF RESTAU-RANTS HERE IN ENGRASSIA, YOU SEE...
HEY! YOU TWO!

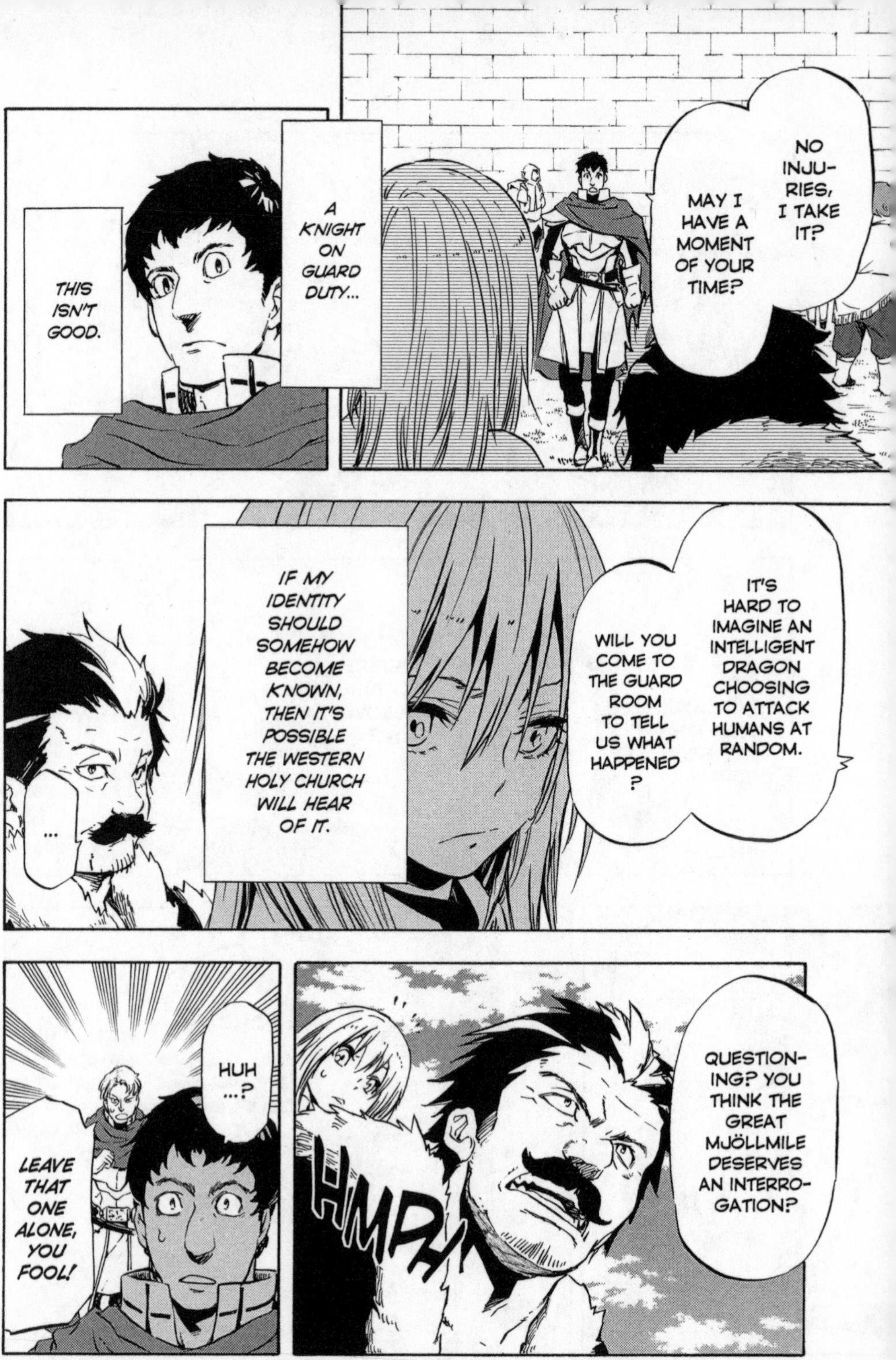
NO INJURIES, I TAKE IT?
MAY I HAVE A MOMENT OF YOUR TIME?
A KNIGHT ON GUARD DUTY...
THIS ISN'T GOOD.
IT'S HARD TO IMAGINE AN INTELLIGENT DRAGON CHOOSING TO ATTACK HUMANS AT RANDOM.
WILL YOU COME TO THE GUARD ROOM TO TELL US WHAT HAPPENED?
IF MY IDENTITY SHOULD SOMEHOW BECOME KNOWN, THEN IT'S POSSIBLE THE WESTERN HOLY CHURCH WILL HEAR OF IT.
...
QUESTIONING? YOU THINK THE GREAT MJÖLLMILE DESERVES AN INTERROGATION?
HMPH
!!
HUH...?
LEAVE THAT ONE ALONE, YOU FOOL!

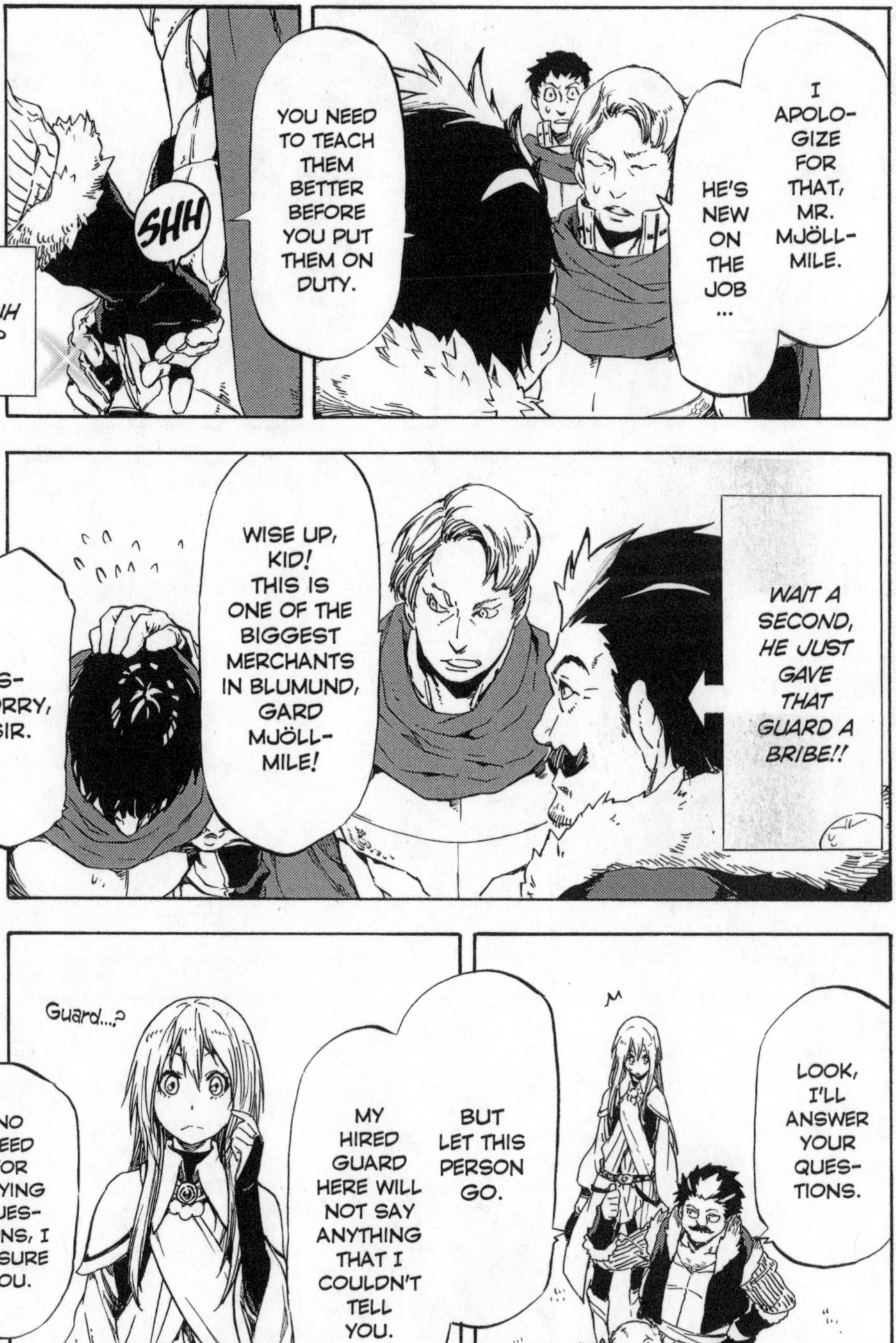
I APOLOGIZE FOR THAT, MR. MJÖLLMILE.
HE'S NEW ON THE JOB...
YOU NEED TO TEACH THEM BETTER BEFORE YOU PUT THEM ON DUTY.
SHH
HUH?
WAIT A SECOND, HE JUST GAVE THAT GUARD A BRIBE!!
WISE UP, KID! THIS IS ONE OF THE BIGGEST MERCHANTS IN BLUMUND, GARD MJÖLLMILE!
S-SORRY, SIR.
LOOK, I'LL ANSWER YOUR QUESTIONS.
BUT LET THIS PERSON GO.
MY HIRED GUARD HERE WILL NOT SAY ANYTHING THAT I COULDN'T TELL YOU.
Guard...?
NO NEED FOR PRYING QUESTIONS, I ASSURE YOU.

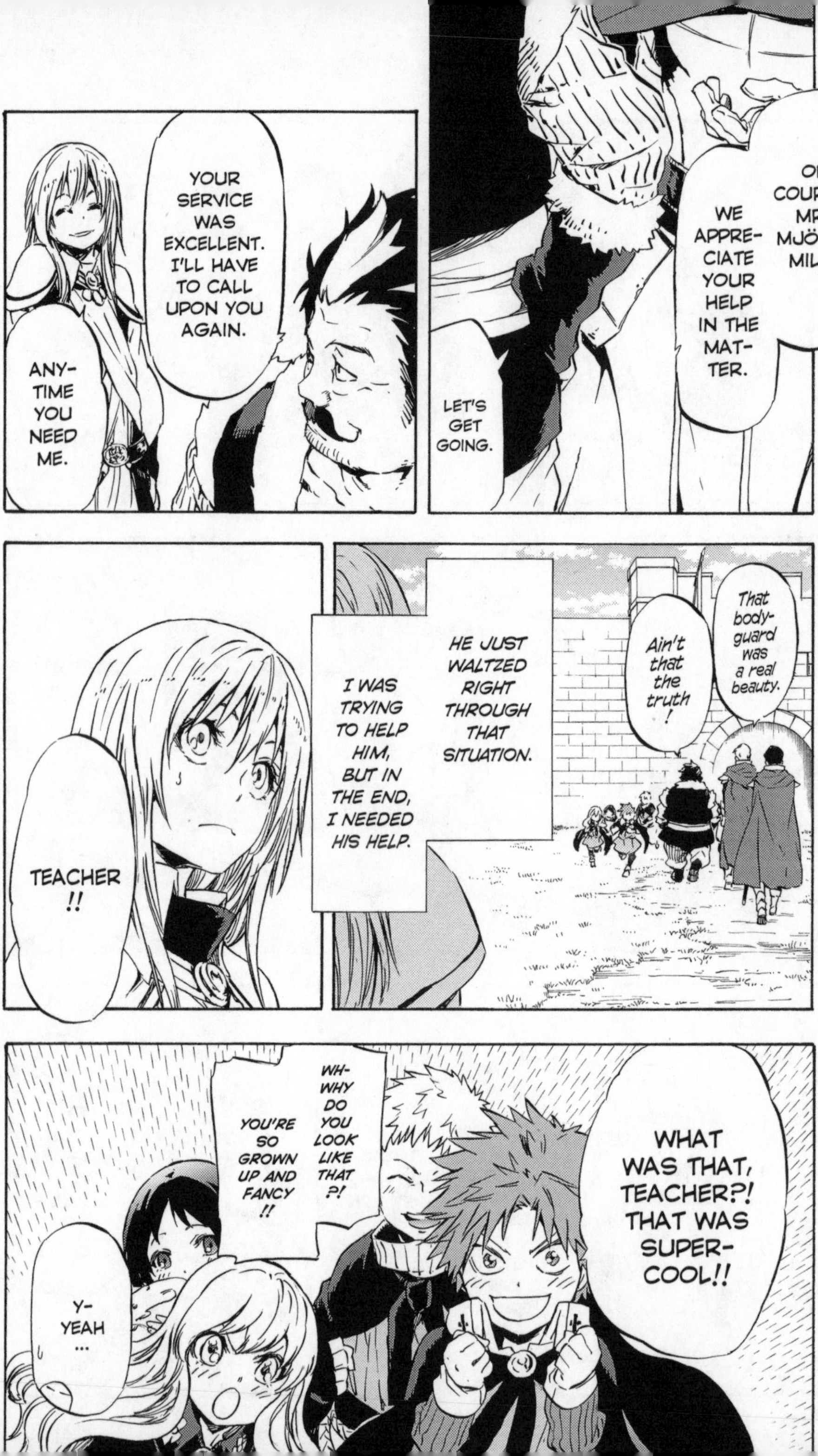

OF COURSE, MR. MJÖLLMILE.
WE APPRECIATE YOUR HELP IN THE MATTER.
LET'S GET GOING.
YOUR SERVICE WAS EXCELLENT. I'LL HAVE TO CALL UPON YOU AGAIN.
ANYTIME YOU NEED ME.
That bodyguard was a real beauty.
Ain't that the truth!
HE JUST WALTZED RIGHT THROUGH THAT SITUATION.
I WAS TRYING TO HELP HIM, BUT IN THE END, I NEEDED HIS HELP.
TEACHER!!
WHAT WAS THAT, TEACHER?! THAT WAS SUPER-COOL!!
WH-WHY DO YOU LOOK LIKE THAT?!
YOU'RE SO GROWN UP AND FANCY!!
Y-YEAH...

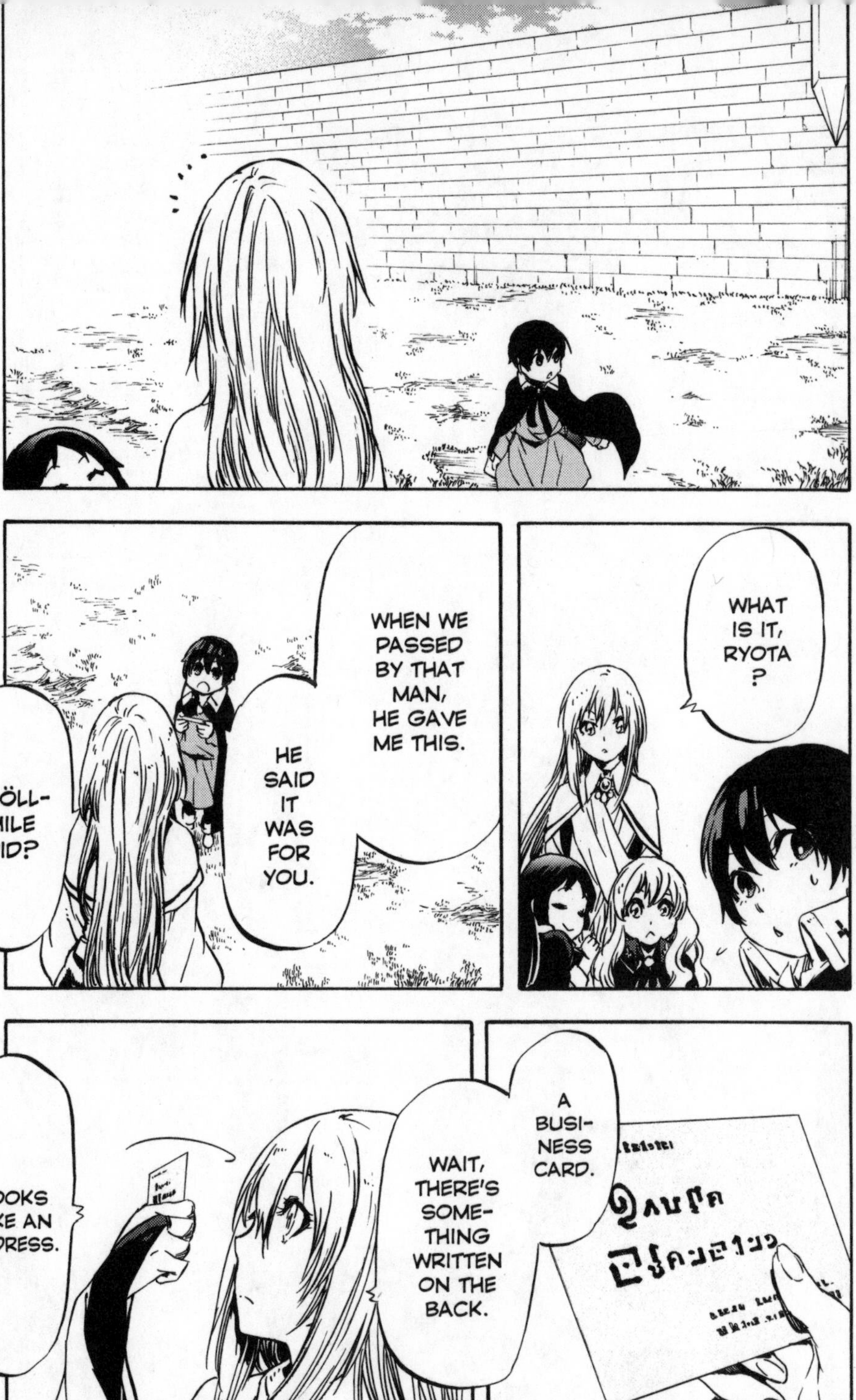
WHAT IS IT, RYOTA?
WHEN WE PASSED BY THAT MAN, HE GAVE ME THIS.
HE SAID IT WAS FOR YOU.
MJÖLL-MILE DID?
A BUSI-NESS CARD.
WAIT, THERE'S SOME-THING WRITTEN ON THE BACK.
LOOKS LIKE AN ADDRESS.

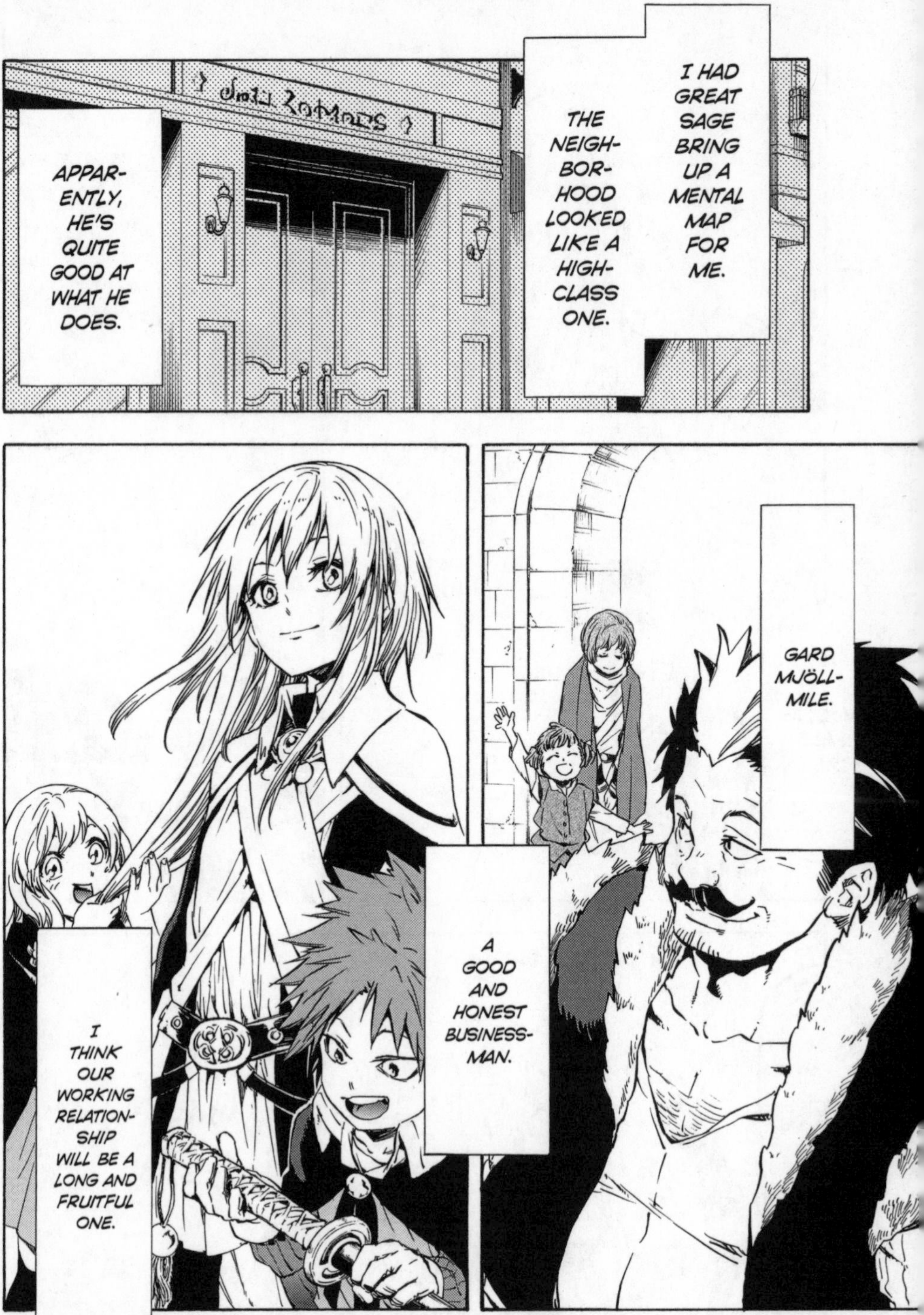
I HAD GREAT SAGE BRING UP A MENTAL MAP FOR ME.
THE NEIGHBORHOOD LOOKED LIKE A HIGH-CLASS ONE.
APPARENTLY, HE'S QUITE GOOD AT WHAT HE DOES.
GARD MJÖLLMILE.
A GOOD AND HONEST BUSINESSMAN.
I THINK OUR WORKING RELATIONSHIP WILL BE A LONG AND FRUITFUL ONE.

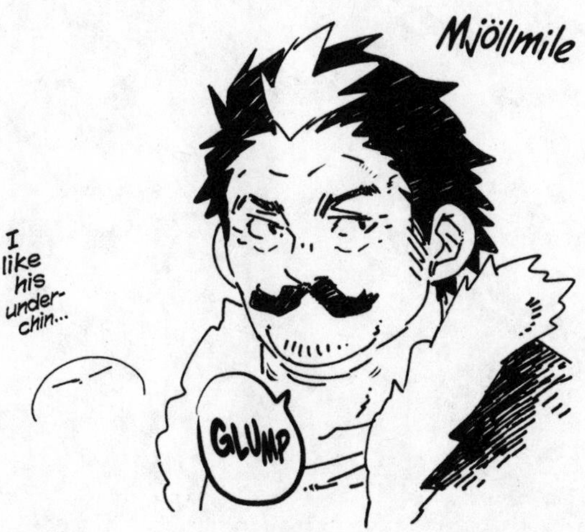
Mjöllmile
I like his under-chin...
GLUMP

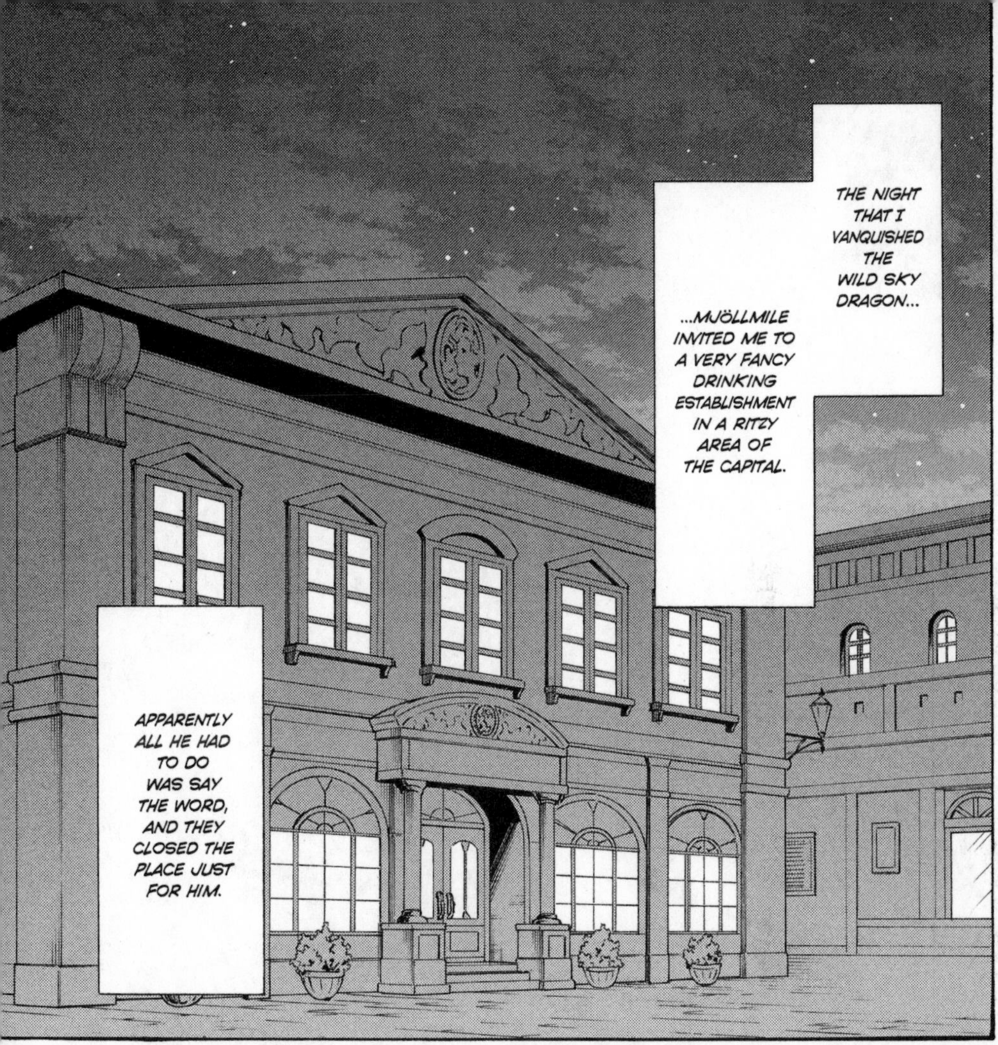
THE NIGHT THAT I VANQUISHED THE WILD SKY DRAGON...
...MJÖLLMILE INVITED ME TO A VERY FANCY DRINKING ESTABLISHMENT IN A RITZY AREA OF THE CAPITAL.
APPARENTLY ALL HE HAD TO DO WAS SAY THE WORD, AND THEY CLOSED THE PLACE JUST FOR HIM.
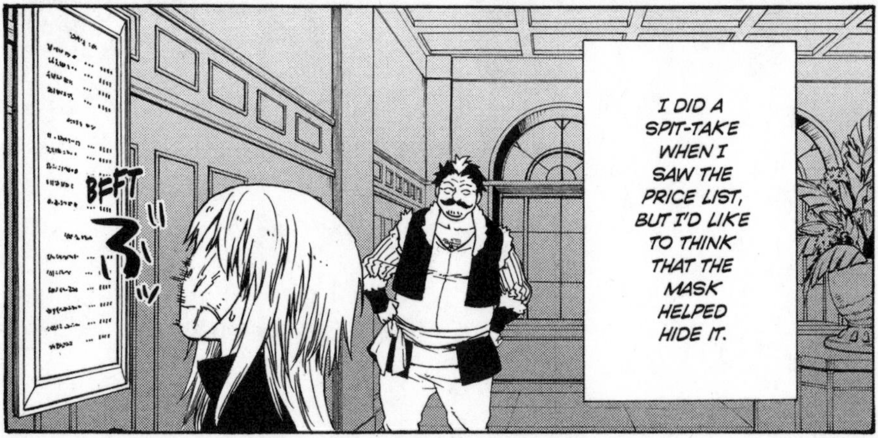
I DID A SPIT-TAKE WHEN I SAW THE PRICE LIST, BUT I'D LIKE TO THINK THAT THE MASK HELPED HIDE IT.
BFFT

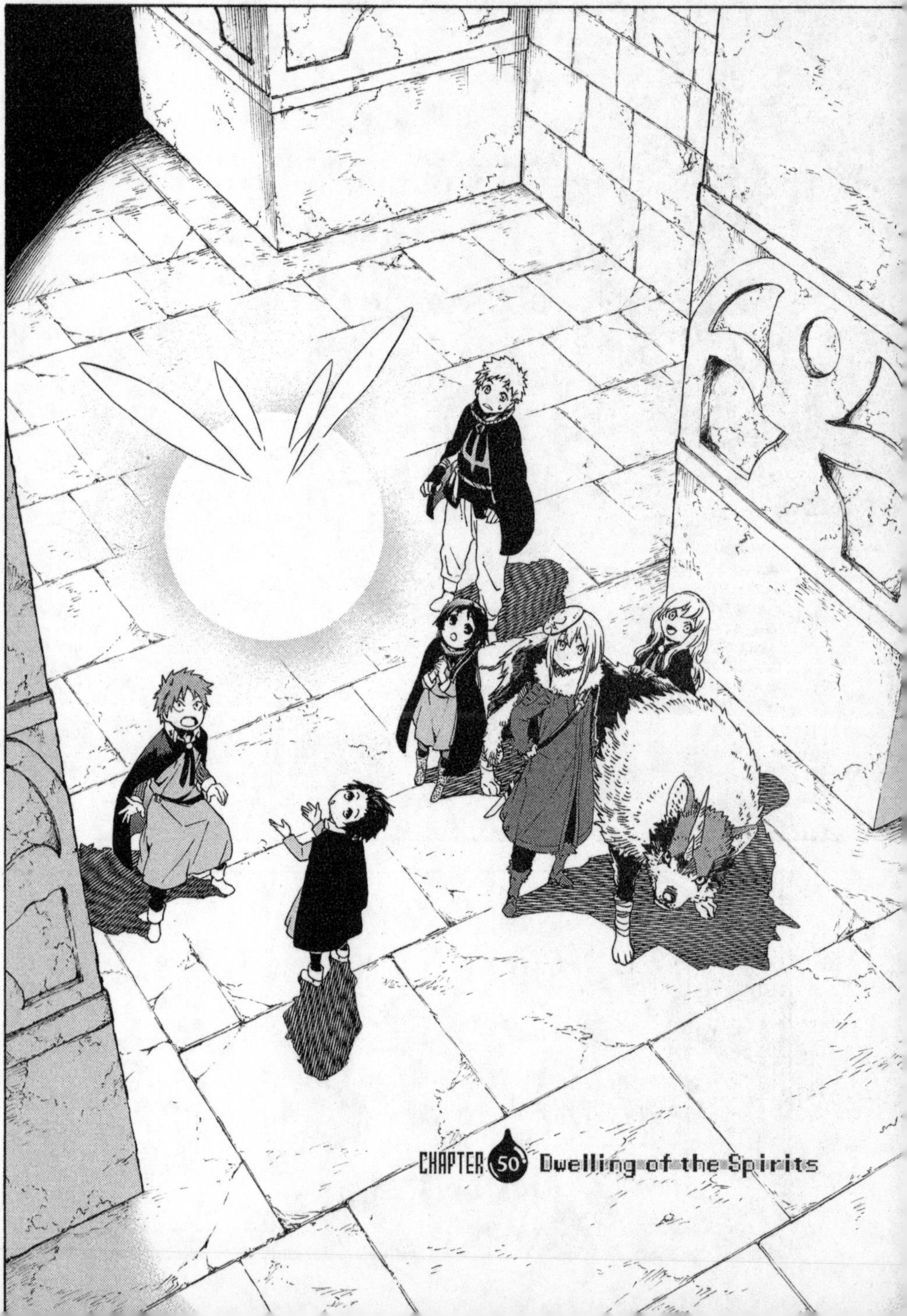
CHAPTER 50 Dwelling of the Spirits

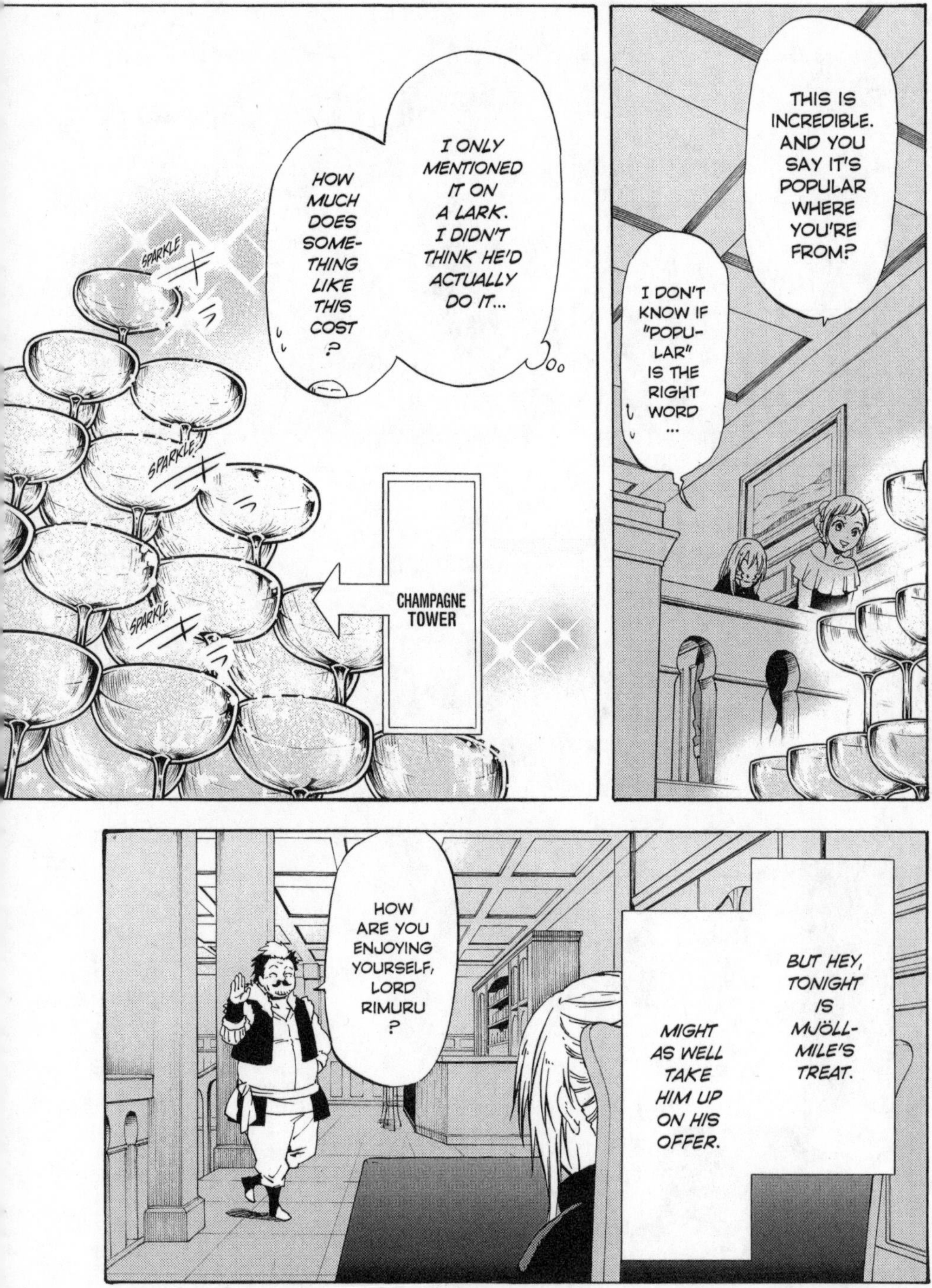
THIS IS INCREDIBLE. AND YOU SAY IT'S POPULAR WHERE YOU'RE FROM?
I DON'T KNOW IF "POPULAR" IS THE RIGHT WORD ...
I ONLY MENTIONED IT ON A LARK. I DIDN'T THINK HE'D ACTUALLY DO IT...
HOW MUCH DOES SOME-THING LIKE THIS COST ?
SPARKLE
SPARKLE
SPARKLE
CHAMPAGNE TOWER
BUT HEY, TONIGHT IS MJÖLL-MILE'S TREAT.
MIGHT AS WELL TAKE HIM UP ON HIS OFFER.
HOW ARE YOU ENJOYING YOURSELF, LORD RIMURU ?

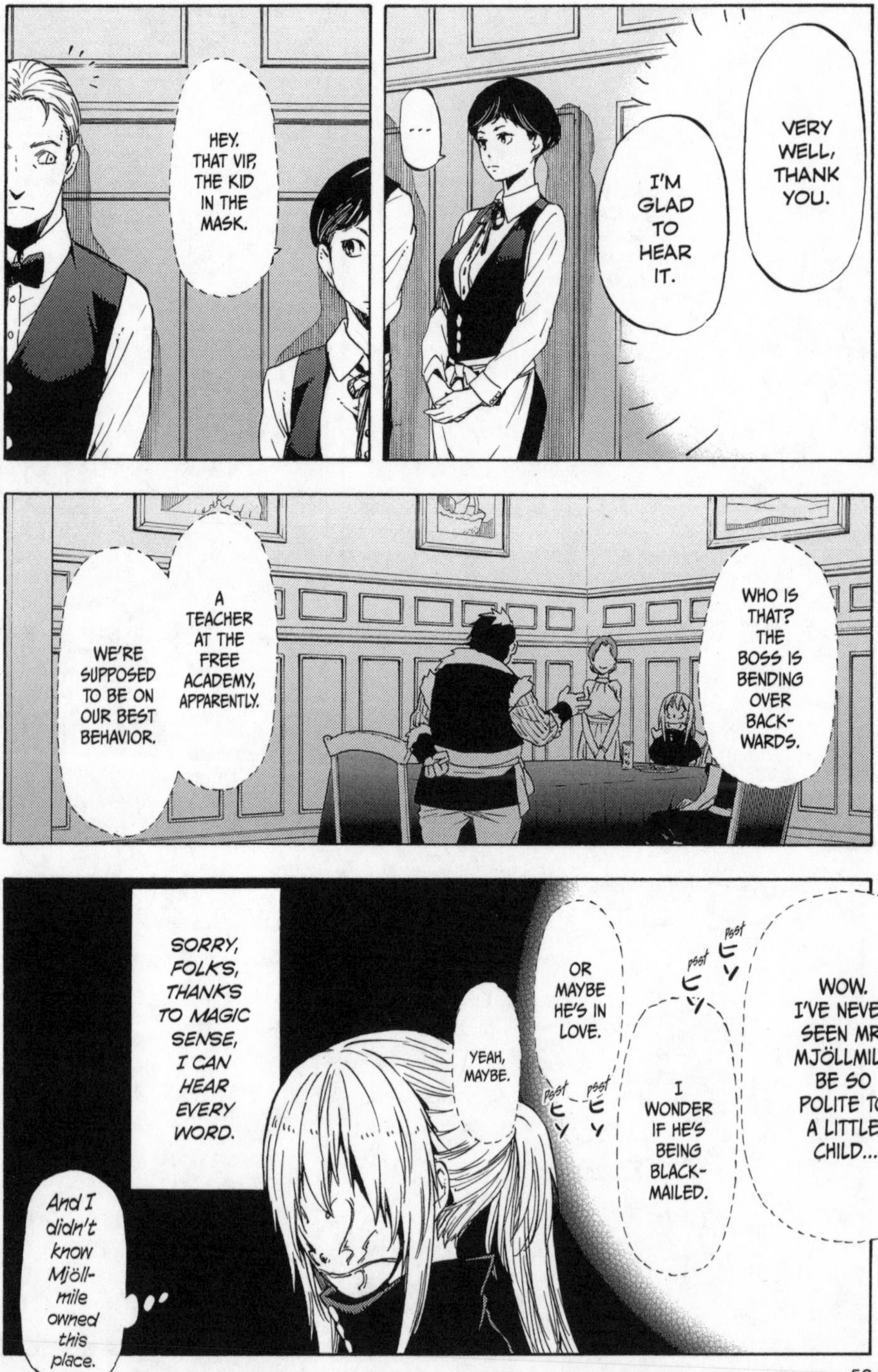
VERY WELL, THANK YOU.
I'M GLAD TO HEAR IT.
...
HEY. THAT VIP, THE KID IN THE MASK.
WHO IS THAT? THE BOSS IS BENDING OVER BACKWARDS.
A TEACHER AT THE FREE ACADEMY, APPARENTLY.
WE'RE SUPPOSED TO BE ON OUR BEST BEHAVIOR.
WOW. I'VE NEVER SEEN MR. MJÖLLMILE BE SO POLITE TO A LITTLE CHILD...
PSST ヒソ
PSST ヒソ
I WONDER IF HE'S BEING BLACKMAILED.
OR MAYBE HE'S IN LOVE.
PSST ヒソ
PSST ヒソ
YEAH, MAYBE.
SORRY, FOLKS, THANKS TO MAGIC SENSE, I CAN HEAR EVERY WORD.
And I didn't know Mjöllmile owned this place.

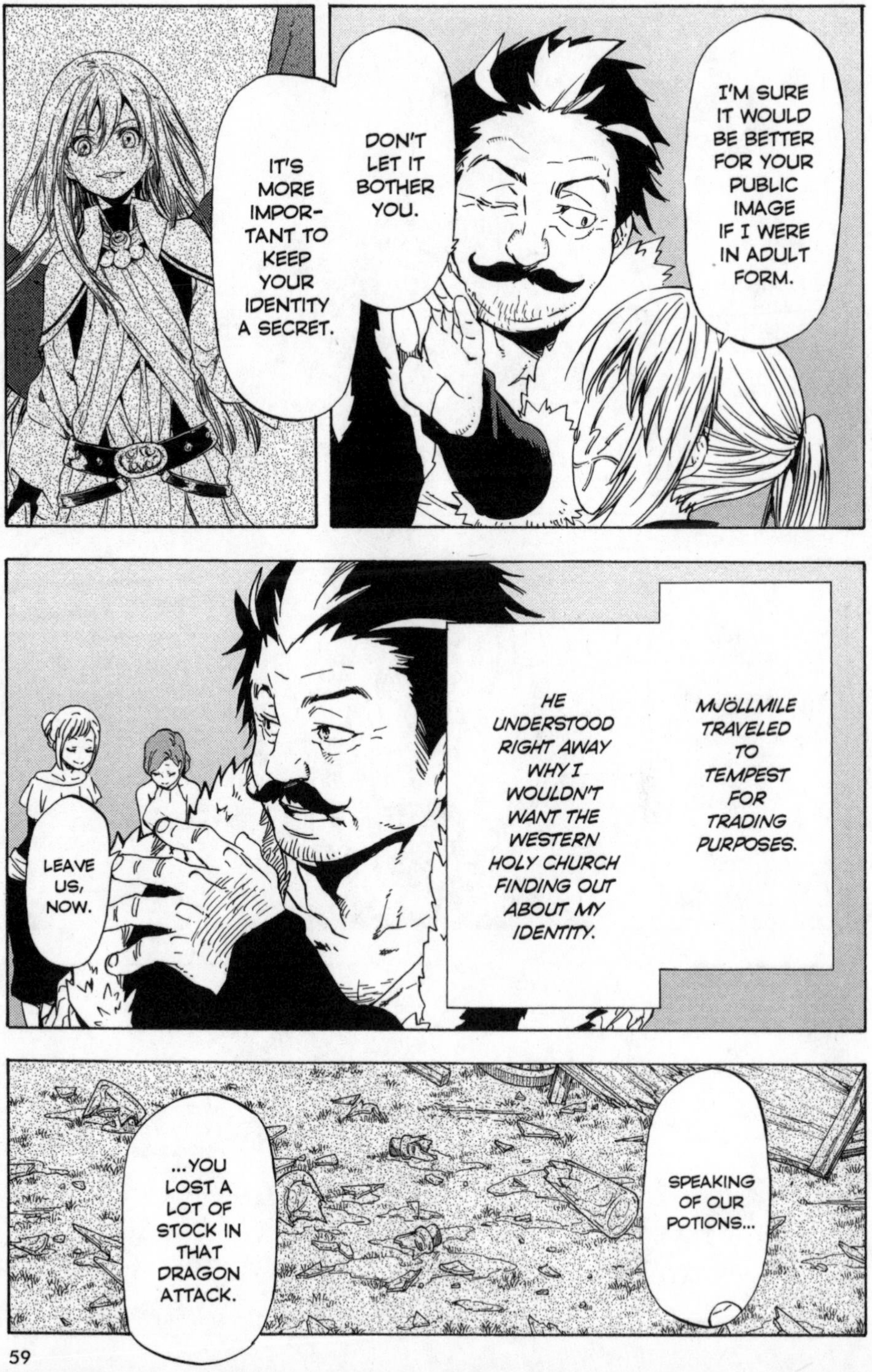
I'M SURE IT WOULD BE BETTER FOR YOUR PUBLIC IMAGE IF I WERE IN ADULT FORM.
DON'T LET IT BOTHER YOU. IT'S MORE IMPOR-TANT TO KEEP YOUR IDENTITY A SECRET.
MJÖLLMILE TRAVELED TO TEMPEST FOR TRADING PURPOSES.
HE UNDERSTOOD RIGHT AWAY WHY I WOULDN'T WANT THE WESTERN HOLY CHURCH FINDING OUT ABOUT MY IDENTITY.
LEAVE US, NOW.
SPEAKING OF OUR POTIONS...
...YOU LOST A LOT OF STOCK IN THAT DRAGON ATTACK.

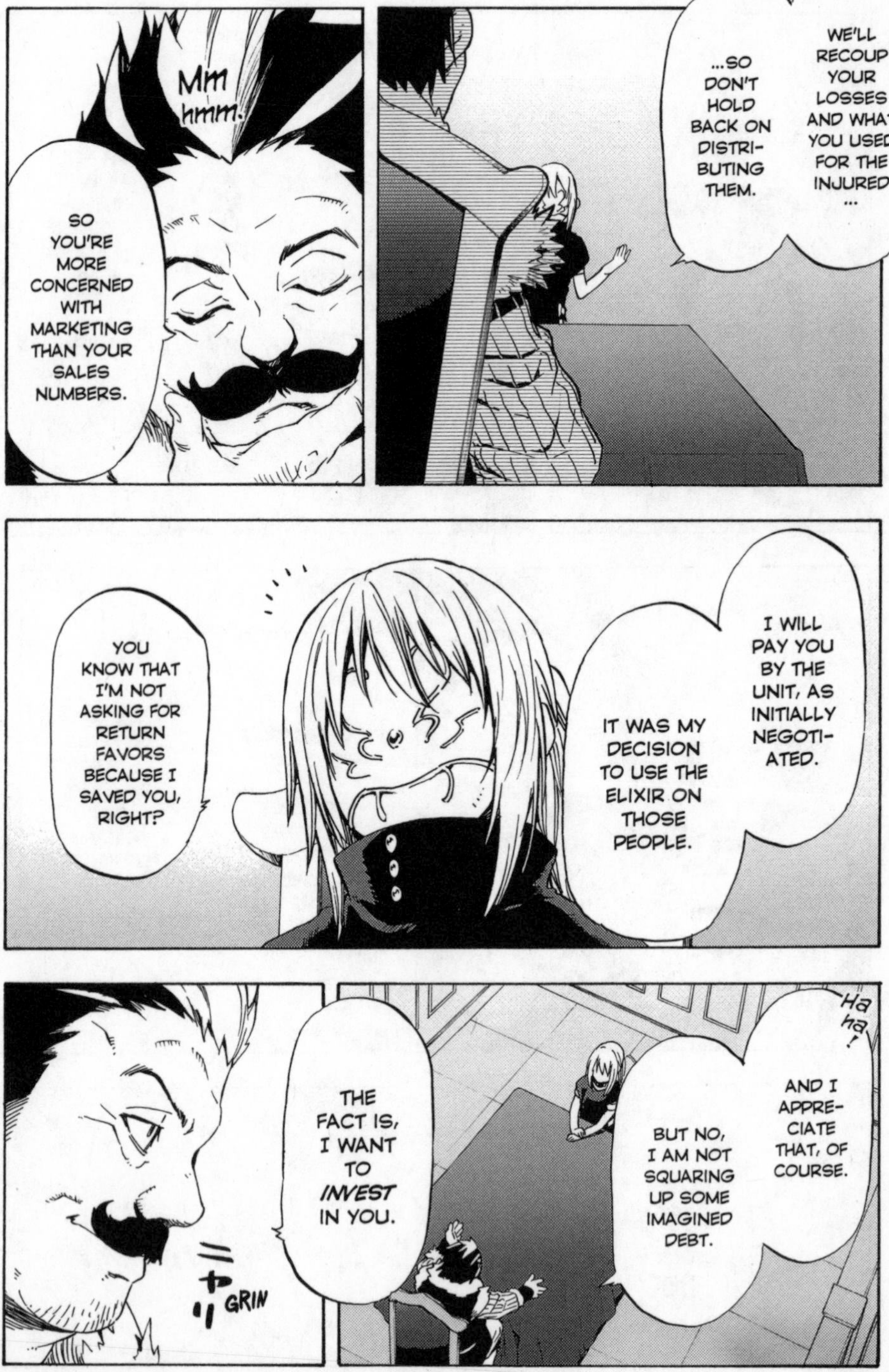
WE'LL RECOUP YOUR LOSSES AND WHAT YOU USED FOR THE INJURED ...
...SO DON'T HOLD BACK ON DISTRI-BUTING THEM.
Mm hmm!
SO YOU'RE MORE CONCERNED WITH MARKETING THAN YOUR SALES NUMBERS.
I WILL PAY YOU BY THE UNIT, AS INITIALLY NEGOTI-ATED.
IT WAS MY DECISION TO USE THE ELIXIR ON THOSE PEOPLE.
YOU KNOW THAT I'M NOT ASKING FOR RETURN FAVORS BECAUSE I SAVED YOU, RIGHT?
Ha ha!
AND I APPRE-CIATE THAT, OF COURSE.
BUT NO, I AM NOT SQUARING UP SOME IMAGINED DEBT.
THE FACT IS, I WANT TO *INVEST* IN YOU.
GRIN

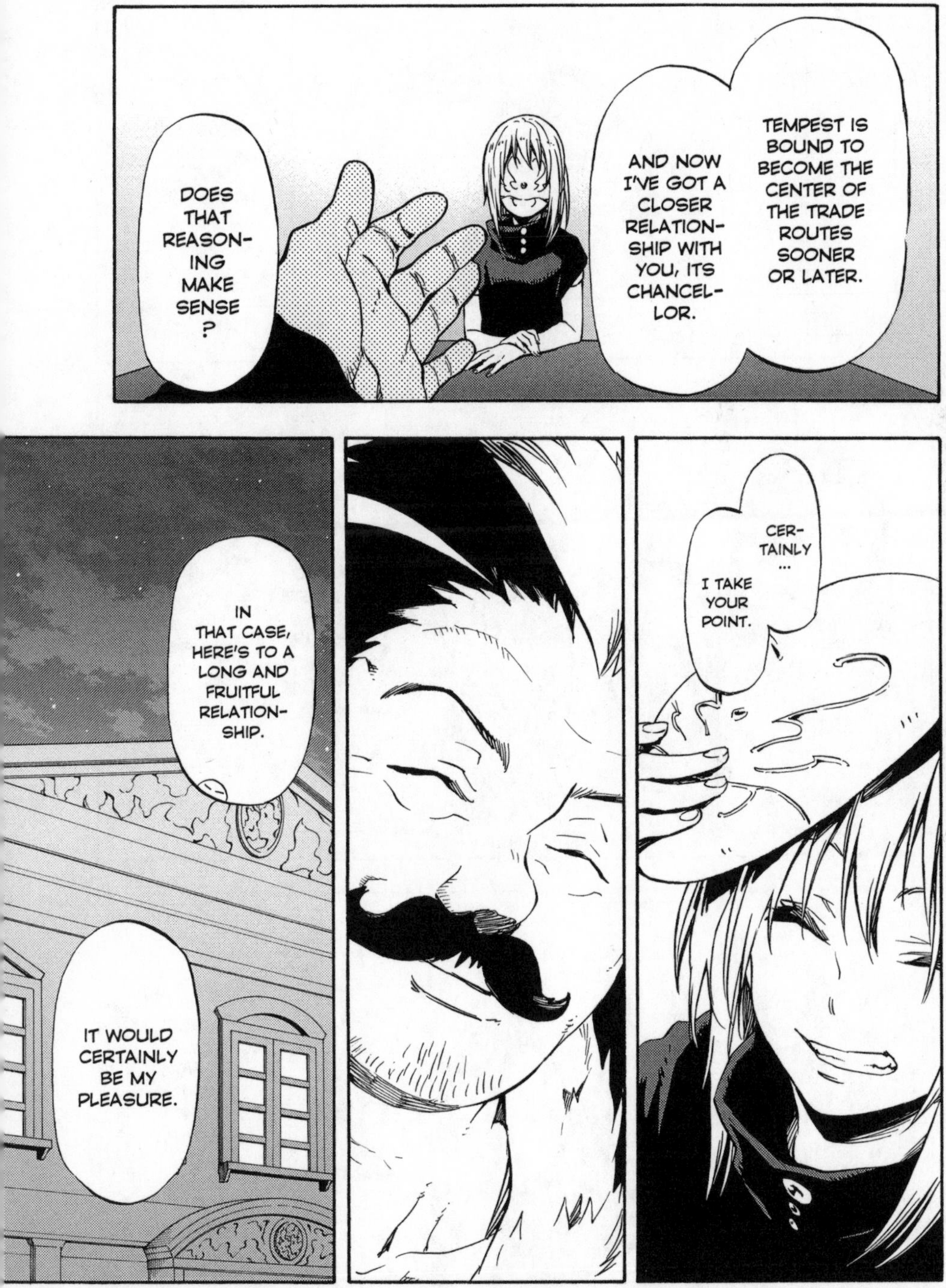
TEMPEST IS BOUND TO BECOME THE CENTER OF THE TRADE ROUTES SOONER OR LATER.
AND NOW I'VE GOT A CLOSER RELATION-SHIP WITH YOU, ITS CHANCEL-LOR.
DOES THAT REASON-ING MAKE SENSE?
CER-TAINLY...
I TAKE YOUR POINT.
IN THAT CASE, HERE'S TO A LONG AND FRUITFUL RELATION-SHIP.
IT WOULD CERTAINLY BE MY PLEASURE.

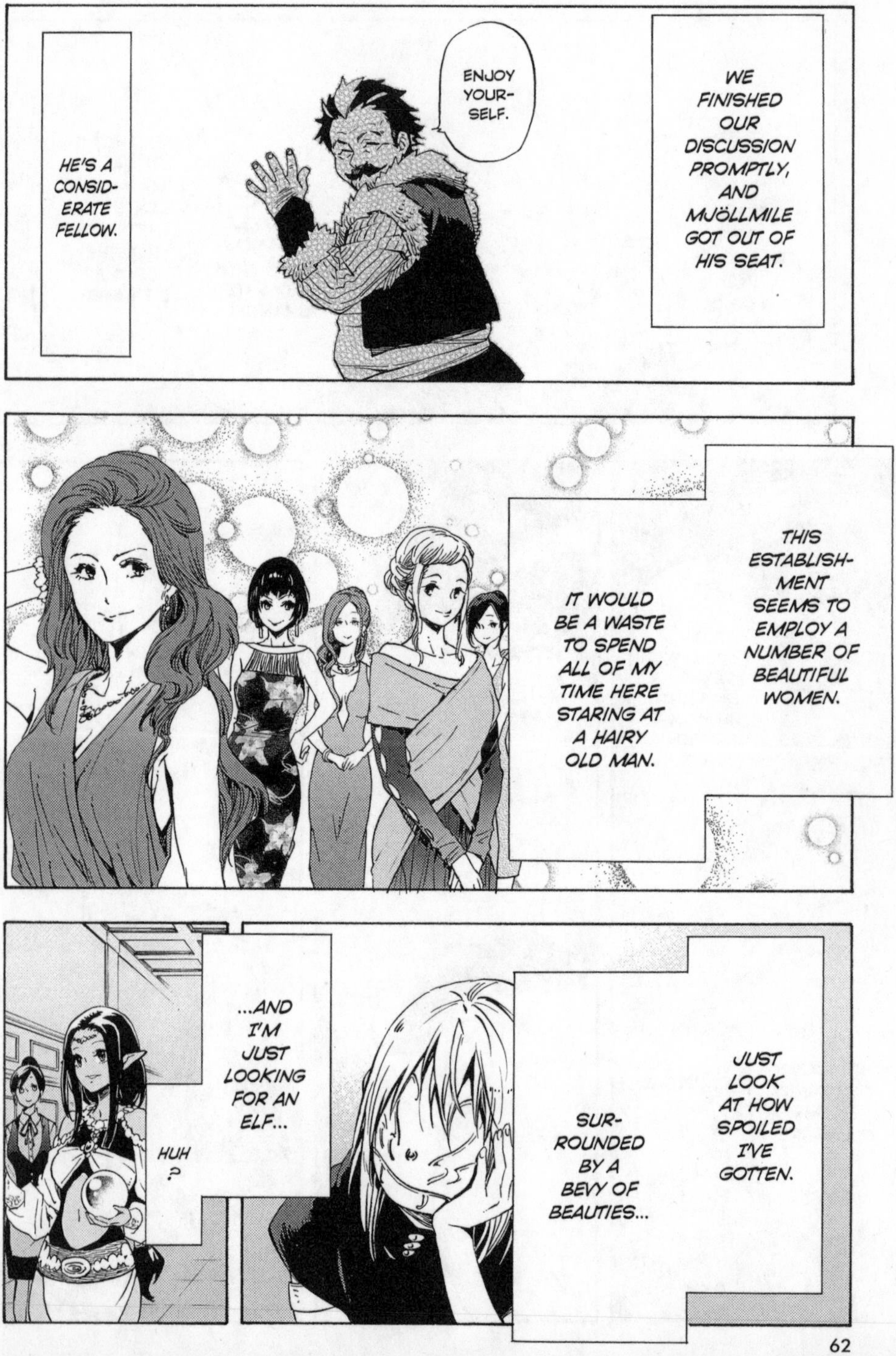
WE FINISHED OUR DISCUSSION PROMPTLY, AND MJÖLLMILE GOT OUT OF HIS SEAT.
ENJOY YOURSELF.
HE'S A CONSIDERATE FELLOW.
THIS ESTABLISHMENT SEEMS TO EMPLOY A NUMBER OF BEAUTIFUL WOMEN.
IT WOULD BE A WASTE TO SPEND ALL OF MY TIME HERE STARING AT A HAIRY OLD MAN.
JUST LOOK AT HOW SPOILED I'VE GOTTEN.
SURROUNDED BY A BEVY OF BEAUTIES...
...AND I'M JUST LOOKING FOR AN ELF...
HUH?

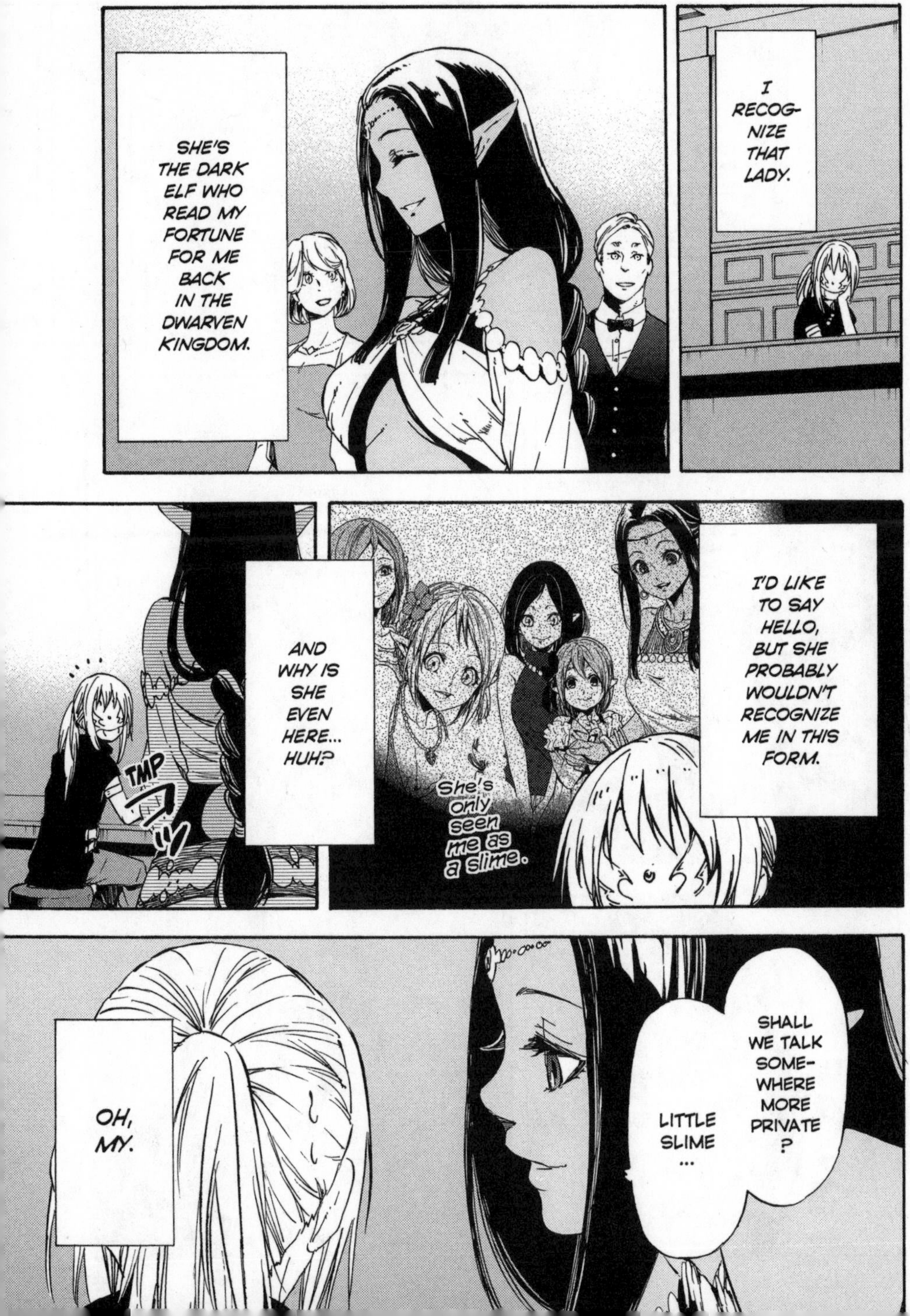
I RECOGNIZE THAT LADY.
SHE'S THE DARK ELF WHO READ MY FORTUNE FOR ME BACK IN THE DWARVEN KINGDOM.
I'D LIKE TO SAY HELLO, BUT SHE PROBABLY WOULDN'T RECOGNIZE ME IN THIS FORM.
She's only seen me as a slime.
AND WHY IS SHE EVEN HERE... HUH?
TMP
SHALL WE TALK SOMEWHERE MORE PRIVATE?
LITTLE SLIME...
OH, MY.

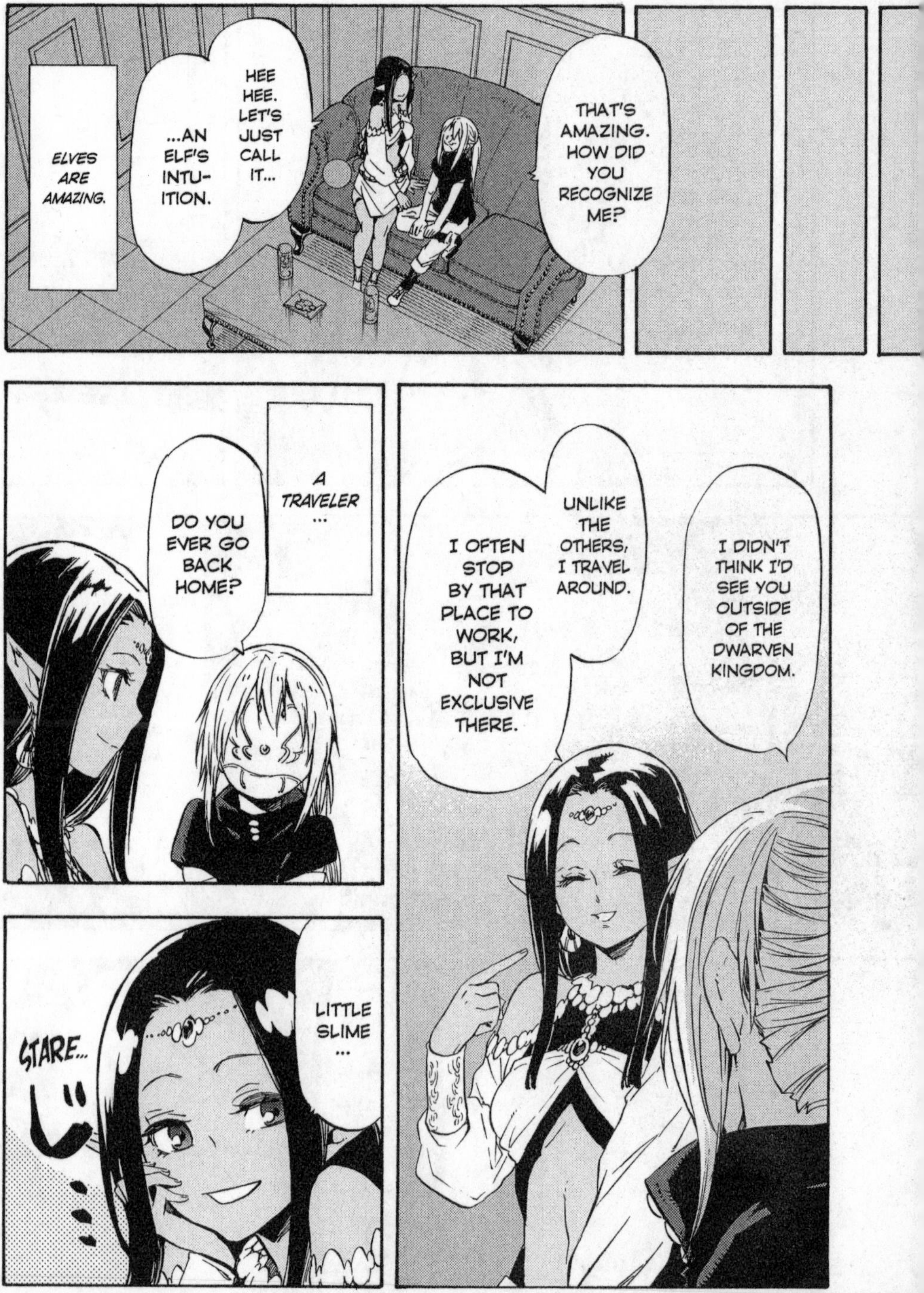
THAT'S AMAZING. HOW DID YOU RECOGNIZE ME?
HEE HEE. LET'S JUST CALL IT...
...AN ELF'S INTU-ITION.
ELVES ARE AMAZING.
I DIDN'T THINK I'D SEE YOU OUTSIDE OF THE DWARVEN KINGDOM.
UNLIKE THE OTHERS, I TRAVEL AROUND.
I OFTEN STOP BY THAT PLACE TO WORK, BUT I'M NOT EXCLUSIVE THERE.
A TRAVELER ...
DO YOU EVER GO BACK HOME?
LITTLE SLIME ...
STARE...

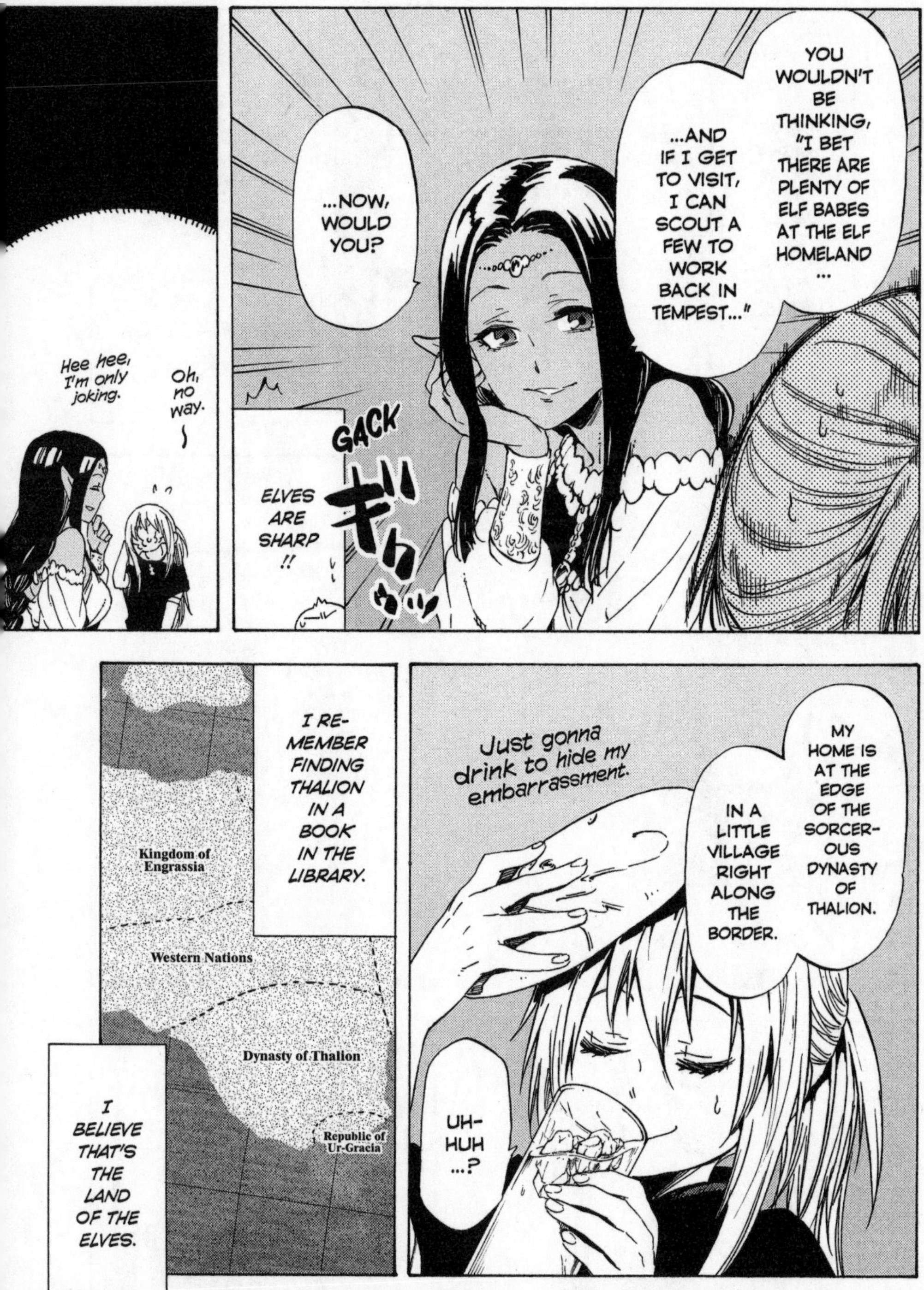
YOU WOULDN'T BE THINKING, "I BET THERE ARE PLENTY OF ELF BABES AT THE ELF HOMELAND ...
...AND IF I GET TO VISIT, I CAN SCOUT A FEW TO WORK BACK IN TEMPEST..."
...NOW, WOULD YOU?
GACK
ELVES ARE SHARP !!
Oh, no way.
Hee hee, I'm only joking.
MY HOME IS AT THE EDGE OF THE SORCEROUS DYNASTY OF THALION.
IN A LITTLE VILLAGE RIGHT ALONG THE BORDER.
Just gonna drink to hide my embarrassment.
UH-HUH ...?
I REMEMBER FINDING THALION IN A BOOK IN THE LIBRARY.
Kingdom of Engrassia
Western Nations
Dynasty of Thalion
Republic of Ur-Gracia
I BELIEVE THAT'S THE LAND OF THE ELVES.

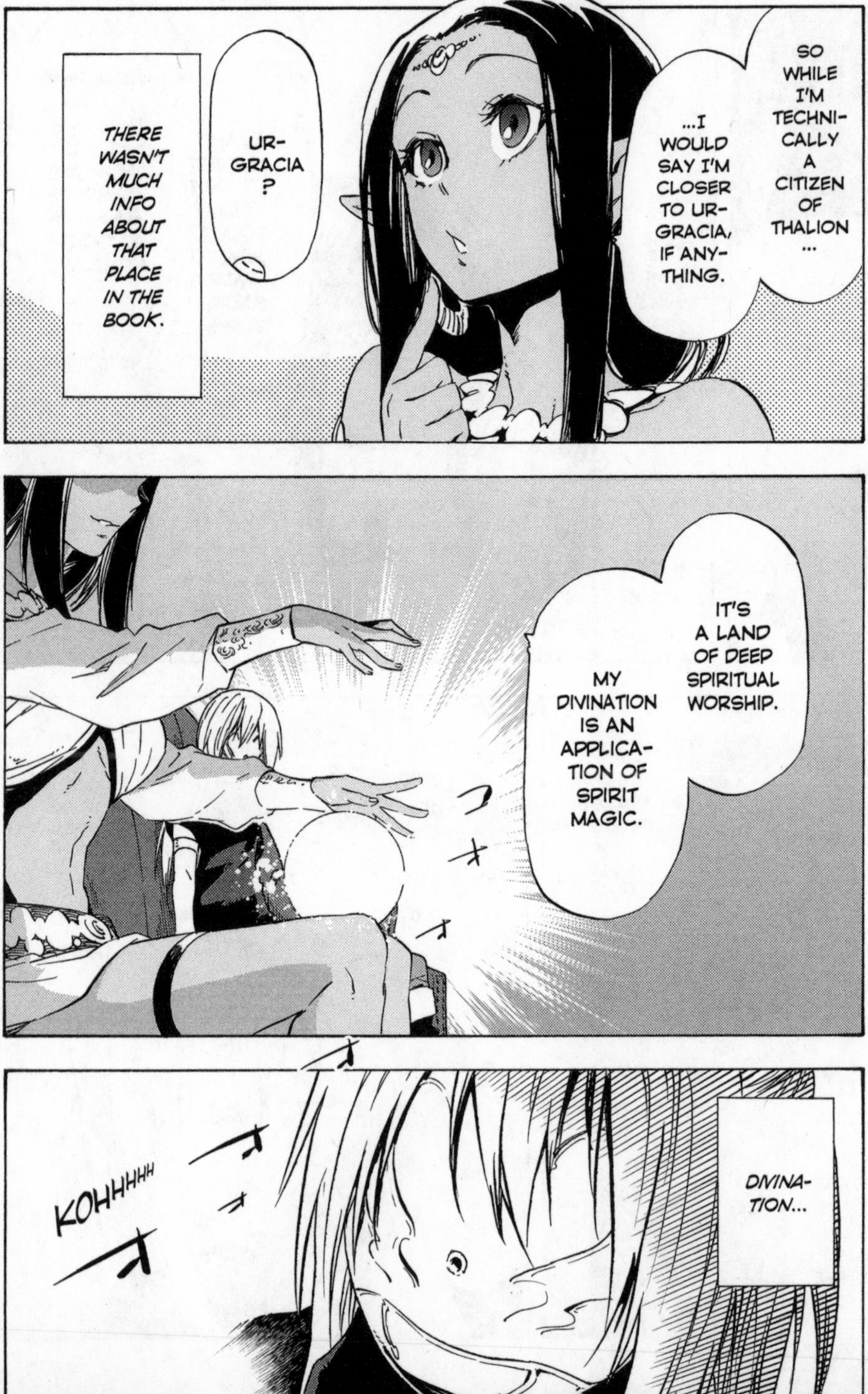
SO WHILE I'M TECHNI-CALLY A CITIZEN OF THALION ...
...I WOULD SAY I'M CLOSER TO UR-GRACIA, IF ANY-THING.
UR-GRACIA ?
THERE WASN'T MUCH INFO ABOUT THAT PLACE IN THE BOOK.
IT'S A LAND OF DEEP SPIRITUAL WORSHIP.
MY DIVINATION IS AN APPLICA-TION OF SPIRIT MAGIC.
DIVINA-TION...
KOHHHHH

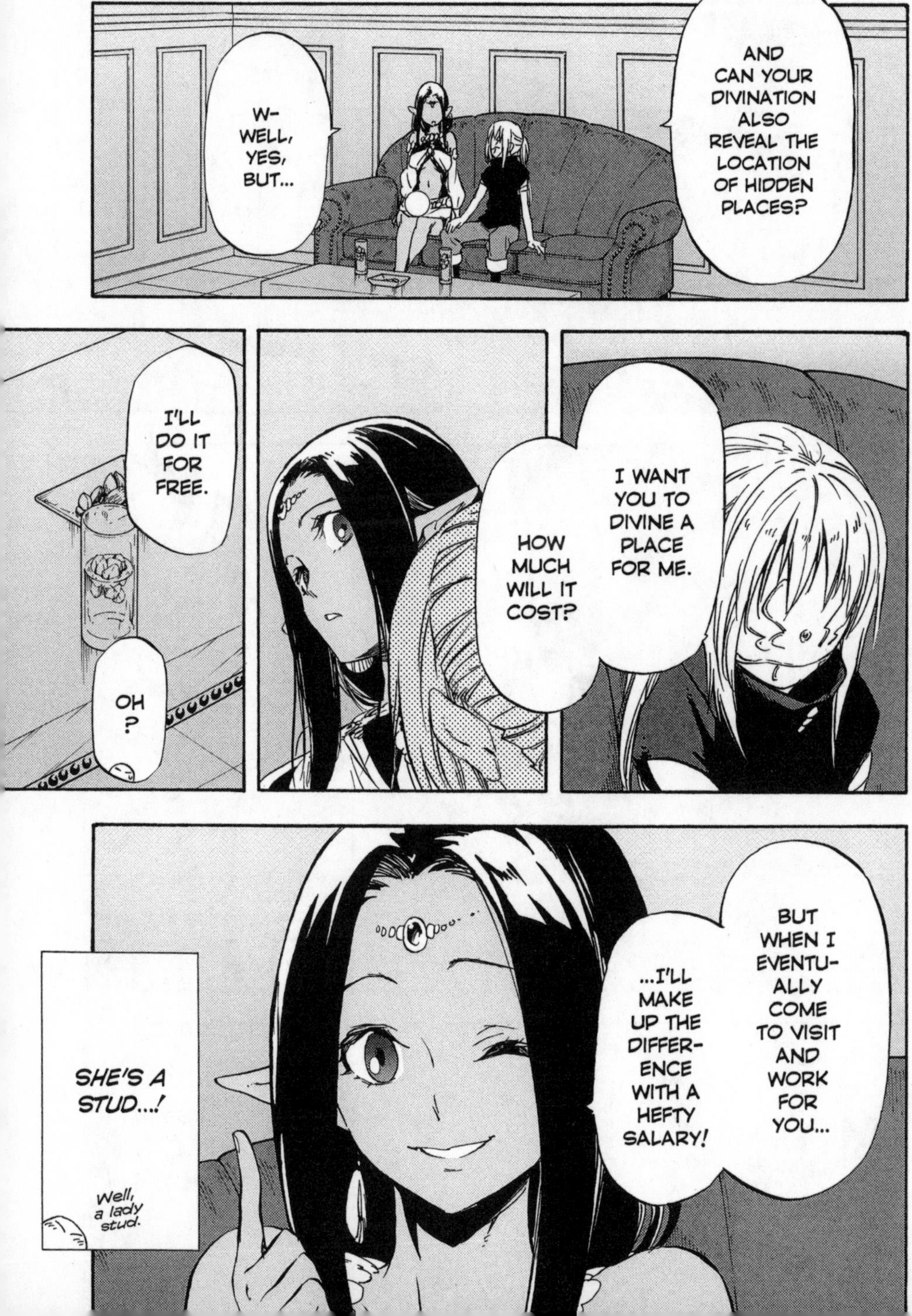
AND CAN YOUR DIVINATION ALSO REVEAL THE LOCATION OF HIDDEN PLACES?
W-WELL, YES, BUT...
I WANT YOU TO DIVINE A PLACE FOR ME.
HOW MUCH WILL IT COST?
I'LL DO IT FOR FREE.
OH?
BUT WHEN I EVENTU-ALLY COME TO VISIT AND WORK FOR YOU...
...I'LL MAKE UP THE DIFFER-ENCE WITH A HEFTY SALARY!
SHE'S A STUD...!
Well, a lady stud.

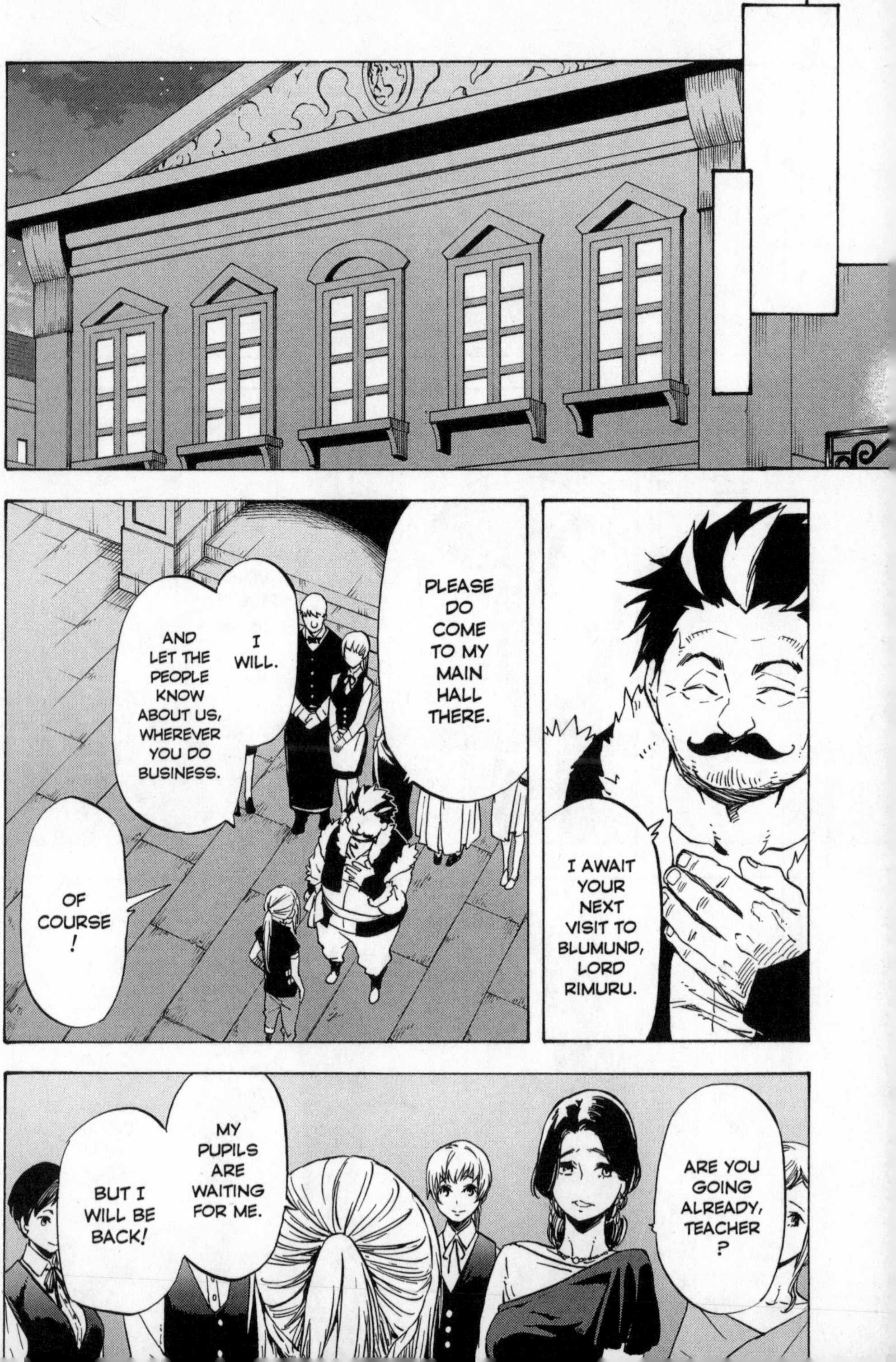
I AWAIT YOUR NEXT VISIT TO BLUMUND, LORD RIMURU.
PLEASE DO COME TO MY MAIN HALL THERE.
I WILL.
AND LET THE PEOPLE KNOW ABOUT US, WHEREVER YOU DO BUSINESS.
OF COURSE!
ARE YOU GOING ALREADY, TEACHER?
MY PUPILS ARE WAITING FOR ME.
BUT I WILL BE BACK!

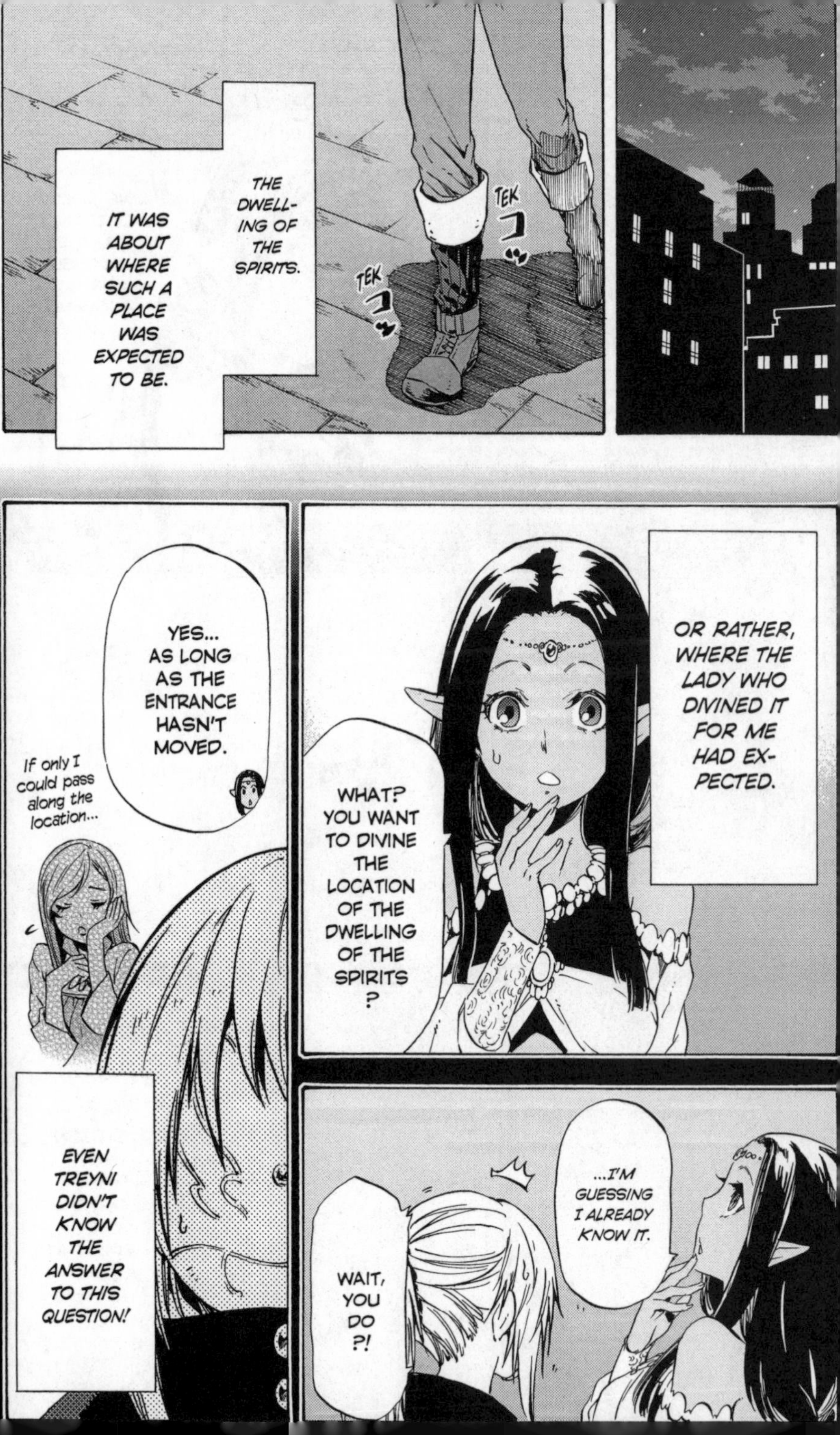
TEK
TEK
THE DWELLING OF THE SPIRITS.
IT WAS ABOUT WHERE SUCH A PLACE WAS EXPECTED TO BE.
OR RATHER, WHERE THE LADY WHO DIVINED IT FOR ME HAD EXPECTED.
WHAT? YOU WANT TO DIVINE THE LOCATION OF THE DWELLING OF THE SPIRITS?
...I'M GUESSING I ALREADY KNOW IT.
WAIT, YOU DO?!
YES... AS LONG AS THE ENTRANCE HASN'T MOVED.
If only I could pass along the location...
EVEN TREYNI DIDN'T KNOW THE ANSWER TO THIS QUESTION!

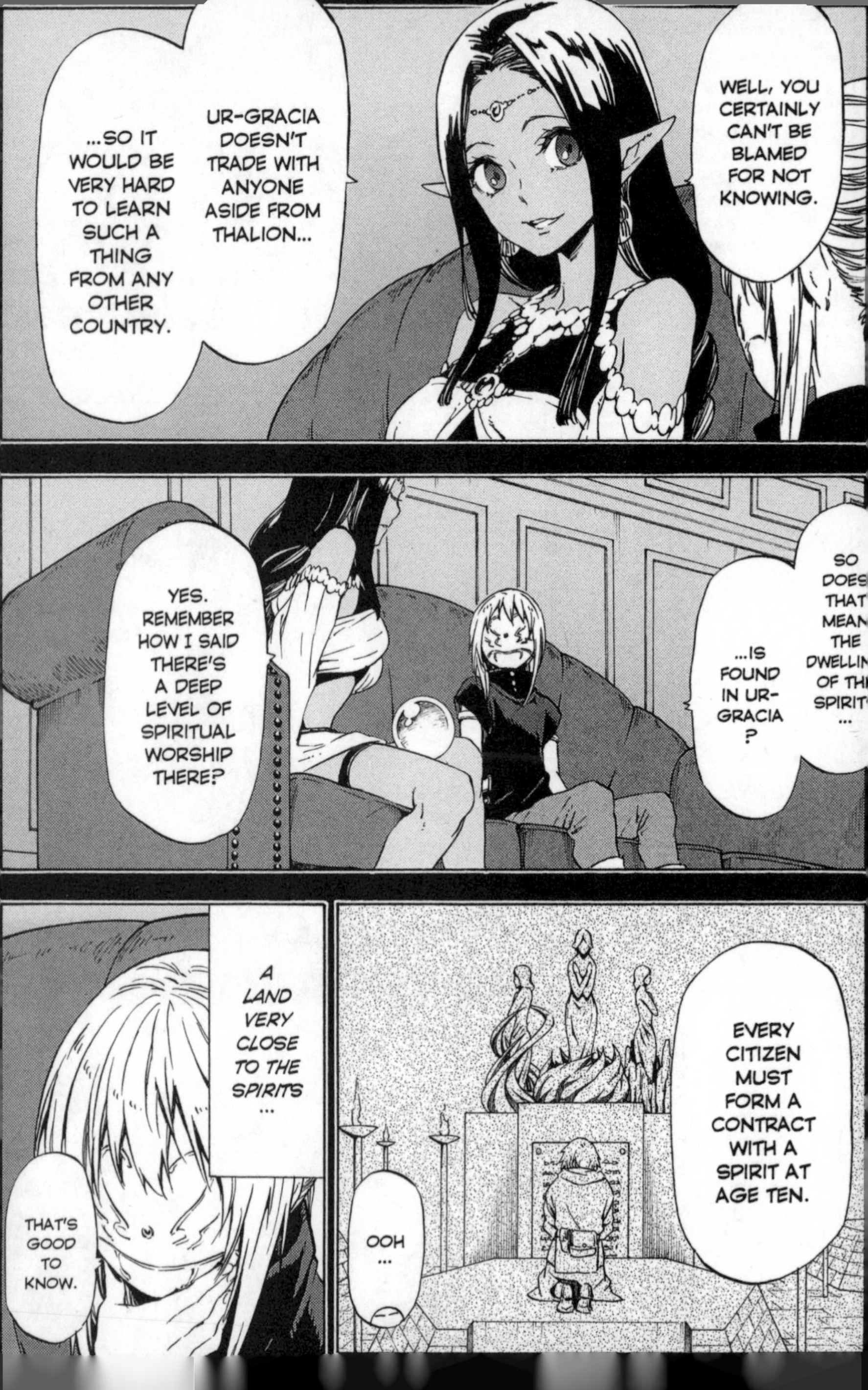
WELL, YOU CERTAINLY CAN'T BE BLAMED FOR NOT KNOWING.
UR-GRACIA DOESN'T TRADE WITH ANYONE ASIDE FROM THALION...
...SO IT WOULD BE VERY HARD TO LEARN SUCH A THING FROM ANY OTHER COUNTRY.
SO DOES THAT MEAN THE DWELLIN OF TH SPIRIT ...
...IS FOUND IN UR-GRACIA ?
YES. REMEMBER HOW I SAID THERE'S A DEEP LEVEL OF SPIRITUAL WORSHIP THERE?
EVERY CITIZEN MUST FORM A CONTRACT WITH A SPIRIT AT AGE TEN.
OOH ...
A LAND VERY CLOSE TO THE SPIRITS ...
THAT'S GOOD TO KNOW.

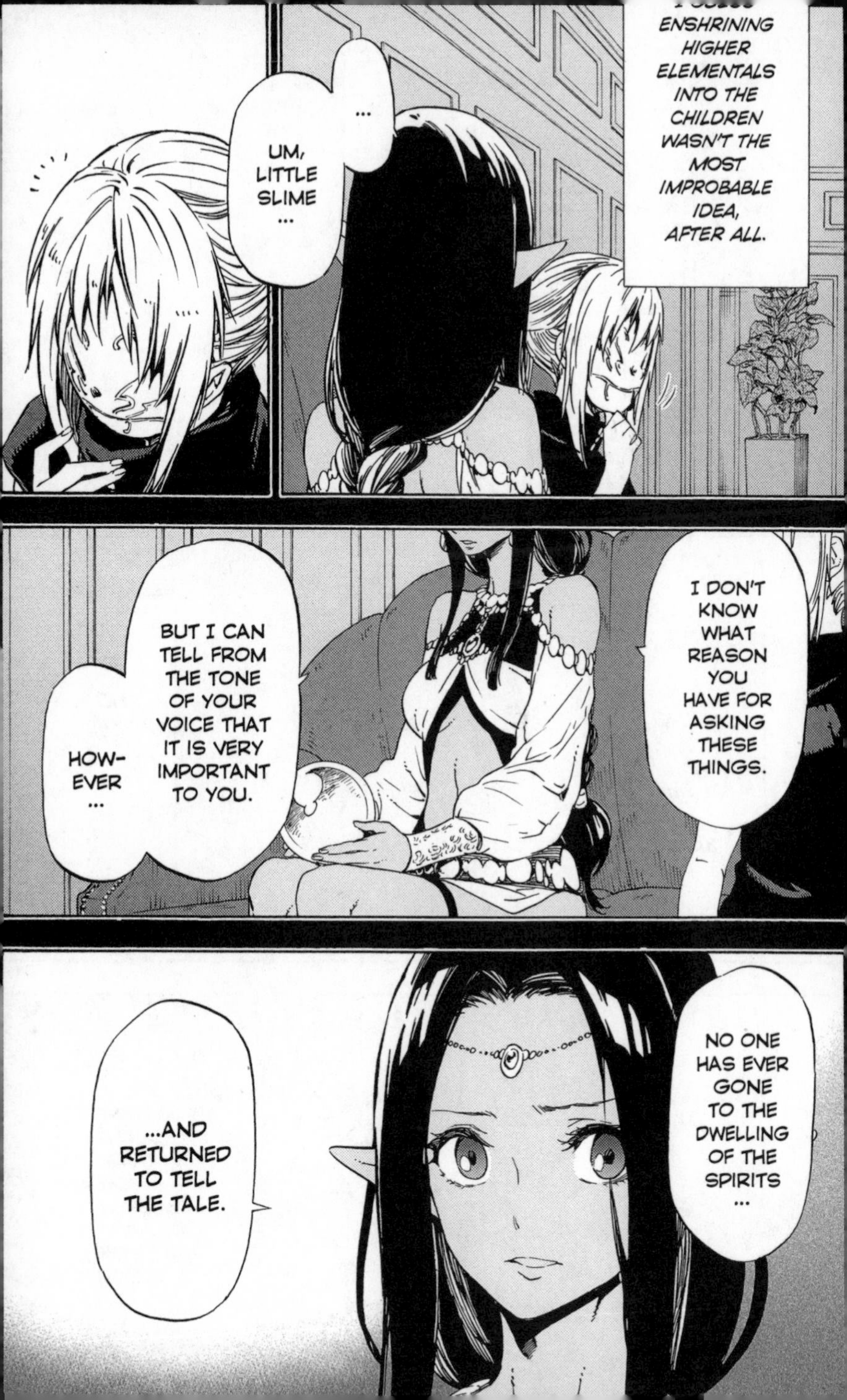
ENSHRINING HIGHER ELEMENTALS INTO THE CHILDREN WASN'T THE MOST IMPROBABLE IDEA, AFTER ALL.
...
UM, LITTLE SLIME ...
I DON'T KNOW WHAT REASON YOU HAVE FOR ASKING THESE THINGS.
BUT I CAN TELL FROM THE TONE OF YOUR VOICE THAT IT IS VERY IMPORTANT TO YOU.
HOW-EVER ...
NO ONE HAS EVER GONE TO THE DWELLING OF THE SPIRITS ...
...AND RETURNED TO TELL THE TALE.

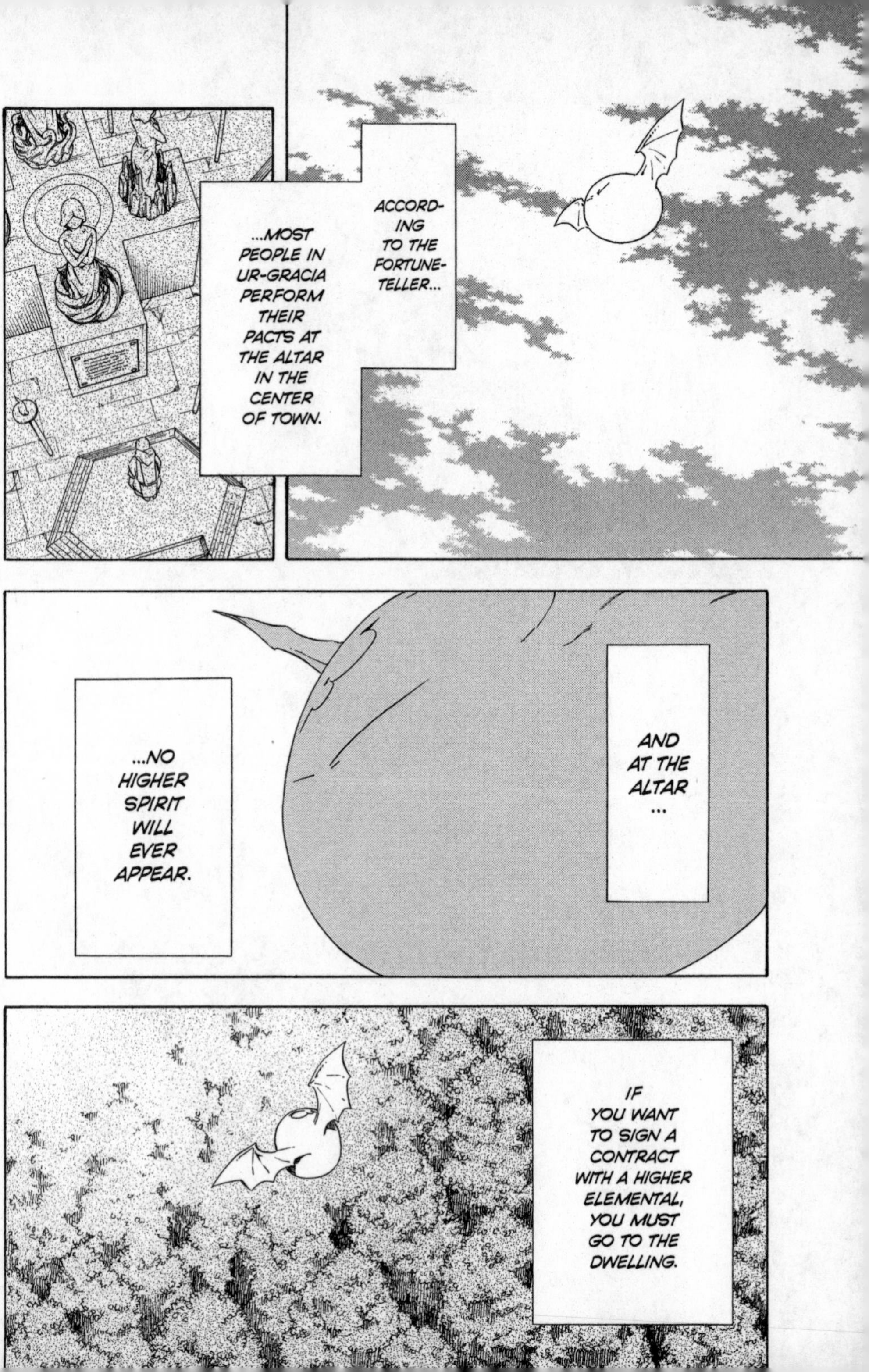
ACCORDING TO THE FORTUNE-TELLER...
...MOST PEOPLE IN UR-GRACIA PERFORM THEIR PACTS AT THE ALTAR IN THE CENTER OF TOWN.
AND AT THE ALTAR...
...NO HIGHER SPIRIT WILL EVER APPEAR.
IF YOU WANT TO SIGN A CONTRACT WITH A HIGHER ELEMENTAL, YOU MUST GO TO THE DWELLING.

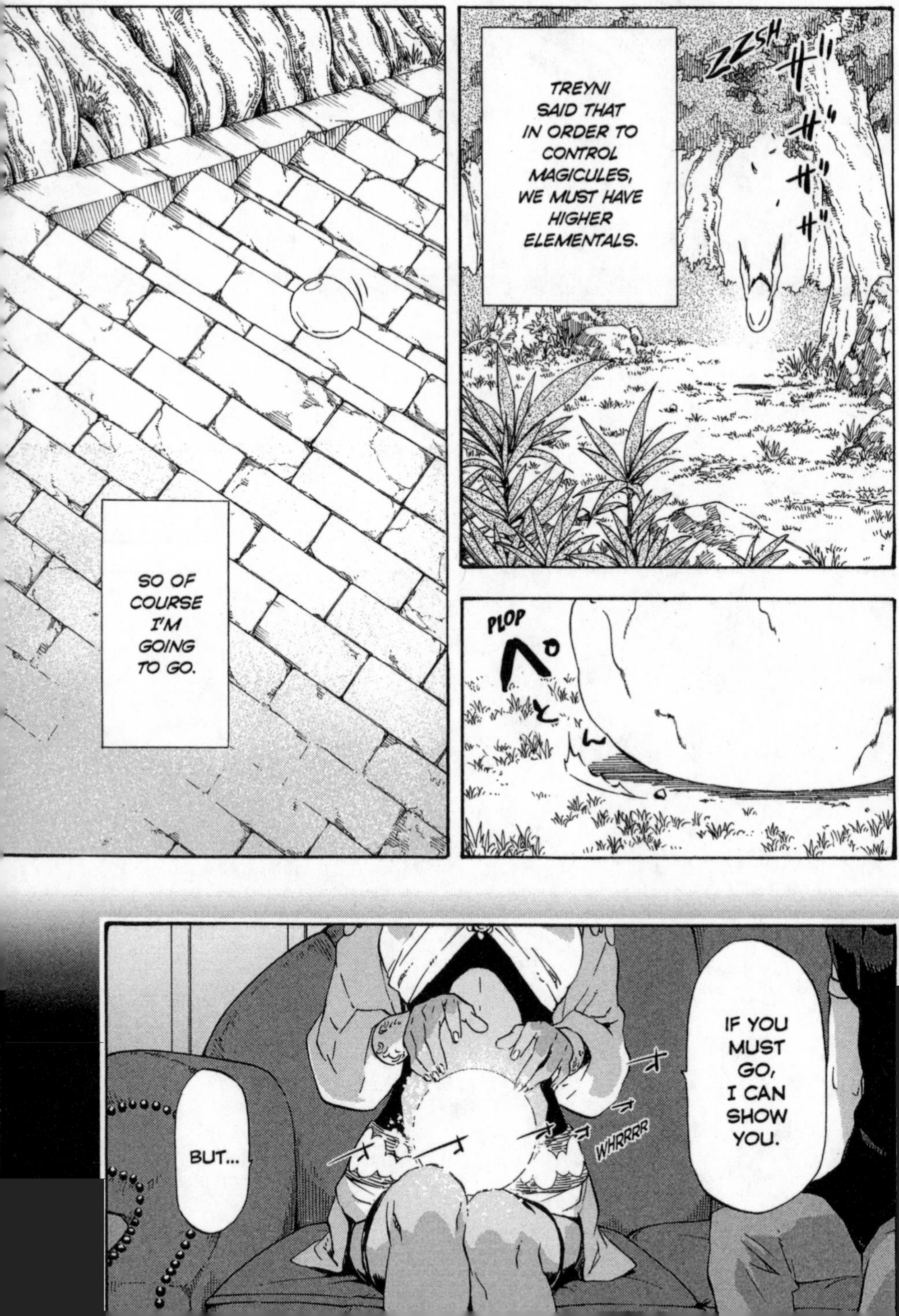
TREYNI SAID THAT IN ORDER TO CONTROL MAGICULES, WE MUST HAVE HIGHER ELEMENTALS.
ZZSH
PLOP
SO OF COURSE I'M GOING TO GO.
IF YOU MUST GO, I CAN SHOW YOU.
WHRRRR
BUT...

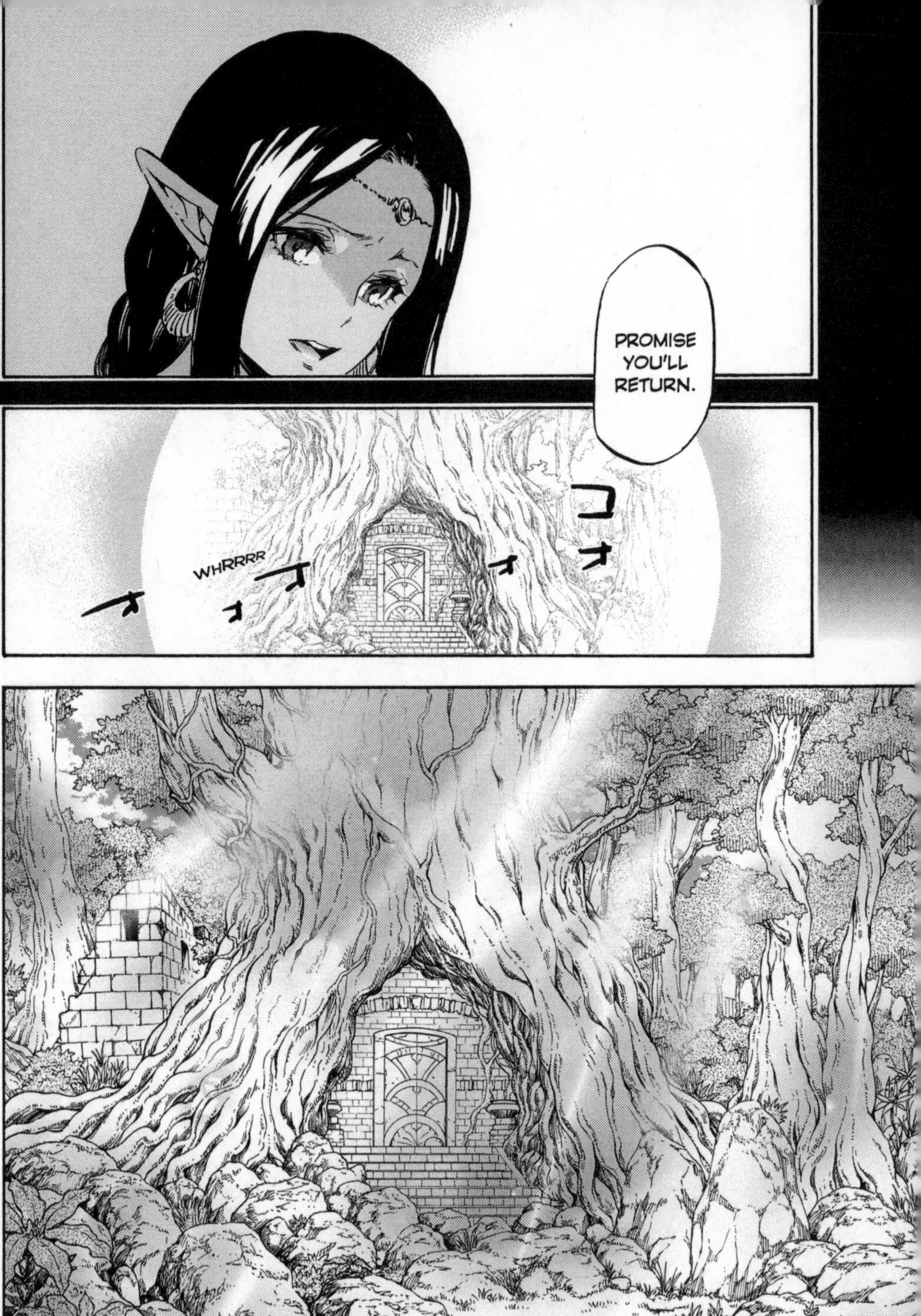
PROMISE YOU'LL RETURN.
WHRRRR

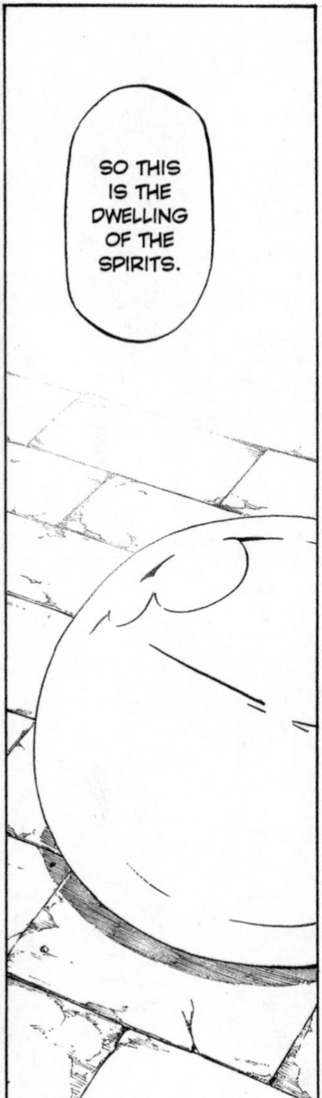
SO THIS IS THE DWELLING OF THE SPIRITS.
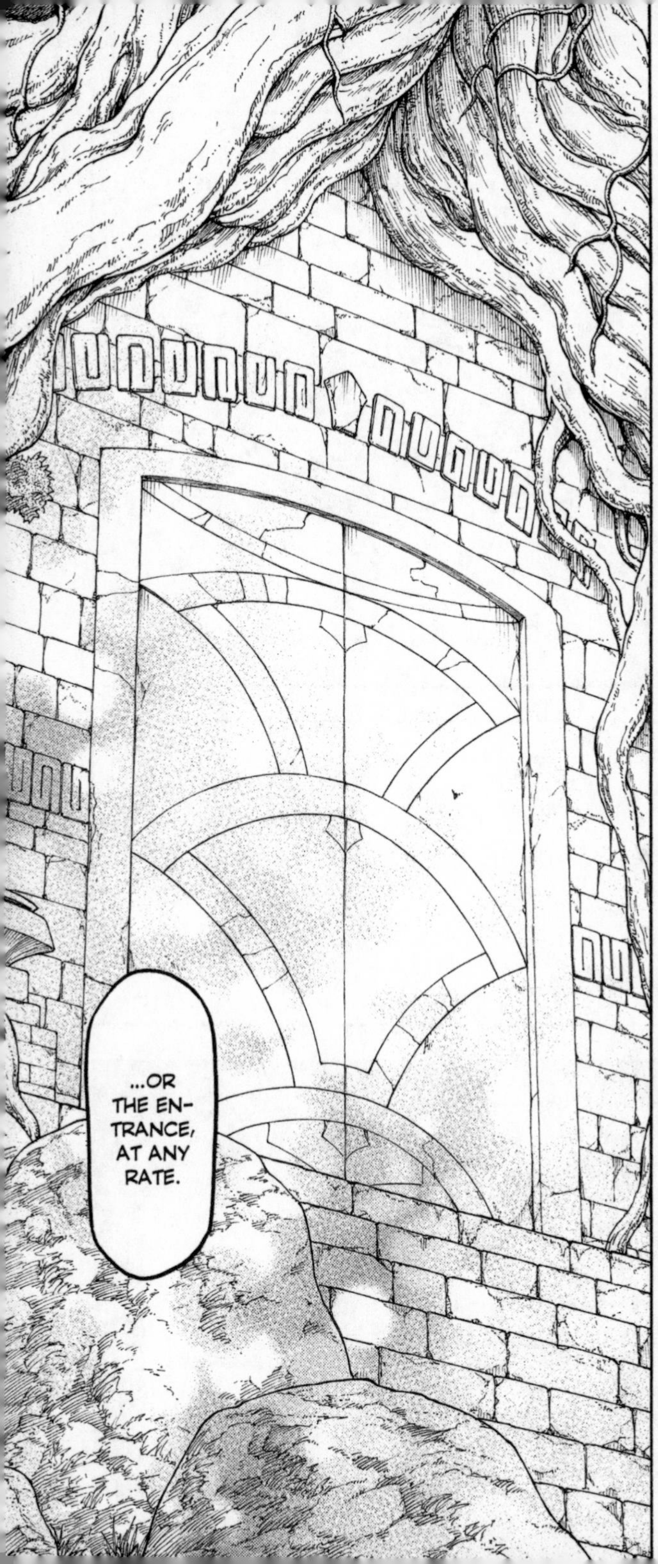
...OR THE EN-TRANCE, AT ANY RATE.

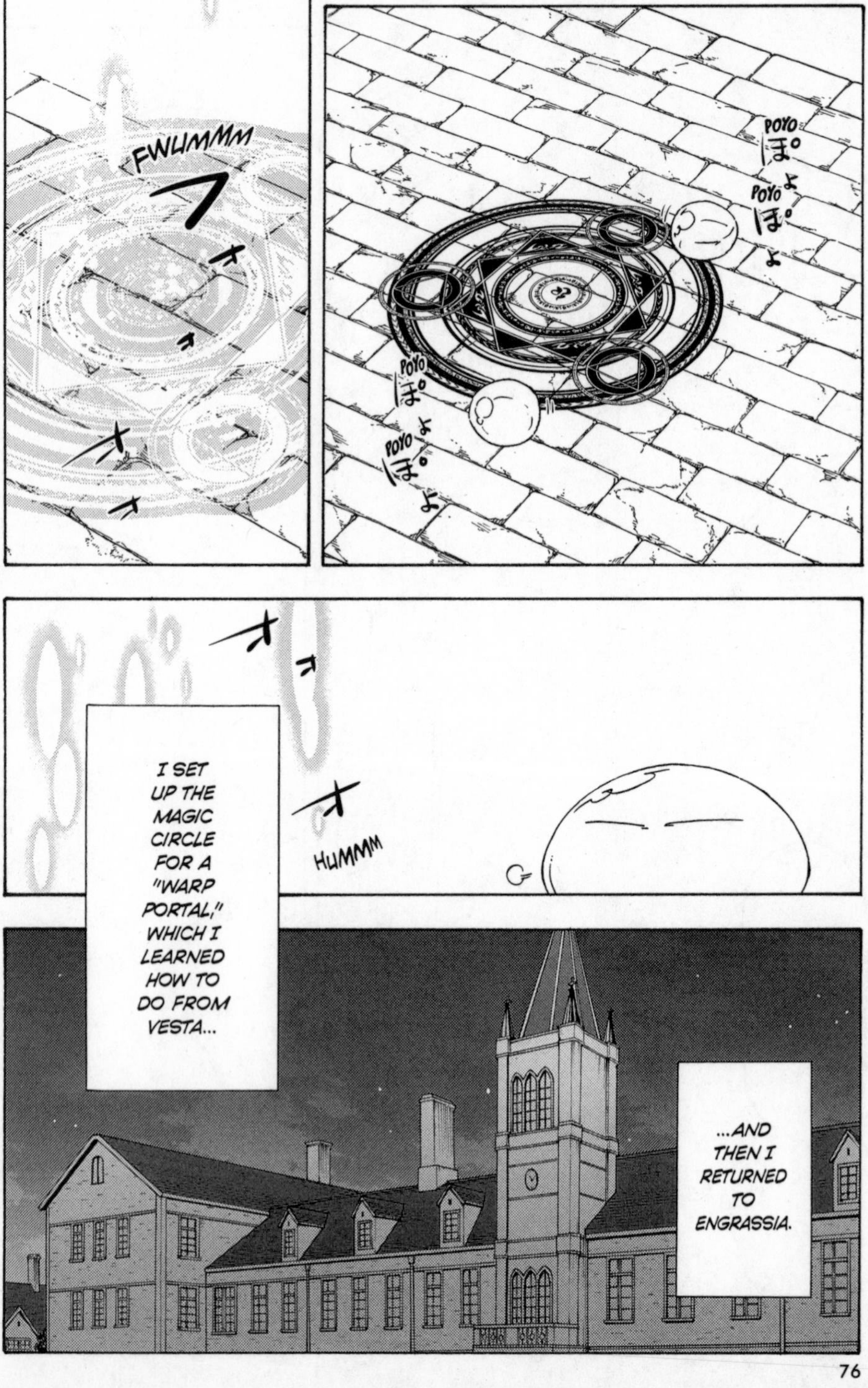
POYO ぽよ
POYO ぽよ
POYO ぽよ
POYO ぽよ
FWUMMM
HUMMM
I SET UP THE MAGIC CIRCLE FOR A "WARP PORTAL," WHICH I LEARNED HOW TO DO FROM VESTA...
...AND THEN I RETURNED TO ENGRASSIA.

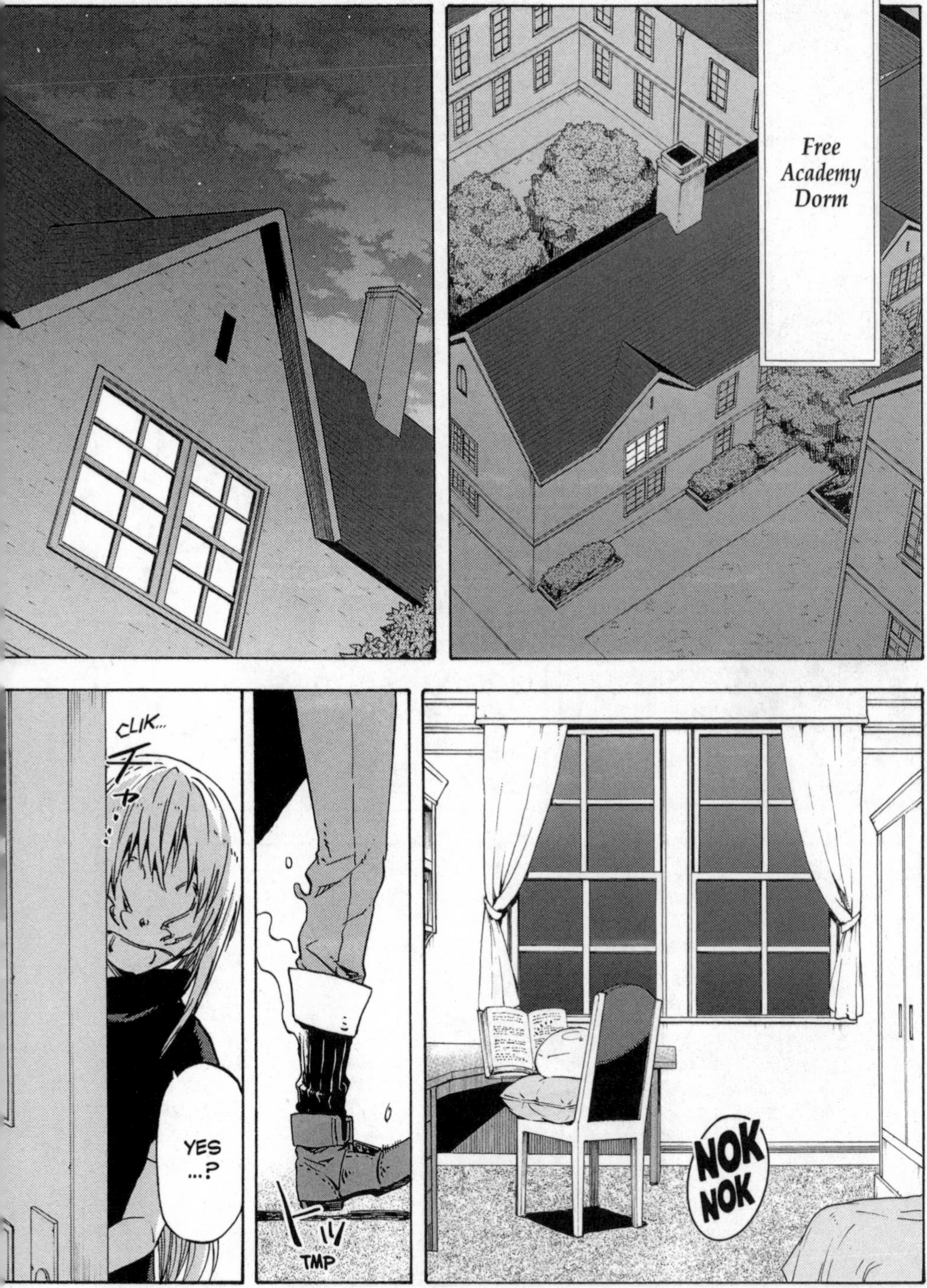

Free Academy Dorm
NOK NOK
TMP
CLIK...
YES ...?

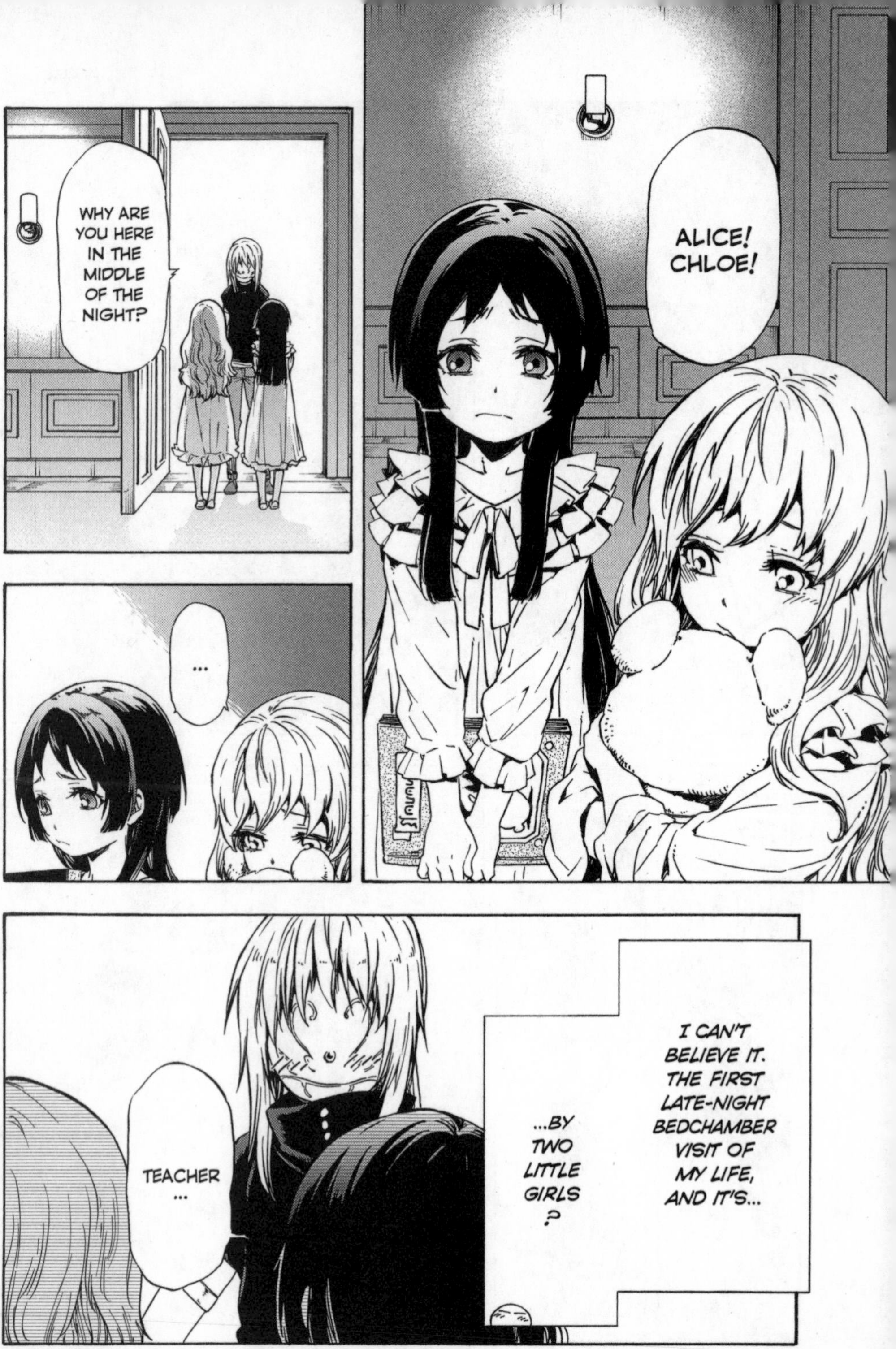
ALICE! CHLOE!
WHY ARE YOU HERE IN THE MIDDLE OF THE NIGHT?
...
I CAN'T BELIEVE IT. THE FIRST LATE-NIGHT BEDCHAMBER VISIT OF MY LIFE, AND IT'S...
...BY TWO LITTLE GIRLS?
TEACHER...

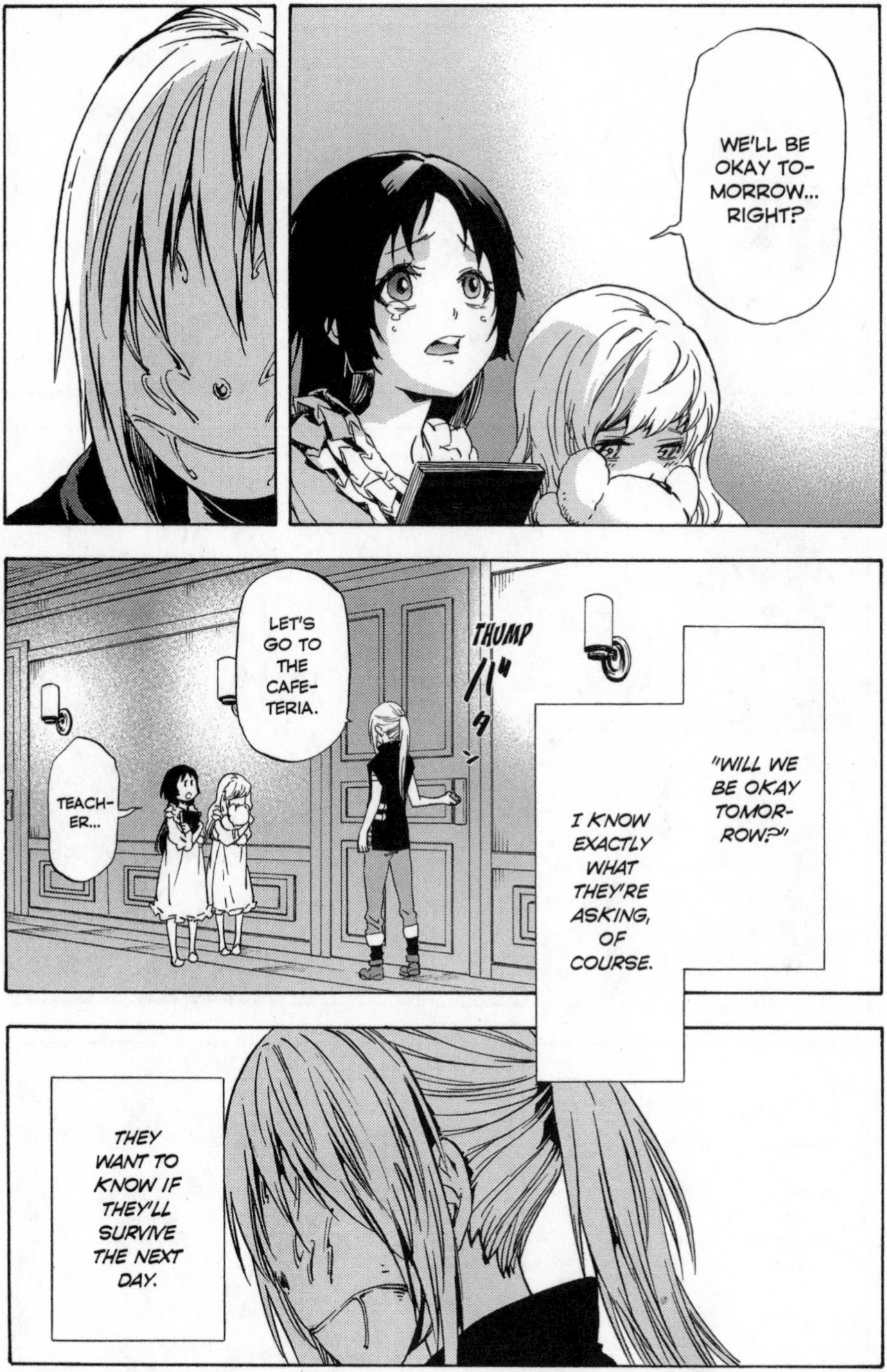
WE'LL BE OKAY TO-MORROW... RIGHT?
"WILL WE BE OKAY TOMOR-ROW?"
I KNOW EXACTLY WHAT THEY'RE ASKING, OF COURSE.
THUMP
LET'S GO TO THE CAFE-TERIA.
TEACHER...
THEY WANT TO KNOW IF THEY'LL SURVIVE THE NEXT DAY.

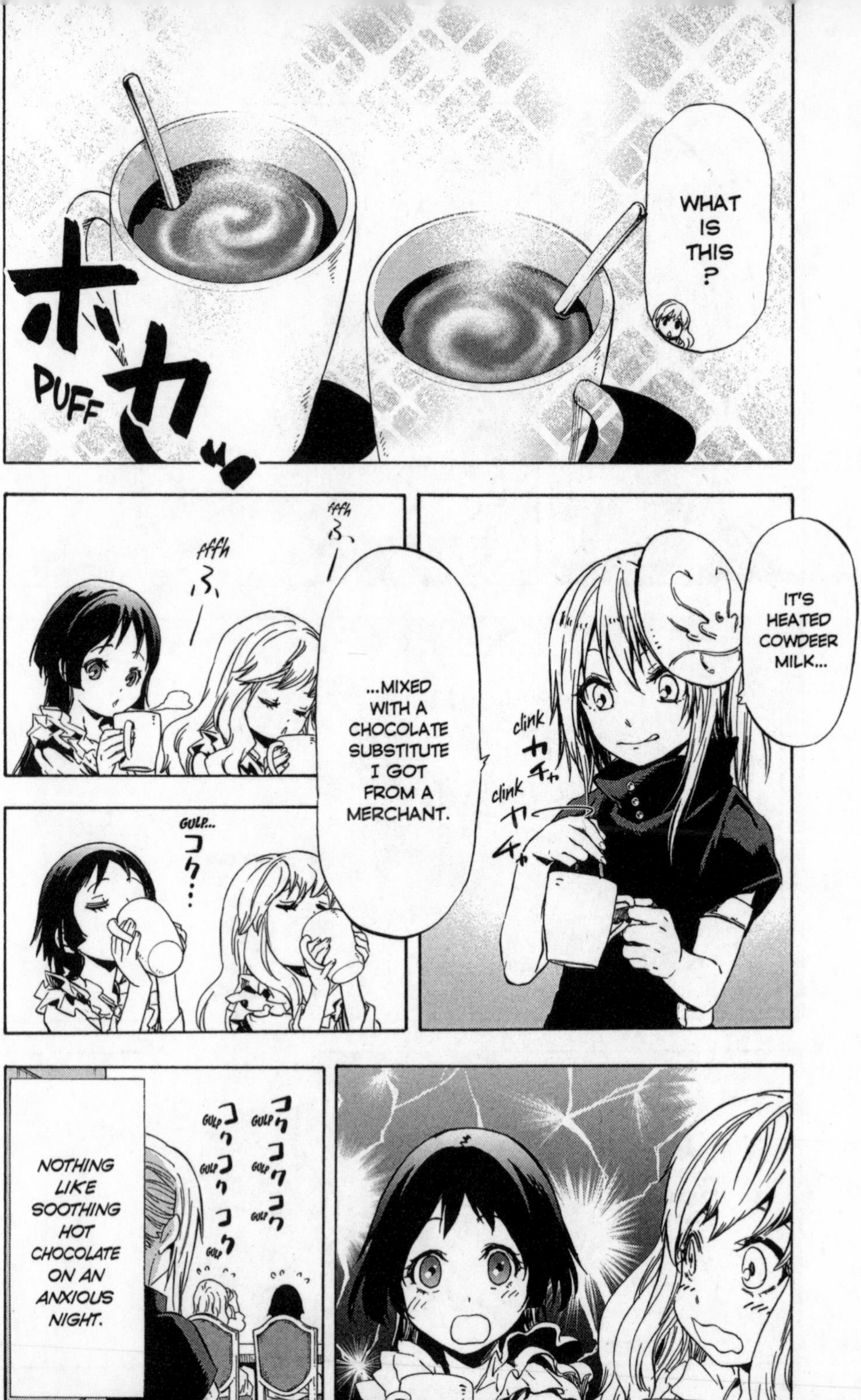

WHAT IS THIS?
PUFF
ホカッ
IT'S HEATED COWDEER MILK...
clink
カチャ
clink
カチャ
...MIXED WITH A CHOCOLATE SUBSTITUTE I GOT FROM A MERCHANT.
fffh
ふー
fffh
ふー
GULP...
コク…
GULP
コクコクコク
GULP
コクコクコク
NOTHING LIKE SOOTHING HOT CHOCOLATE ON AN ANXIOUS NIGHT.

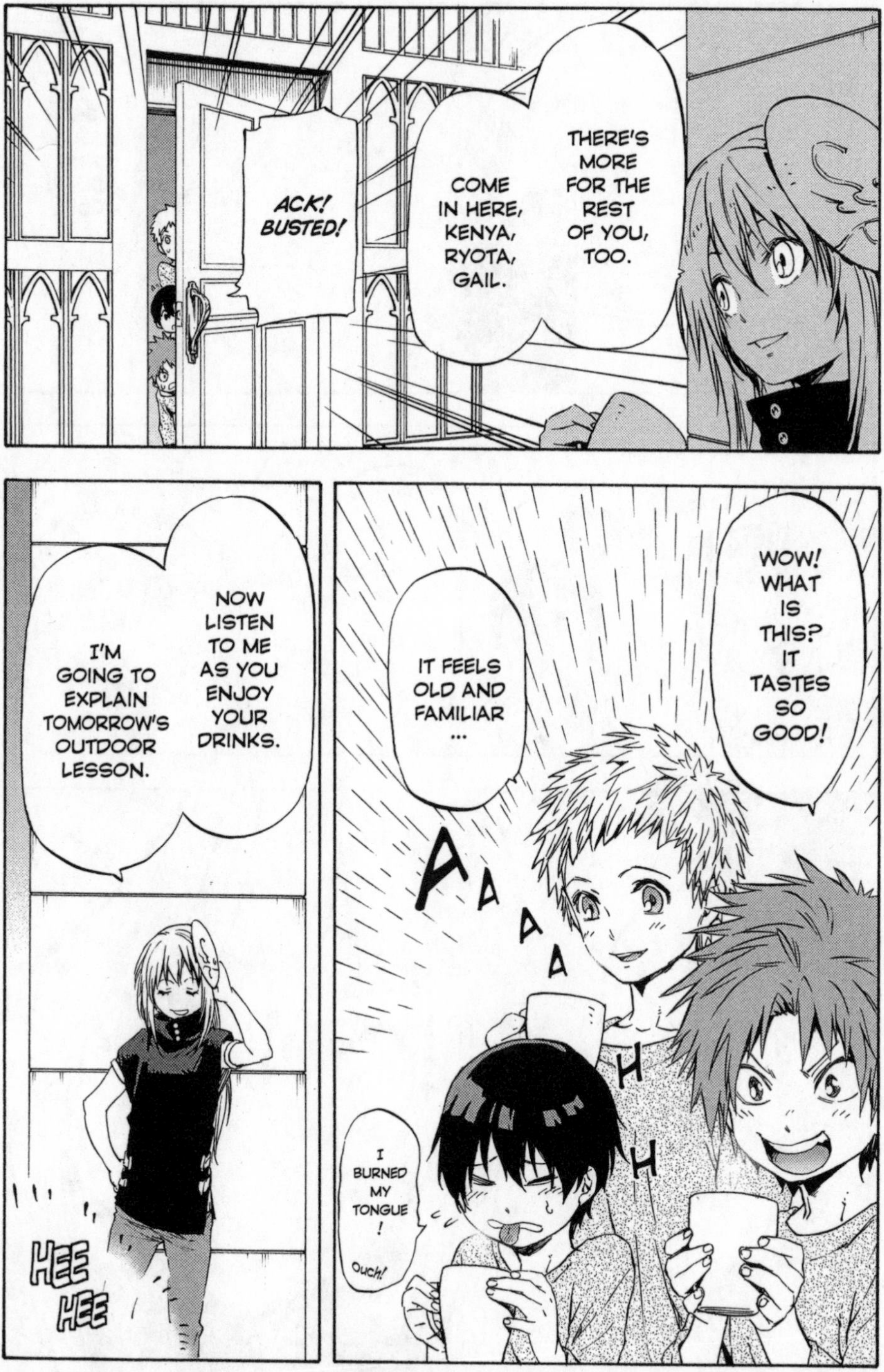
THERE'S MORE FOR THE REST OF YOU, TOO.
COME IN HERE, KENYA, RYOTA, GAIL.
ACK! BUSTED!
WOW! WHAT IS THIS? IT TASTES SO GOOD!
IT FEELS OLD AND FAMILIAR ...
AAAAHHH
I BURNED MY TONGUE!
Ouch!
NOW LISTEN TO ME AS YOU ENJOY YOUR DRINKS.
I'M GOING TO EXPLAIN TOMORROW'S OUTDOOR LESSON.
HEE HEE

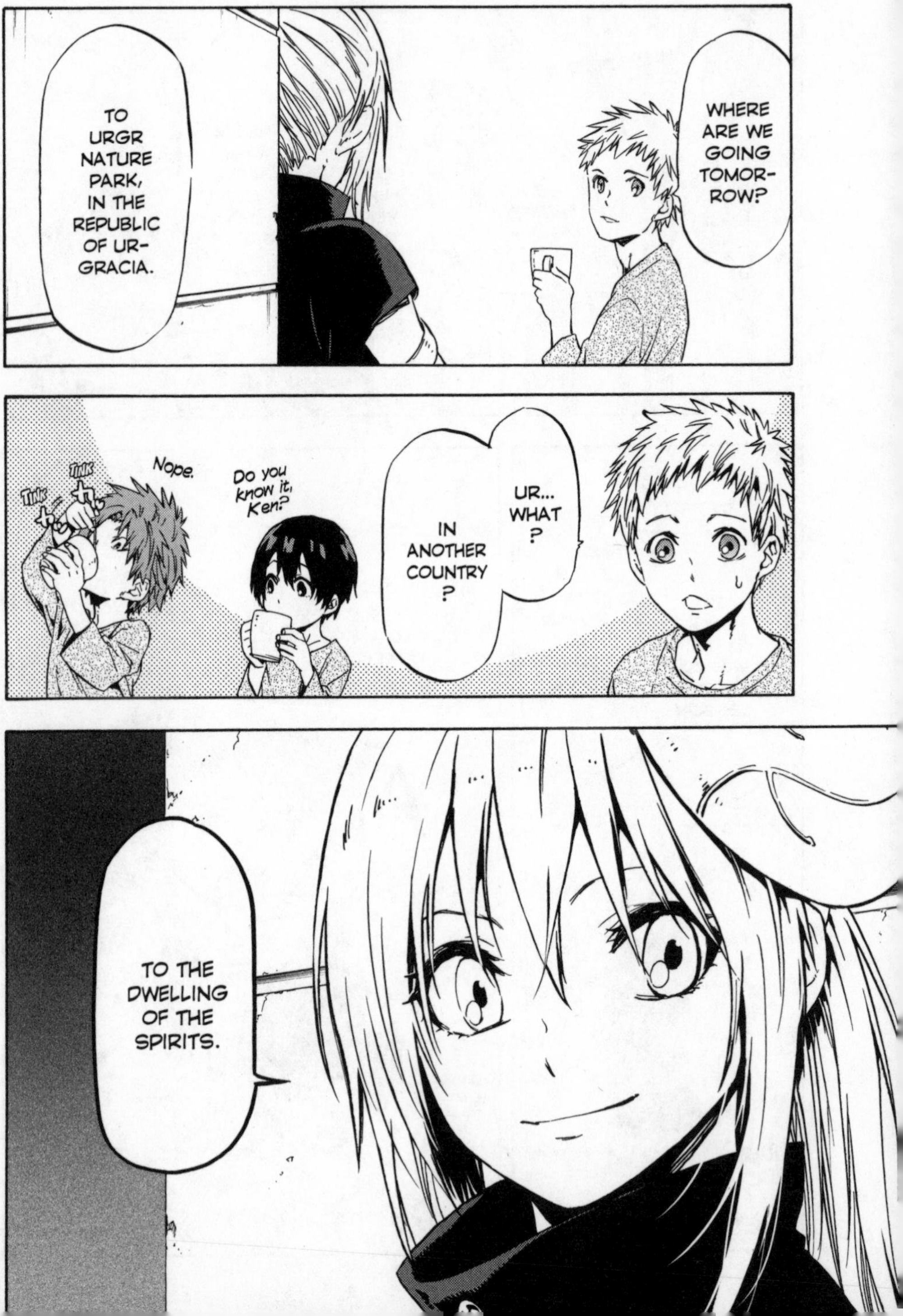
WHERE ARE WE GOING TOMORROW?
TO URGR NATURE PARK, IN THE REPUBLIC OF URGRACIA.
UR... WHAT?
IN ANOTHER COUNTRY?
Do you know it, Ken?
Nope.
TINK
TINK
...
TO THE DWELLING OF THE SPIRITS.

Hot chocolate
with slime-mallows

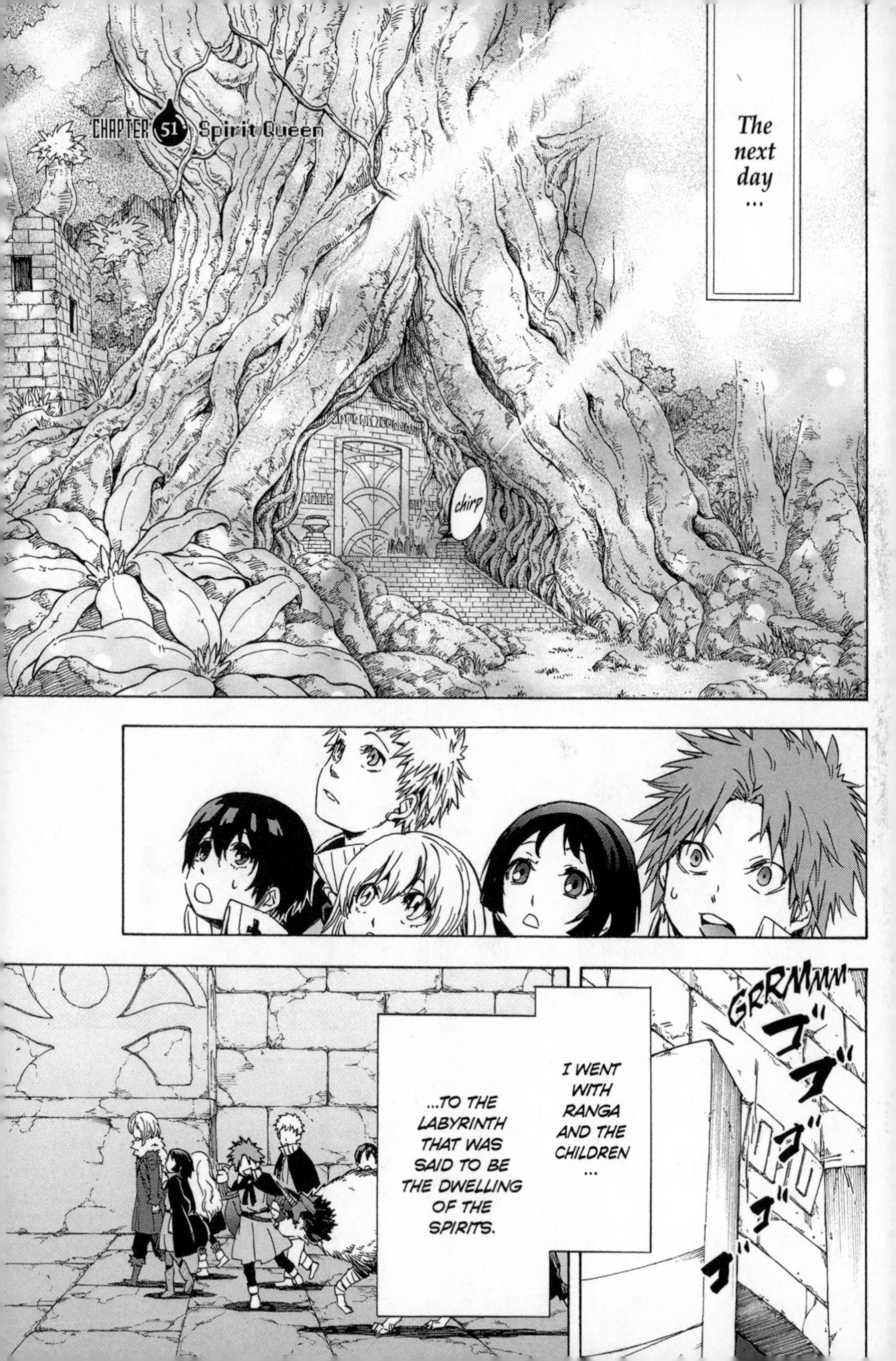
CHAPTER 51 Spirit Queen
The next day ...
chirp
GRRMMM
I WENT WITH RANGA AND THE CHILDREN ...
...TO THE LABYRINTH THAT WAS SAID TO BE THE DWELLING OF THE SPIRITS.

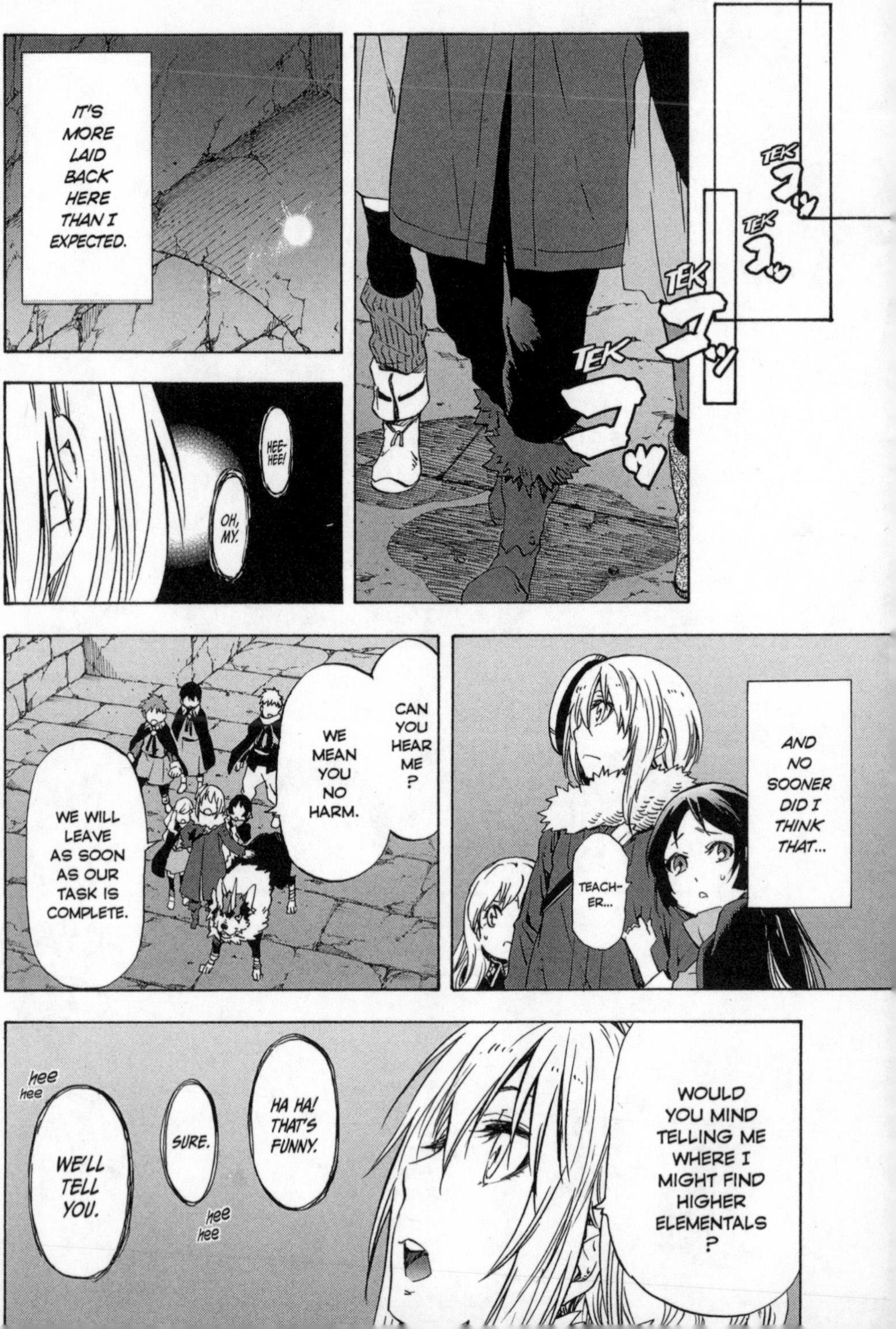
TEK
TEK
TEK
TEK
IT'S MORE LAID BACK HERE THAN I EXPECTED.
HEE-HEE!
OH, MY.
AND NO SOONER DID I THINK THAT...
TEACHER...
CAN YOU HEAR ME?
WE MEAN YOU NO HARM.
WE WILL LEAVE AS SOON AS OUR TASK IS COMPLETE.
WOULD YOU MIND TELLING ME WHERE I MIGHT FIND HIGHER ELEMENTALS?
HA HA! THAT'S FUNNY.
SURE.
hee hee
WE'LL TELL YOU.
hee hee

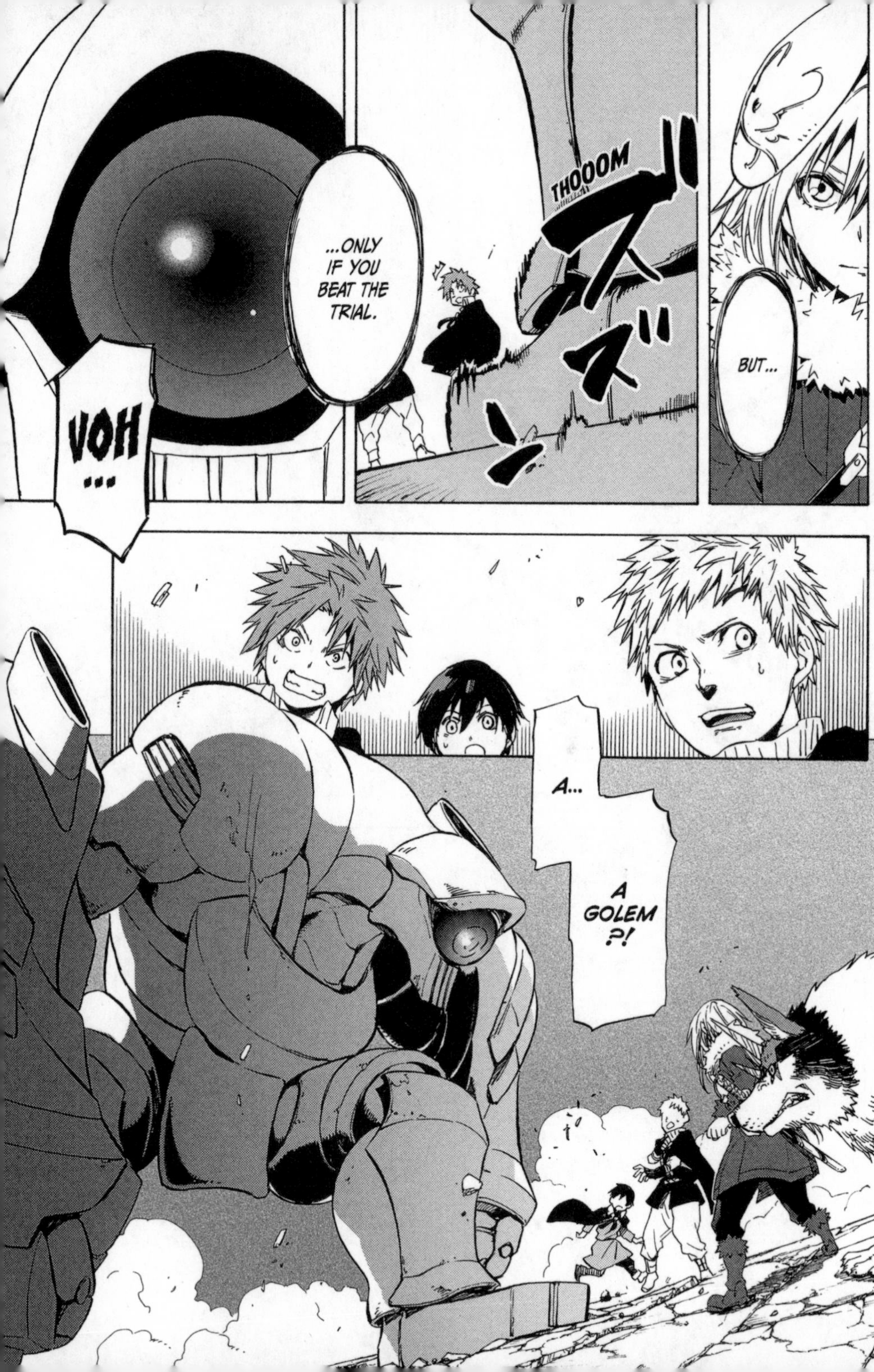
BUT...
...ONLY IF YOU BEAT THE TRIAL.
THOOOM
VOH...
A...
A GOLEM?!

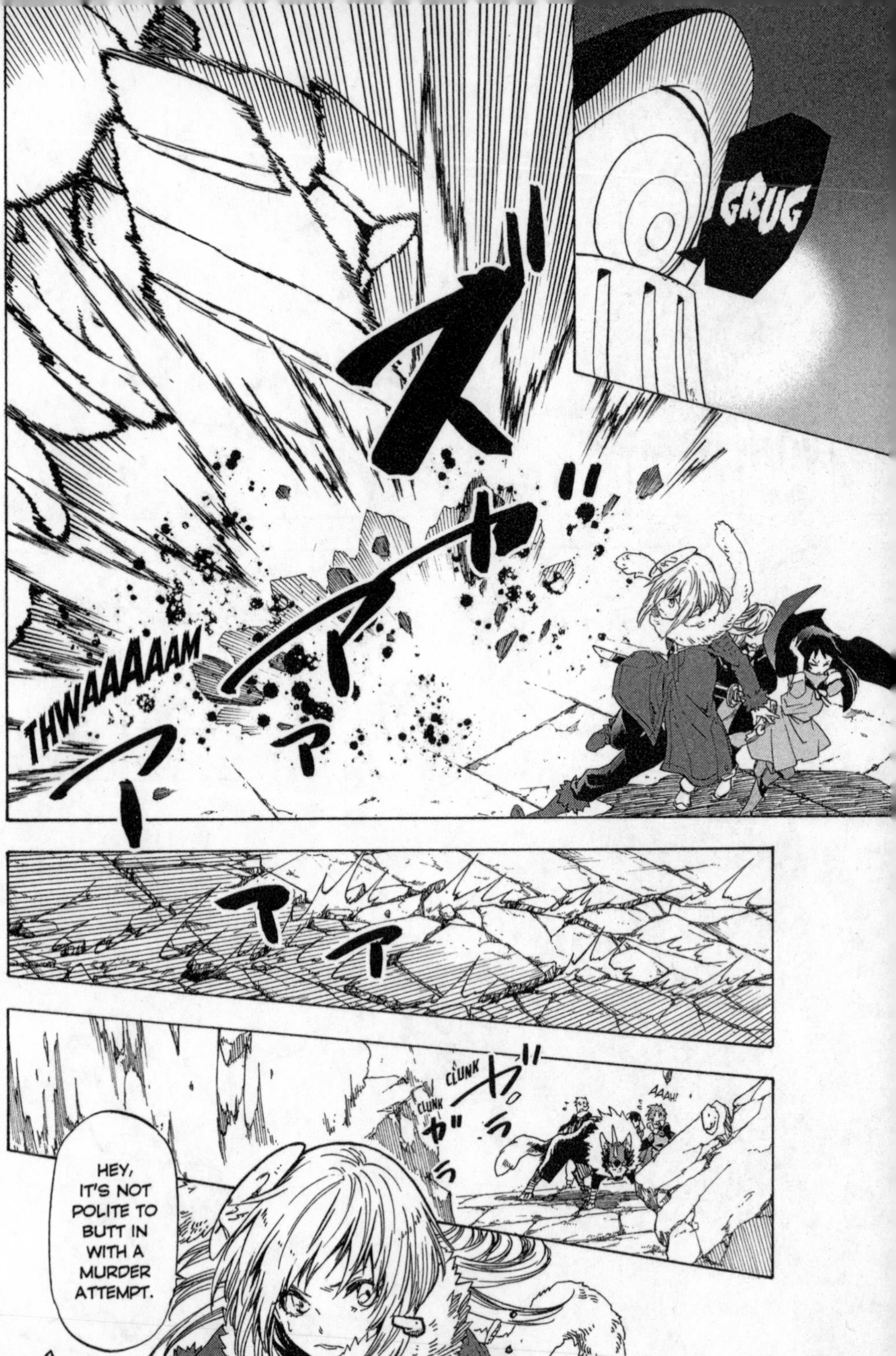
GRUG
THWAAAAAM
AAAH!
CLUNK
CLUNK
HEY, IT'S NOT POLITE TO BUTT IN WITH A MURDER ATTEMPT.

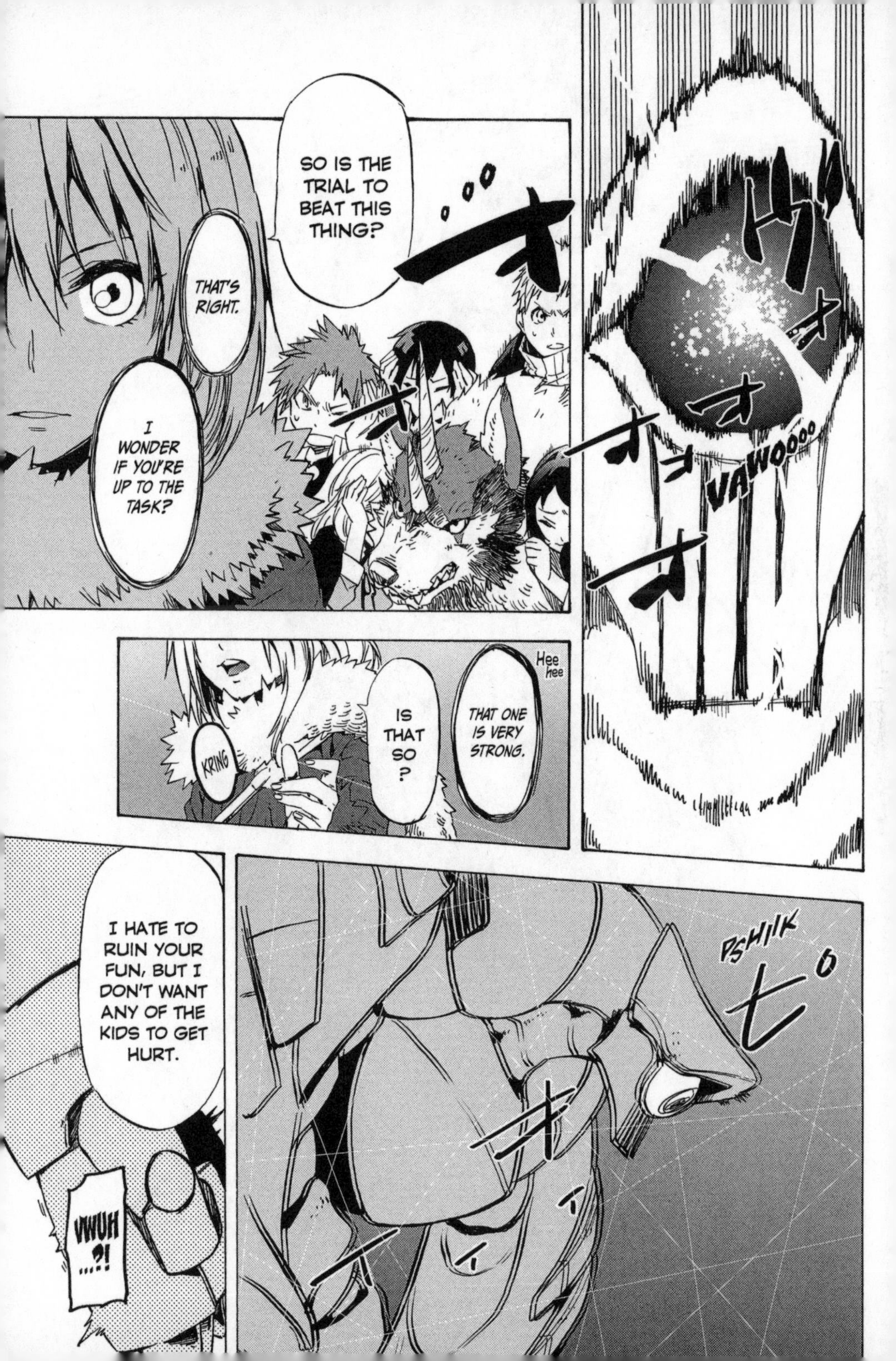

VAWOOOO
SO IS THE TRIAL TO BEAT THIS THING?
THAT'S RIGHT.
I WONDER IF YOU'RE UP TO THE TASK?
Hee hee
THAT ONE IS VERY STRONG.
IS THAT SO?
KRING
PSHIIK
I HATE TO RUIN YOUR FUN, BUT I DON'T WANT ANY OF THE KIDS TO GET HURT.
VWUH ...?!

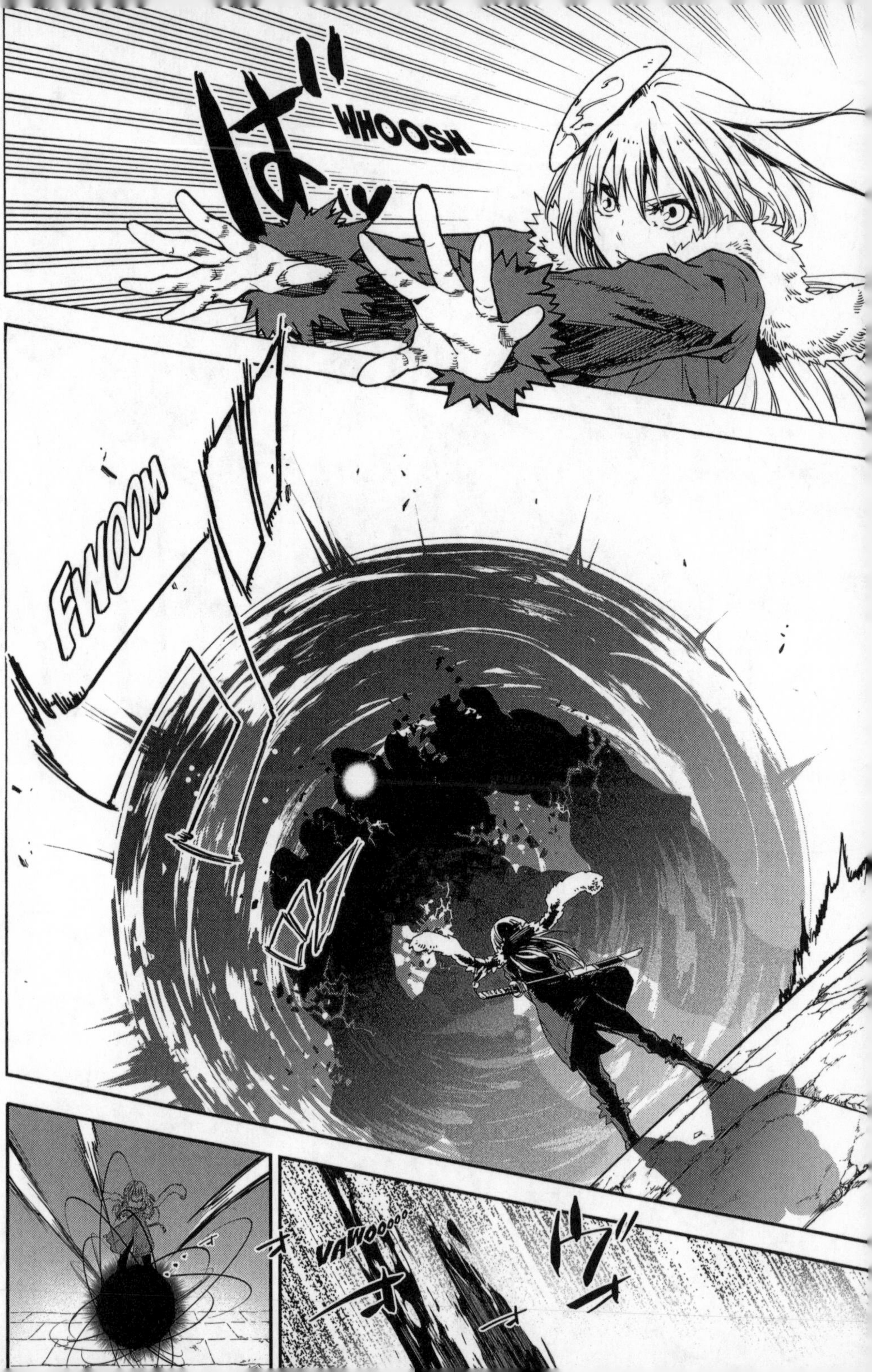
ばっ
WHOOSH
FWOOM
ドヴォオオオオ
VAWOOOOO...

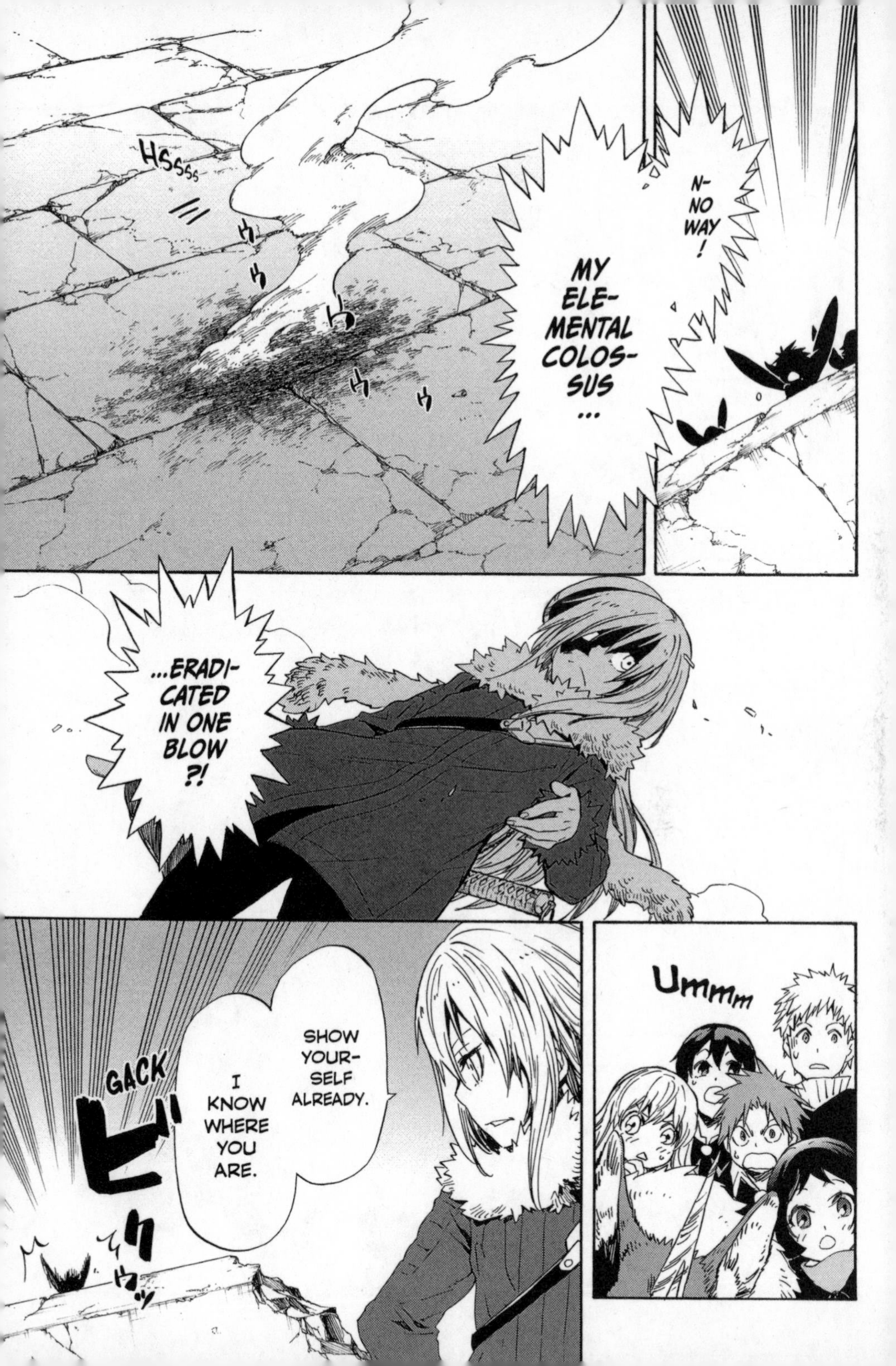
N-NO WAY!
HSsss
MY ELEMENTAL COLOSSUS...
...ERADICATED IN ONE BLOW?!
Ummm
SHOW YOURSELF ALREADY.
I KNOW WHERE YOU ARE.
GACK

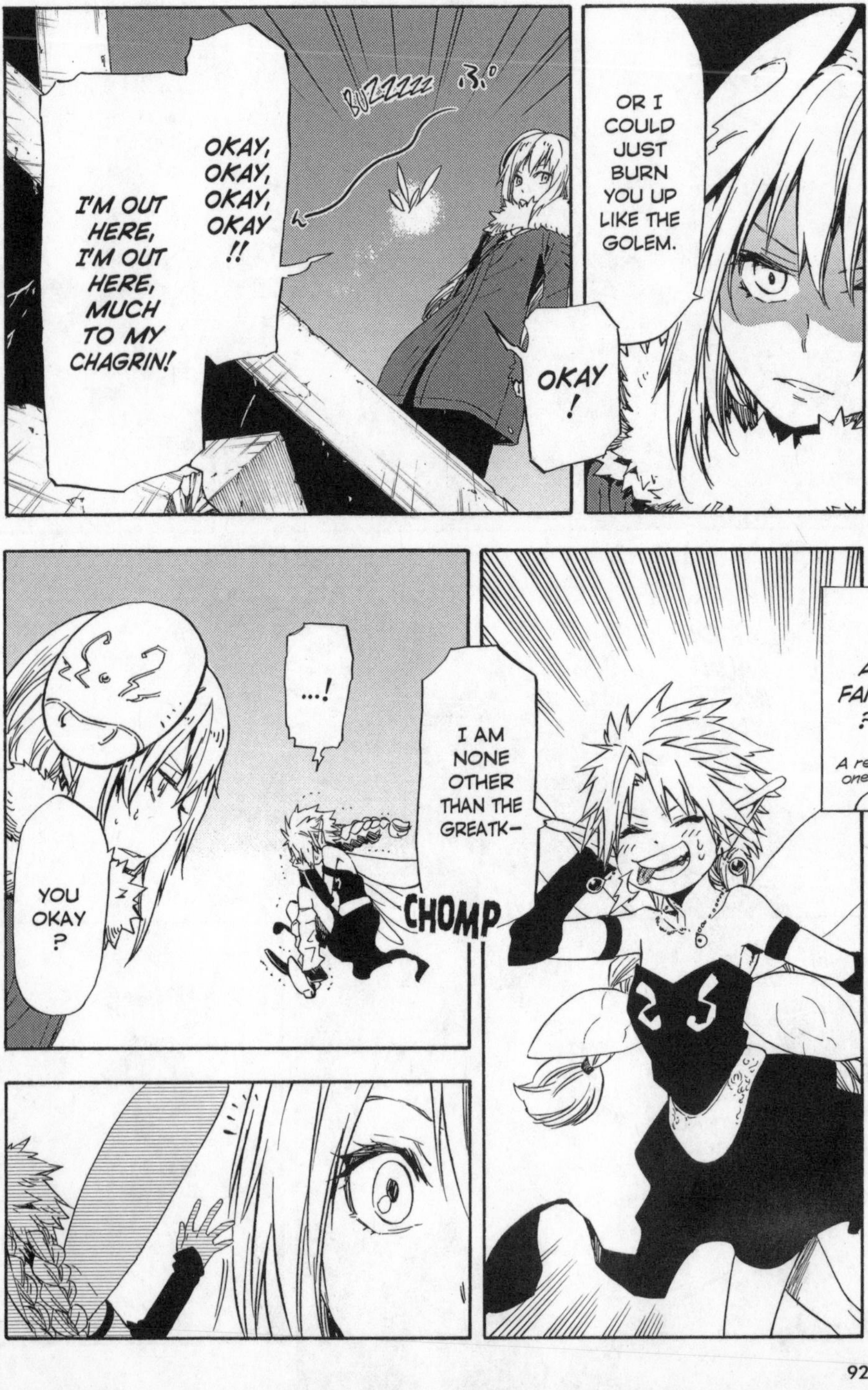
OR I COULD JUST BURN YOU UP LIKE THE GOLEM.
OKAY!
BUZZZZZ
OKAY, OKAY, OKAY, OKAY!!
I'M OUT HERE, I'M OUT HERE, MUCH TO MY CHAGRIN!
A FAIRY?
A real one?
I AM NONE OTHER THAN THE GREATK—
CHOMP
...!
YOU OKAY?

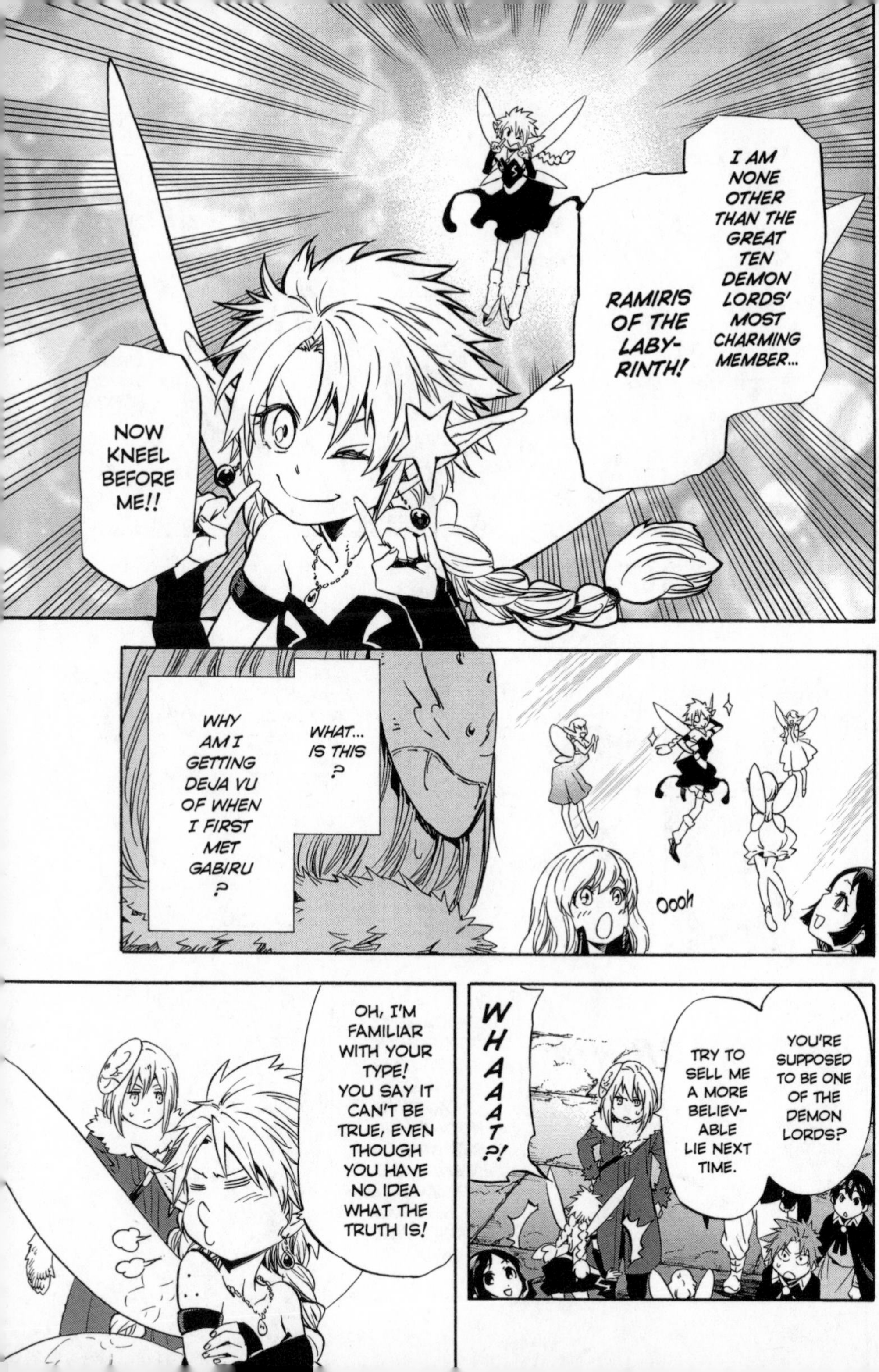
I AM NONE OTHER THAN THE GREAT TEN DEMON LORDS' MOST CHARMING MEMBER...
RAMIRIS OF THE LABY-RINTH!
NOW KNEEL BEFORE ME!!
Oooh
WHAT... IS THIS ?
WHY AM I GETTING DEJA VU OF WHEN I FIRST MET GABIRU ?
YOU'RE SUPPOSED TO BE ONE OF THE DEMON LORDS?
TRY TO SELL ME A MORE BELIEV-ABLE LIE NEXT TIME.
WHAAAAT?!
OH, I'M FAMILIAR WITH YOUR TYPE! YOU SAY IT CAN'T BE TRUE, EVEN THOUGH YOU HAVE NO IDEA WHAT THE TRUTH IS!

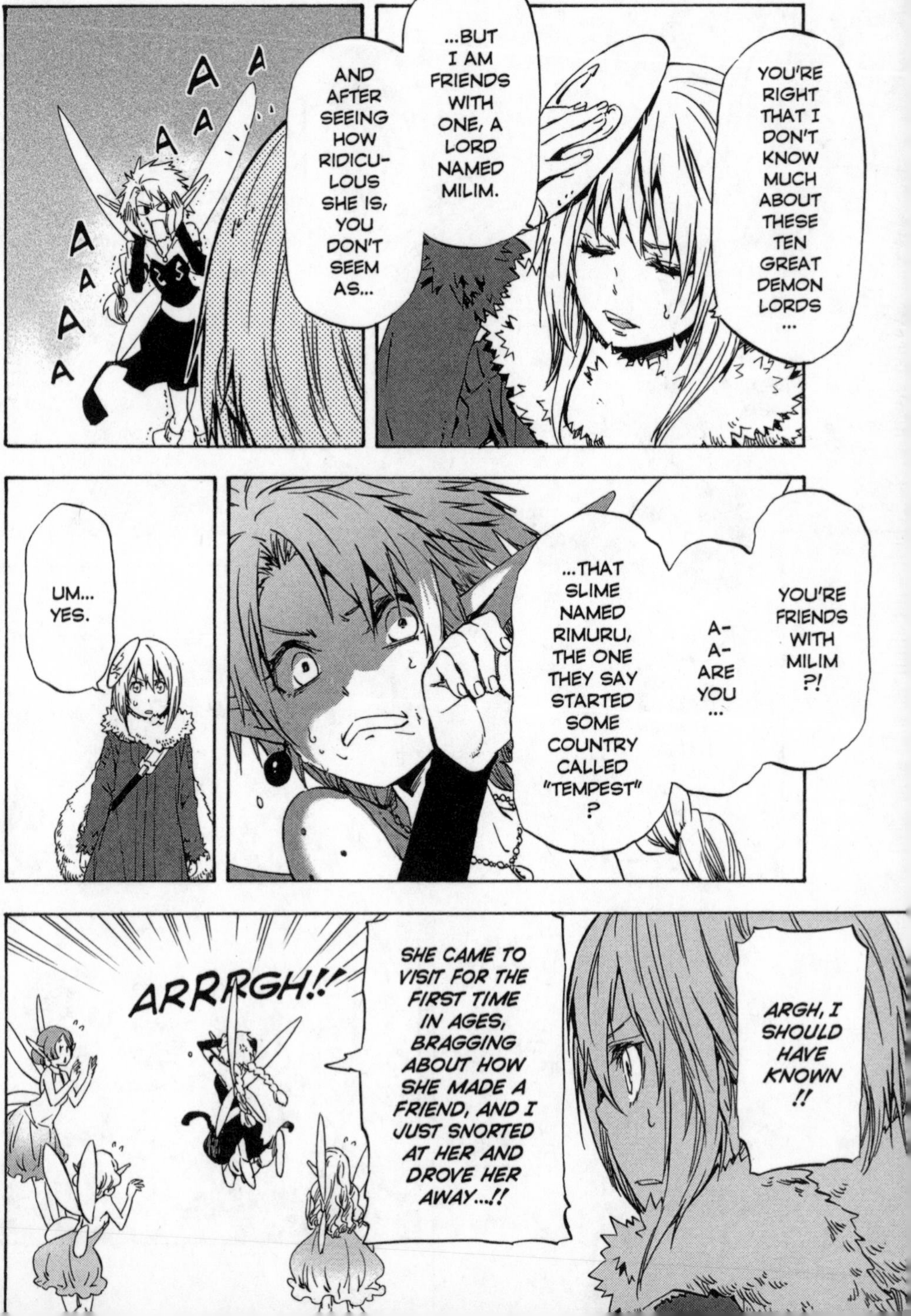
YOU'RE RIGHT THAT I DON'T KNOW MUCH ABOUT THESE TEN GREAT DEMON LORDS ...
...BUT I AM FRIENDS WITH ONE, A LORD NAMED MILIM.
AND AFTER SEEING HOW RIDICU-LOUS SHE IS, YOU DON'T SEEM AS...
A A A A A A A A A A
YOU'RE FRIENDS WITH MILIM ?!
A- A- ARE YOU ...
...THAT SLIME NAMED RIMURU, THE ONE THEY SAY STARTED SOME COUNTRY CALLED "TEMPEST" ?
UM... YES.
ARGH, I SHOULD HAVE KNOWN !!
SHE CAME TO VISIT FOR THE FIRST TIME IN AGES, BRAGGING ABOUT HOW SHE MADE A FRIEND, AND I JUST SNORTED AT HER AND DROVE HER AWAY...!!
ARRRGH!!

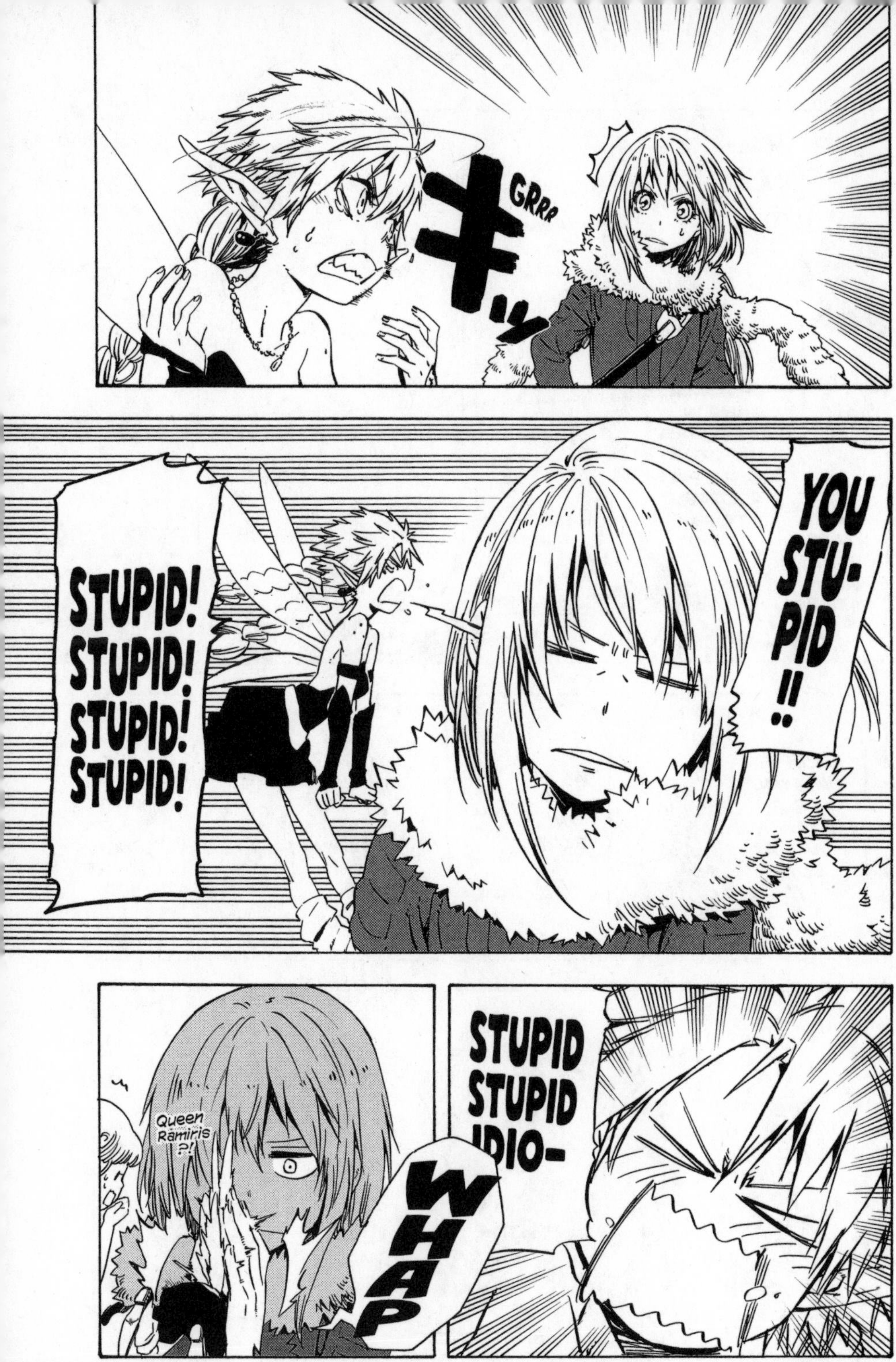
GRRR
YOU STU-PID!!
STUPID! STUPID! STUPID! STUPID!
STUPID STUPID IDIO-
WHAP
Queen Ramiris?!

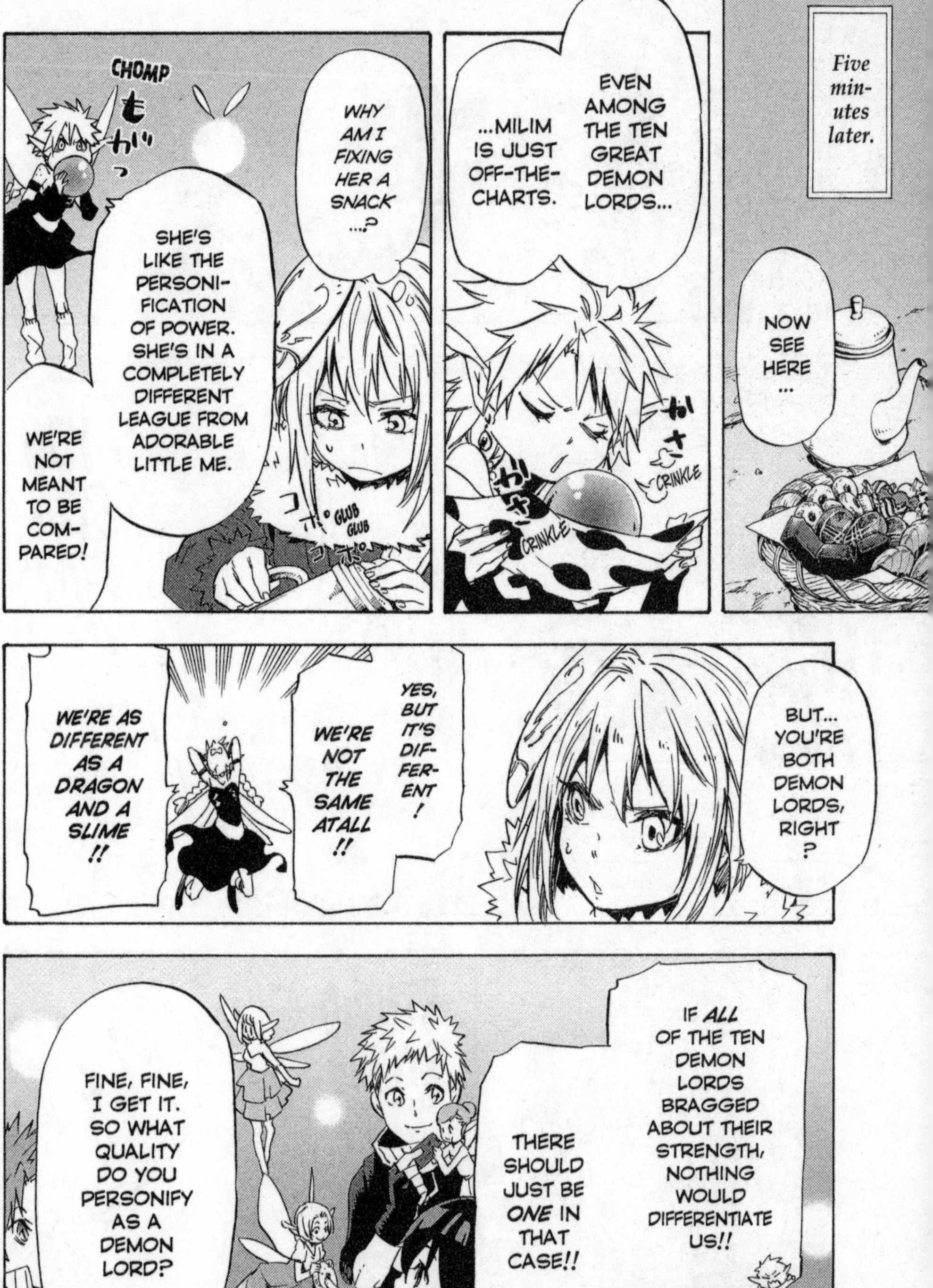
Five minutes later.
NOW SEE HERE...
EVEN AMONG THE TEN GREAT DEMON LORDS...
...MILIM IS JUST OFF-THE-CHARTS.
CRINKLE
CRINKLE
WHY AM I FIXING HER A SNACK...?
CHOMP
SHE'S LIKE THE PERSONIFICATION OF POWER. SHE'S IN A COMPLETELY DIFFERENT LEAGUE FROM ADORABLE LITTLE ME.
GLUB GLUB
WE'RE NOT MEANT TO BE COMPARED!
BUT... YOU'RE BOTH DEMON LORDS, RIGHT?
YES, BUT IT'S DIFFERENT!
WE'RE NOT THE SAME AT ALL!!
WE'RE AS DIFFERENT AS A DRAGON AND A SLIME!!
IF ALL OF THE TEN DEMON LORDS BRAGGED ABOUT THEIR STRENGTH, NOTHING WOULD DIFFERENTIATE US!!
THERE SHOULD JUST BE ONE IN THAT CASE!!
FINE, FINE, I GET IT. SO WHAT QUALITY DO YOU PERSONIFY AS A DEMON LORD?

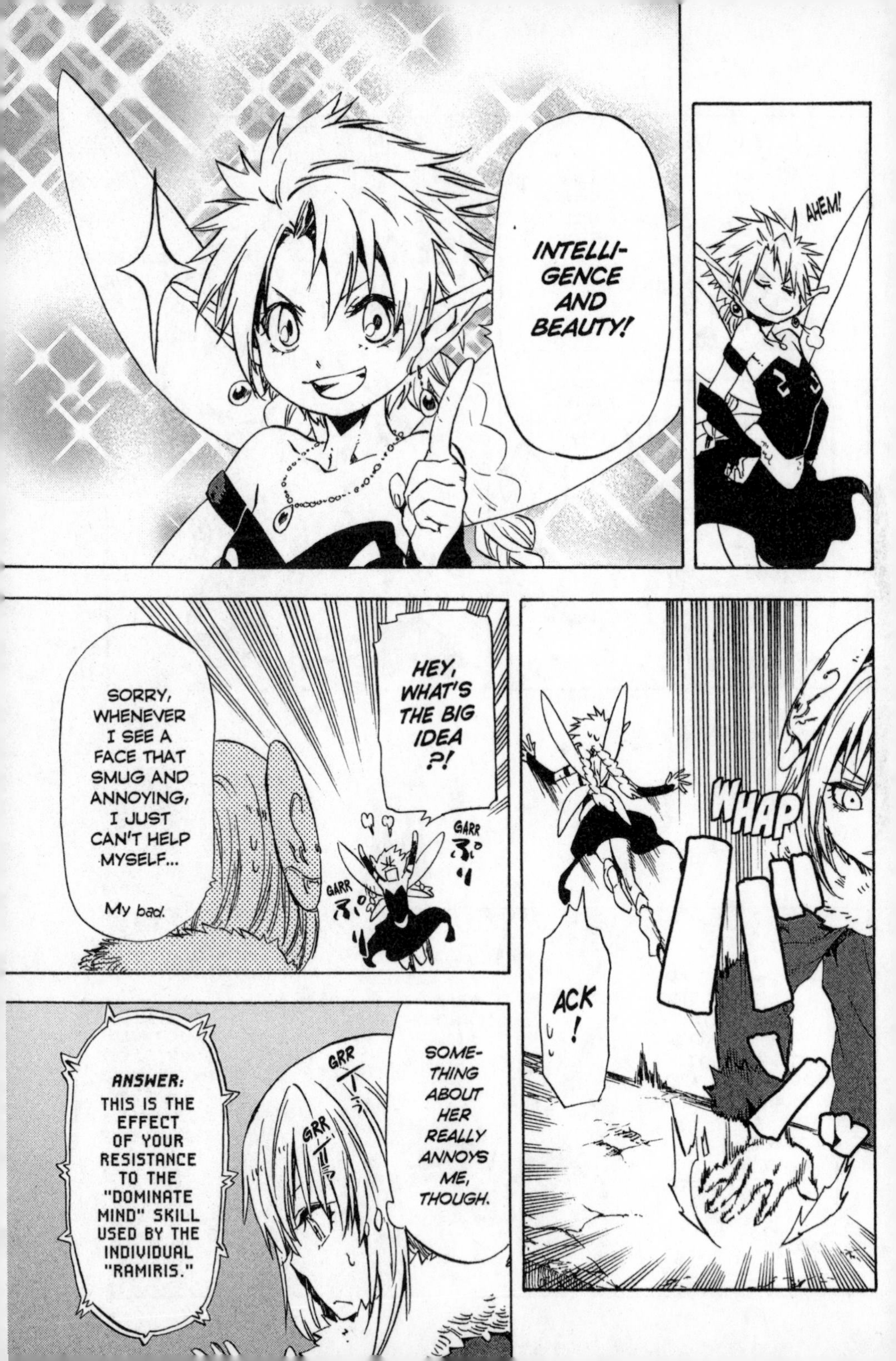
AHEM!
INTELLI-GENCE AND BEAUTY!
WHAP
ACK!
HEY, WHAT'S THE BIG IDEA?!
GARR
GARR
SORRY, WHENEVER I SEE A FACE THAT SMUG AND ANNOYING, I JUST CAN'T HELP MYSELF...
My bad.
SOME-THING ABOUT HER REALLY ANNOYS ME, THOUGH.
GRR
GRR
ANSWER: THIS IS THE EFFECT OF YOUR RESISTANCE TO THE "DOMINATE MIND" SKILL USED BY THE INDIVIDUAL "RAMIRIS."

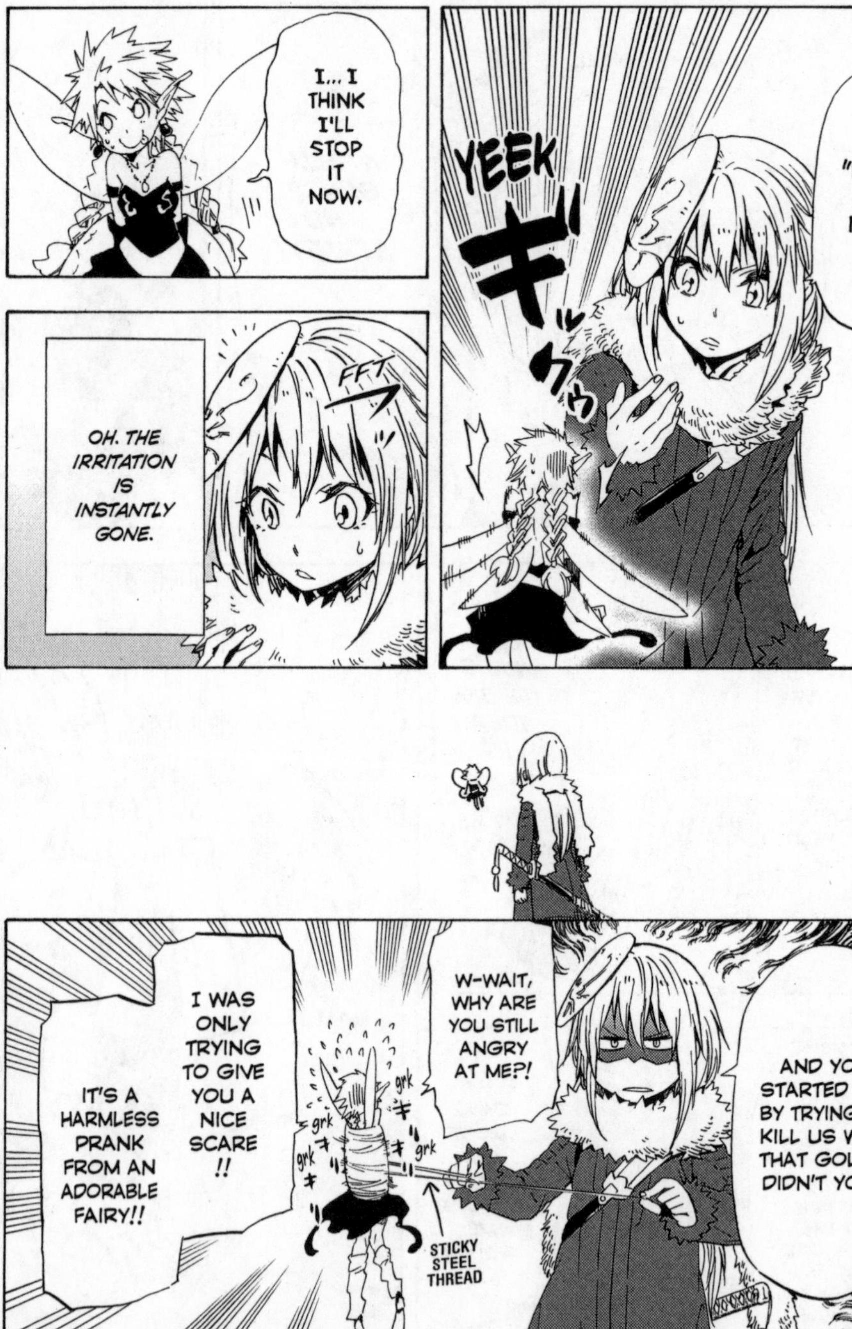
"DOMINATE MIND" ...?
YEEK
I... I THINK I'LL STOP IT NOW.
OH. THE IRRITATION IS INSTANTLY GONE.
FFT
AND YOU STARTED OFF BY TRYING TO KILL US WITH THAT GOLEM, DIDN'T YOU?
W-WAIT, WHY ARE YOU STILL ANGRY AT ME?!
grk grk grk grk
STICKY STEEL THREAD
I WAS ONLY TRYING TO GIVE YOU A NICE SCARE!!
IT'S A HARMLESS PRANK FROM AN ADORABLE FAIRY!!

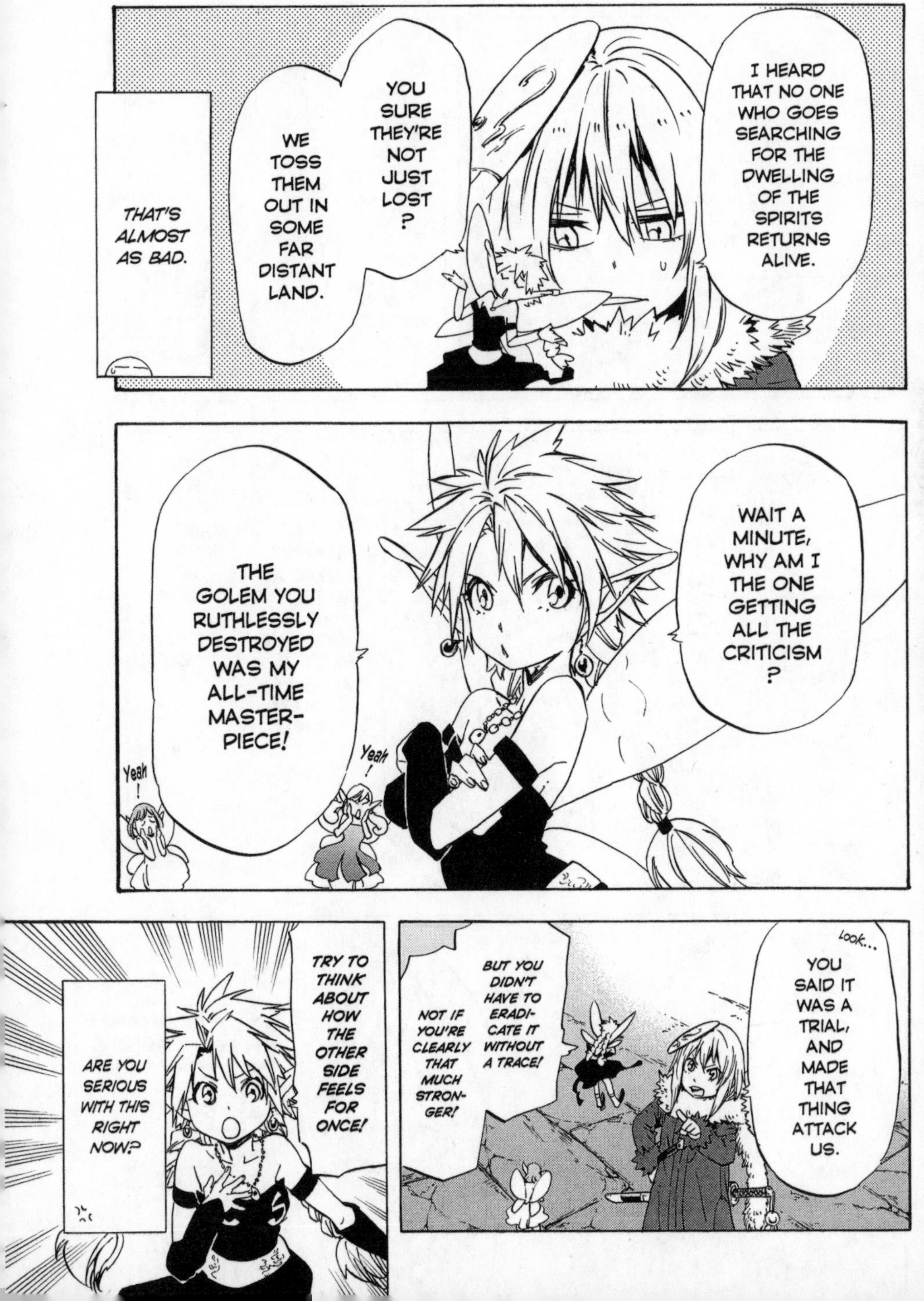
I HEARD THAT NO ONE WHO GOES SEARCHING FOR THE DWELLING OF THE SPIRITS RETURNS ALIVE.
YOU SURE THEY'RE NOT JUST LOST?
WE TOSS THEM OUT IN SOME FAR DISTANT LAND.
THAT'S ALMOST AS BAD.
WAIT A MINUTE, WHY AM I THE ONE GETTING ALL THE CRITICISM?
THE GOLEM YOU RUTHLESSLY DESTROYED WAS MY ALL-TIME MASTER-PIECE!
Yeah!
Yeah!
Look...
YOU SAID IT WAS A TRIAL, AND MADE THAT THING ATTACK US.
BUT YOU DIDN'T HAVE TO ERADI-CATE IT WITHOUT A TRACE!
NOT IF YOU'RE CLEARLY THAT MUCH STRON-GER!
TRY TO THINK ABOUT HOW THE OTHER SIDE FEELS FOR ONCE!
ARE YOU SERIOUS WITH THIS RIGHT NOW?

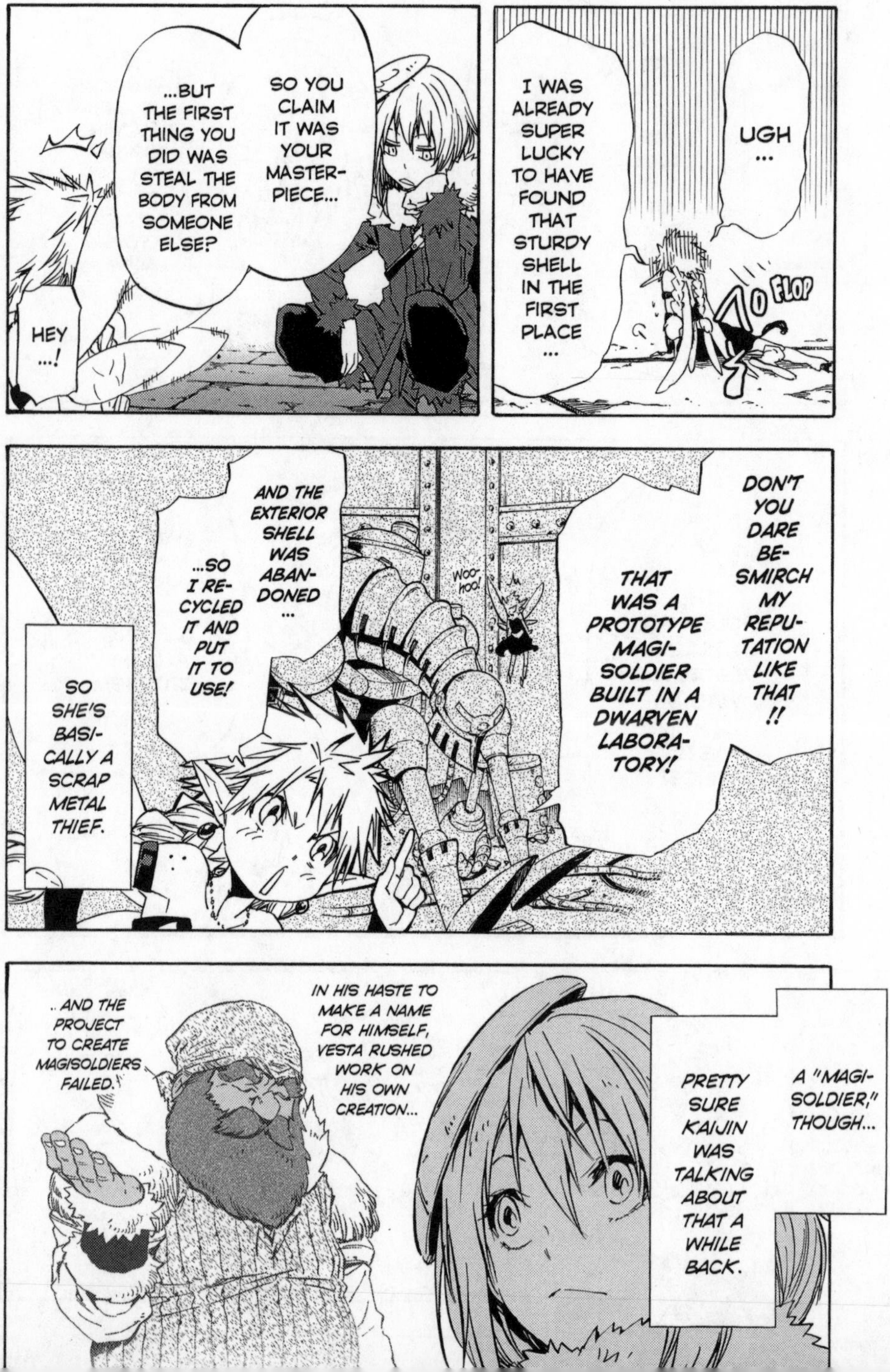
UGH ...
I WAS ALREADY SUPER LUCKY TO HAVE FOUND THAT STURDY SHELL IN THE FIRST PLACE ...
FLOP
SO YOU CLAIM IT WAS YOUR MASTERPIECE...
...BUT THE FIRST THING YOU DID WAS STEAL THE BODY FROM SOMEONE ELSE?
HEY ...!
DON'T YOU DARE BESMIRCH MY REPUTATION LIKE THAT !!
THAT WAS A PROTOTYPE MAGI-SOLDIER BUILT IN A DWARVEN LABORATORY!
WOO-HOO!
AND THE EXTERIOR SHELL WAS ABANDONED ...
...SO I RECYCLED IT AND PUT IT TO USE!
SO SHE'S BASICALLY A SCRAP METAL THIEF.
A "MAGI-SOLDIER," THOUGH...
PRETTY SURE KAIJIN WAS TALKING ABOUT THAT A WHILE BACK.
IN HIS HASTE TO MAKE A NAME FOR HIMSELF, VESTA RUSHED WORK ON HIS OWN CREATION...
.. AND THE PROJECT TO CREATE MAGISOLDIERS FAILED.

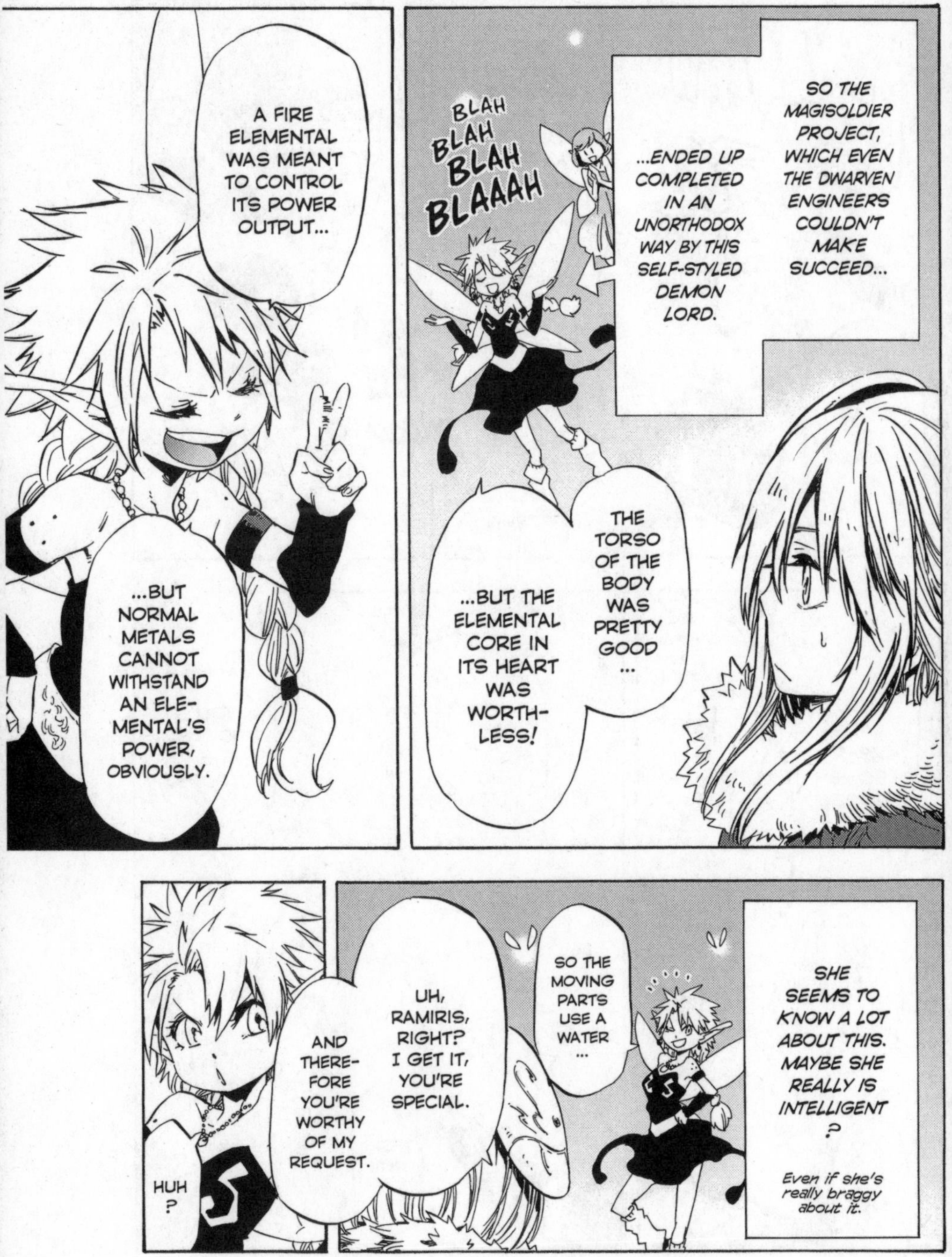
SO THE MAGISOLDIER PROJECT, WHICH EVEN THE DWARVEN ENGINEERS COULDN'T MAKE SUCCEED...
...ENDED UP COMPLETED IN AN UNORTHODOX WAY BY THIS SELF-STYLED DEMON LORD.
BLAH BLAH BLAH BLAAAH
THE TORSO OF THE BODY WAS PRETTY GOOD...
...BUT THE ELEMENTAL CORE IN ITS HEART WAS WORTHLESS!
A FIRE ELEMENTAL WAS MEANT TO CONTROL ITS POWER OUTPUT...
...BUT NORMAL METALS CANNOT WITHSTAND AN ELEMENTAL'S POWER, OBVIOUSLY.
SHE SEEMS TO KNOW A LOT ABOUT THIS. MAYBE SHE REALLY IS INTELLIGENT?
Even if she's really braggy about it.
SO THE MOVING PARTS USE A WATER...
UH, RAMIRIS, RIGHT? I GET IT, YOU'RE SPECIAL.
AND THEREFORE YOU'RE WORTHY OF MY REQUEST.
HUH?

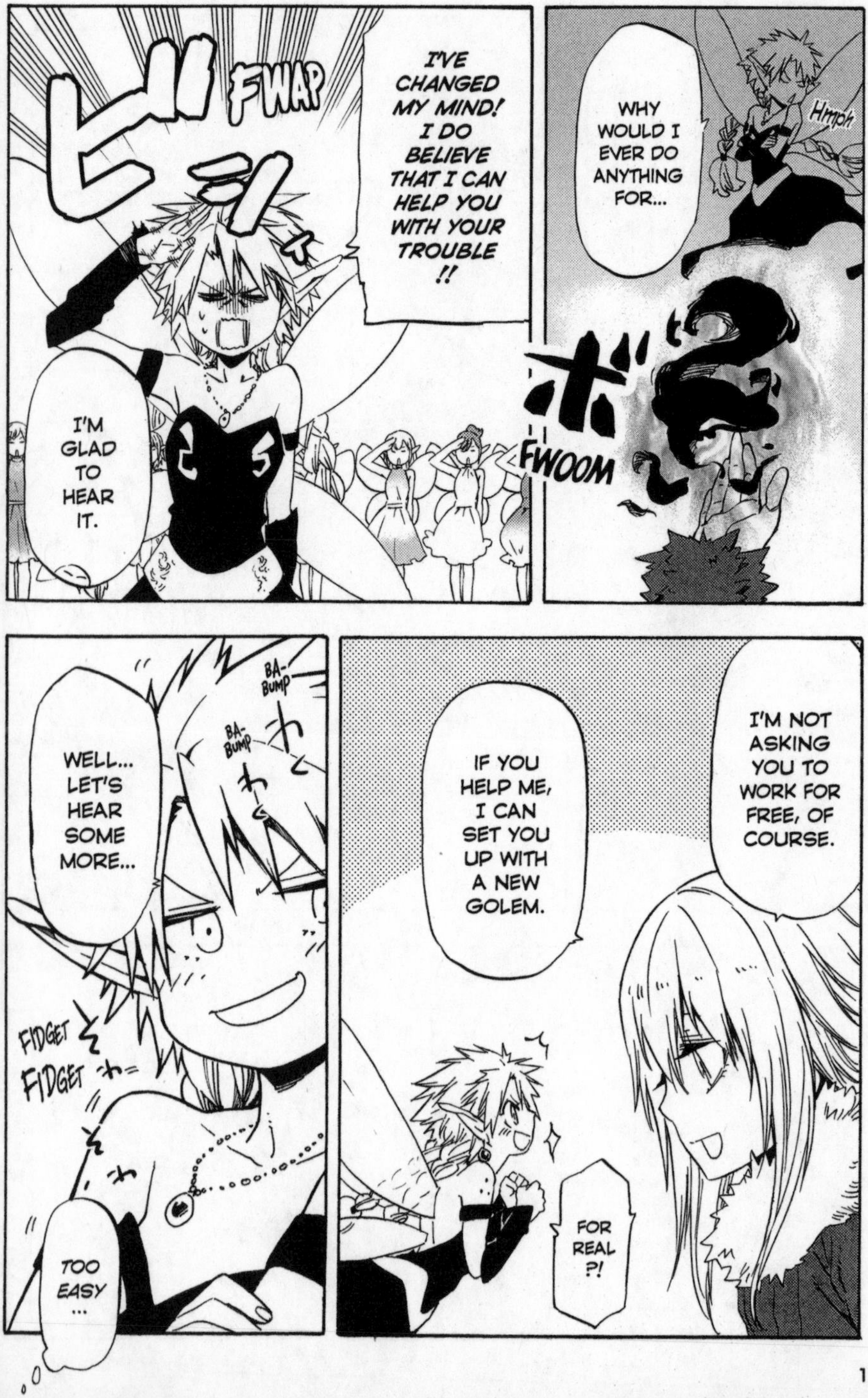
Hmph
WHY WOULD I EVER DO ANYTHING FOR...
FWOOM
I'VE CHANGED MY MIND! I DO BELIEVE THAT I CAN HELP YOU WITH YOUR TROUBLE !!
FWAP
I'M GLAD TO HEAR IT.
I'M NOT ASKING YOU TO WORK FOR FREE, OF COURSE.
IF YOU HELP ME, I CAN SET YOU UP WITH A NEW GOLEM.
FOR REAL ?!
BA-BUMP
BA-BUMP
WELL... LET'S HEAR SOME MORE...
FIDGET
FIDGET
TOO EASY ...

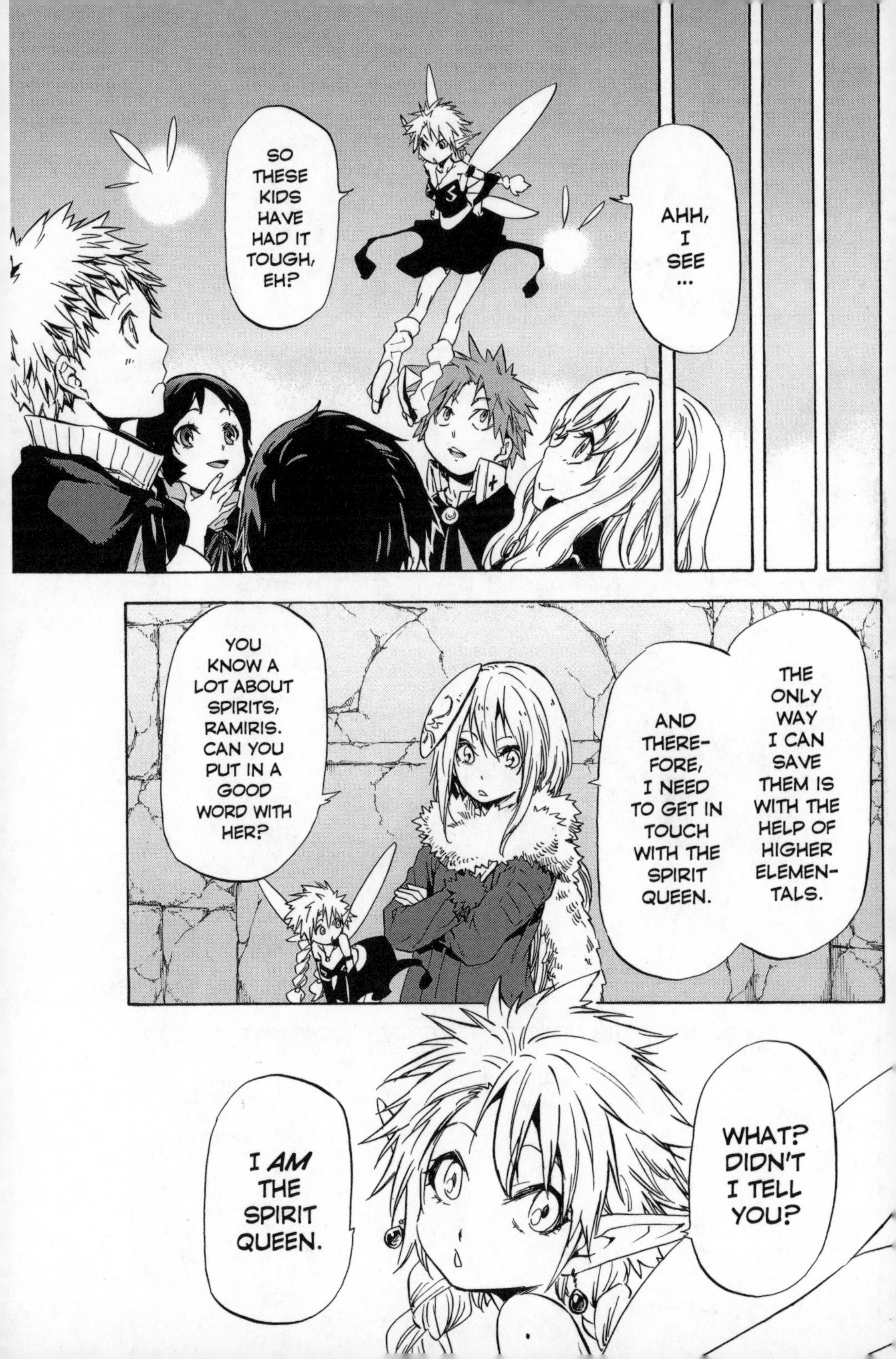
AHH, I SEE...
SO THESE KIDS HAVE HAD IT TOUGH, EH?
THE ONLY WAY I CAN SAVE THEM IS WITH THE HELP OF HIGHER ELEMENTALS.
AND THEREFORE, I NEED TO GET IN TOUCH WITH THE SPIRIT QUEEN.
YOU KNOW A LOT ABOUT SPIRITS, RAMIRIS. CAN YOU PUT IN A GOOD WORD WITH HER?
WHAT? DIDN'T I TELL YOU?
I *AM* THE SPIRIT QUEEN.

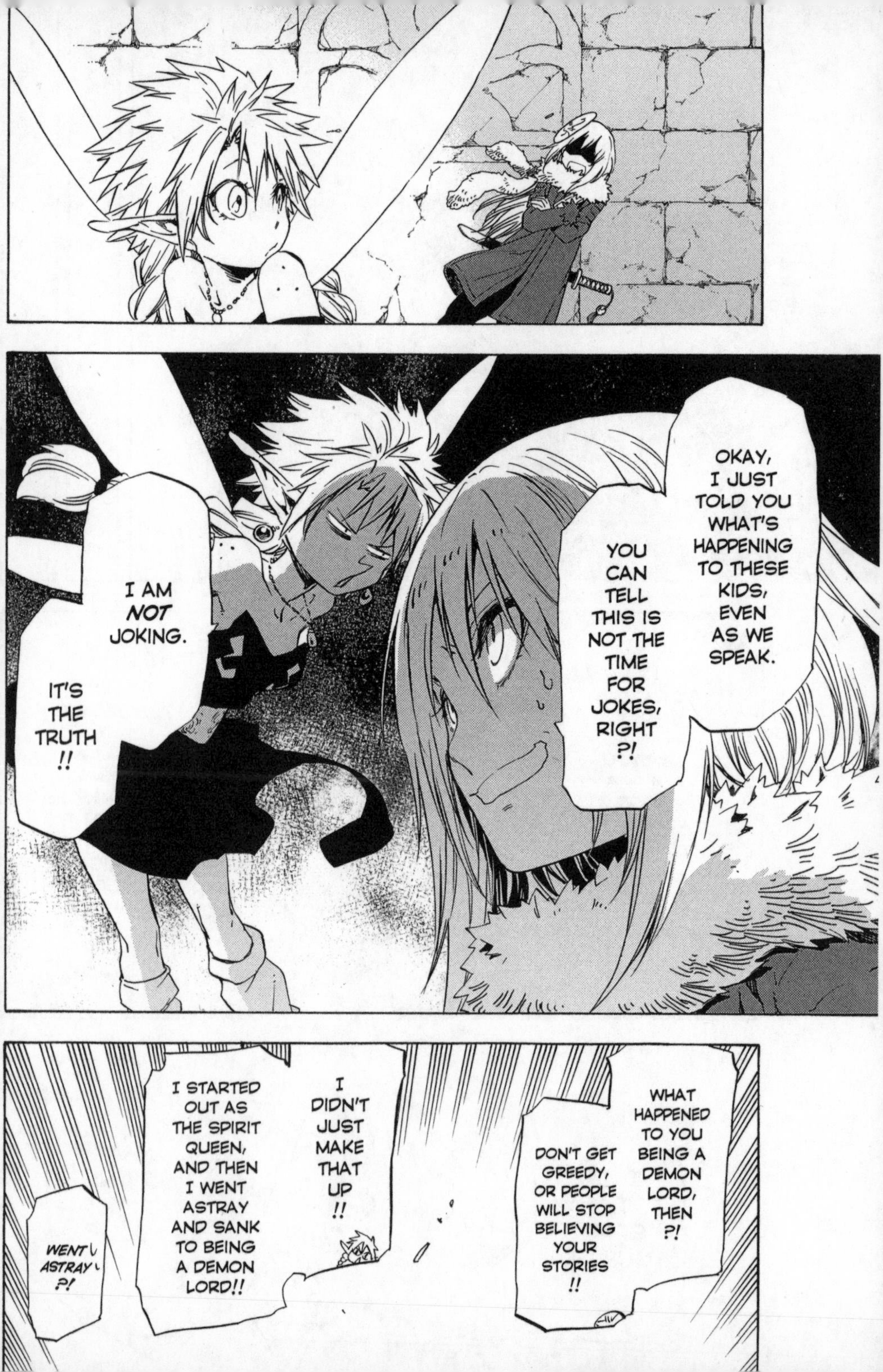
OKAY, I JUST TOLD YOU WHAT'S HAPPENING TO THESE KIDS, EVEN AS WE SPEAK.
YOU CAN TELL THIS IS NOT THE TIME FOR JOKES, RIGHT?!
I AM *NOT* JOKING.
IT'S THE TRUTH!!
WHAT HAPPENED TO YOU BEING A DEMON LORD, THEN?!
DON'T GET GREEDY, OR PEOPLE WILL STOP BELIEVING YOUR STORIES!!
I DIDN'T JUST MAKE THAT UP!!
I STARTED OUT AS THE SPIRIT QUEEN, AND THEN I WENT ASTRAY AND SANK TO BEING A DEMON LORD!!
WENT ASTRAY?!

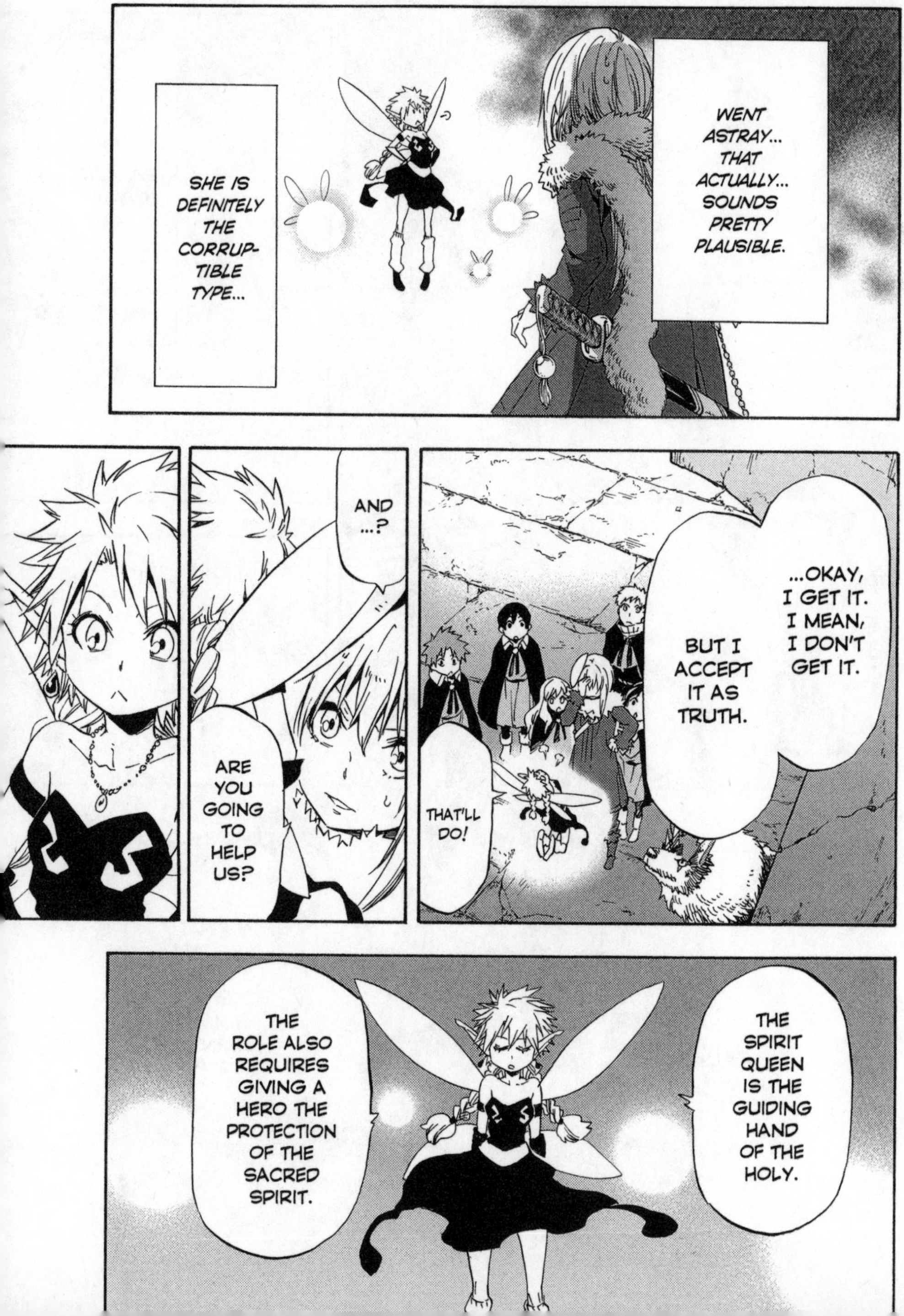
WENT ASTRAY... THAT ACTUALLY... SOUNDS PRETTY PLAUSIBLE.
SHE IS DEFINITELY THE CORRUP-TIBLE TYPE...
...OKAY, I GET IT. I MEAN, I DON'T GET IT.
BUT I ACCEPT IT AS TRUTH.
THAT'LL DO!
AND ...?
ARE YOU GOING TO HELP US?
THE SPIRIT QUEEN IS THE GUIDING HAND OF THE HOLY.
THE ROLE ALSO REQUIRES GIVING A HERO THE PROTECTION OF THE SACRED SPIRIT.

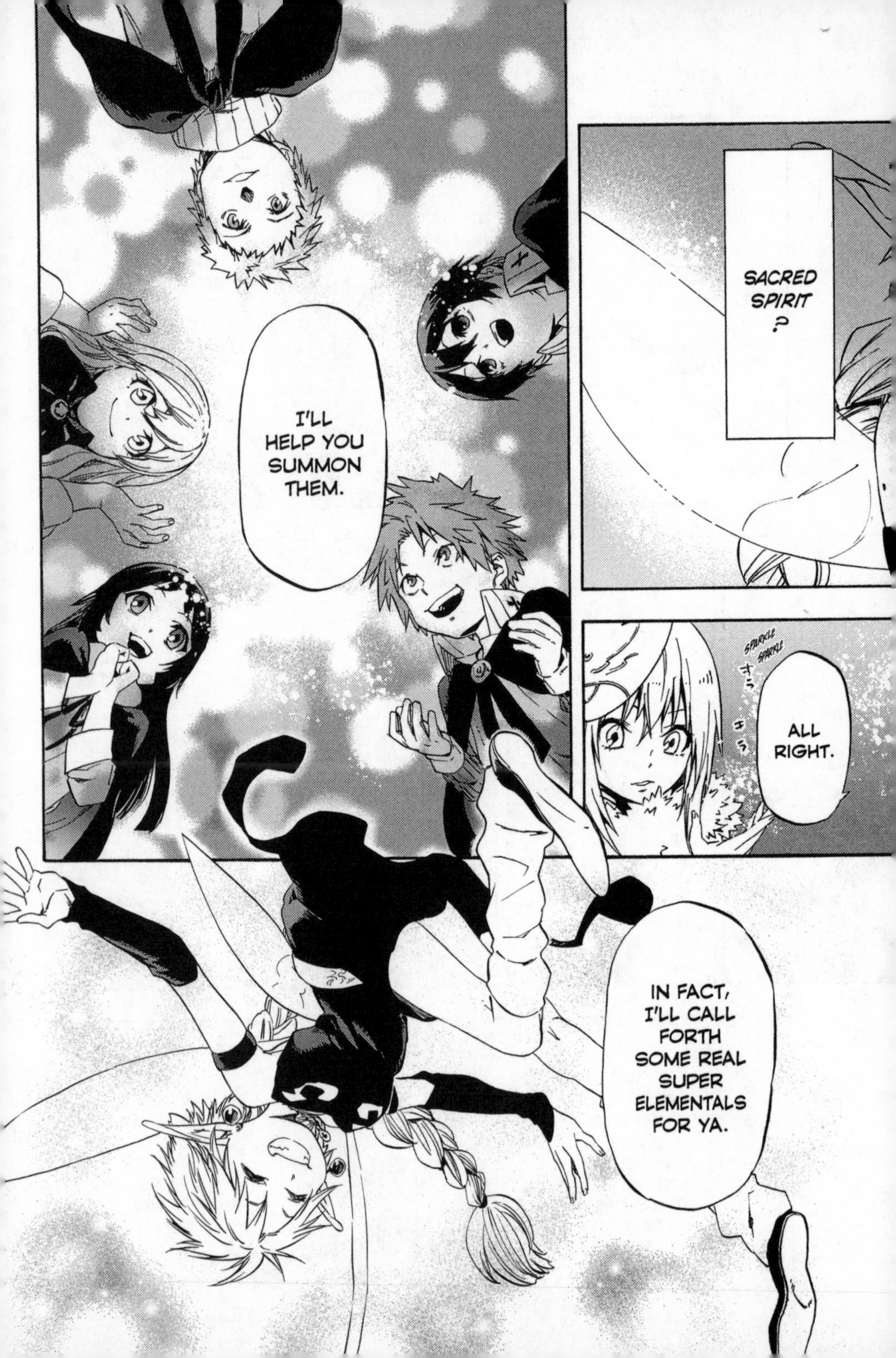
SACRED SPIRIT?
SPARKLE SPARKLE
ALL RIGHT.
I'LL HELP YOU SUMMON THEM.
IN FACT, I'LL CALL FORTH SOME REAL SUPER ELEMENTALS FOR YA.

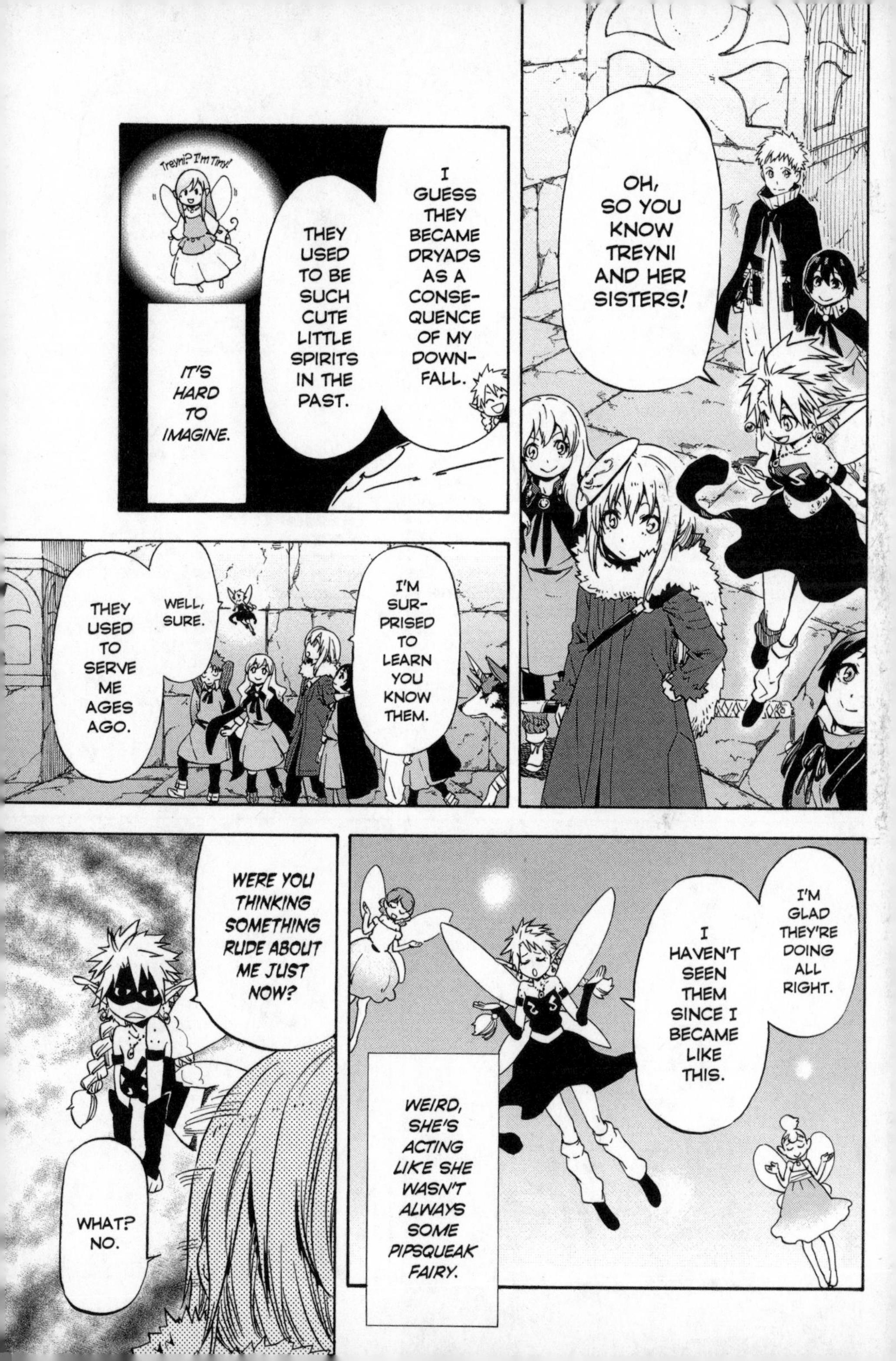
OH, SO YOU KNOW TREYNI AND HER SISTERS!
I GUESS THEY BECAME DRYADS AS A CONSEQUENCE OF MY DOWNFALL.
THEY USED TO BE SUCH CUTE LITTLE SPIRITS IN THE PAST.
Treyni? I'm Tiny!
IT'S HARD TO IMAGINE.
I'M SURPRISED TO LEARN YOU KNOW THEM.
WELL, SURE.
THEY USED TO SERVE ME AGES AGO.
I'M GLAD THEY'RE DOING ALL RIGHT.
I HAVEN'T SEEN THEM SINCE I BECAME LIKE THIS.
WEIRD, SHE'S ACTING LIKE SHE WASN'T ALWAYS SOME PIPSQUEAK FAIRY.
WERE YOU THINKING SOMETHING RUDE ABOUT ME JUST NOW?
WHAT? NO.

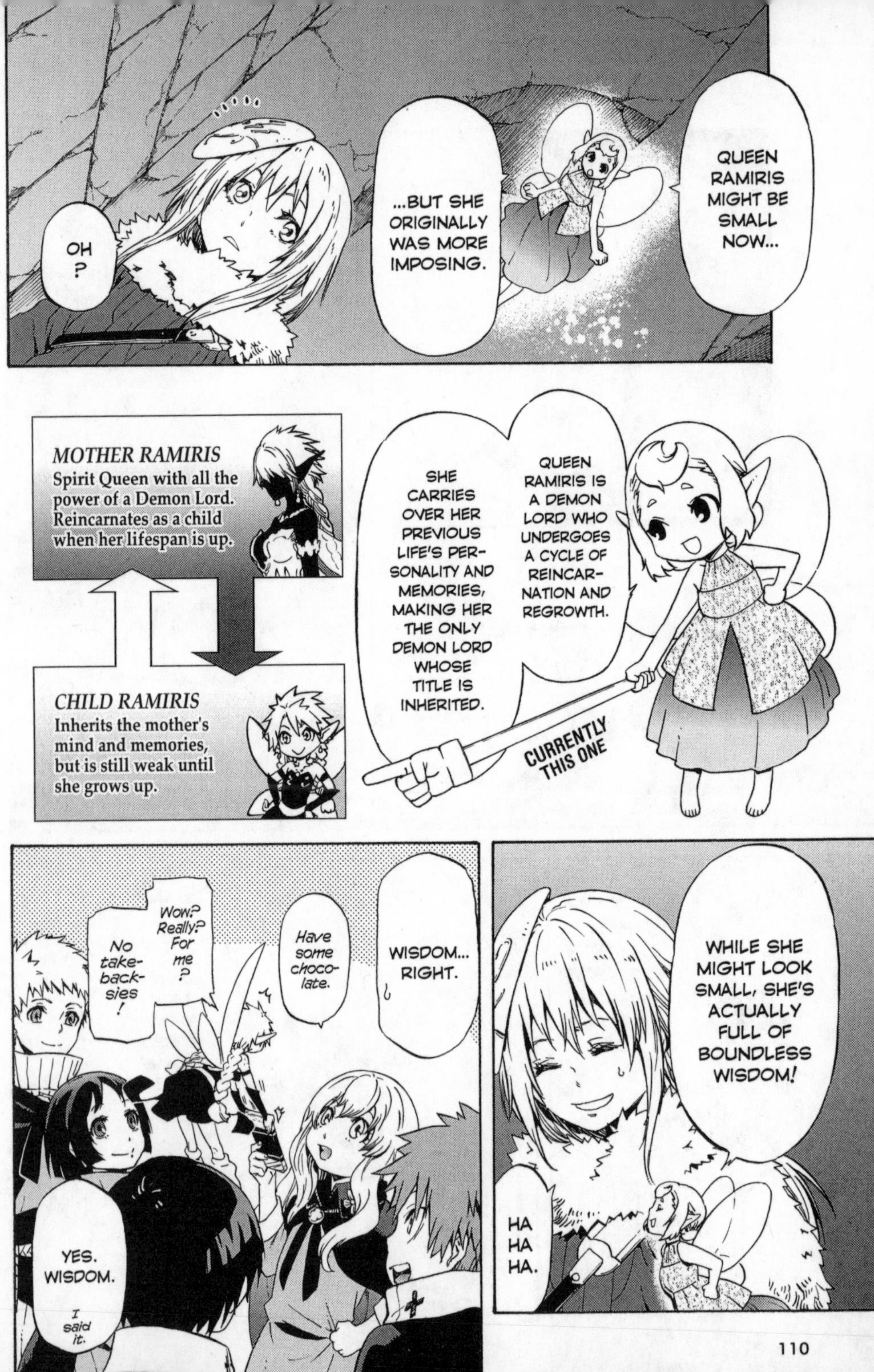
QUEEN RAMIRIS MIGHT BE SMALL NOW...
...BUT SHE ORIGINALLY WAS MORE IMPOSING.
OH?
QUEEN RAMIRIS IS A DEMON LORD WHO UNDERGOES A CYCLE OF REINCARNATION AND REGROWTH.
SHE CARRIES OVER HER PREVIOUS LIFE'S PERSONALITY AND MEMORIES, MAKING HER THE ONLY DEMON LORD WHOSE TITLE IS INHERITED.
CURRENTLY THIS ONE
MOTHER RAMIRIS
Spirit Queen with all the power of a Demon Lord. Reincarnates as a child when her lifespan is up.
CHILD RAMIRIS
Inherits the mother's mind and memories, but is still weak until she grows up.
WHILE SHE MIGHT LOOK SMALL, SHE'S ACTUALLY FULL OF BOUNDLESS WISDOM!
HA HA HA.
WISDOM... RIGHT.
Have some chocolate.
Wow? Really? For me?
No take-backsies!
YES. WISDOM.
I said it.

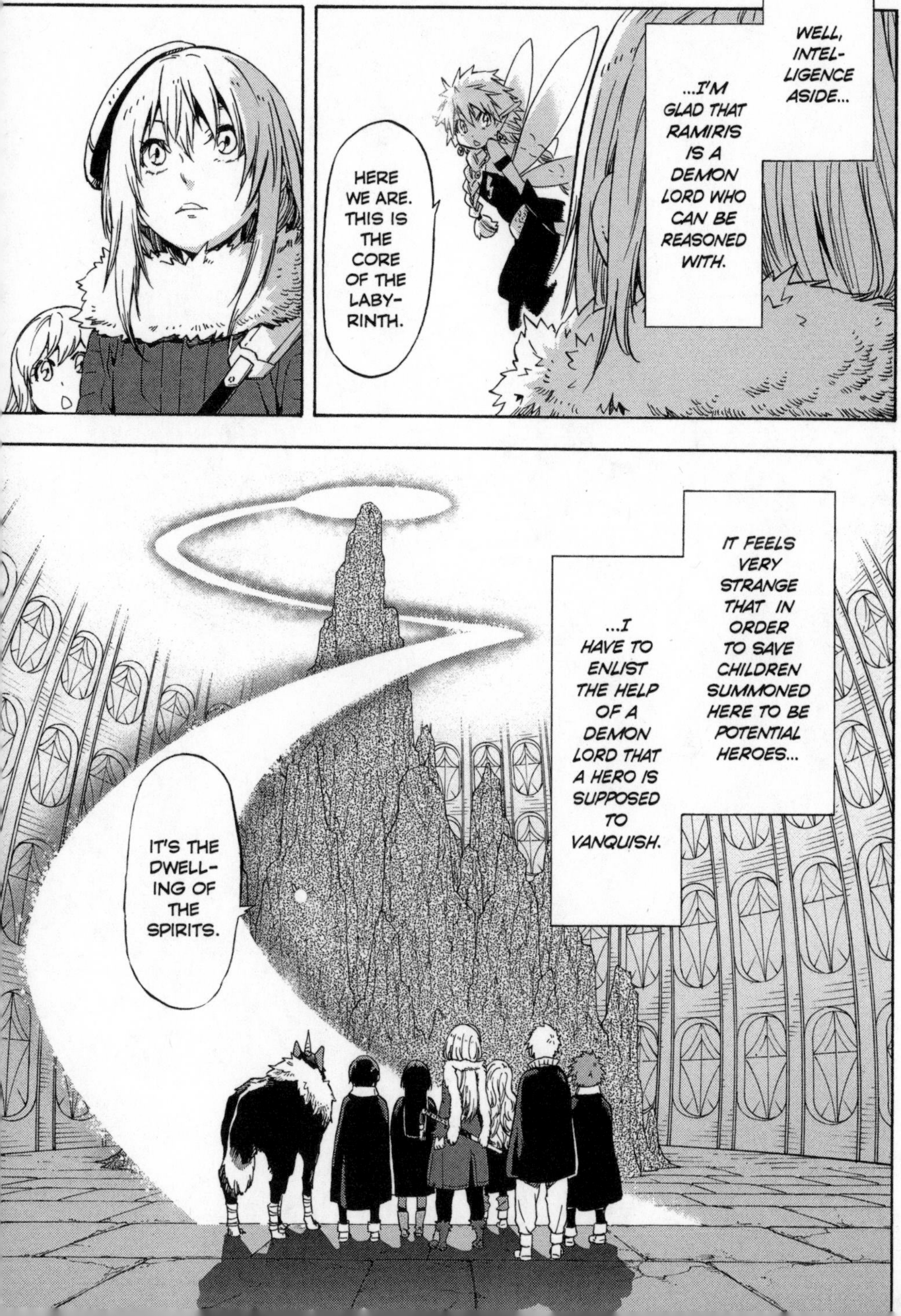
WELL, INTELLIGENCE ASIDE...
...I'M GLAD THAT RAMIRIS IS A DEMON LORD WHO CAN BE REASONED WITH.
HERE WE ARE. THIS IS THE CORE OF THE LABYRINTH.
IT FEELS VERY STRANGE THAT IN ORDER TO SAVE CHILDREN SUMMONED HERE TO BE POTENTIAL HEROES...
...I HAVE TO ENLIST THE HELP OF A DEMON LORD THAT A HERO IS SUPPOSED TO VANQUISH.
IT'S THE DWELLING OF THE SPIRITS.

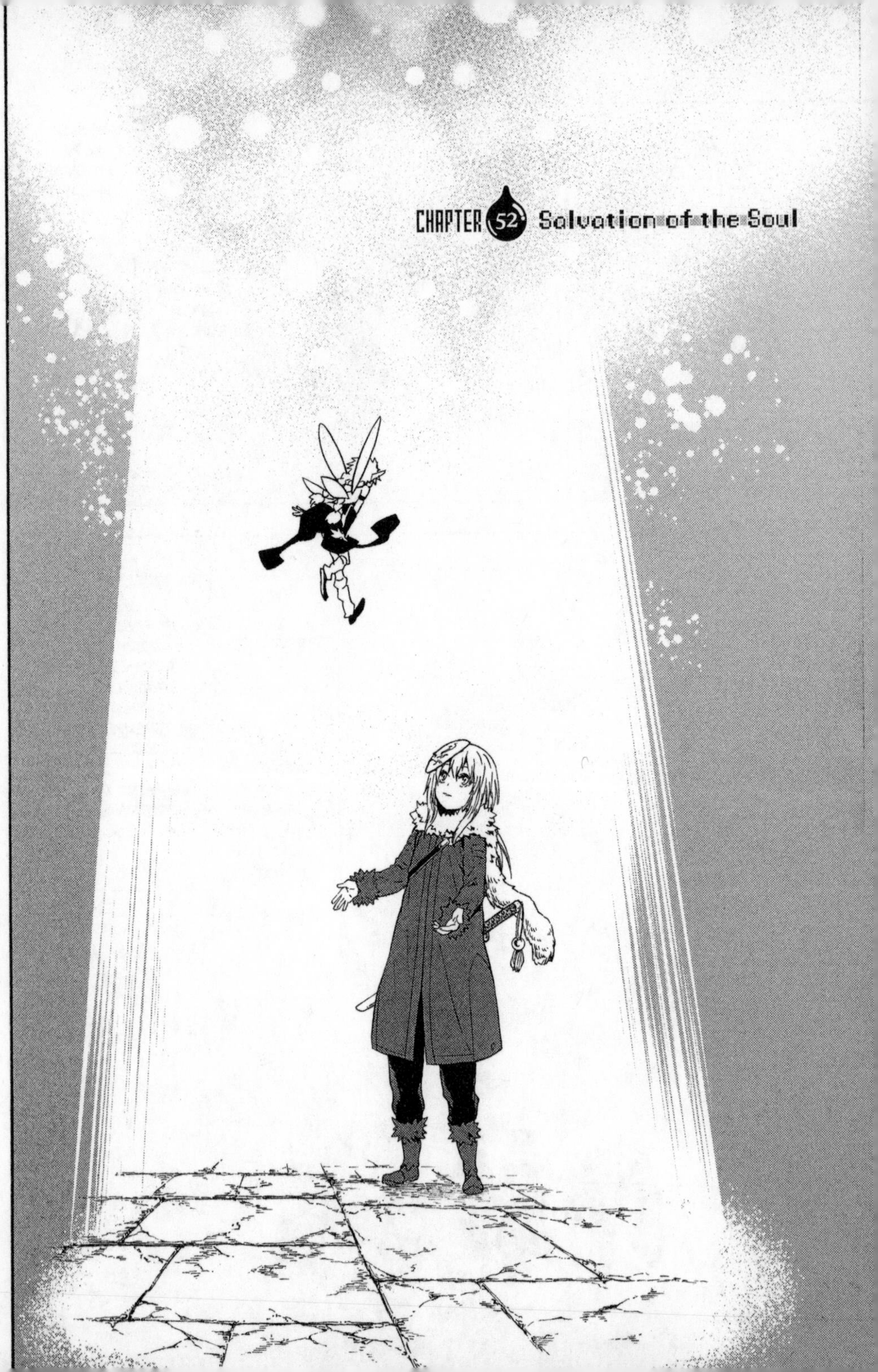
CHAPTER 52 Salvation of the Soul

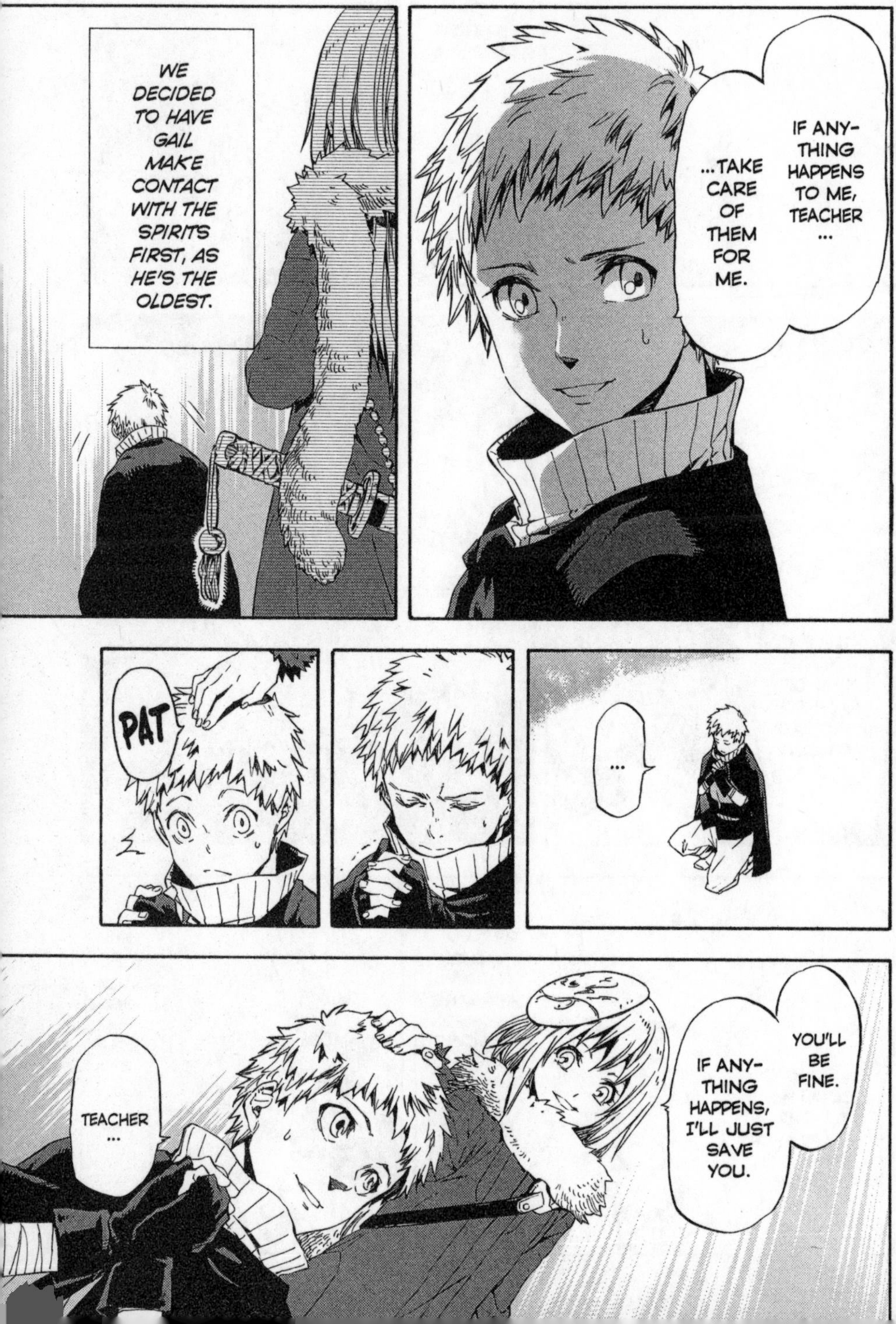
IF ANY-THING HAPPENS TO ME, TEACHER...
...TAKE CARE OF THEM FOR ME.
WE DECIDED TO HAVE GAIL MAKE CONTACT WITH THE SPIRITS FIRST, AS HE'S THE OLDEST.
...
PAT
YOU'LL BE FINE.
IF ANY-THING HAPPENS, I'LL JUST SAVE YOU.
TEACHER...

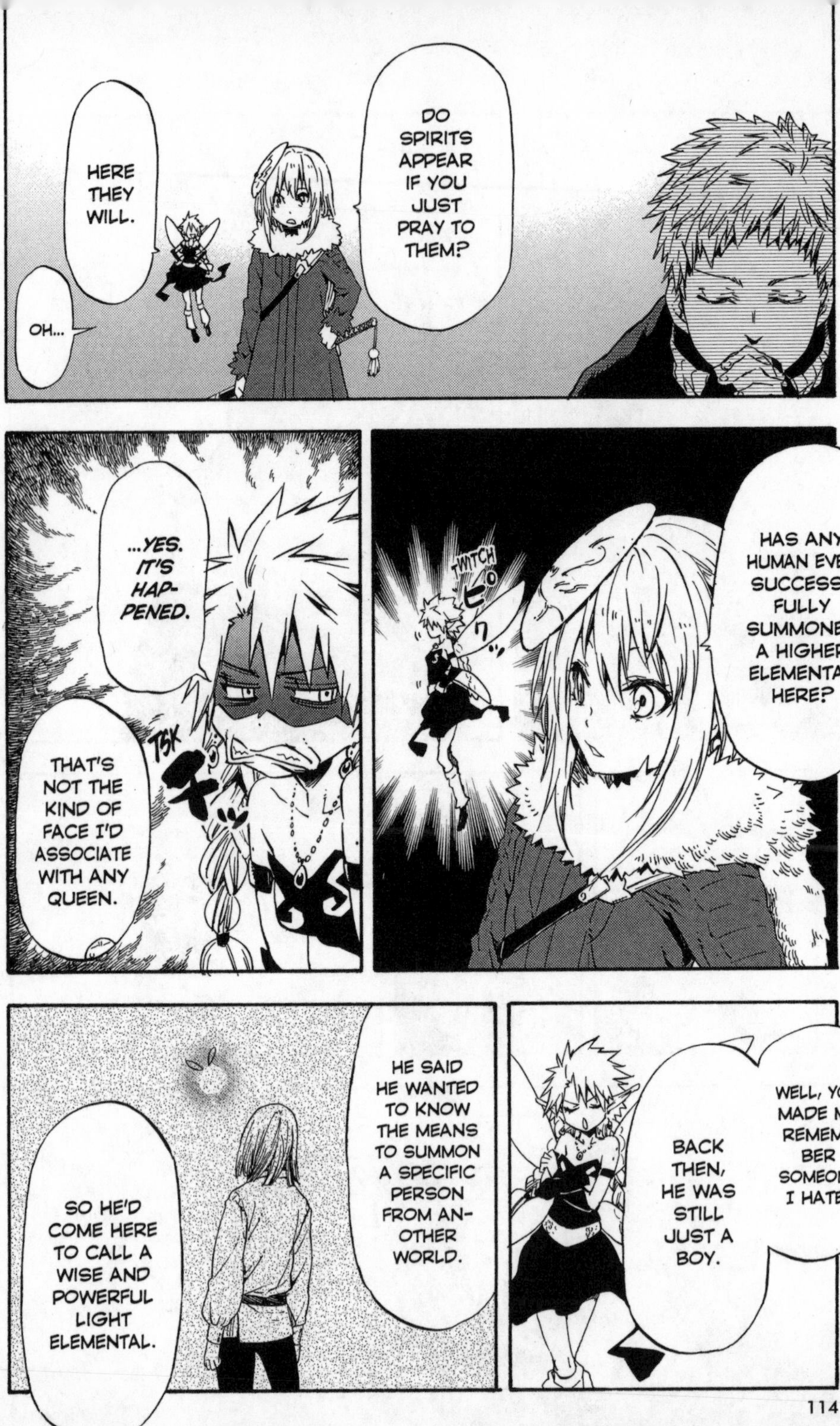
DO SPIRITS APPEAR IF YOU JUST PRAY TO THEM?
HERE THEY WILL.
OH...
HAS ANY HUMAN EVER SUCCESSFULLY SUMMONED A HIGHER ELEMENTAL HERE?
TWITCH
...YES. IT'S HAPPENED.
TSK
THAT'S NOT THE KIND OF FACE I'D ASSOCIATE WITH ANY QUEEN.
WELL, YOU MADE ME REMEMBER SOMEONE I HATE.
BACK THEN, HE WAS STILL JUST A BOY.
HE SAID HE WANTED TO KNOW THE MEANS TO SUMMON A SPECIFIC PERSON FROM ANOTHER WORLD.
SO HE'D COME HERE TO CALL A WISE AND POWERFUL LIGHT ELEMENTAL.

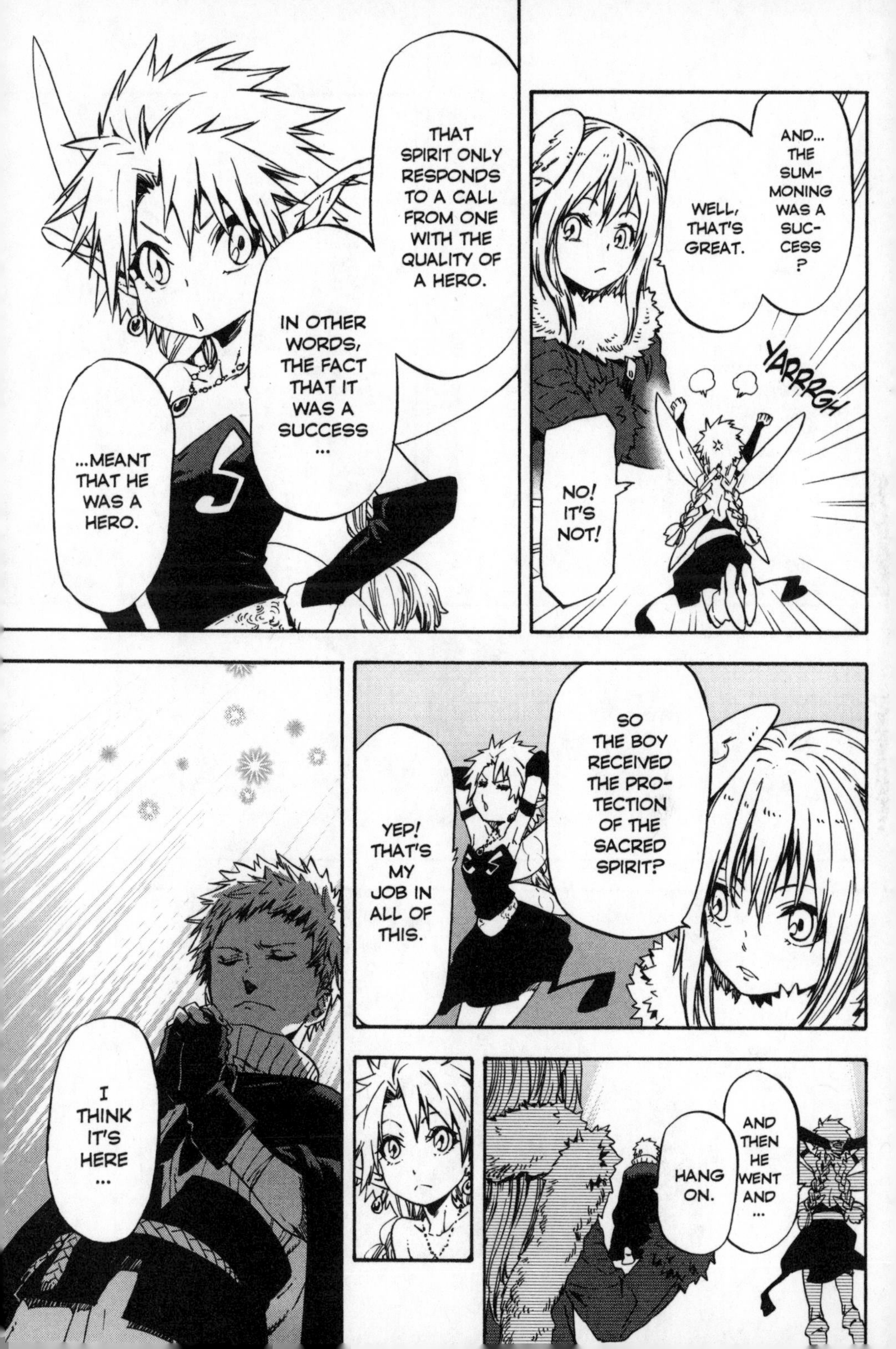
AND... THE SUMMONING WAS A SUCCESS?
WELL, THAT'S GREAT.
YARRRGH
NO! IT'S NOT!
THAT SPIRIT ONLY RESPONDS TO A CALL FROM ONE WITH THE QUALITY OF A HERO.
IN OTHER WORDS, THE FACT THAT IT WAS A SUCCESS...
...MEANT THAT HE WAS A HERO.
SO THE BOY RECEIVED THE PROTECTION OF THE SACRED SPIRIT?
YEP! THAT'S MY JOB IN ALL OF THIS.
AND THEN HE WENT AND...
HANG ON.
I THINK IT'S HERE...

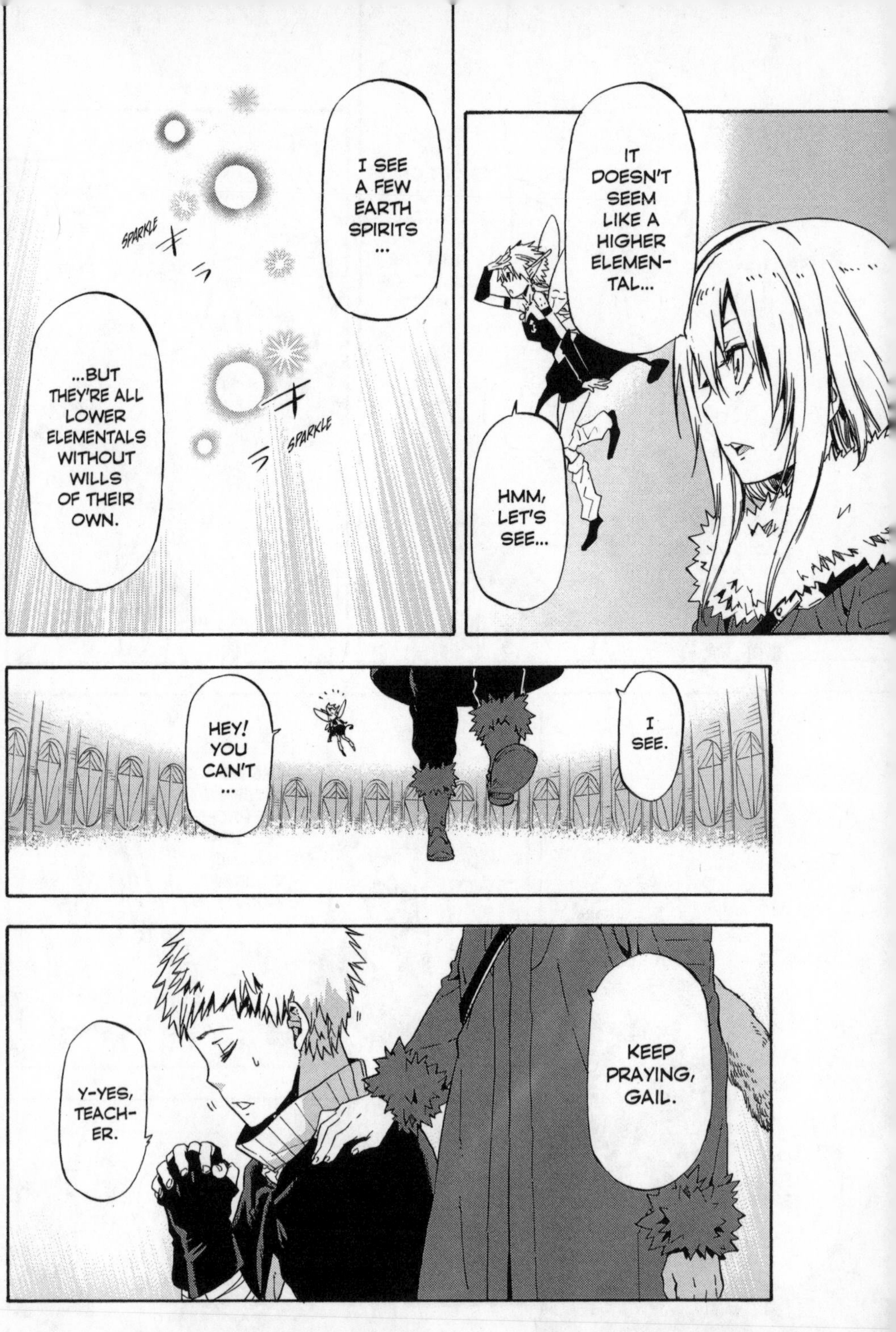
IT DOESN'T SEEM LIKE A HIGHER ELEMENTAL...
HMM, LET'S SEE...
I SEE A FEW EARTH SPIRITS...
SPARKLE
...BUT THEY'RE ALL LOWER ELEMENTALS WITHOUT WILLS OF THEIR OWN.
SPARKLE
I SEE.
HEY! YOU CAN'T...
KEEP PRAYING, GAIL.
Y-YES, TEACHER.

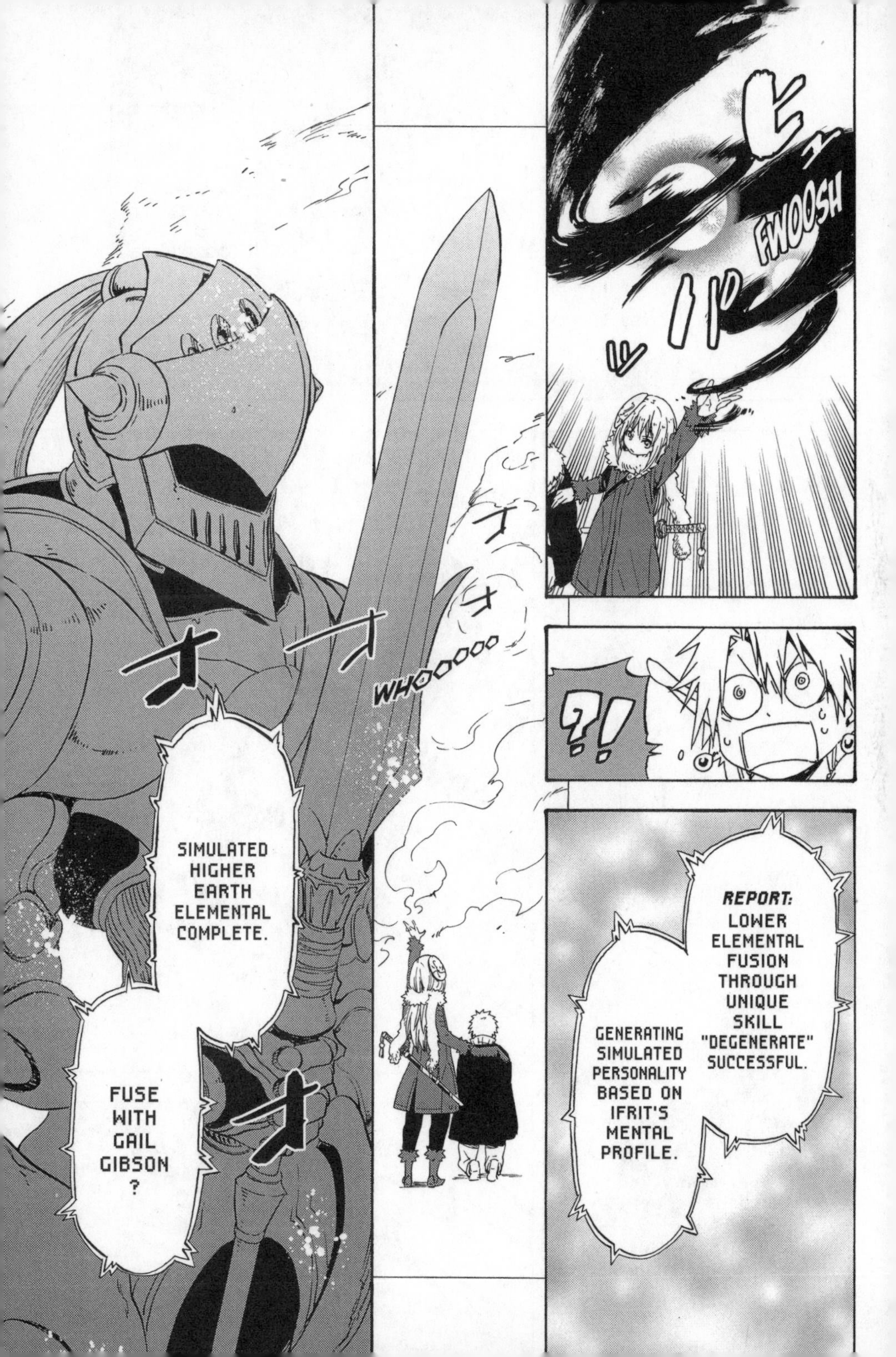
FWOOSH
?!
REPORT: LOWER ELEMENTAL FUSION THROUGH UNIQUE SKILL "DEGENERATE" SUCCESSFUL.
GENERATING SIMULATED PERSONALITY BASED ON IFRIT'S MENTAL PROFILE.
WHOOOOO
SIMULATED HIGHER EARTH ELEMENTAL COMPLETE.
FUSE WITH GAIL GIBSON ?

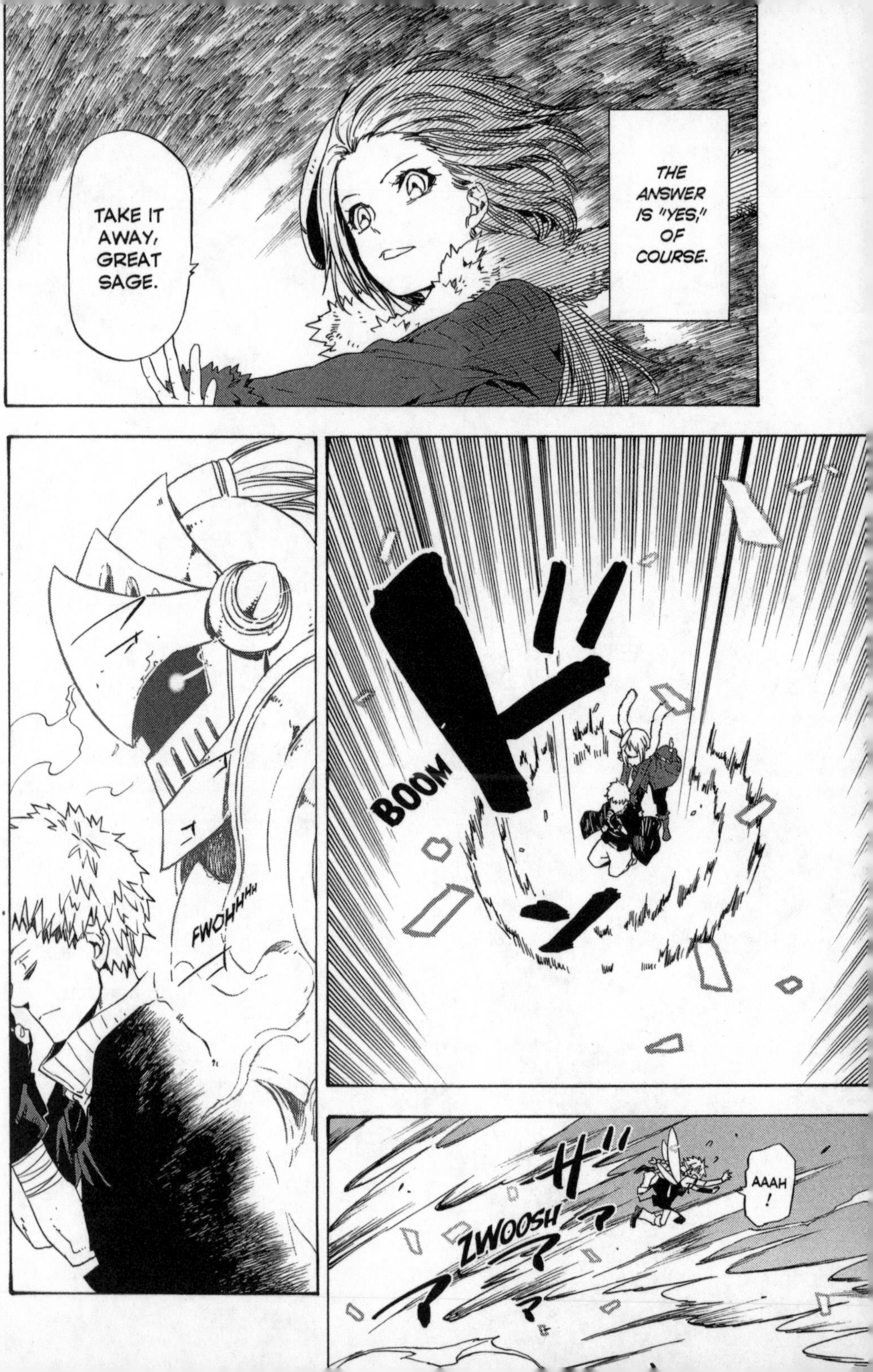
THE ANSWER IS "YES," OF COURSE.
TAKE IT AWAY, GREAT SAGE.
BOOM
AAAH!
ZWOOSH
FWOHHHH

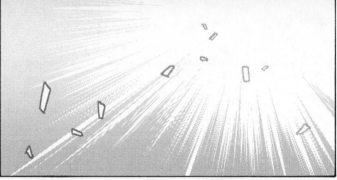

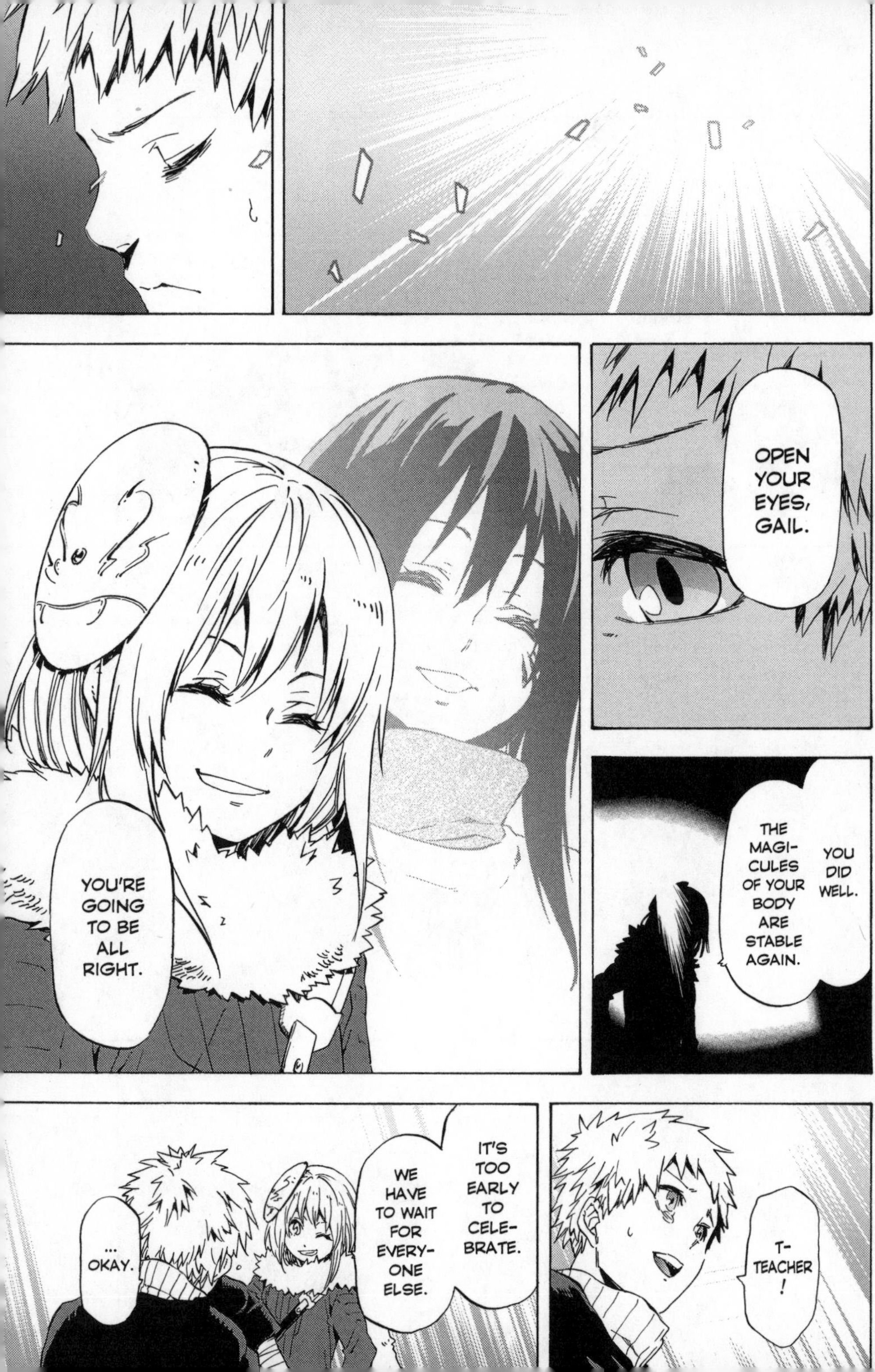
OPEN YOUR EYES, GAIL.
YOU DID WELL.
THE MAGICULES OF YOUR BODY ARE STABLE AGAIN.
YOU'RE GOING TO BE ALL RIGHT.
T-TEACHER!
IT'S TOO EARLY TO CELEBRATE.
WE HAVE TO WAIT FOR EVERYONE ELSE.
... OKAY.

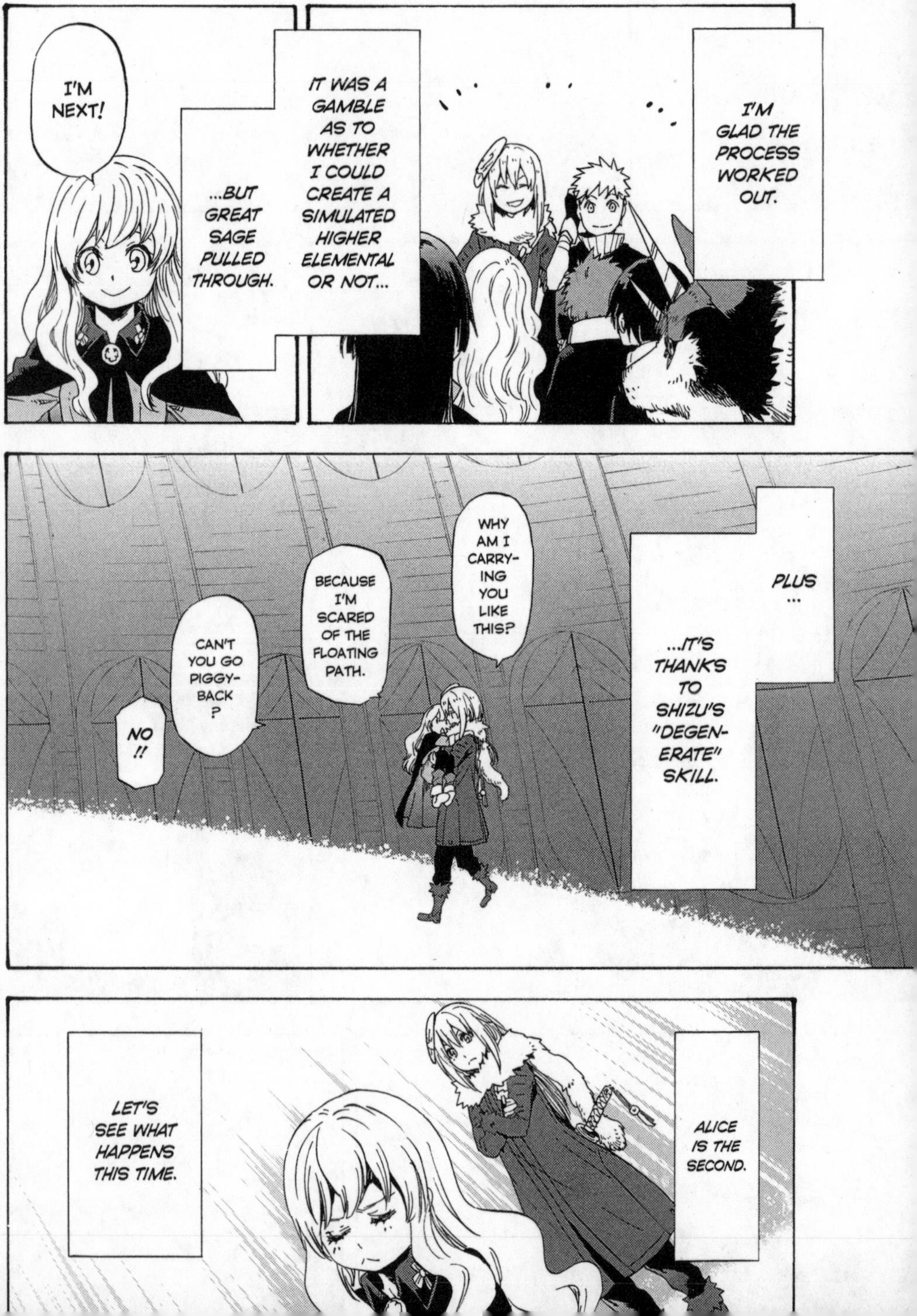

...
..
..
I'M GLAD THE PROCESS WORKED OUT.
IT WAS A GAMBLE AS TO WHETHER I COULD CREATE A SIMULATED HIGHER ELEMENTAL OR NOT...
...BUT GREAT SAGE PULLED THROUGH.
I'M NEXT!
PLUS...
...IT'S THANKS TO SHIZU'S "DEGENERATE" SKILL.
WHY AM I CARRYING YOU LIKE THIS?
BECAUSE I'M SCARED OF THE FLOATING PATH.
CAN'T YOU GO PIGGYBACK?
NO!!
ALICE IS THE SECOND.
LET'S SEE WHAT HAPPENS THIS TIME.

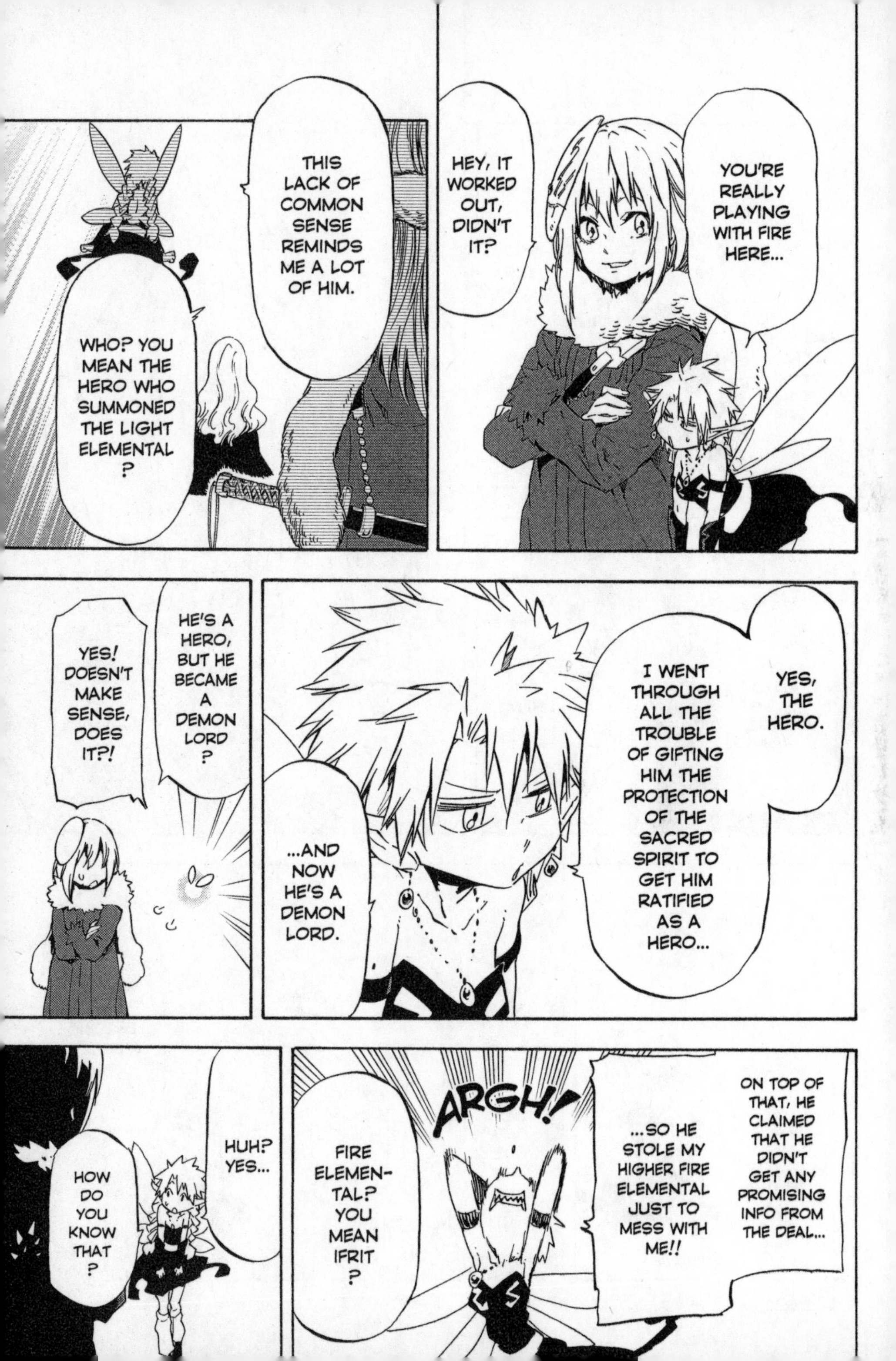
YOU'RE REALLY PLAYING WITH FIRE HERE...
HEY, IT WORKED OUT, DIDN'T IT?
THIS LACK OF COMMON SENSE REMINDS ME A LOT OF HIM.
WHO? YOU MEAN THE HERO WHO SUMMONED THE LIGHT ELEMENTAL?
YES, THE HERO.
I WENT THROUGH ALL THE TROUBLE OF GIFTING HIM THE PROTECTION OF THE SACRED SPIRIT TO GET HIM RATIFIED AS A HERO...
...AND NOW HE'S A DEMON LORD.
HE'S A HERO, BUT HE BECAME A DEMON LORD?
YES! DOESN'T MAKE SENSE, DOES IT?!
ON TOP OF THAT, HE CLAIMED THAT HE DIDN'T GET ANY PROMISING INFO FROM THE DEAL...
...SO HE STOLE MY HIGHER FIRE ELEMENTAL JUST TO MESS WITH ME!!
ARGH!
FIRE ELEMENTAL? YOU MEAN IFRIT?
HUH? YES...
HOW DO YOU KNOW THAT?

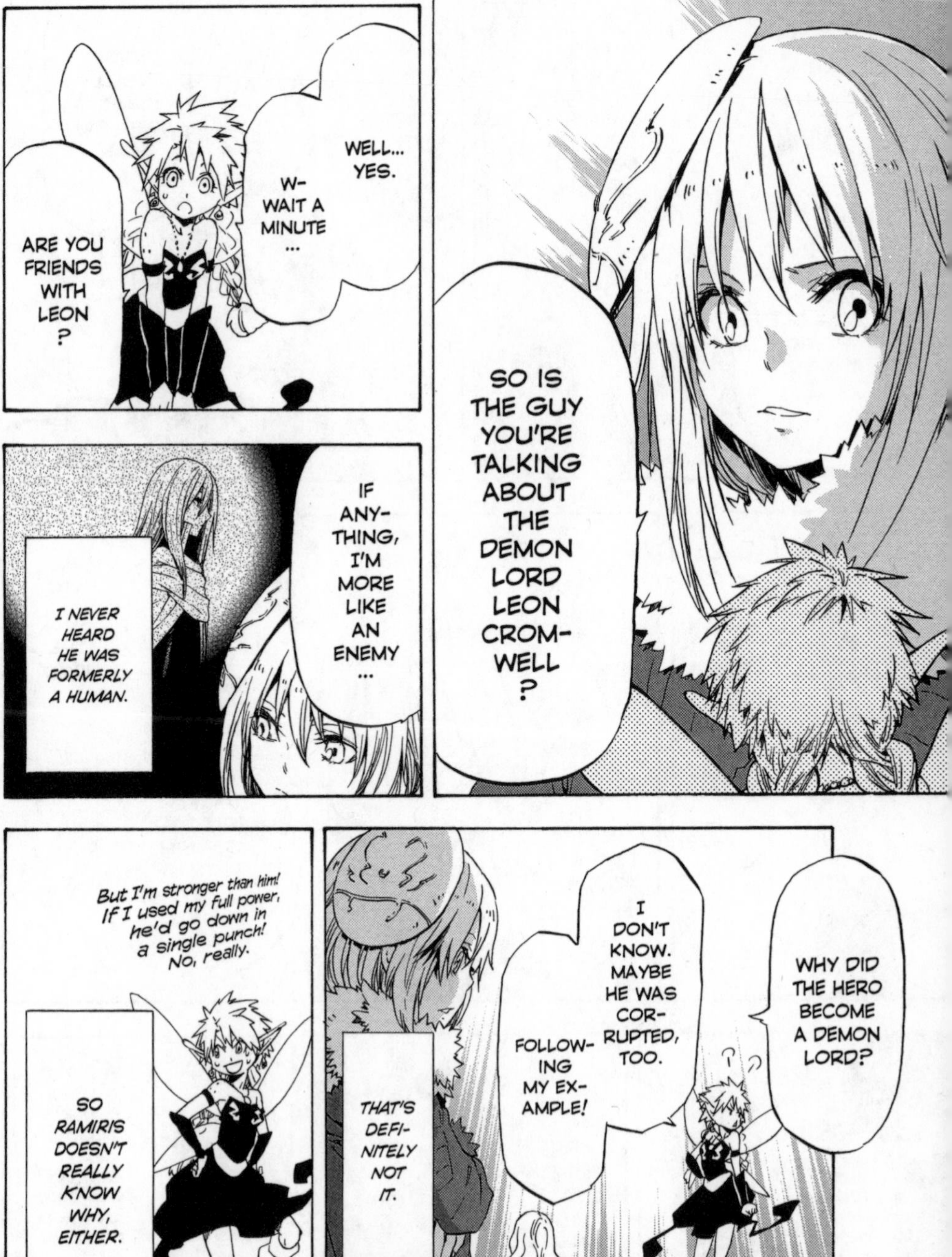
SO IS THE GUY YOU'RE TALKING ABOUT THE DEMON LORD LEON CROMWELL?
WELL... YES.
W-WAIT A MINUTE...
ARE YOU FRIENDS WITH LEON?
IF ANYTHING, I'M MORE LIKE AN ENEMY...
I NEVER HEARD HE WAS FORMERLY A HUMAN.
WHY DID THE HERO BECOME A DEMON LORD?
I DON'T KNOW. MAYBE HE WAS CORRUPTED, TOO.
FOLLOWING MY EXAMPLE!
THAT'S DEFINITELY NOT IT.
But I'm stronger than him! If I used my full power, he'd go down in a single punch! No, really.
SO RAMIRIS DOESN'T REALLY KNOW WHY, EITHER.

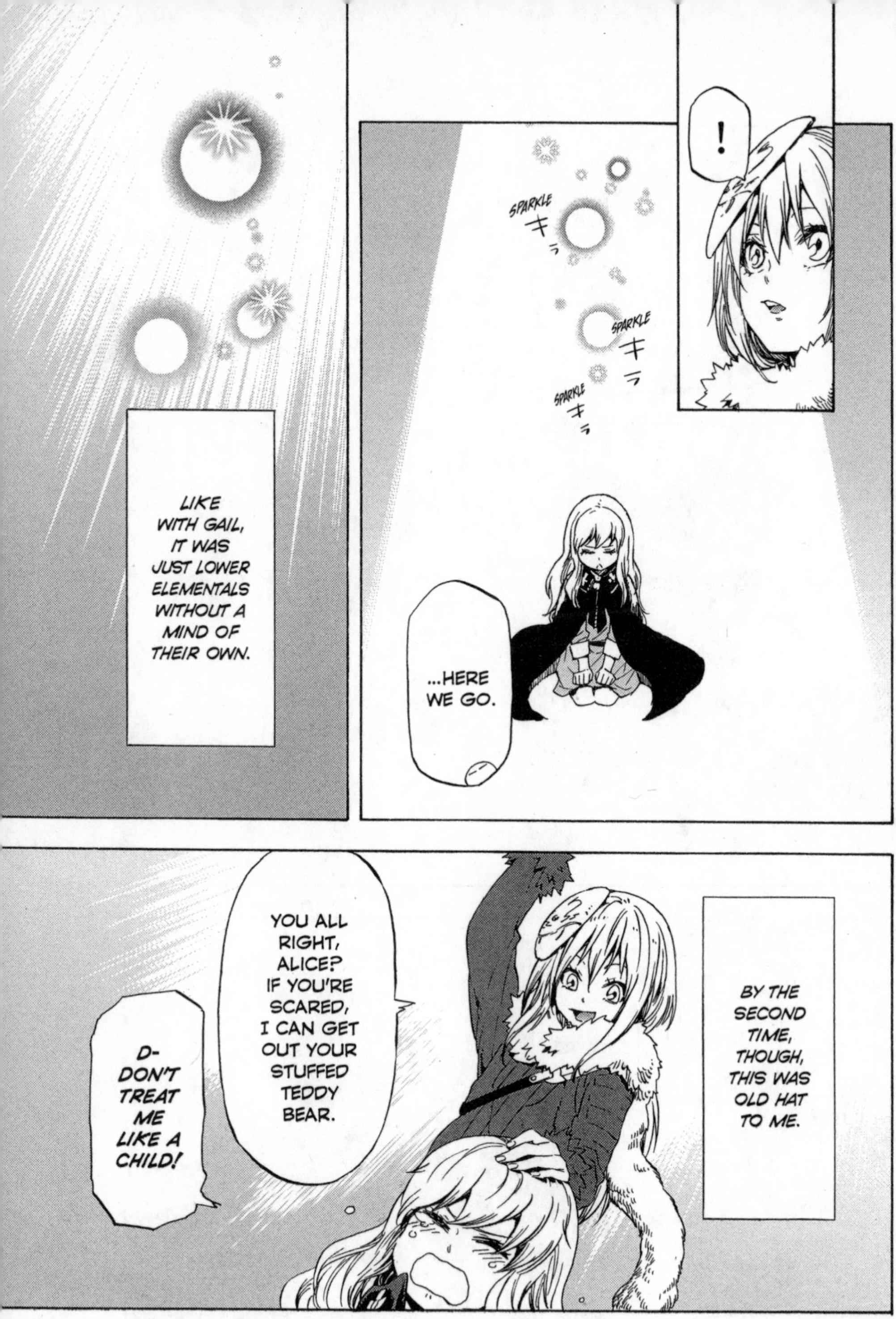
!
SPARKLE キラ
SPARKLE キラ
SPARKLE キラ
...HERE WE GO.
LIKE WITH GAIL, IT WAS JUST LOWER ELEMENTALS WITHOUT A MIND OF THEIR OWN.
BY THE SECOND TIME, THOUGH, THIS WAS OLD HAT TO ME.
YOU ALL RIGHT, ALICE? IF YOU'RE SCARED, I CAN GET OUT YOUR STUFFED TEDDY BEAR.
D-DON'T TREAT ME LIKE A CHILD!

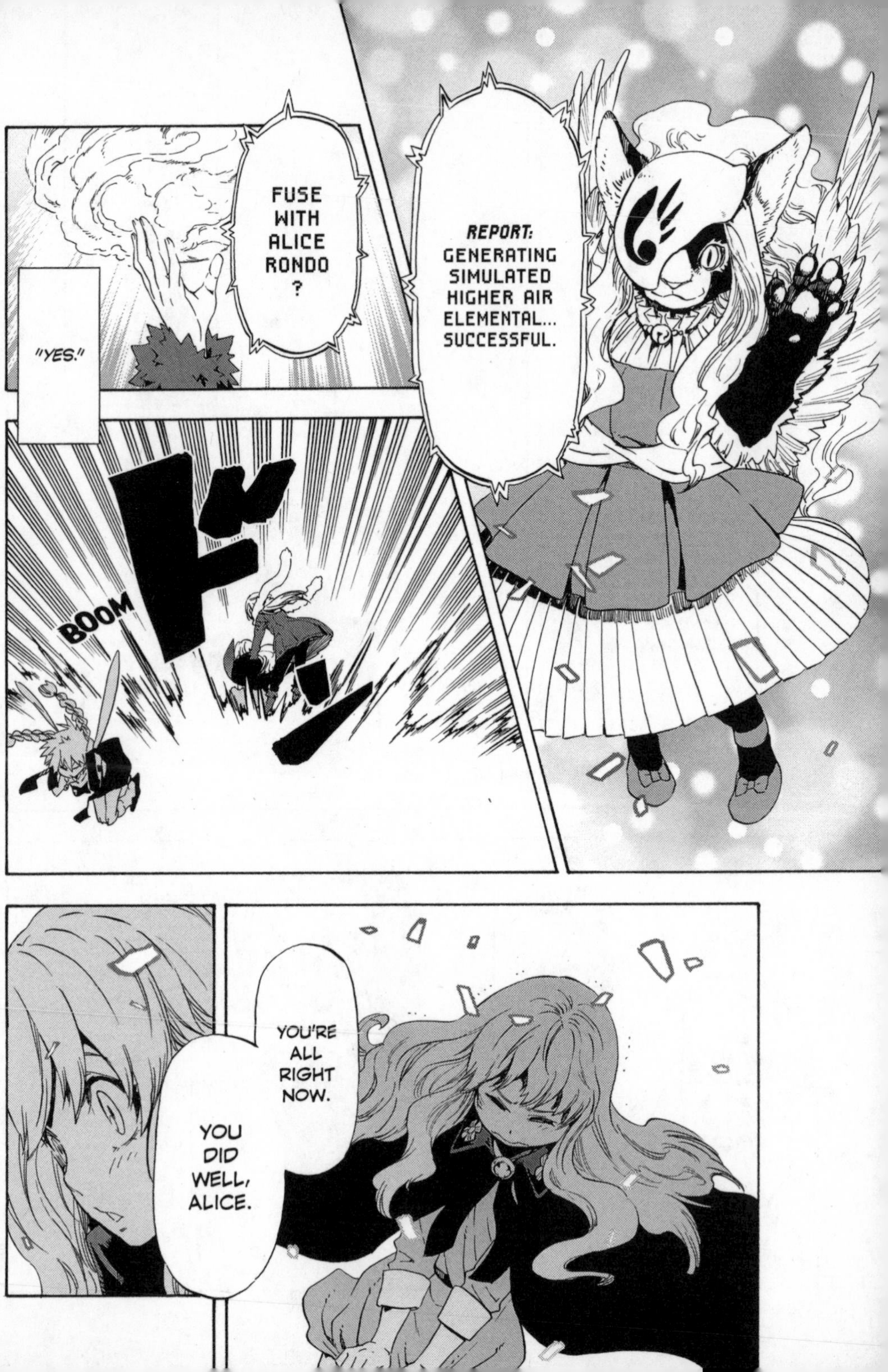

REPORT: GENERATING SIMULATED HIGHER AIR ELEMENTAL... SUCCESSFUL.
FUSE WITH ALICE RONDO ?
"YES."
BOOM
YOU'RE ALL RIGHT NOW.
YOU DID WELL, ALICE.

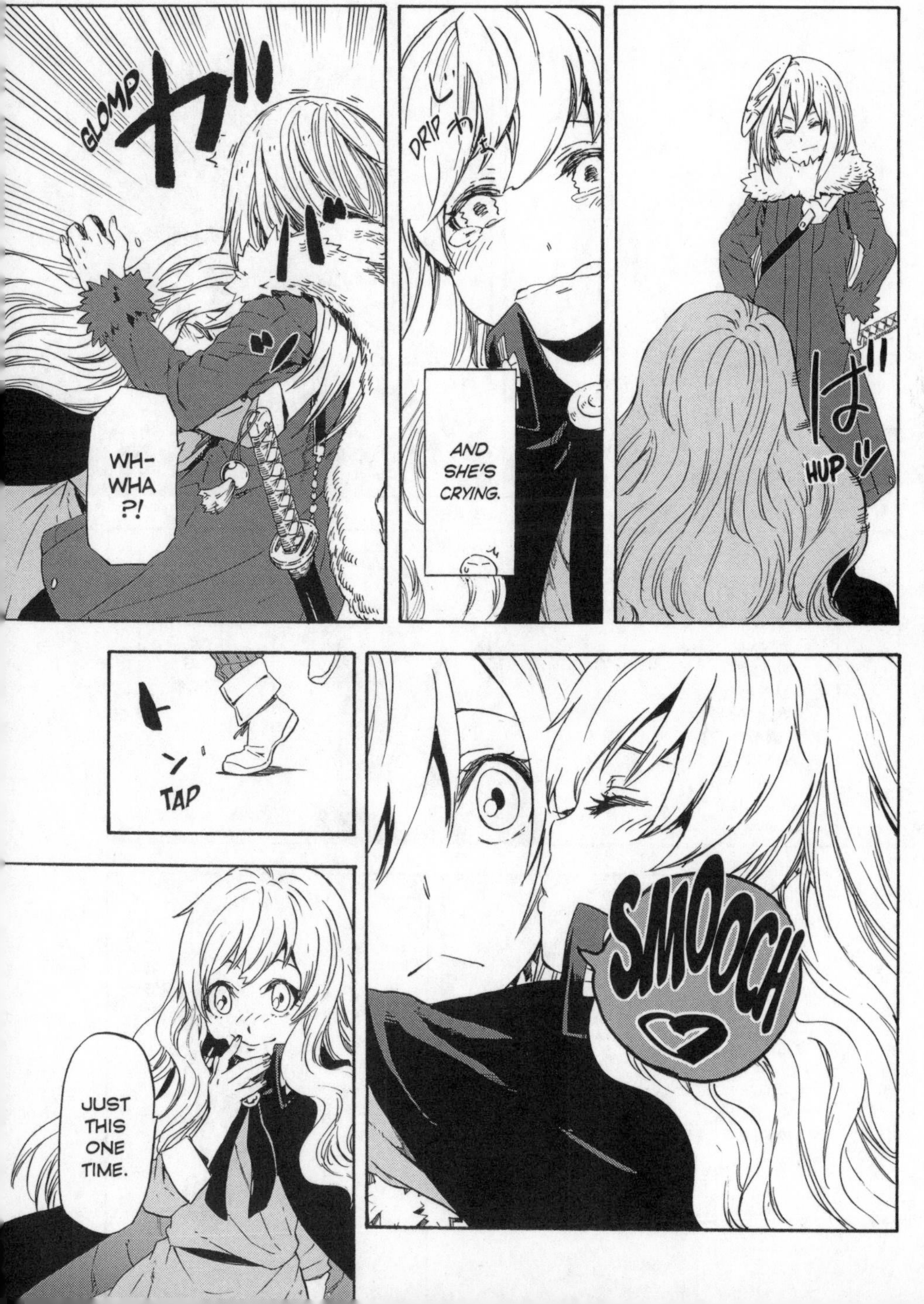
ばッ
HUP
DRIP
AND SHE'S CRYING.
GLOMP
WH-WHA?!
SMOOCH
トン
TAP
JUST THIS ONE TIME.

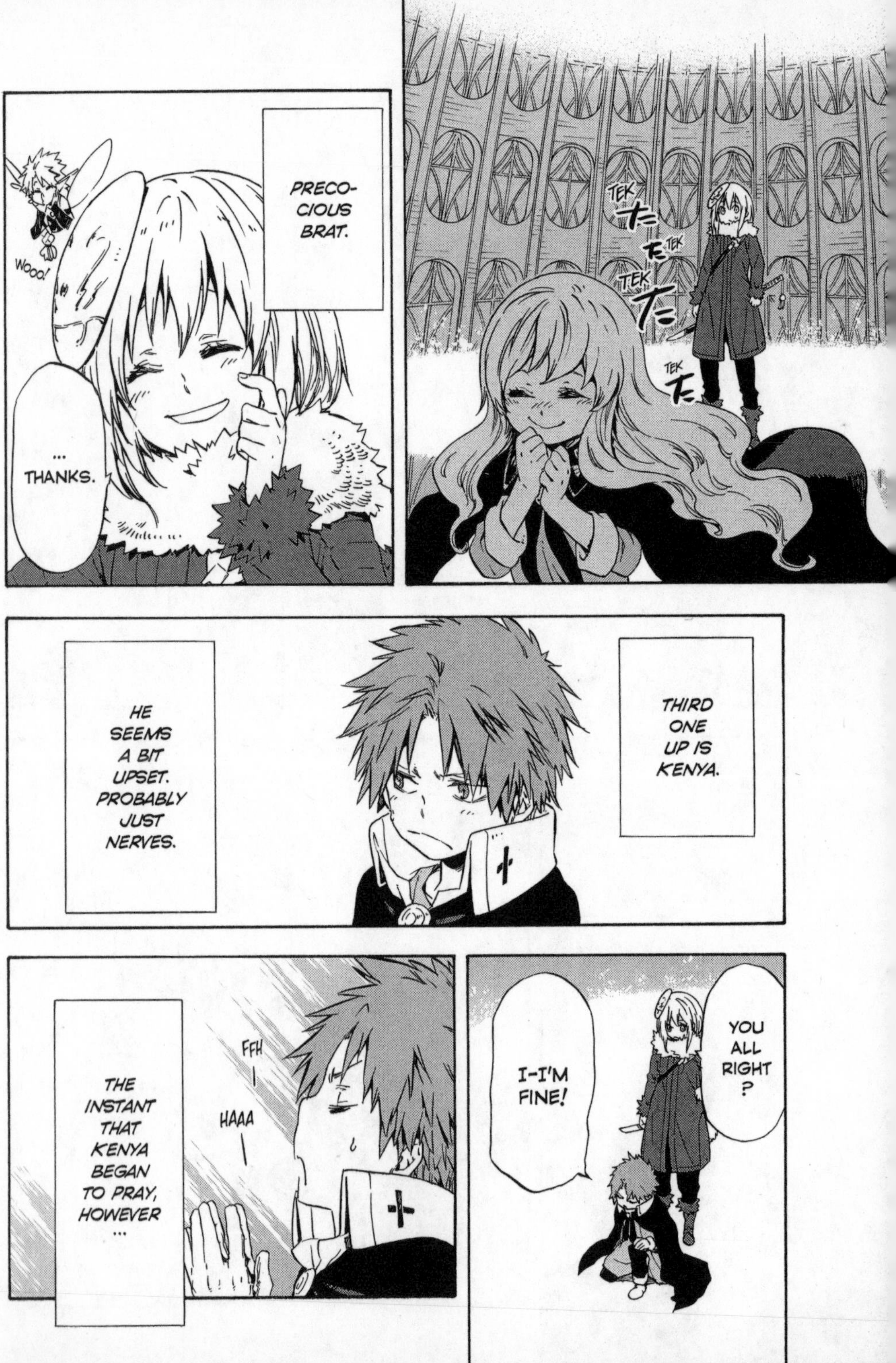
TEK
TEK
TEK
TEK
PRECOCIOUS BRAT.
WOOO!
... THANKS.
THIRD ONE UP IS KENYA.
HE SEEMS A BIT UPSET. PROBABLY JUST NERVES.
YOU ALL RIGHT?
I-I'M FINE!
FFH-
HAAA-
THE INSTANT THAT KENYA BEGAN TO PRAY, HOWEVER...

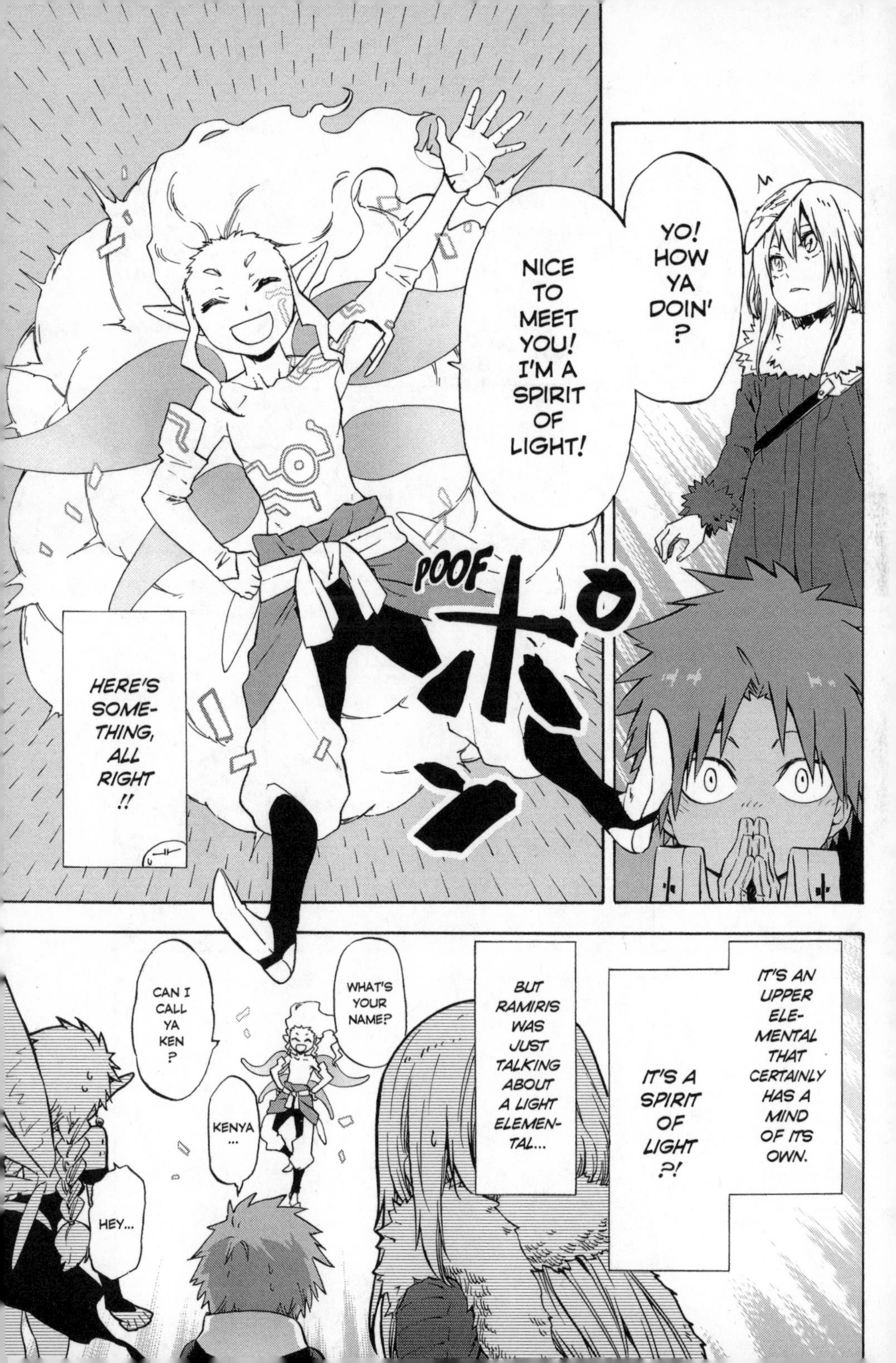
YO! HOW YA DOIN'?
NICE TO MEET YOU! I'M A SPIRIT OF LIGHT!
POOF
HERE'S SOMETHING, ALL RIGHT!!
IT'S AN UPPER ELEMENTAL THAT CERTAINLY HAS A MIND OF ITS OWN.
IT'S A SPIRIT OF LIGHT?!
BUT RAMIRIS WAS JUST TALKING ABOUT A LIGHT ELEMENTAL...
WHAT'S YOUR NAME?
CAN I CALL YA KEN?
KENYA...
HEY...

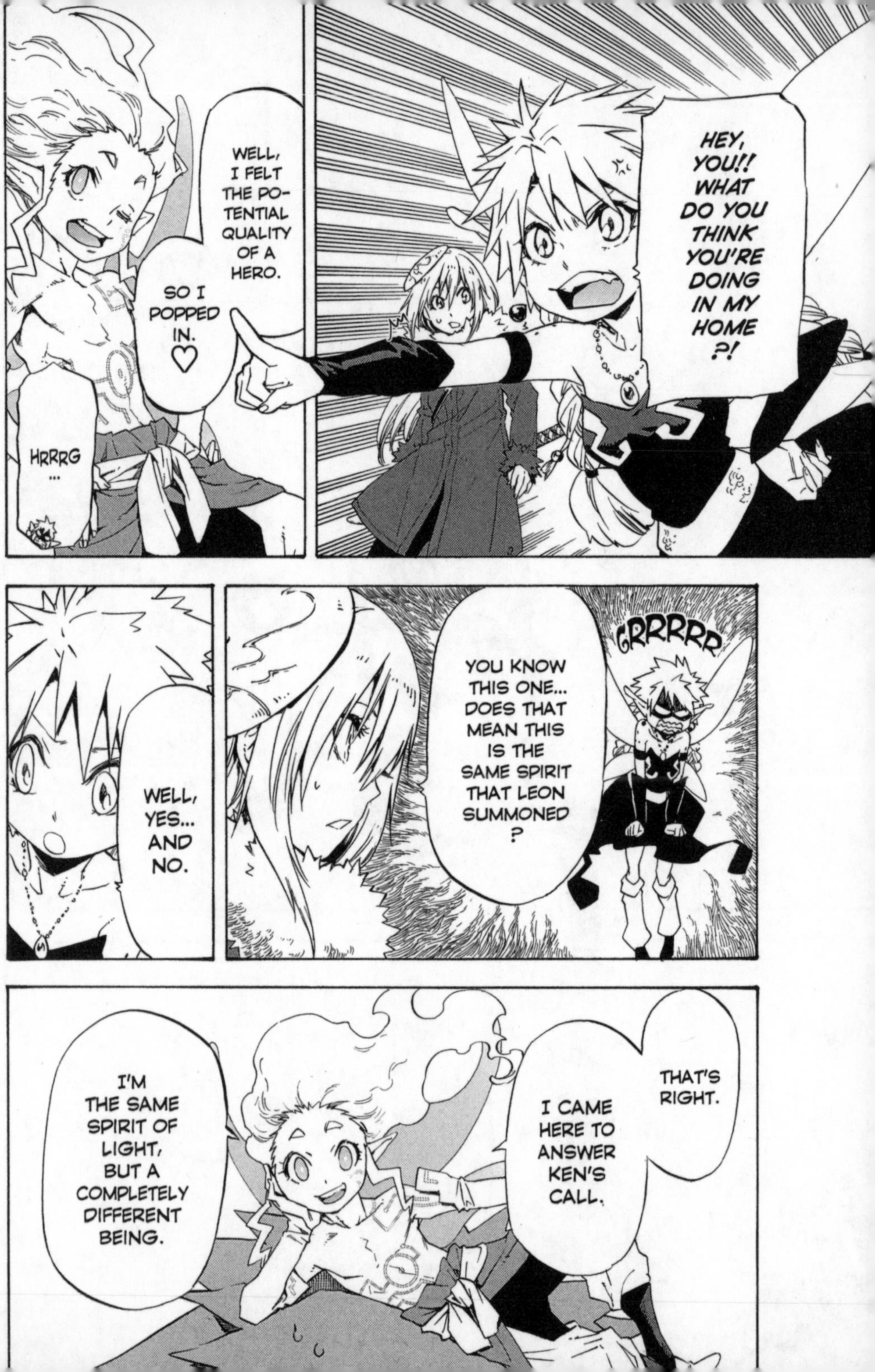
HEY, YOU!! WHAT DO YOU THINK YOU'RE DOING IN MY HOME ?!
WELL, I FELT THE PO-TENTIAL QUALITY OF A HERO.
SO I POPPED IN. ♡
HRRRG ...
GRRRRR
YOU KNOW THIS ONE... DOES THAT MEAN THIS IS THE SAME SPIRIT THAT LEON SUMMONED ?
WELL, YES... AND NO.
THAT'S RIGHT.
I CAME HERE TO ANSWER KEN'S CALL.
I'M THE SAME SPIRIT OF LIGHT, BUT A COMPLETELY DIFFERENT BEING.

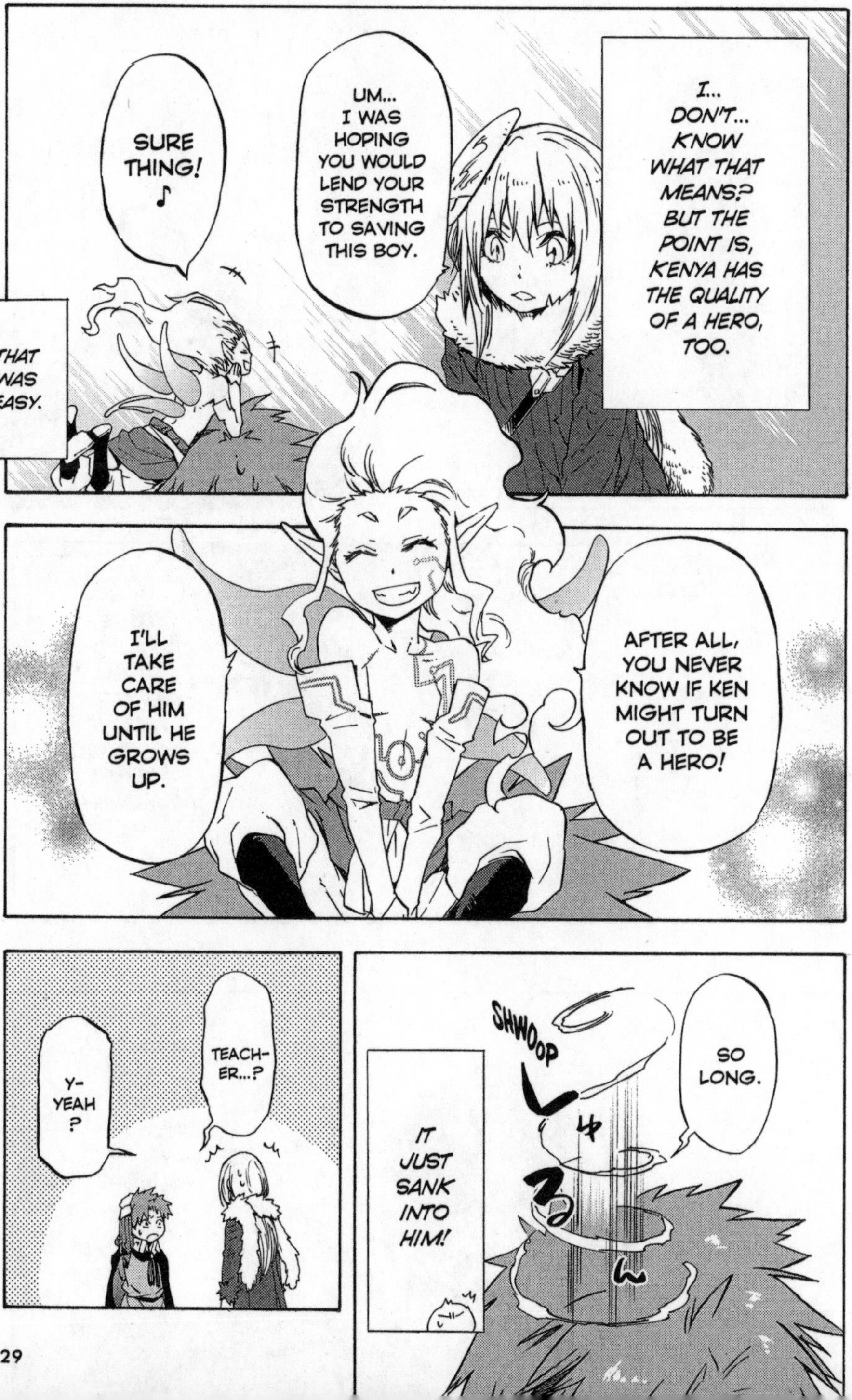
I... DON'T... KNOW WHAT THAT MEANS? BUT THE POINT IS, KENYA HAS THE QUALITY OF A HERO, TOO.
UM... I WAS HOPING YOU WOULD LEND YOUR STRENGTH TO SAVING THIS BOY.
SURE THING! ♪
THAT WAS EASY.
AFTER ALL, YOU NEVER KNOW IF KEN MIGHT TURN OUT TO BE A HERO!
I'LL TAKE CARE OF HIM UNTIL HE GROWS UP.
SO LONG.
SHWOOP
IT JUST SANK INTO HIM!
TEACHER...?
Y-YEAH?

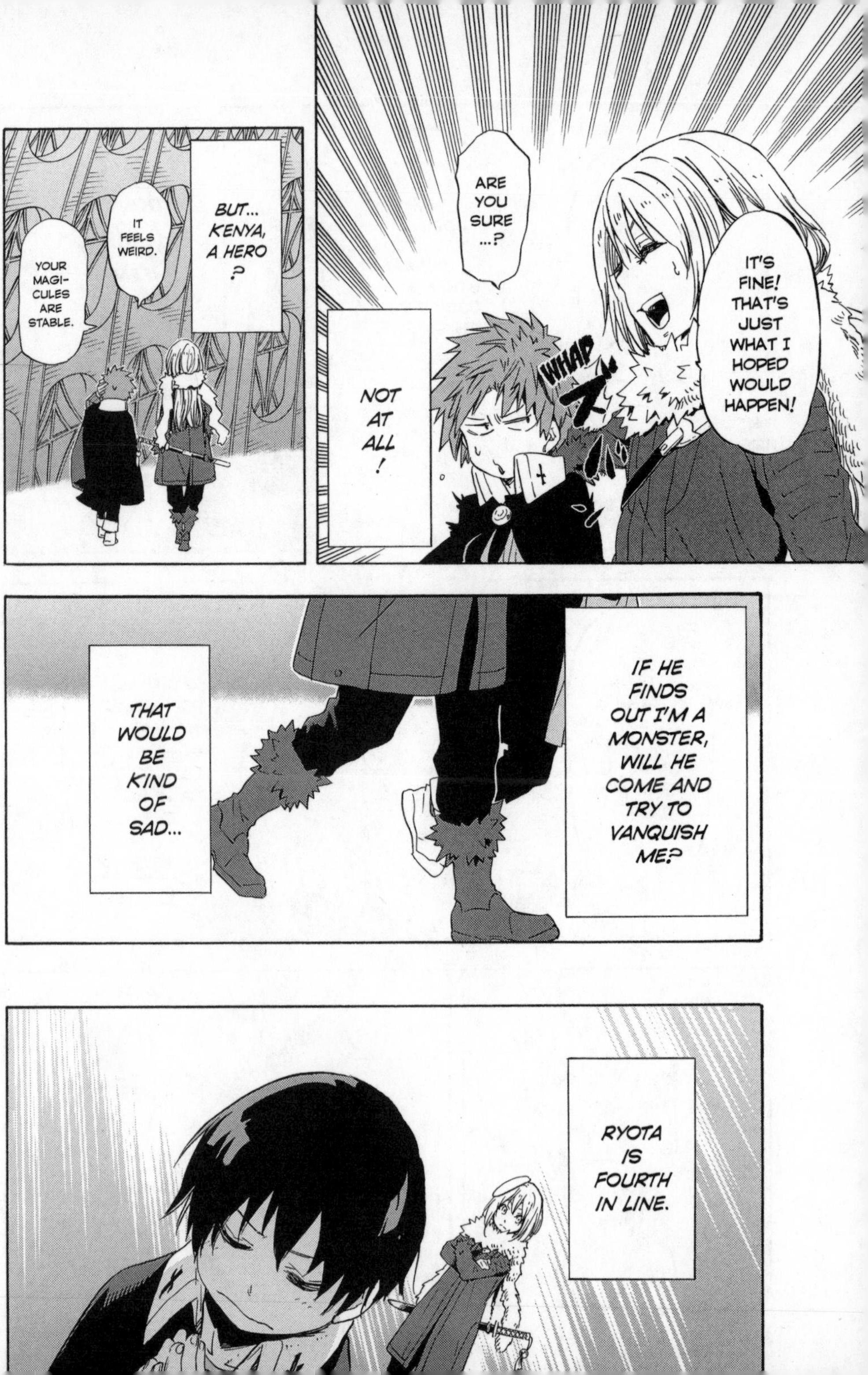
ARE YOU SURE ...?
IT'S FINE! THAT'S JUST WHAT I HOPED WOULD HAPPEN!
WHAP
NOT AT ALL!
BUT... KENYA, A HERO?
IT FEELS WEIRD.
YOUR MAGI-CULES ARE STABLE.
IF HE FINDS OUT I'M A MONSTER, WILL HE COME AND TRY TO VANQUISH ME?
THAT WOULD BE KIND OF SAD...
RYOTA IS FOURTH IN LINE.

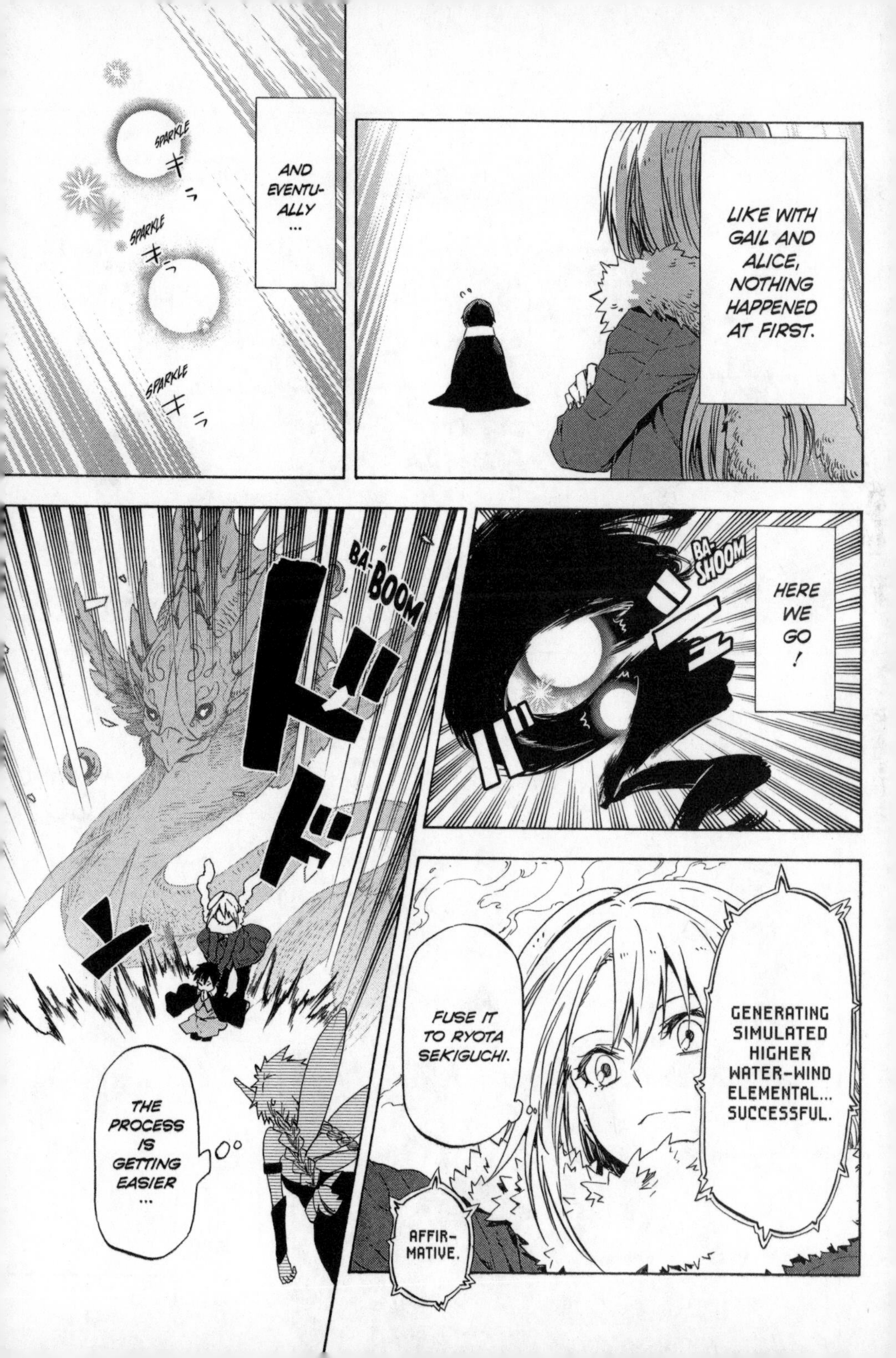

LIKE WITH GAIL AND ALICE, NOTHING HAPPENED AT FIRST.
AND EVENTU-ALLY ...
SPARKLE
SPARKLE
SPARKLE
BA-SHOOM
HERE WE GO!
GENERATING SIMULATED HIGHER WATER-WIND ELEMENTAL... SUCCESSFUL.
FUSE IT TO RYOTA SEKIGUCHI.
AFFIR-MATIVE.
BA-BOOM
THE PROCESS IS GETTING EASIER ...

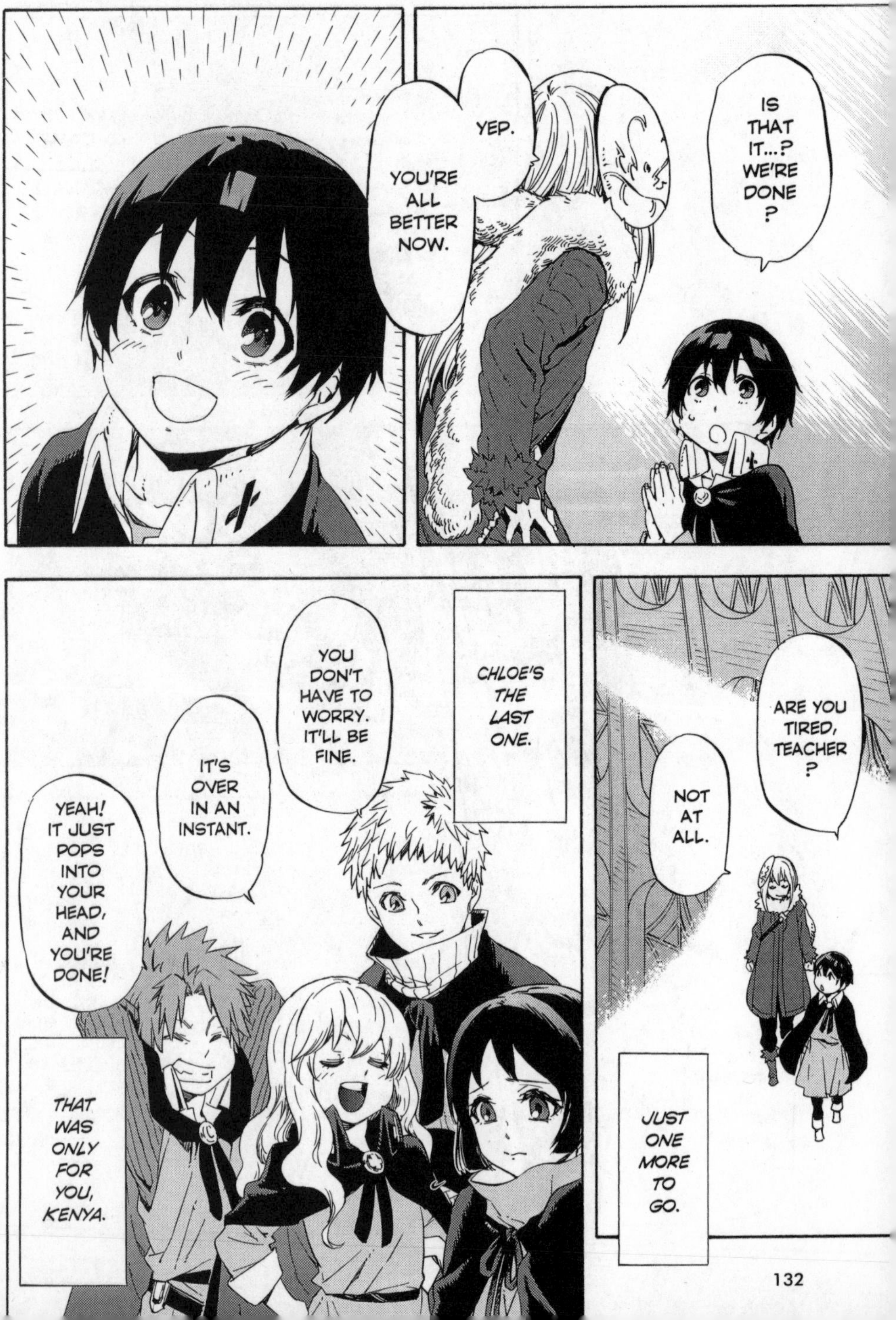
IS THAT IT...? WE'RE DONE?
YEP.
YOU'RE ALL BETTER NOW.
ARE YOU TIRED, TEACHER?
NOT AT ALL.
JUST ONE MORE TO GO.
CHLOE'S THE LAST ONE.
YOU DON'T HAVE TO WORRY. IT'LL BE FINE.
IT'S OVER IN AN INSTANT.
YEAH! IT JUST POPS INTO YOUR HEAD, AND YOU'RE DONE!
THAT WAS ONLY FOR YOU, KENYA.

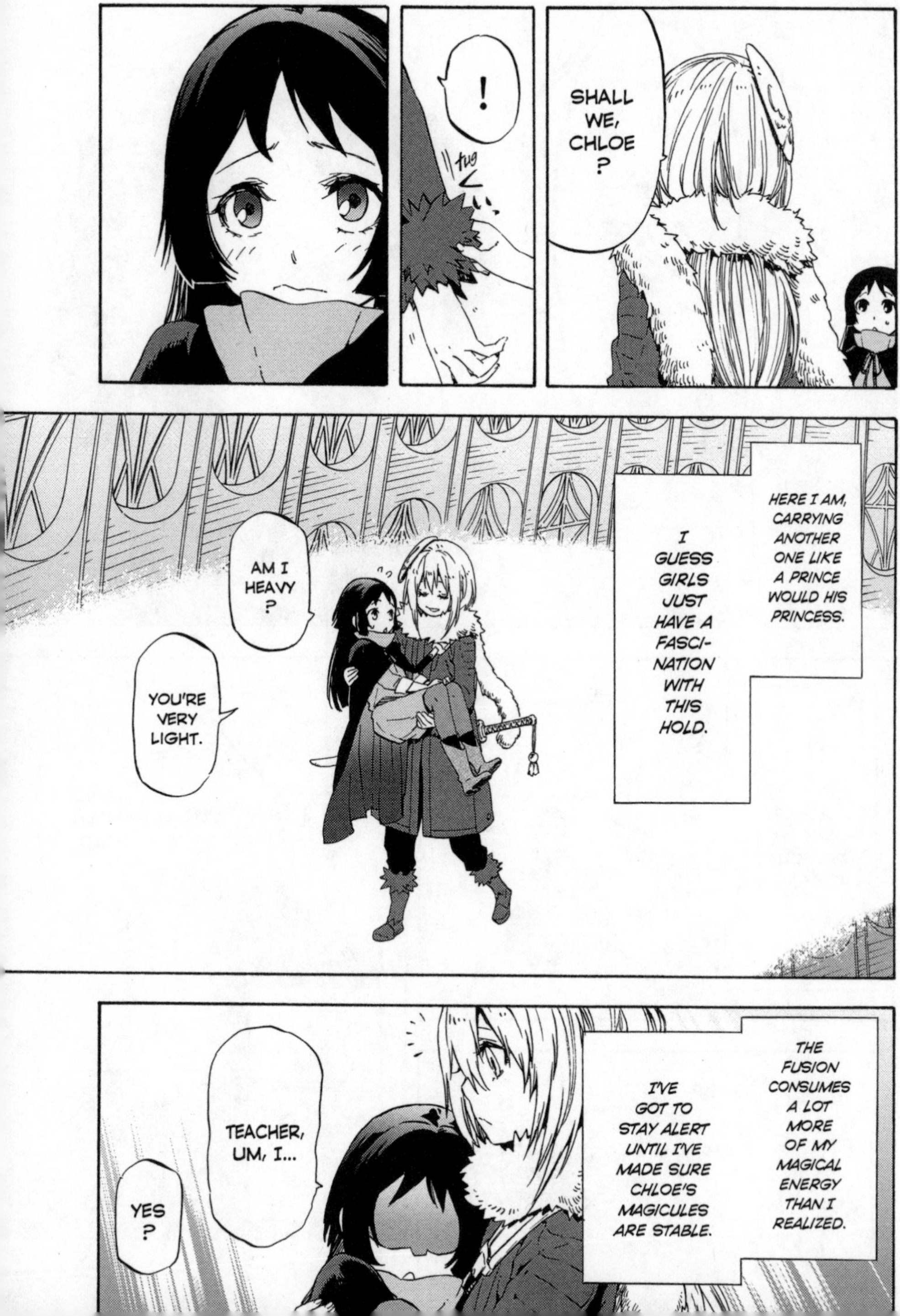
SHALL WE, CHLOE?
!
tug
HERE I AM, CARRYING ANOTHER ONE LIKE A PRINCE WOULD HIS PRINCESS.
I GUESS GIRLS JUST HAVE A FASCINATION WITH THIS HOLD.
AM I HEAVY?
YOU'RE VERY LIGHT.
THE FUSION CONSUMES A LOT MORE OF MY MAGICAL ENERGY THAN I REALIZED.
I'VE GOT TO STAY ALERT UNTIL I'VE MADE SURE CHLOE'S MAGICULES ARE STABLE.
TEACHER, UM, I...
YES?

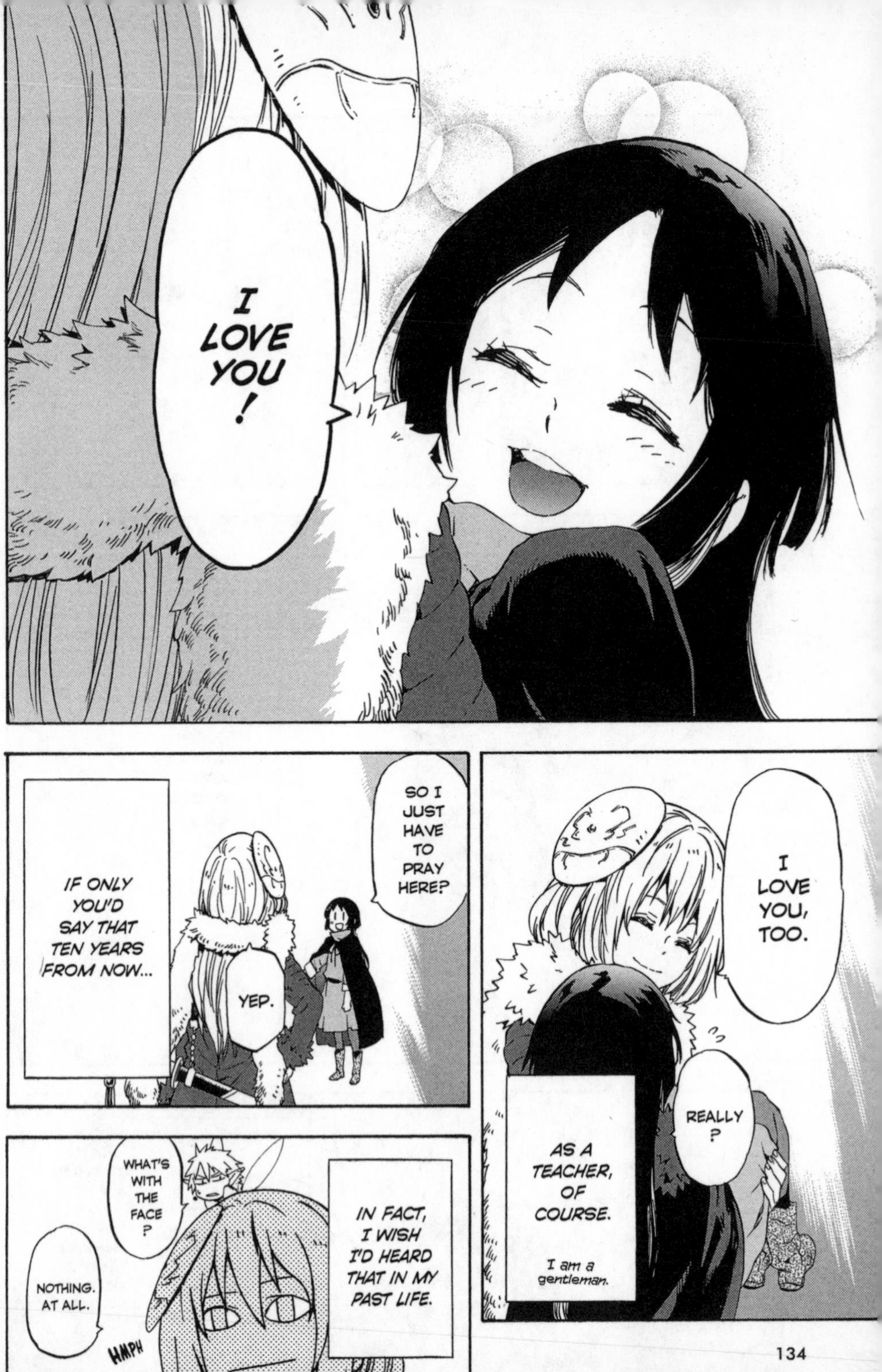
I LOVE YOU!
I LOVE YOU, TOO.
REALLY?
AS A TEACHER, OF COURSE.
I am a gentleman.
SO I JUST HAVE TO PRAY HERE?
YEP.
IF ONLY YOU'D SAY THAT TEN YEARS FROM NOW...
IN FACT, I WISH I'D HEARD THAT IN MY PAST LIFE.
WHAT'S WITH THE FACE?
NOTHING. AT ALL.
HMPH

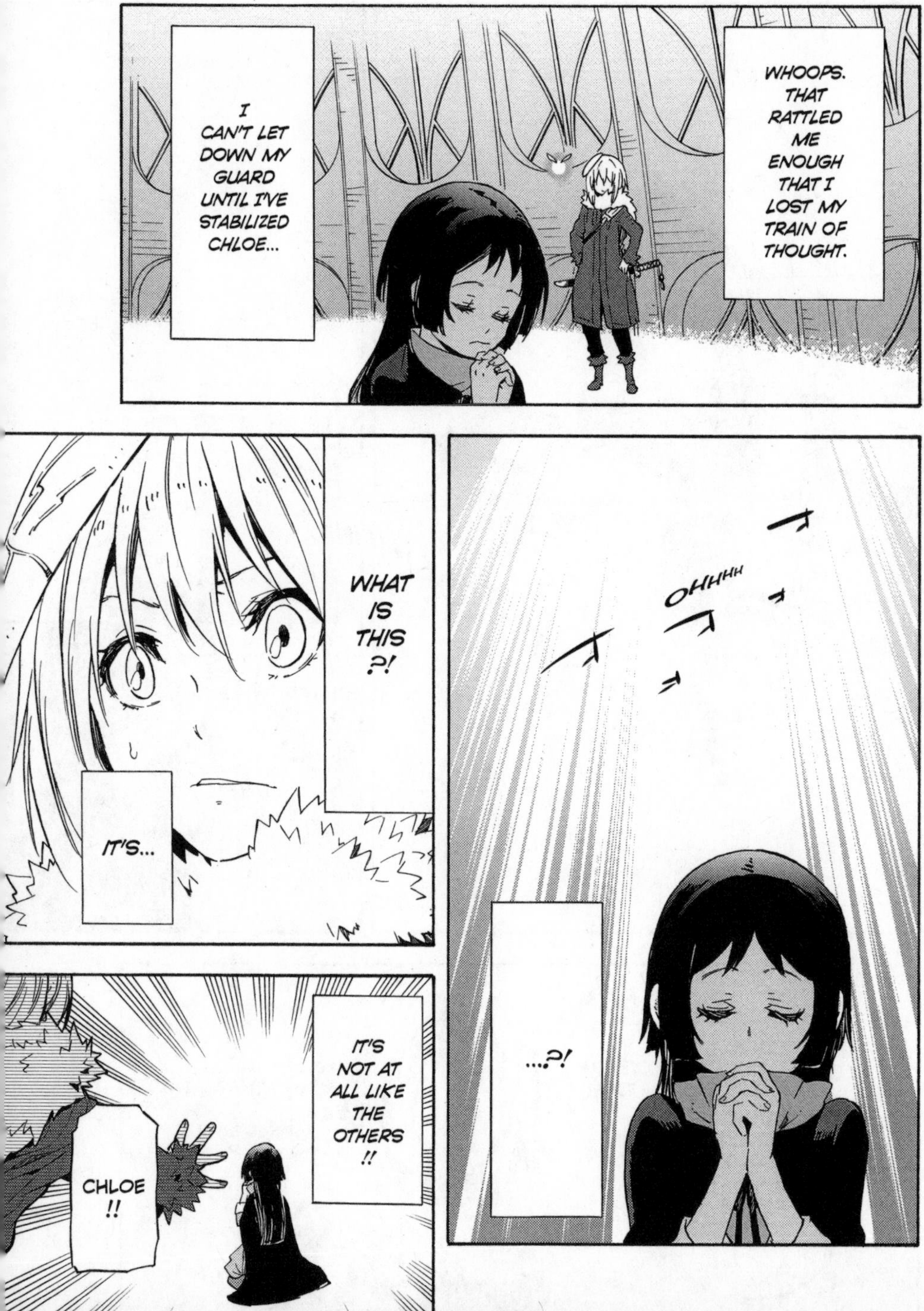
WHOOPS. THAT RATTLED ME ENOUGH THAT I LOST MY TRAIN OF THOUGHT.
I CAN'T LET DOWN MY GUARD UNTIL I'VE STABILIZED CHLOE...
OHHHH
...?!
WHAT IS THIS ?!
IT'S...
IT'S NOT AT ALL LIKE THE OTHERS !!
CHLOE !!

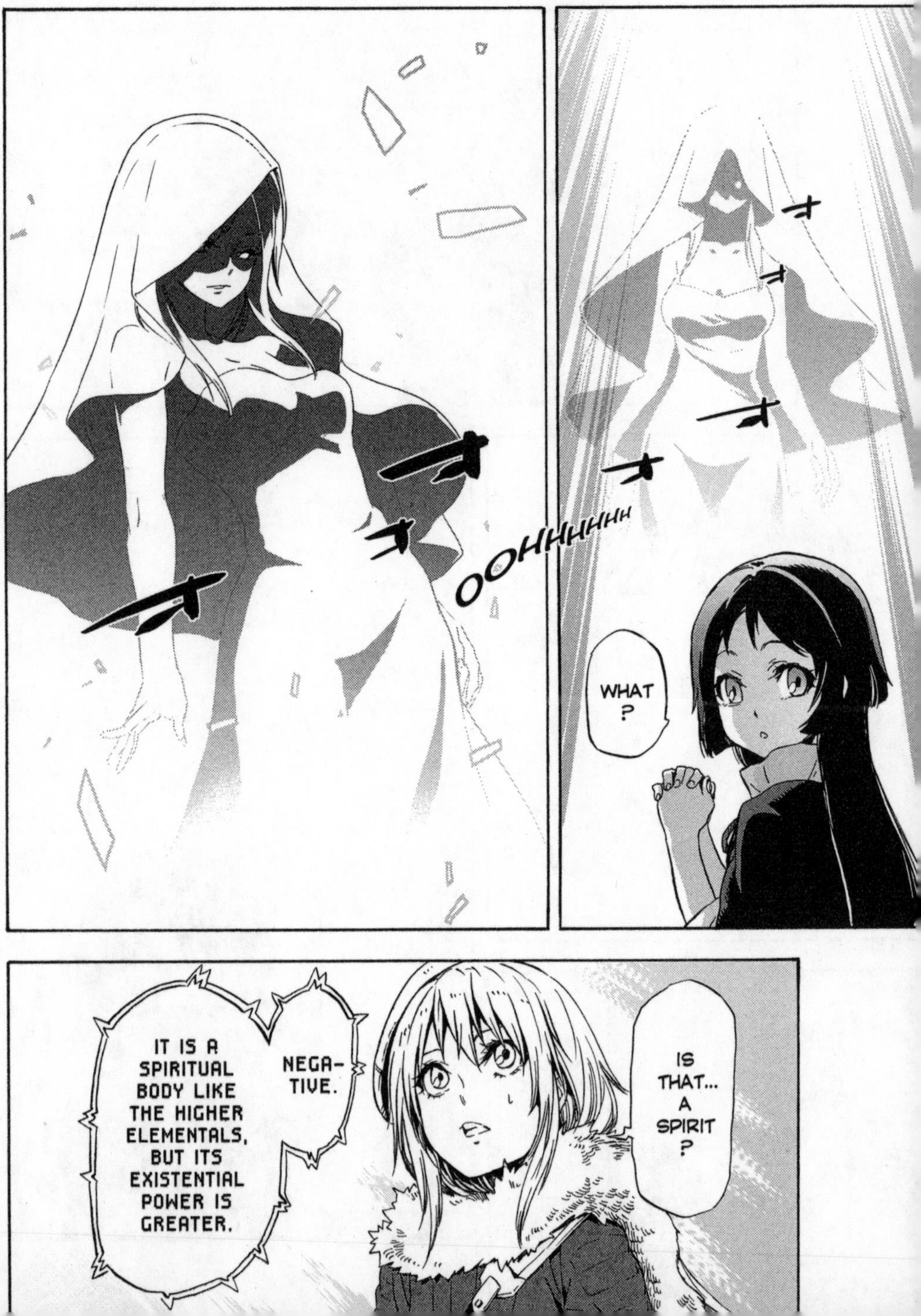
OOHHHHHH
WHAT?
IS THAT... A SPIRIT?
NEGA-TIVE.
IT IS A SPIRITUAL BODY LIKE THE HIGHER ELEMENTALS, BUT ITS EXISTENTIAL POWER IS GREATER.

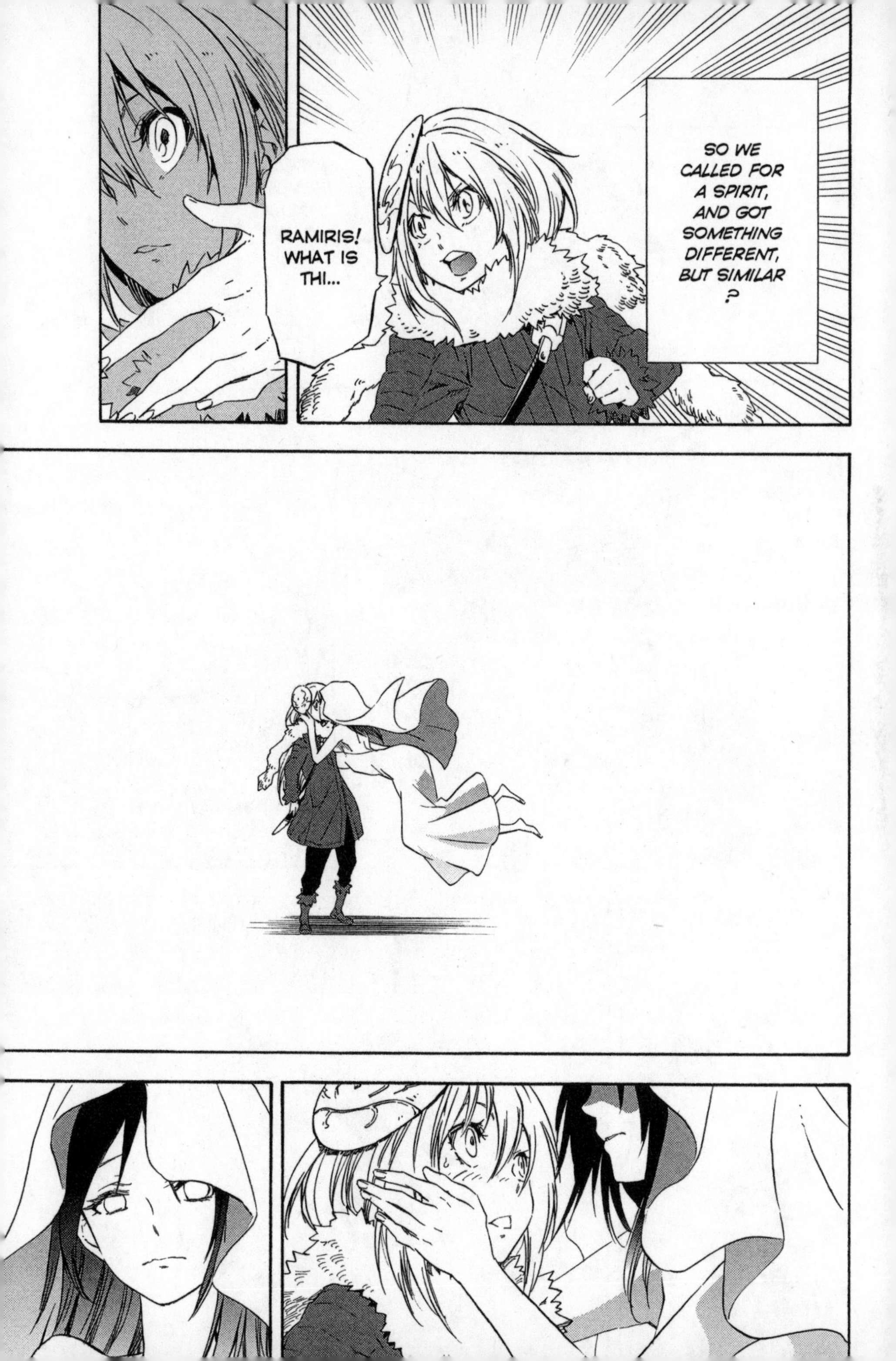
SO WE CALLED FOR A SPIRIT, AND GOT SOMETHING DIFFERENT, BUT SIMILAR?
RAMIRIS! WHAT IS THI...

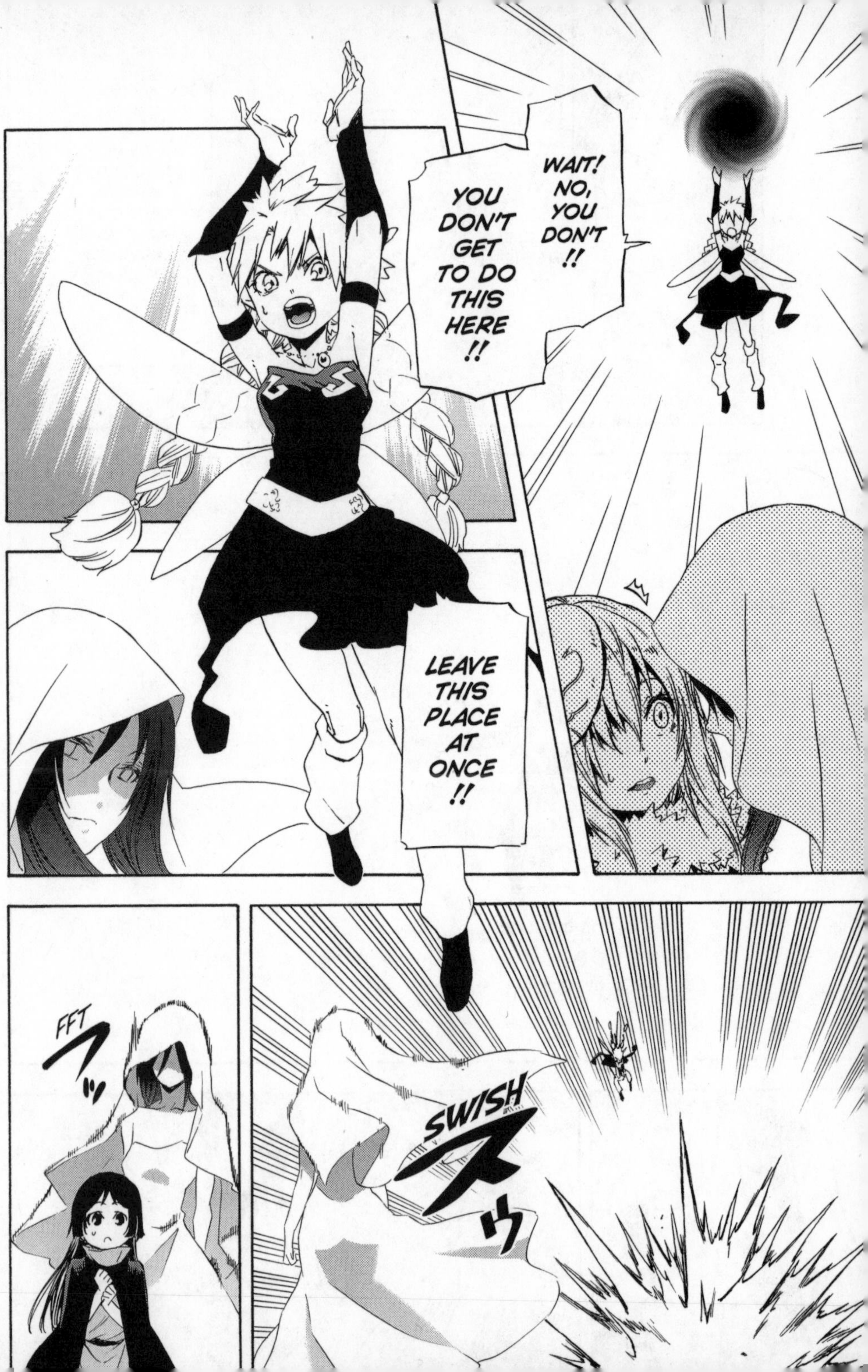
WAIT! NO, YOU DON'T!!
YOU DON'T GET TO DO THIS HERE!!
LEAVE THIS PLACE AT ONCE!!
SWISH
FFT

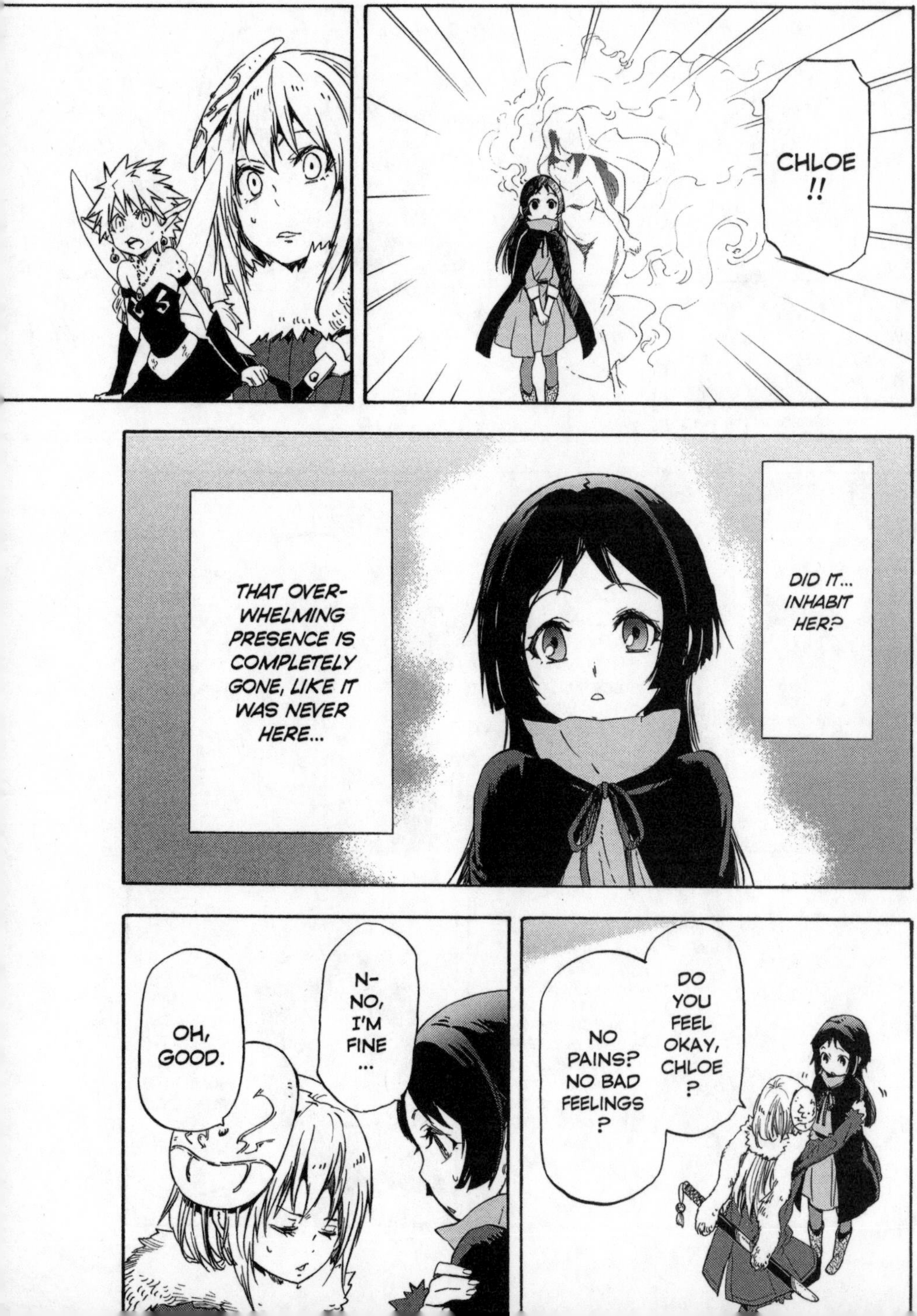
CHLOE !!
DID IT... INHABIT HER?
THAT OVER-WHELMING PRESENCE IS COMPLETELY GONE, LIKE IT WAS NEVER HERE...
DO YOU FEEL OKAY, CHLOE?
NO PAINS? NO BAD FEELINGS?
N-NO, I'M FINE...
OH, GOOD.

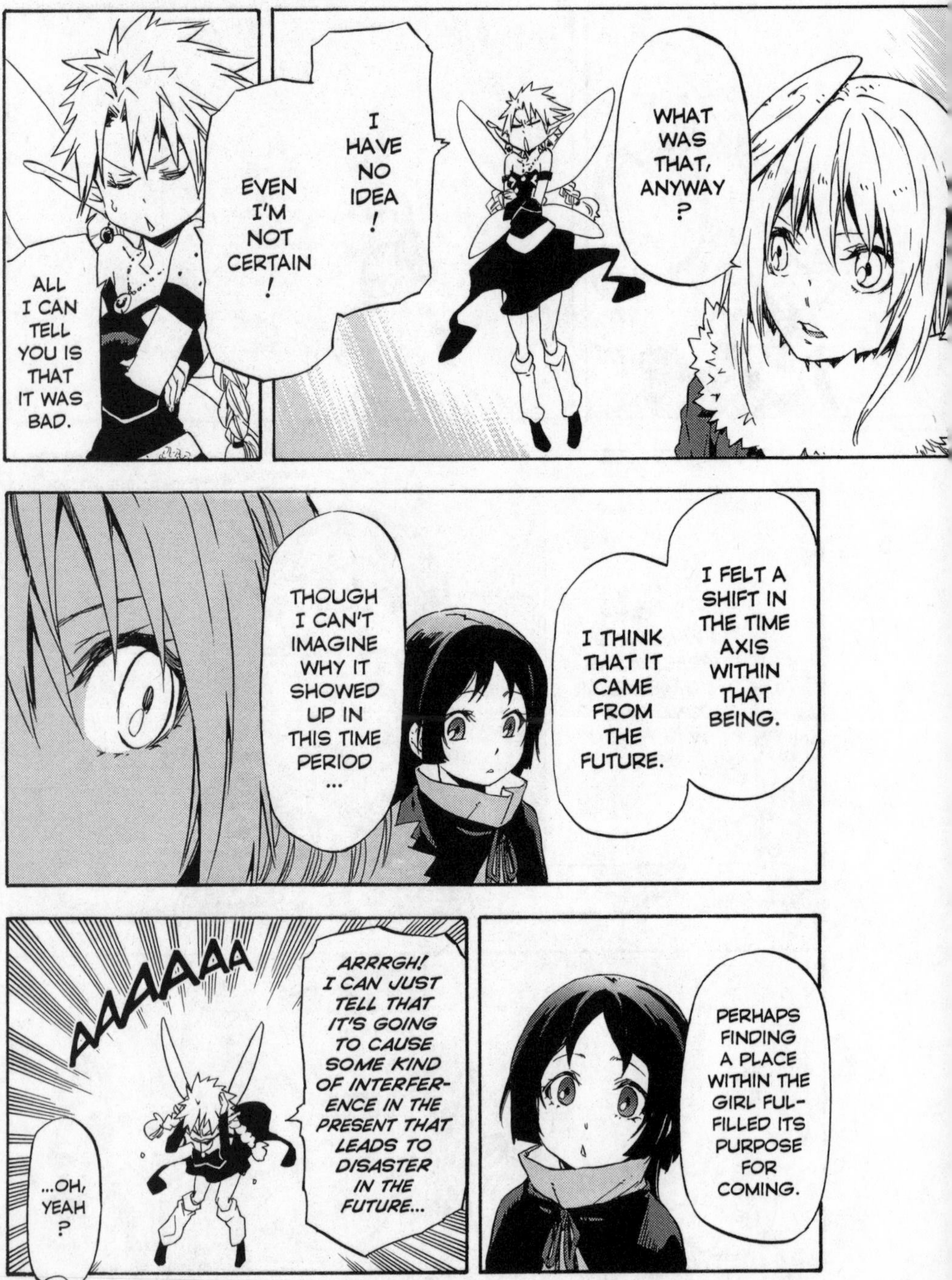
WHAT WAS THAT, ANYWAY?
I HAVE NO IDEA!
EVEN I'M NOT CERTAIN!
ALL I CAN TELL YOU IS THAT IT WAS BAD.
I FELT A SHIFT IN THE TIME AXIS WITHIN THAT BEING.
I THINK THAT IT CAME FROM THE FUTURE.
THOUGH I CAN'T IMAGINE WHY IT SHOWED UP IN THIS TIME PERIOD...
PERHAPS FINDING A PLACE WITHIN THE GIRL FUL-FILLED ITS PURPOSE FOR COMING.
ARRRGH! I CAN JUST TELL THAT IT'S GOING TO CAUSE SOME KIND OF INTERFER-ENCE IN THE PRESENT THAT LEADS TO DISASTER IN THE FUTURE...
AAAAAA
...OH, YEAH?

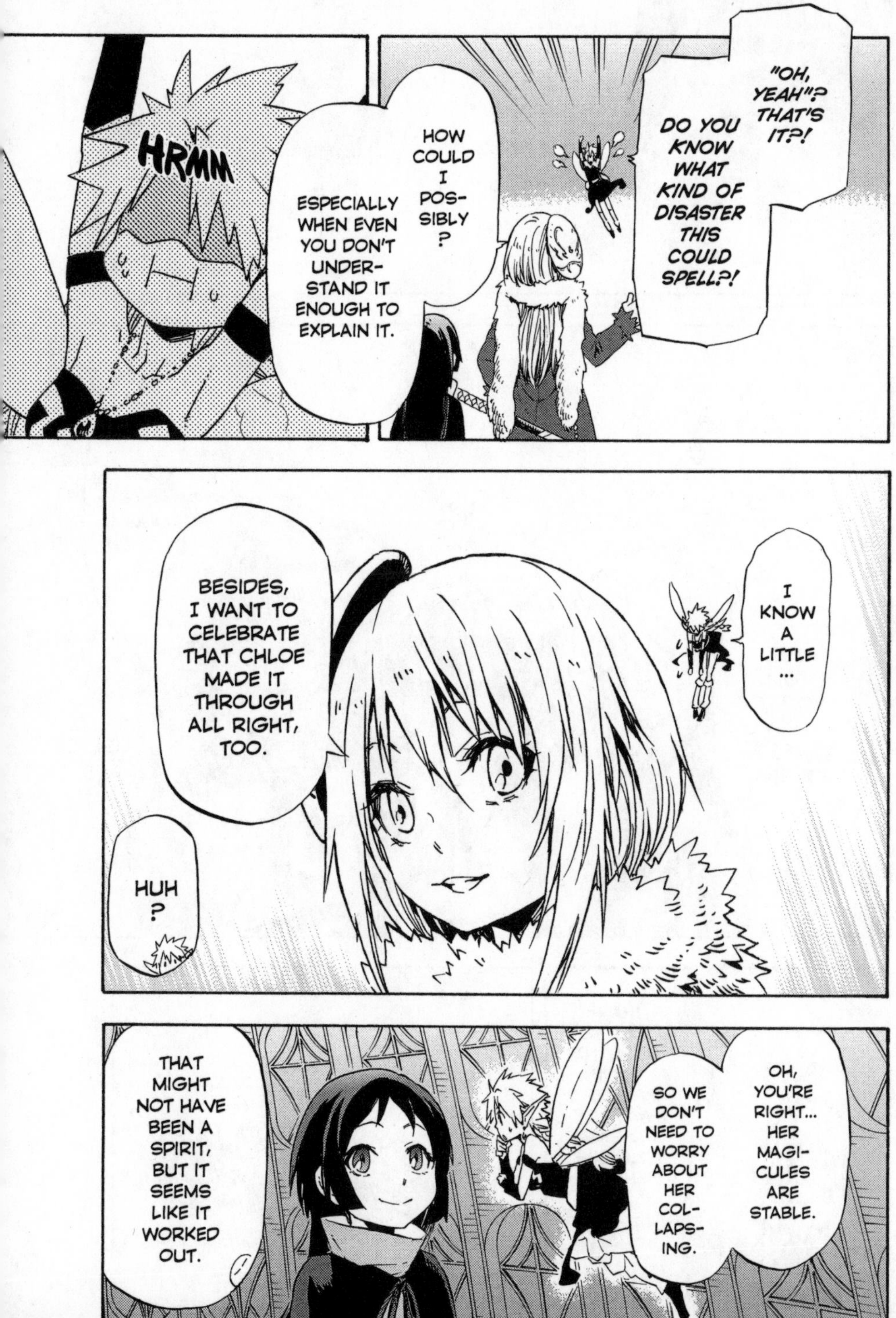
"OH, YEAH"? THAT'S IT?!
DO YOU KNOW WHAT KIND OF DISASTER THIS COULD SPELL?!
HOW COULD I POSSIBLY?
ESPECIALLY WHEN EVEN YOU DON'T UNDERSTAND IT ENOUGH TO EXPLAIN IT.
HRMM
I KNOW A LITTLE...
BESIDES, I WANT TO CELEBRATE THAT CHLOE MADE IT THROUGH ALL RIGHT, TOO.
HUH?
OH, YOU'RE RIGHT... HER MAGICULES ARE STABLE.
SO WE DON'T NEED TO WORRY ABOUT HER COLLAPSING.
THAT MIGHT NOT HAVE BEEN A SPIRIT, BUT IT SEEMS LIKE IT WORKED OUT.

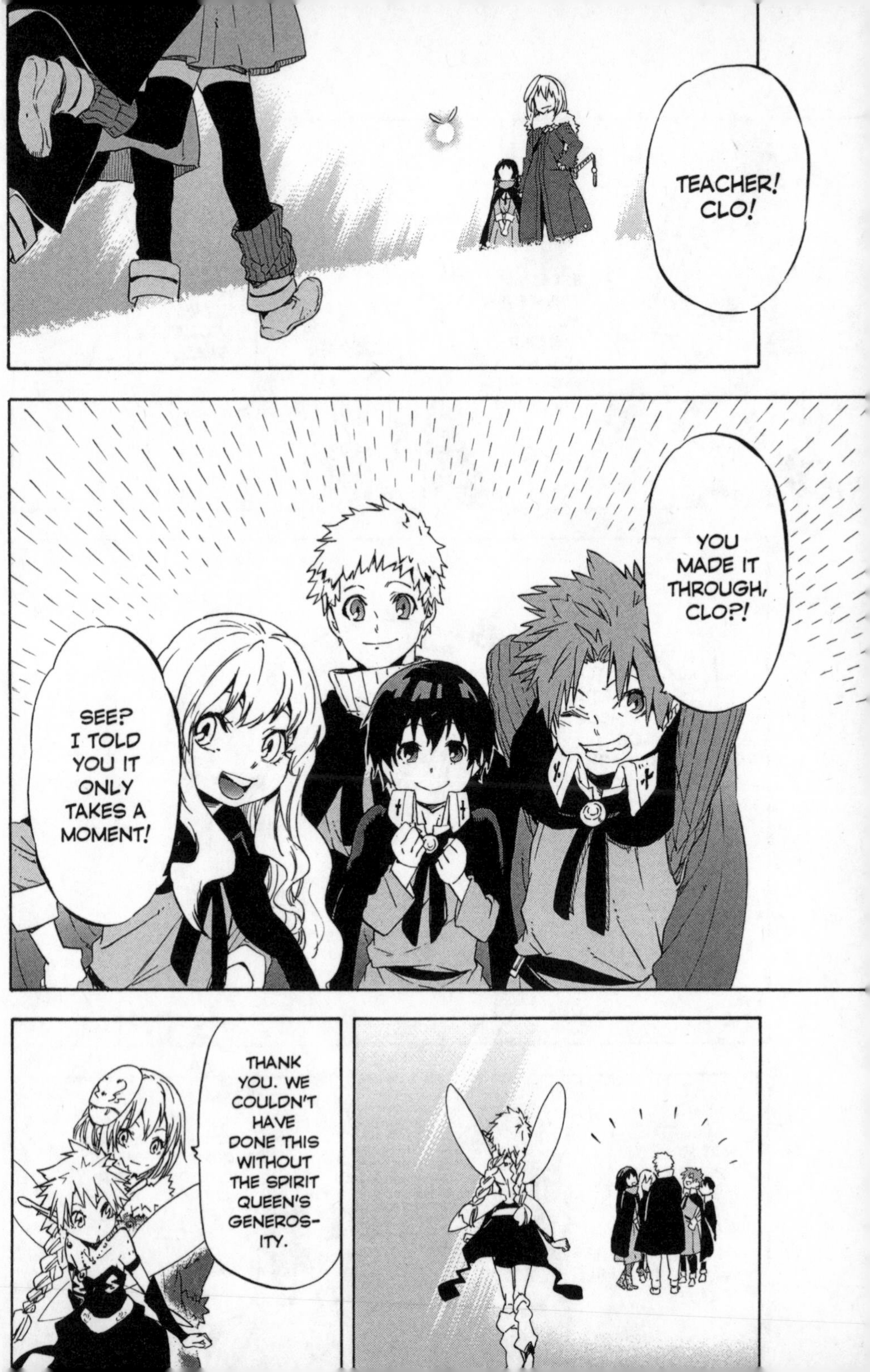
TEACHER! CLO!
YOU MADE IT THROUGH, CLO?!
SEE? I TOLD YOU IT ONLY TAKES A MOMENT!
THANK YOU. WE COULDN'T HAVE DONE THIS WITHOUT THE SPIRIT QUEEN'S GENEROS-ITY.

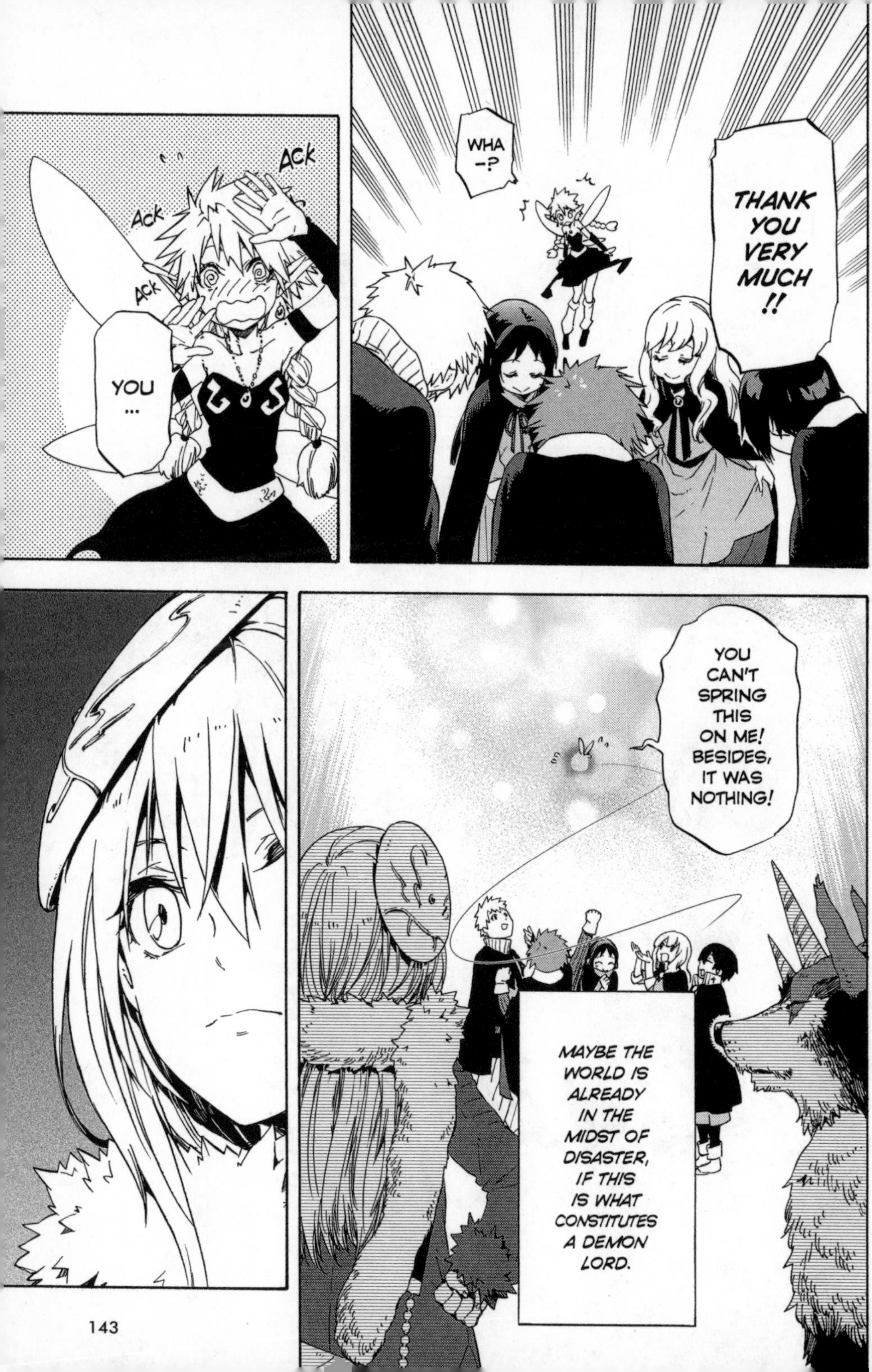
THANK YOU VERY MUCH !!
WHA -?
Ack
Ack
Ack
YOU ...
YOU CAN'T SPRING THIS ON ME! BESIDES, IT WAS NOTHING!
MAYBE THE WORLD IS ALREADY IN THE MIDST OF DISASTER, IF THIS IS WHAT CONSTITUTES A DEMON LORD.

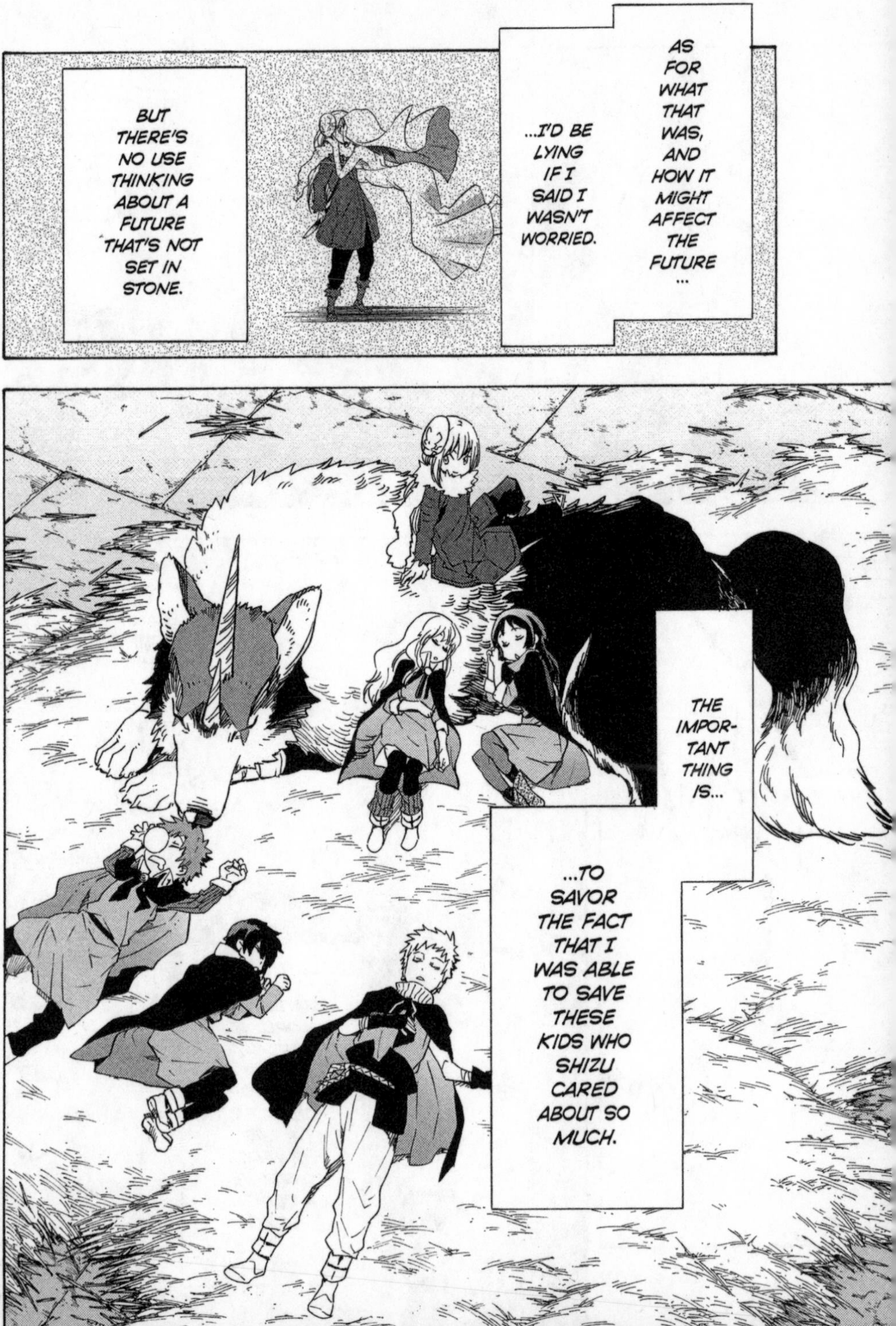
AS FOR WHAT THAT WAS, AND HOW IT MIGHT AFFECT THE FUTURE...
...I'D BE LYING IF I SAID I WASN'T WORRIED.
BUT THERE'S NO USE THINKING ABOUT A FUTURE THAT'S NOT SET IN STONE.
THE IMPOR-TANT THING IS...
...TO SAVOR THE FACT THAT I WAS ABLE TO SAVE THESE KIDS WHO SHIZU CARED ABOUT SO MUCH.

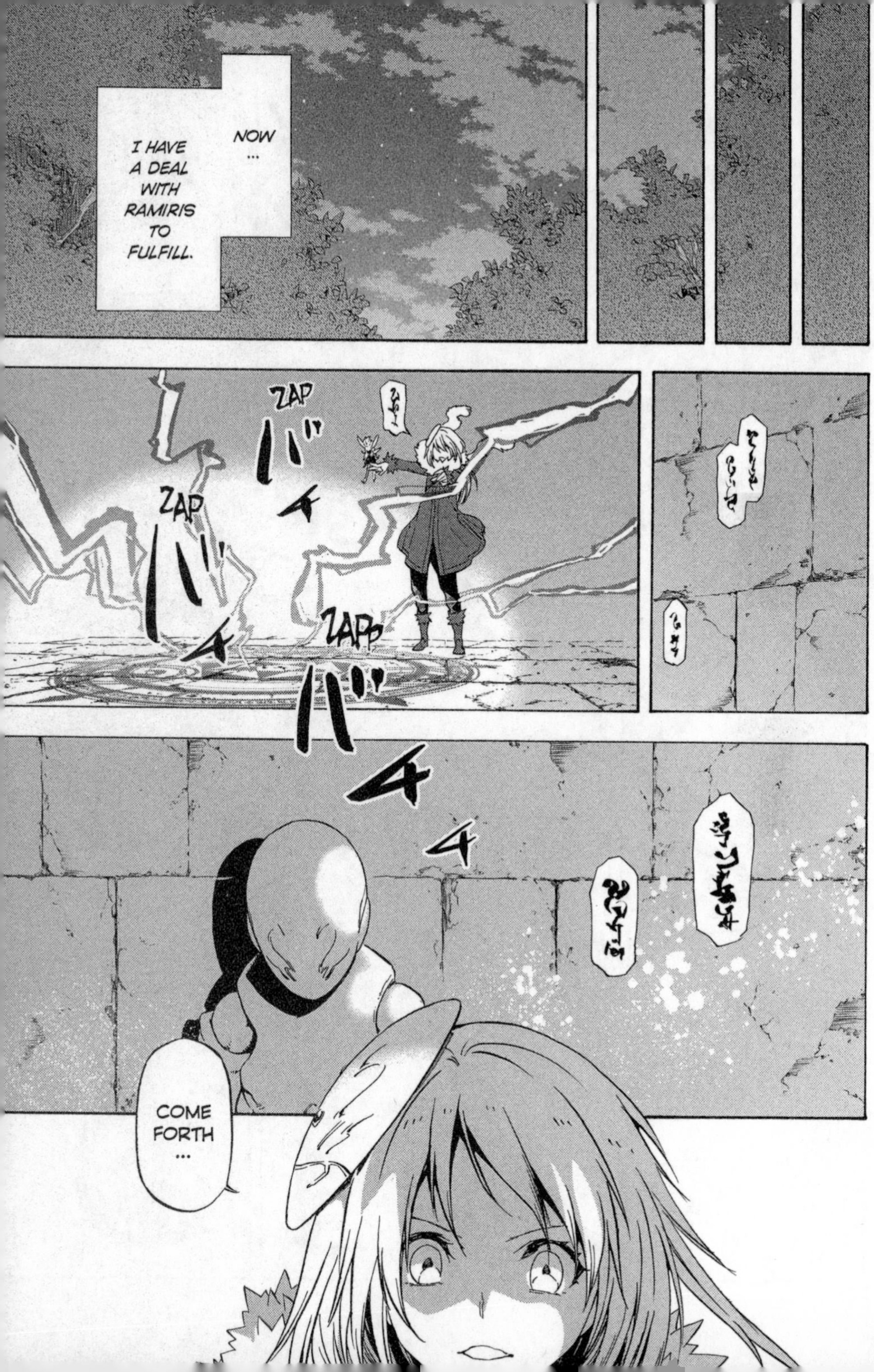
NOW ...
I HAVE A DEAL WITH RAMIRIS TO FULFILL.
ZAP
ZAP
ZAPP
COME FORTH ...

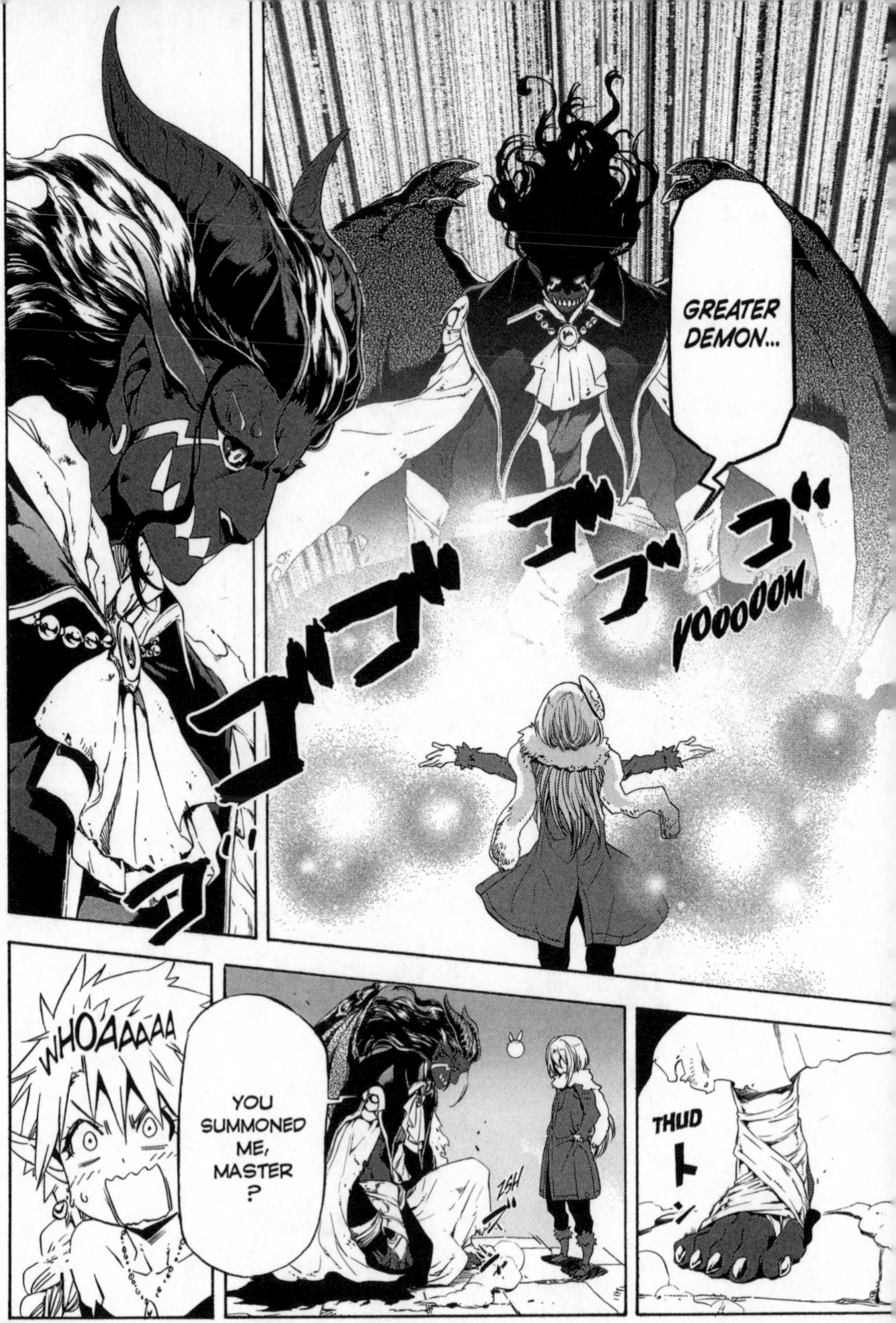
GREATER DEMON...
VOOOOOM
THUD
YOU SUMMONED ME, MASTER?
ZSH
WHOAAAAA

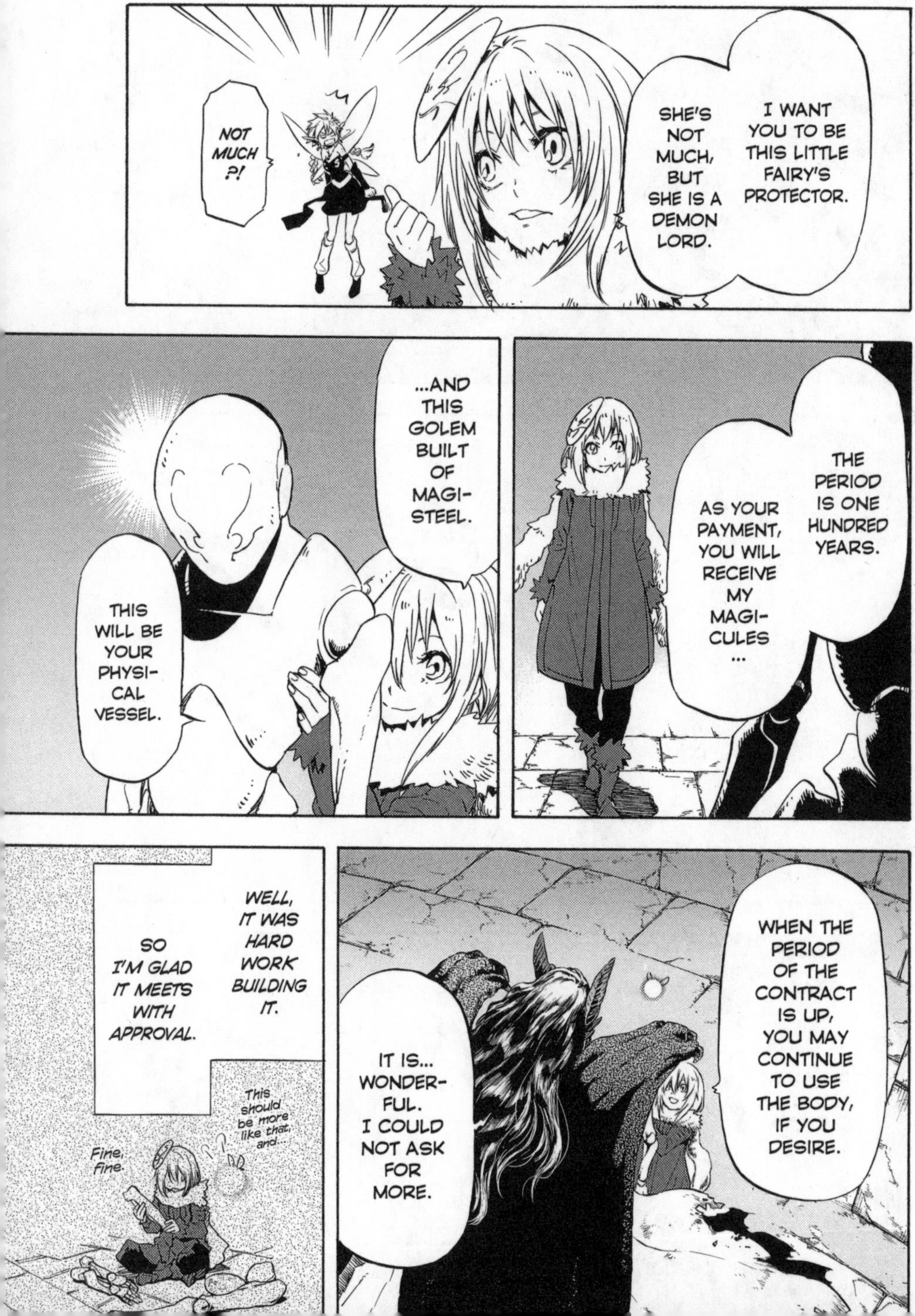
I WANT YOU TO BE THIS LITTLE FAIRY'S PROTECTOR.
SHE'S NOT MUCH, BUT SHE IS A DEMON LORD.
NOT MUCH ?!
THE PERIOD IS ONE HUNDRED YEARS.
AS YOUR PAYMENT, YOU WILL RECEIVE MY MAGICULES ...
...AND THIS GOLEM BUILT OF MAGISTEEL.
THIS WILL BE YOUR PHYSICAL VESSEL.
WHEN THE PERIOD OF THE CONTRACT IS UP, YOU MAY CONTINUE TO USE THE BODY, IF YOU DESIRE.
IT IS... WONDERFUL. I COULD NOT ASK FOR MORE.
WELL, IT WAS HARD WORK BUILDING IT.
SO I'M GLAD IT MEETS WITH APPROVAL.
This should be more like that, and...
Fine, fine.

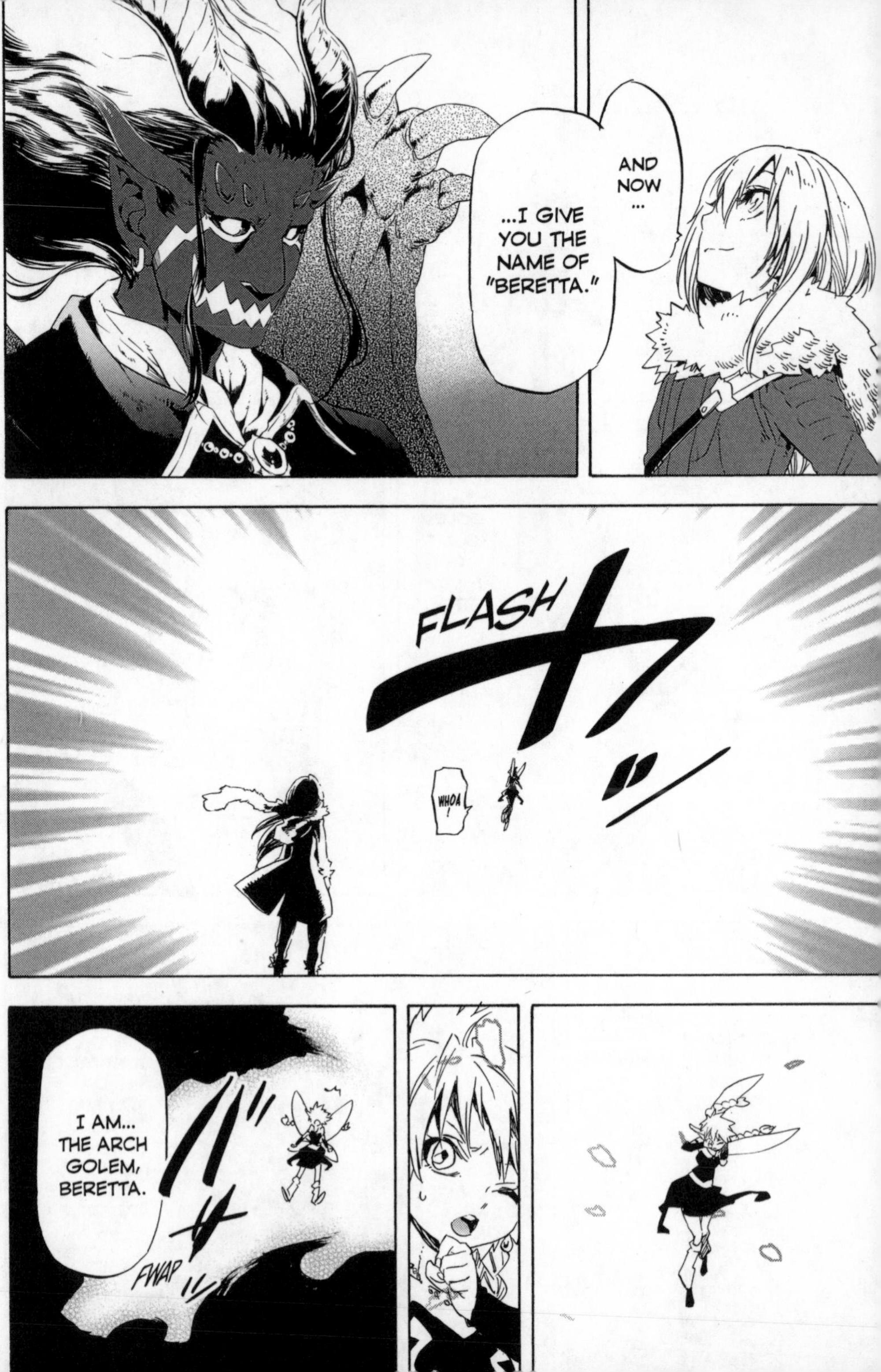
AND NOW ...
...I GIVE YOU THE NAME OF "BERETTA."
FLASH
WHOA!
I AM... THE ARCH GOLEM, BERETTA.
FWAP

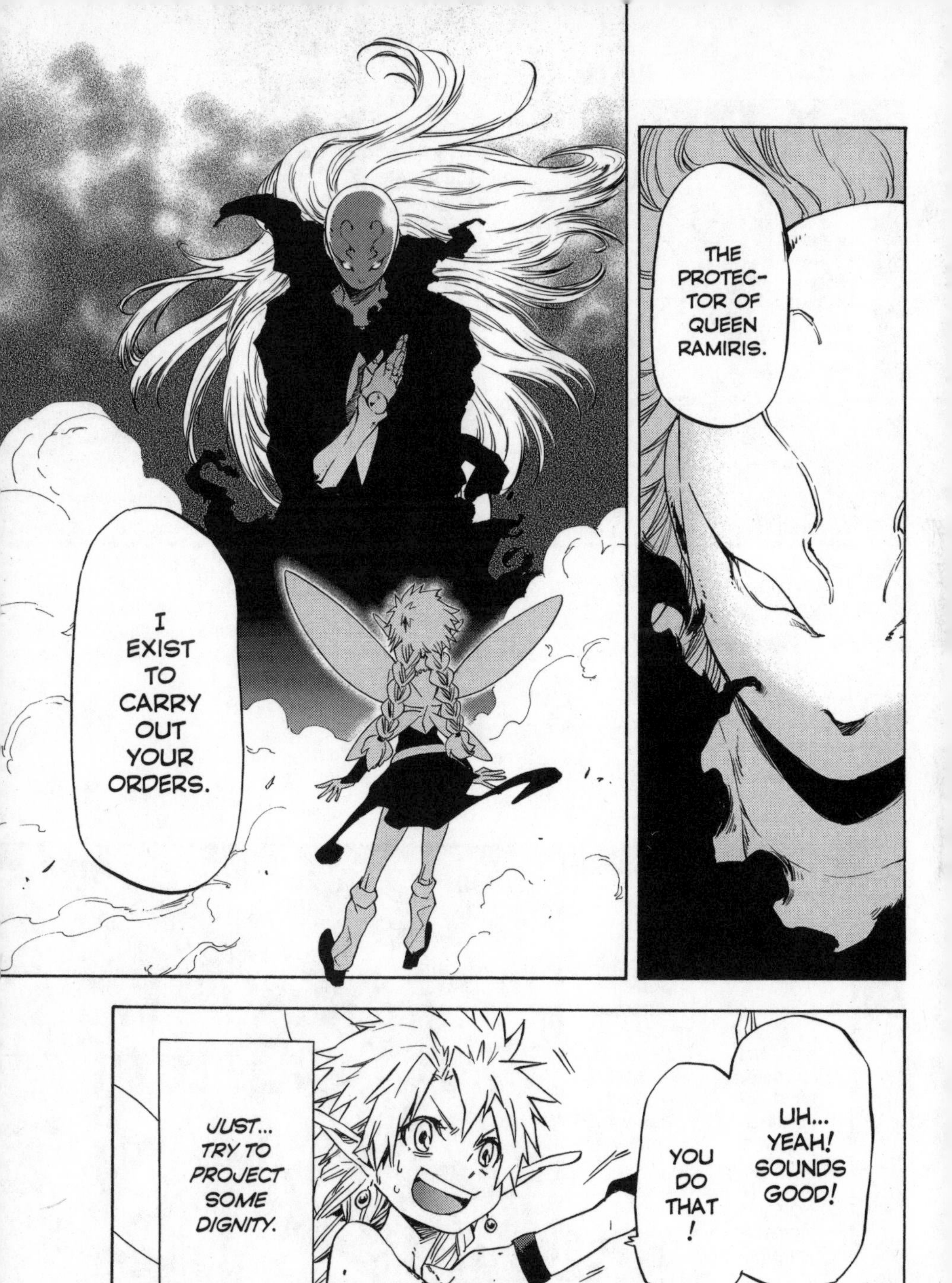
THE PROTECTOR OF QUEEN RAMIRIS.
I EXIST TO CARRY OUT YOUR ORDERS.
UH... YEAH! SOUNDS GOOD!
YOU DO THAT!
JUST... TRY TO PROJECT SOME DIGNITY.

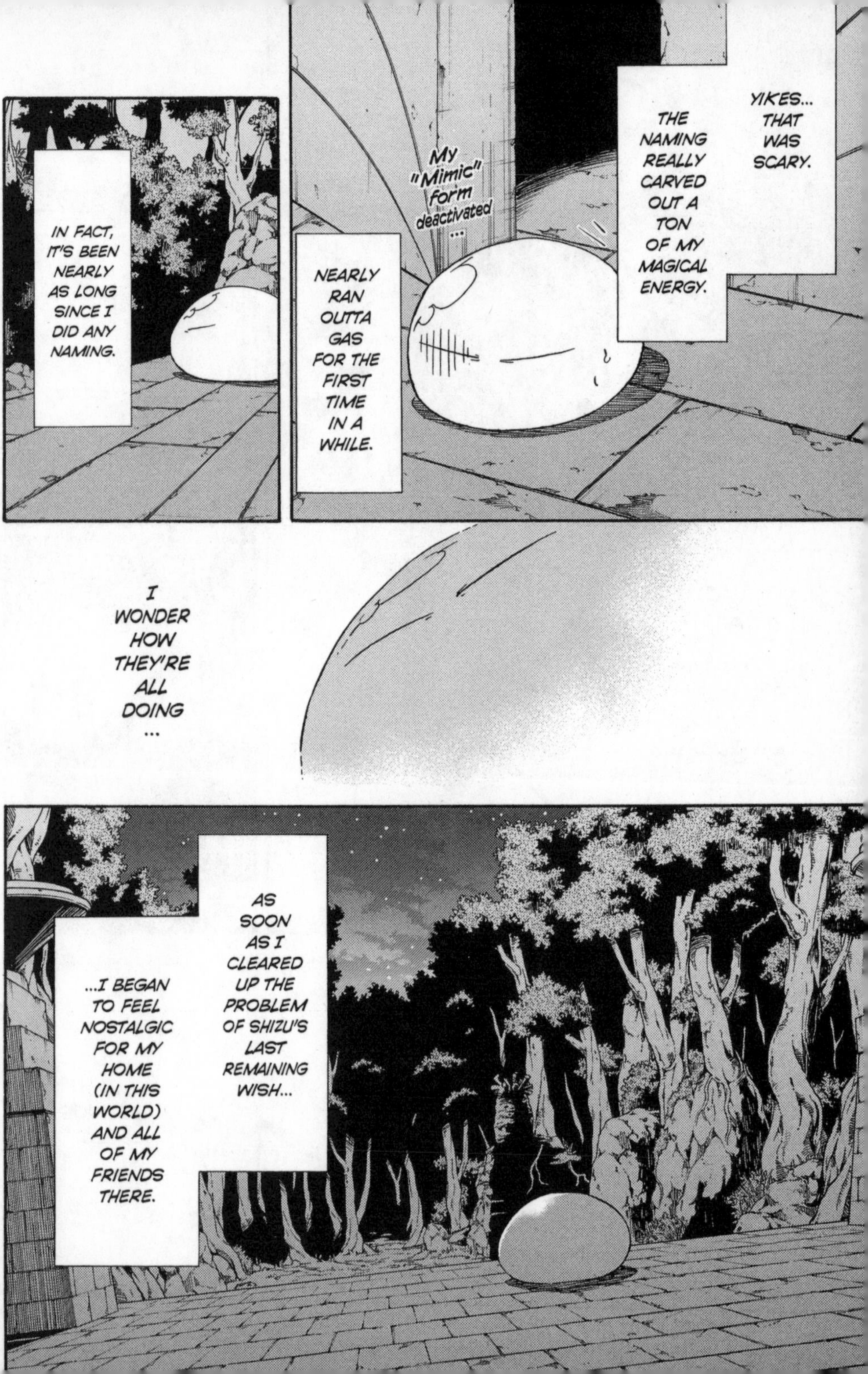
YIKES... THAT WAS SCARY.
THE NAMING REALLY CARVED OUT A TON OF MY MAGICAL ENERGY.
My "Mimic" form deactivated...
NEARLY RAN OUTTA GAS FOR THE FIRST TIME IN A WHILE.
IN FACT, IT'S BEEN NEARLY AS LONG SINCE I DID ANY NAMING.
I WONDER HOW THEY'RE ALL DOING...
AS SOON AS I CLEARED UP THE PROBLEM OF SHIZU'S LAST REMAINING WISH...
...I BEGAN TO FEEL NOSTALGIC FOR MY HOME (IN THIS WORLD) AND ALL OF MY FRIENDS THERE.

Reincarnate
in Volume 12?

→YES

NO

Bonus Short Story

Veldora's Slime Observation Journal

~SWEETS~

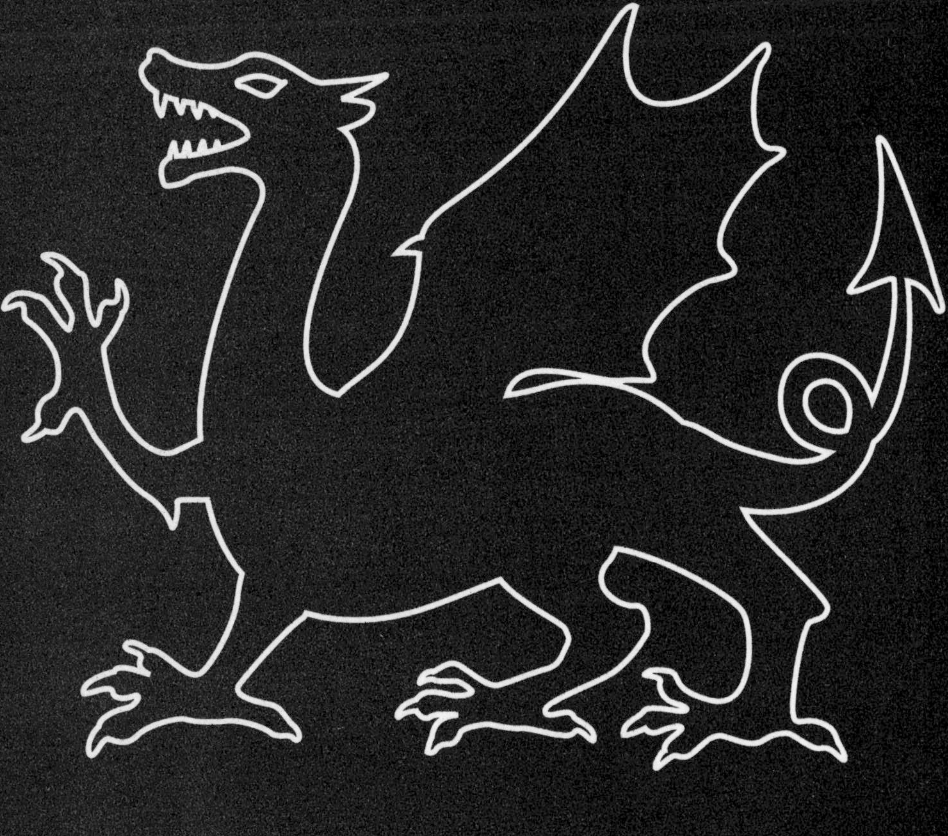

Veldora's Slime Observation Journal
~SWEETS~

◆TEACHING JOB◆

It's a boar.
No, it's a bore.
It is so very difficult and boring to work hard.
But I will do my best.

Once Ifrit has declared that he will be working seriously, I cannot very well shirk my duties.

Meanwhile, Rimuru has been flitting around here and there in search of ways to save the children. He did not have success searching for useful information at the library, but that is of no concern. Surely he will find a way.

But now…
Rimuru has returned to the capital city of Rimuru. Mostly to see his companions, but also to give himself a breather.

Yes, taking a breather is a very important thing. "Shirking duties" sounds so bad, but when you call it "taking a breather," all is forgiven.

"Don't you agree, Ifrit?"

"It sounds extremely convenient to me."

I'm getting nowhere with him. Ifrit's gone back to his old hardheaded ways. Then again, he's essentially always like that.

"Ahh, those crimuru puffs do look delicious. There are many wonderful-looking dishes out there, but few so consistently elicit such universal expressions of delight. It must be quite a delicacy…"

"I agree. Despite the fact that I do not require food to survive, I have begun to take an interest in the sense of taste."

"So you get it, too! A gift bestowed by my teachings."

"Or in other words, it's your fault, Master Veldora."

…I am not certain I appreciate that way of saying it. But more importantly, it is a good thing that Ifrit is developing more interests.

First it was shogi, then go, then reading. He's even become quite adept in the ways of "Veldora-style Killing Arts." And all of these things are because of me.

Be grateful, Ifrit!

Pleased with the effect I was having, I resumed working on analysis. In truth, I have not been slacking off lately. And not because I am afraid of Rimuru, I assure you. It was my own decision—that I could not simply continue my present course.

I want to get out into the open and adventure with Rimuru. Or if not travel, then I would like to view Rimuru's exploits from a close distance.

And in order to do that, I must break free of this detestable "Unlimited Imprisonment."

Heh heh heh. You can sing my praises, if you wish.

"Understood: Reporting that recent progress has been commendable."

Gwah—?!
I-I didn't know you were here, Rimuru.

"Affirmative: The opinion that a breather is necessary is judged to be worth testing."

Ha…ha ha ha. You need not coddle me now.
Sweet words often contain traps.

I have learned much in my life, and I have no desire to receive an even tougher daily quota. I intend to continue analyzing, of course! I made my case very quickly and fervently.

In fact, I was so hasty about it that I forgot to turn my words into proper thoughts.

In response, Rimuru tossed something to me. And not just me; it fell before Ifrit as well.

"Are these...crimuru puffs?"

"What?! You mean, actual treats?!"

It wasn't until Ifrit pointed it out that I realized Rimuru's items were none other than the crimuru puffs everyone was eating outside.

"Announcement: To serve as a breather, I have attempted to re-create the taste information. Please enjoy."

I-is this true?!
Such a thing cannot exist in this sealed, isolated space. But there it is, before my eyes, a most delectable sight.

"Wh-what should we do?"

"They are gifts from Lord Rimuru, so I believe we should gratefully enjoy them."

That is very brave of you, Ifrit. But I am of the unparalleled dragonkind, feared by one and all. Crimuru puffs will not intimidate the likes of me!

I downed the object in one bite.

"Gyawawawa!! What is this?! What! Is! This? It is...so...yummyyy! This was it! This was the height of bliss all along!!"

I was enraptured. How could it be this good?

I'd seen how Rimuru obsessed over food, and wanted to try it someday, but I never realized how great it could be.

This bliss. It is the absolute zenith of pleasure.

I savored the delight of the sensation, but alas, happiness is a short-lived sensation. The flavor in my mouth soon drained away, leaving me sad and lonely.

Now I had to consider my actions. Why did I eat the entire thing in one bite? Ifrit is nibbling at his, bit by tiny bit...

"I'm not giving you any."

Hrrgh...

Perhaps I should make use of the law of survival of the fittest and...

"..."

I-I am merely joking, of course. Ifrit and I are friends, so I would never do such a thing to him.

Nay, I simply request seconds!

"Denied: Because re-creating taste information is extremely inefficient, overuse will cause delays in work. The experiment was a success, so there are no further taste re-creations planned for now."

Hwaaa?!
You can't do this to me...

"Suggestion: If there is some extra room to spare based on the pace of internal analysis..."

Meaning I just have to try harder?
Oh, I will do it.
You will see! I will try my hardest!

With a new goal in mind, my motivation soared to heights never before seen. I resumed my analytical work with unprecedented ferocity.

"Maybe you're a lot easier to trick than I thought, Master Veldora..."

But secretly, I thought, *Oh, Ifrit, you are a fool.*

I tried to remember and re-create that wonderful taste, but I could not. As Rimuru said, re-creating taste information is quite difficult.

In the outside world, Rimuru is surrounded by his companions, who are all eating the crimuru puffs together. Treyni, in fact, has stealthily consumed four of them. I must learn from her gluttonous example.

Four of them. I am jealous.

I only got to eat one. I must demand fairness. But all that I can do is sigh and lament my poor fortune.

Whoops. I was so focused on Treyni that I nearly missed Rimuru say that he had discovered a valuable key to saving the children.

And that key? Fusion with Ifrit.

"With me?"

"Not you, specifically, but with spirits. I doubt that the potential effect is limited only to flame elementals."

While we discussed the matter, Rimuru and the others arrived at the same conclusion. Treyni summoned a Sylphide, one of the higher wind elementals, as a demonstration to the group.

"The poor wretch."

"Who, the one named Gabiru?"

"Indeed. Treyni has a wicked personality. She chose him specifically because she knew the spirit would treat him cruelly."

"That makes sense. Sylphide is of the same rank as me and will not obey the weak. Wind elementals have a carefree disposition, so they will not respond to a summons from any whom they do not feel a connection to."

"Is that right? And how was it for you?"

"Me? As long as I had the chance to rage, I was happy."

"Strange, given that you are so calm and rational now."

"That is thanks to you, Master Veldora. And learning about the game shogi has succeeded in giving me a rational, thoughtful side."

Ah, yes. Like people, spirits can grow and evolve through their experiences.

All of this has gone in accordance with my knowledge on the subject, ignoring the case of Ifrit.

Wind spirits are fickle, fire spirits are violent, earth spirits are easygoing, and water spirits are rational, generally speaking. Some can break these molds, but generally they fit under these descriptions.

Now that I have displayed some of my vast knowledge, I might soon hear more praises of myself. Kwaaa ha ha ha!

Wait, I should not be laughing. They are still talking outside.

Apparently, a lower elemental will not be capable of controlling the magicules of the children, so the group has decided to head for the Dwelling of the Spirits, the place where the Spirit Queen presides.

As a matter of fact, I think I may know her…

I heard Treyni talking about the Spirit Queen before, and the conversation struck a memory of mine. In fact, if it is who I am thinking of…

But never mind that. In any case, we do not know where it is. No point in interrupting without proper information.

"Ifrit, would you happen to know where that place is?"

"Sadly, no. When I chose to follow Demon Lord Leon,
I parted ways forever with the Spirit Queen."

Ah. Well, there's no helping that.

I was hoping I could win some points and haggle for another
crimuru puff, but I suppose I'll have to give up on that one.

On the other hand…

Even the freewheeling, audacious Shion is generous enough
to leave the pastries for others. And yet Treyni, the one to
whom I ceded my territory, does not know the meaning of
moderation.

"You can see why she's in power."

"I must learn from her example."

"No, that wasn't the point! Don't copy her!"

Why not?

The way she naturally and subtly gets whatever she wants?
She has mastered the art of blending in and getting away
with it. I must observe her actions and learn from them.

◆GARD MJÖLLMILE THE MERCHANT◆

Rimuru and the children are enjoying an outdoor picnic.
They seem to be having a good time eating their lunch,
although it is a bit deformed from careless treatment. The
lunch was apparently created by one "Yoshida," like the
crimuru puffs.

When I am back in my body, I will become friends with this
Yoshida! And then I will dine upon those pastries every
day. It is with this desire in mind that I focus on observation
today.

And once again—one almost expects it at this point—some
trouble arose.

Oddly enough, it was the appearance of a sky dragon. This beast's threat level is "Calamity."

"Heh heh heh. You were once of that same strength level, but you could easily win in a fight now, wouldn't you say?"

"Indeed, Master. Even before my training in here, I would have matched up well against it. Now, I dare say I could defeat it without trouble."

"But of course you can. The effort you have made here will not go to waste," I told Ifrit, hoping that the same message would reach Rimuru as well. I hope for him to be in a good mood, that he might perform that taste re-creation again. And this time, I hope to try out spiciness and rich umami, not just sweetness. And I mean to use whatever means of flattery I can.

Still, I would prefer sweets most of all.

"You're pretty easy to figure out, Master Veldora. Though I suppose I'm no different, given that I'm going along with this."

Kwa ha ha ha.

Listen to Ifrit talk! I am not easy; I am clever. One must not confuse the two.

"These threat levels that humans devised are rather crude, aren't they, Master? They use only the amount of magical energy as the basis, rather than strength. I just cannot fathom how even Charybdis was considered a Calamity."

"Where else could it be? Above Calamity, there is only Disaster, the rank for demon lords, and Catastrophe, those beings that reign atop all life. And by the standards of human strength, everything at Calamity and above is dangerous. There is little point to splitting the ranks even finer," I told Ifrit. He looked impressed.

"How very wise, Master Veldora. One never knows when the occasional insight or wisdom might escape your lips!"

I don't feel as though he is complimenting me. That put me in a poor mood. As Rimuru commanded me, I was acting as Ifrit's training partner, but I decided to secretly strengthen my regiment.

Heh heh heh. Now that will increase the load upon Ifrit's shoulders and cause him grief. Naturally it will mean a heavier load for myself, but I hardly notice. I will do anything to pick on my target.

"I seem to recall that the habitat for sky dragons was quite far from here, however. Why would it be in a place like this?"

"So you noticed. It might have flown over Falmuth on the way from the dragon's nest, but that does not seem practical."

"Yes. Sky dragons' main source of food is monsters; they rarely attack humans. They are merciless to those who invade their territory, but it is almost unheard of for them to act aggressively outside of those bounds."

"Perhaps something is utilizing them for dark ends."

"...Are you reading too many holy manga texts, Master?"

Very well! I shall increase the burden a bit more to make Ifrit suffer.

"Gaaaaah!! I'm joking, only joking! I was only jealous of how insightful you are, Master Veldora!"

Ah, so that is why!

Jealous of me? Hah. Why, Ifrit, you little scamp.

"I suppose I cannot blame you. My wisdom is so vast and scintillating that I do understand why you would feel that way."

My mood restored, I lessened the load upon Ifrit.

Now that things have calmed down, I turned my attention

to the sky dragon's attack. The city is protected by powerful magical barriers and fields, meaning that they cannot be infiltrated from either the skies or underground. One assumes that the denser the population within, the stronger the protection.

This is simply because there would be more powerful mages in their midst. Much like one would use legion magic to nullify anti-military magics, city defenses place a high priority on stopping monster attacks. I am certain that many mages must be expending magical power in shifts, day and night, to maintain the barriers. One might call this "urban magic," or even "nation magic."

Those last two types of magic are in essence the same as other types, just on much larger scales. They are forms of ritual magic, which are more efficient when large groups of casters execute them.

In any case, unlike legion magic, which is crafted for offensive and defensive use, this kind of magic is refined and evolved for defense alone. I can handle it myself, but I believe that even Charybdis would find it very difficult to break this barrier.

At any rate, a city as vast as the capital of great Engrassia should be fine...

"But there are many who failed to escape in time."

"Yes. Rimuru is heading to assist them."

"I would assume that vanquishing that little sky dragon should come first."

But of course, Ifrit. Conspiracy or no, once Rimuru is in the picture, the matter is as good as solved.

No, what caught my attention was one of the humans who failed to flee in time. He looks like a merchant, but the healing potions he carries are extremely powerful.

Humans die so easily that many of them rush only to save

themselves. This man, however, went to save a fallen woman. I was impressed; it was not a typical act.

For one thing, such a powerful potion would be very valuable. And this was a merchant, who makes his living in maximizing profits, using such an expensive product to save the life of a stranger.

This is what makes humans so fascinating. It is often in the face of great danger that one finally sees their true nature.

But now it appears as though the merchant's luck has run dry. The sky dragon turned its attention on him instead.

"Look out, Mister..." cried a wee child, but the man promptly shouted, "I know it's there!"

"Do you suppose he was trying to attract the attention of the sky dragon?" asked Ifrit.

"But of course. It is an admirable course of action!"

I was moved by his courage. And that was not the end of it.

"Who do you think I am? I'm too important to die in a silly spot like this. Now begone, before you get in my way!" he shouted to the woman and her daughter.

Well done! I've included these lines of dialogue into my list of speeches I wish to say one day!

I like this man. He stands fast in the face of danger, not because he is frozen with fear, but because he offers himself as a target so that the woman and child can flee in safety! His daring is commendable. And I know that Rimuru would not abandon a man of such caliber.

Sure enough, my expectations were met. Rimuru slaughtered the sky dragon in seconds, then spoke to the merchant.

"Huh? This bottle... This is our healing solution."

Ohh?

So that is the connection here. Another example of fate bring-ing souls together.

The merchant named himself as Gard Mjöllmile. He is a great trader in Blumund, enough that he is well-known even here in the larger kingdom of Engrassia. Not only that, but with the generous way he greased the palms of the guards and knights, he knows how to make his way through society.

"I will have to learn from his example."

"Perhaps you should learn how to make money first, Master."

"Kwa ha ha! Very sassy of you!"

"I'm worried that you would end up giving away too much, Master Veldora..."

Why must Ifrit be such a worrywart? But I will admit, his concern is perhaps warranted. I shall have to study up on these mortal matters first.

In that sense, it is good fortune that we have become ac-quainted with Mjöllmile. After my prison is broken, I shall ask him for lessons in his arts. Then I, too, will earn bribes and work as a bodyguard!

This is what one calls a "win-win situation," I believe! The thought fills me with excitement for the future.

◆DWELLING OF THE SPIRITS◆

So Mjöllmile proved himself to be a formidable man. I never understood until now what kind of power a truly wealthy merchant can wield. No longer will I disparage bribes. Now I will think of them as a helpful allowance that can be claimed every day!

Not only does he do business in his homeland, but he also owns a number of very profitable shops in his trading part-ner of Engrassia. He invited Rimuru to one of them, which turned out to be a business that serves drinks.

Like "Butterflies of the Night," the bar in the dwarven kingdom, this is the sort of place that employs attractive women to shower its patrons with delightful attention. Why, this seems the sort of business that was designed just for me. I'm even more impressed with this Mjöllmile.

Rimuru looks shocked at the price list.

"The cheapest drink on the menu is a silver coin. They only use coppers for tips, it would seem. That's quite a pricey establishment."

"Do you know about this stuff, Ifrit?"

"No, not very well, but I do recall that a single silver coin would buy three good meals all at once."

That would be based on Ifrit's memories with Shizue Izawa. I am not familiar with the coins typically used in commerce, so this is very helpful information.

According to Ifrit, outside of the city center, two silvers is enough to stay at an inn. In other words, two drinks at this bar would cost as much as a night's stay.

"Does it seem expensive to you?"

"It does. As far as I can remember, there was only a hand- ful of occasions that we used such an extravagant business's services."

Yes, that does seem to check out. Shizue Izawa did make a respectable living, but this kind of expense would be a waste for one who does not drink liquor.

But for me? A paradise!

"Ifrit! One day in the future, we shall have to greet the dawn drinking in such a place!!"

"Understood. I would be happy to drink on your tab, Master Veldora!"

What? I have to foot the bill? Why, Ifrit, you scheming rascal.

Still, the thought of this experience filled me with excitement.

Rimuru entered the bar, and before I knew it, he'd done something preposterous!

"This is incredible. And you say it's popular where you're from?"

"I don't know if 'popular' is the right word…"

And behold! A great tower of glasses with the beverage poured onto the top to spill over the edges!! One, two, three…fifty-five glasses in all!!

This is apparently known as a "champagne tower." That means fifty-five silvers spent on this extravagance alone.

"No, M-Master Veldora! That number's not correct! He ordered a more expensive drink, so each glass would cost more like ten silver coins. And it's being poured to overflowing, which is more than the usual amount, so…"

"Gyargh! Th-then how many coins will this cost?!"

"Five hundred and fifty, at the very minimum!! But I would bet it's at least twice as much…"

Unfathomable. Only on very rare occasions have I ever felt fear, but this bold expenditure of Rimuru's is fearsome, indeed. While it might be on the house, how can one take advantage of such largess so easily?

But it does make me wonder. When I am receiving the gift of Rimuru's generosity, will I be able to wield it to such a degree as well?

"I believe that would be correct, Master."

"As I thought. I cannot wait, then. Heh heh heh."

Now the thought of Rimuru treating me to a night on the town is even better. With my keen knowledge of where the limits are, I believe that I can make the most of it without being scolded.

One by one, I learn things that make me wiser. And what better way to gain wisdom than to return to observing Rimuru. There are so many things to learn from him.

At the moment, he is wrapping up his negotiations with Mjöllmile. Clearly they feel this is a mutually beneficial partnership.

I suppose I must confirm it, then. This smells like money to me! I hope to one day be good friends with Mjöllmile, too.

Despite the surroundings, however, Rimuru seems downcast to me. He must be worried about the little children.

"Do you think so? I get the feeling he's searching for someone..."

"Someone? But who would Rimuru know among this bunch?"

The only people Rimuru knows here are his coworkers at the school. Plus that Yuuki boy, and the man with the godly hands, master of all pastry creation, Yoshida.

"No, that's not what I mean. Lord Rimuru seems to have an abnormal interest in elves, so I suspected that he was attempting to find some at this establishment, as he did in previous cases."

"Elves? Like the ones at the bar in Dwargon?"

"Yes, exactly, though it doesn't seem likely here."

Ifrit was correct. It would be one thing if he had an arrangement to meet them here, but they would not just coincidentally be at this distant place today.

Or so I thought, until the elf who performed the divinations at the dwarven kingdom showed her face moments later!

"Shall we talk somewhere more private, little slime?" she asked, seeing right through him, despite the fact that he was in human form. She is extremely observant.

Of course, one would expect that quality from an individual capable of the advanced magical arts of divination.

The unnamed elf carried on a pleasant chat with Rimuru. It would seem that she can nearly read his mind, in fact. This is very impressive, as even I have found difficulty in skimming meaning from the surface level of Rimuru's thoughts. I wish that I could learn this art from her.

Fortunately for me, Rimuru was thinking at this exact moment that he wished he could scout her to work back in Tempest.

Splendid. I am entirely behind the idea, and I hope it does come about.

The chance meeting with the elf turned out to be a very fruitful one, indeed. Rimuru was mourning the fact that he had no clues to the location of the Dwelling of the Spirit Queen, but the elf was able to divine the answer for him.

The only problem was something she said after that: "No one has ever gone to the Dwelling of the Spirits and returned to tell the tale."

While she was deadly serious when giving this warning, it only confirmed something that I suspected. The Spirit Queen is merely another name for a being I already know. I've never interacted with her directly, but I've heard of her personality—she is quite a mischievous one.

I suppose I shall just have to wait to find out what happens when Rimuru finally meets her!

◆SPIRIT QUEEN◆

On the day after Rimuru calmed down the frightened children with hot chocolate, the group arrived at the place in question.

But back to that hot chocolate: I wish to add that it looked very delicious. I requested a cup to try for myself, but was denied. It is unfair. I will also add that I am in a very dejected mood at the moment.

"Ah, something showed up!"

"Oh, I nearly missed it. What is happening now?" I replied, setting aside the diary that I keep as a daily ritual, and glancing outside.

What I saw was a golem, an object animated by magic. It appears to be attacking Rimuru and the children.

"As a matter of fact, they've been talking to someone for a moment already. Apparently, this is a trial they must pass to learn the location of the higher elementals."

"Ah. A trial, you say."

"That seems to be it."

So that clears that up. But it is a foolish negotiation to make with the likes of Rimuru. Ordinary circumstances aside, he is currently on edge trying to solve the children's quandary, and attempting to keep them safe in this dangerous place.

What will a golem be able to do against...

"Hell Flare, that looked like."

"Its firepower is incredible..."

"I do believe he mediated its power, but it would not do to anger him any further."

The fight was over in an instant. Rimuru used Sticky Steel Thread to immobilize the golem, then dispatched it with Hell Flare.

"Did you say Lord Rimuru was angry?"

"Can't you tell? Rimuru is the type to get angrier about trouble for his companions than for his own affairs. He'll be furious after seeing the danger the children were just put in by that stunt."

"I see."

"It's all in moderation, you see. How far can you go before you anger him? Once you know the answer, he is not so frightening. We are quite lucky in that regard. We have the opportunity to observe him day-in and day-out, giving us the chance to accurately determine the answer!"

"That will be very helpful."

Indeed. I would agree with that.

Whoever it is that is attempting to bargain with Rimuru probably learned their lesson by now. He furiously called them out into the open at last.

"Okay, okay, okay, okay! I'm out here, I'm out here, much to my chagrin!"

It was a fairy. In fact, it was exactly the person I expected it would be.

"Ah, Queen Ramiris! It is so good to see her again. She looks the same as when I became Lord Cromwell's servant. That is a relief."

"Aha. So Ramiris was the Spirit Queen after all."

"Does that mean you are familiar with her, Master Veldora?"

"I remember her as 'Ramiris of the Labyrinth.' I never met her in person, but I do recall that she was one of the Demon Lords."

"Ah, by that name. Queen Ramiris is known by many names, in fact. Her appearance has changed at different times, so it is an element of confusion for many."

That does seem to add up.

The Ramiris here is a little pipsqueak, but the image from my memory is of a beautiful woman. They are so different that it is nearly impossible to reconcile, and one might be forgiven for not realizing they are the same person.

But this is undoubtedly her.

"I am none other than the great Ten Demon Lords' most diminutive member, Ramiris of the Labyrinth!" she said, which cleared that question up. "Now kneel before me!!"

I must compliment her pluck in exhibiting such pride and arrogance in Rimuru's presence. But that actually seemed to have relaxed Rimuru's caution toward her. He doubts her insistence that she is a demon lord.

"Even I remember that Ramiris was a demon lord."

"It is absolutely true. Her powers were preserved; it was merely her aspect that shifted to the role."

It is a very rare thing to happen, but there can be no quibbling with the outcome. I have heard tale of the circumstances, and it seems to me that she is fortunate that is all that happened to her.

Treyni lamented that she'd been left behind, but even if she had been there, she would have been helpless. The trio of dryad sisters will be delighted to hear that Ramiris is alive and well.

Rimuru is eyeing her with skepticism, but I cannot blame him. After all, Ramiris is nearly devoid of all of her power in this state. I believe that she must have undergone a number of reincarnations after her fall from grace.

"I did not realize that the dryad named Treyni has been alive much longer than I have," murmured Ifrit.

"D-don't be a fool!! You must never speak to a woman about her age!"

"P-pardon me, Master!"

"Be careful. It is only you and I here, but if we should emerge into the outside world and have cause to converse in this manner, be cautious at all times not to bring up dangerous topics such as this."

"I will mark these words upon my heart."

That is good to hear. I've learned much in my time as well. Rimuru might be careless, but even I have bitter memories of my own.

Ah yes, there was that day in my tempestuous youth. I called one of my elder sisters an old—no, I shall not repeat it here. Just the memory is summoning a wave of fear that—why did I say "fear"? I feel no fear. Ahem.

The point is, even I have my weak points. Everyone does. It is entirely normal.

"Incidentally, I first met Treyni several millennia ago. After offering my protection for a while, I left her in charge of the forest she created to be my dwelling. The thing about dryads, however, is that they are tree-dwelling spirits, and spend their time sleeping. She might be thousands of years old, but her lifetime of actual activity is not nearly that long."

"Ah, I see. So while you say they fell from grace, there is little fundamental change. When we are in the spiritual plane, we are essentially dormant the majority of the time."

Well, there you have it.

Few keep their wits about them for as long as I do continuously. That is the reality of things, and so counting their living years is rather pointless, as far as gauging them by the human lifespan.

And therefore, it should be even easier to avoid the pointless question of a lady's age.

That wraps up this little conversation. Now it is time to forget about the bitter memories of yore and return to what Rimuru is doing.

Rimuru and Ramiris seem to have found common ground in the topic of Milim, surprisingly enough.

He set up a picnic of snacks, which she is now devouring as though they belong to her. Oh, to enjoy sweets when one is that size...I find that jealousy threatens to consume me!

If you please, could I have some—

"Request denied. There is not enough leeway to produce it."

No fair!
Rimuru's coldness makes me sad.

"Suggestion. If an increase in progress is detected, the extra leeway to produce a taste re-creation may arise..."

It shall be done! I will do whatever it takes. But I am already at the limit of the number of calculations I can perform in a second. Any more than this...

"Announcement. Rather than a single consciousness, the use of multiple consciousnesses of identical capability may theoretically increase processing speed..."

My word! I did not think of this.

It is a good thing that Rimuru knows so much. And as luck would have it, I just recently acquired the ability to split my consciousness into multiple parts!!

"I will do it. I will do anything. I will use parallel consciousness to up the speed of my processing!!"

"Um, Master Veldora, are you sure about this?!"

"Am I sure? Of course I'm sure! Nothing is impossible for me. If I don't do this now, when will I ever?!"

"It's a trick! Lord Rimuru is setting a clever trap for you!!"

"Silence!! Rimuru would never lie to me! By working harder

in here, I give Rimuru extra power. And by doing that, he will be able to send me a re-creation of sweet pastries and all their rich flavor information! How can I not try it?"

"W-well, if you're sure…"
I nodded firmly.

"As long as you're fine with it, Master, I won't argue against it anymore."

There! Now Ifrit is on my side, too. I shall have no regrets!

I returned to the task of decoding with renewed fervor.

◆SALVATION OF THE SOUL◆

It did not work.

Splitting my consciousness to perform parallel calculations turned out to be exhausting beyond measure.

"Somehow, I did not foresee this being as difficult as it is."

"Uh, I would think anyone should understand that. I mean, it's impossible."

Is Ifrit saying that I'm just that incredible? It is an ironic response, but I do think that he is complimenting me underneath. It must be that *tsundere* thing.

"Heh heh heh. Save your compliments."

"It wasn't a compliment…"

Oh, don't be shy now.

At any rate, I shall take a short break.

The first step will be to accustom myself to two minds, and then I can work my way up to three, four, and more. It said that if I maintain the same persona with each of them in tandem, my efficiency will be greater.

Rimuru would not be incorrect about this, so I have been taking care to keep the same capacity with each split consciousness. It is what made me so exhausted, but apparently if I take a break with just one side, there is no problem.

"Wouldn't that mean that you were no longer able to slack off that way? Are you sure that's what you want?"

"Huh?"

Now that Ifrit mentions it... Maybe I've been tricked...

"Announcement. Cookie taste re-creation successful."

Aaah!! Ten cookies suddenly appeared before my eyes.

Ten! Not one or two measly specimens, but a full ten.

Look how generous Rimuru is to me. There is no way that he would be tricking me. I left one of my consciousnesses working while I enjoyed my cookies.

Naturally, I shared one of them with Ifrit.

Ahh, such sweetness! It is so very, very delicious!! As I ate my cookies, savoring their delicate flavor, I listened in on what Rimuru was talking about. He was in the midst of some new mad scheme...

"Is this real?"

"It is real."

I cannot believe it. Summoning spirits and fusing them with the children!

There is no point in asking if such a thing is possible. It is already happening as I watch.

*"Generating simulated higher water-wind elemental...
Successful."*

I have never even heard of such an element before, but he made it work...

Rimuru quickly and deftly fused the summoned spirit to Ryota Sekiguchi. I don't know whether to be aghast or impressed. Even Ifrit cannot keep his mouth shut.

"Lord Rimuru is amazing."

"This is beyond what the word 'amazing' can describe," I replied, rattled.

But just when I thought nothing could shock me—a source of energy that rivals my own!!

What the girl named Chloe called forth was no spirit, but something indefinable from a dimension beyond the spirit realm. Ramiris tried to stop it from happening, but she was no match for it. The being made its home within Chloe in moments.

But I was more curious about the kiss that she gave him. In fact...

"I feel as though I recognized her," I said.

"You know that being?"

"I cannot remember, but she felt familiar."

What a strange thing. I have no memory or knowledge of such a being. And yet...what is this sensation I feel?

I suppose the answer will not be forthcoming.

Chloe emerged unscathed, and that settled the matter of the children's survival for good. Now is the time to celebrate! Rimuru seems to feel the same way, so we concluded the process with no more mention of the strange event at its close. Incidentally, Rimuru fulfilled a promise to Ramiris and fashioned her a new golem.

"...Come forth, Greater Demon..."

He did not just give her a simple golem, but fashioned his own precision body and attached a greater demon to it. This, too, is simply preposterous.

Ramiris's golem was known as the Elemental Colossus and was quite an excellent specimen…but the Arch-Golem he just created is far beyond that. For one thing, he once again stole my magical energy to give her golem the name of Beretta.

I am used to this by now, but I do wish that he would pace himself.

Now, as for the problem…

"It does occur to me that if Lord Rimuru was able to summon demons, could he not have infused the children with demons instead of elemental spirits?" Ifrit wondered.

In fact, it was such a sharp observation, I had no answer. I hadn't considered it myself, but I suppose that in terms of sheer possibility, he could have done it…

A greater demon is a lower creature, and in terms of magical energy only, it is far inferior to a higher elemental. But demons are clever in their use of magicules, and if an autonomous individual with a firm mind of its own was summoned, I think it highly possible that it could have stopped the children's bodies from going out of control.

"Negative. An autonomous demon is pure malice and would likely wreak evil on the children. Therefore, the idea was considered off-limits."

Ah. So Rimuru had been aware of it, then. And that answer certainly makes sense!

Yes, a summoned demon would obey Rimuru's orders. But it might be difficult to get one to obey a child. The problem with demons is that they will obey, but only to a point. It might teach the child wicked tricks, and lead them down the path to temptation.

A Demon Lord like Ramiris is one thing, but a young child

does not have a fully formed moral compass. They might take a demon at its word, and be led astray into great disaster.

So Rimuru decided not to attempt summoning demons to attach to the children.

"And that is why, Ifrit. Sometimes I cannot believe the shallow limits of your intelligence. Learn to use your mind! Think beneath the surface, as Rimuru and I do!"

I am glad that I did not agree with his idea out loud when he brought it up. If I had, then Rimuru might have been disappointed with me. The lesson is, it is dangerous to leap to agreeing with simple opinions and statements.

With that in mind, I decided to change the topic.

"More importantly, Ifrit, that golem body that Rimuru created was a splendid one indeed."

"Uh...yes."

"When I am brought back, I will ask Rimuru to make one for you, too!"

"Oh! That would be wonderful!!"

"Just leave it all to me. Kwaaaa ha ha ha!!"

I laughed long and loud, to cover up the fact that I had nearly just made a fool of myself.

To be reincarnated in Volume 12!

THAT TIME MY HEART RACED AT THE RECORDING

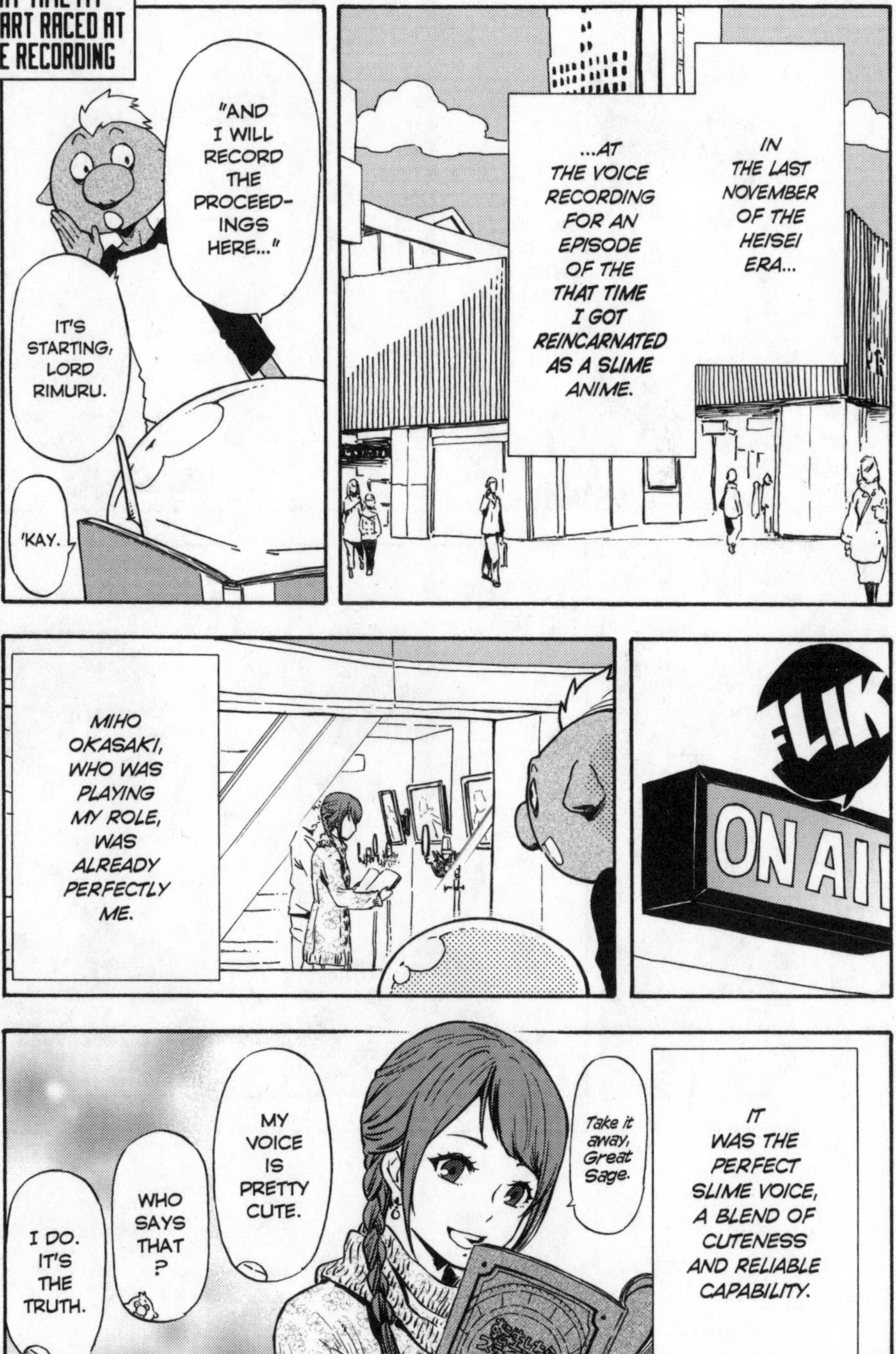
IN THE LAST NOVEMBER OF THE HEISEI ERA...
...AT THE VOICE RECORDING FOR AN EPISODE OF THE THAT TIME I GOT REINCARNATED AS A SLIME ANIME.
"AND I WILL RECORD THE PROCEEDINGS HERE..."
IT'S STARTING, LORD RIMURU.
'KAY.
FLIK
ON AI
MIHO OKASAKI, WHO WAS PLAYING MY ROLE, WAS ALREADY PERFECTLY ME.
IT WAS THE PERFECT SLIME VOICE, A BLEND OF CUTENESS AND RELIABLE CAPABILITY.
Take it away, Great Sage.
MY VOICE IS PRETTY CUTE.
WHO SAYS THAT?
I DO. IT'S THE TRUTH.

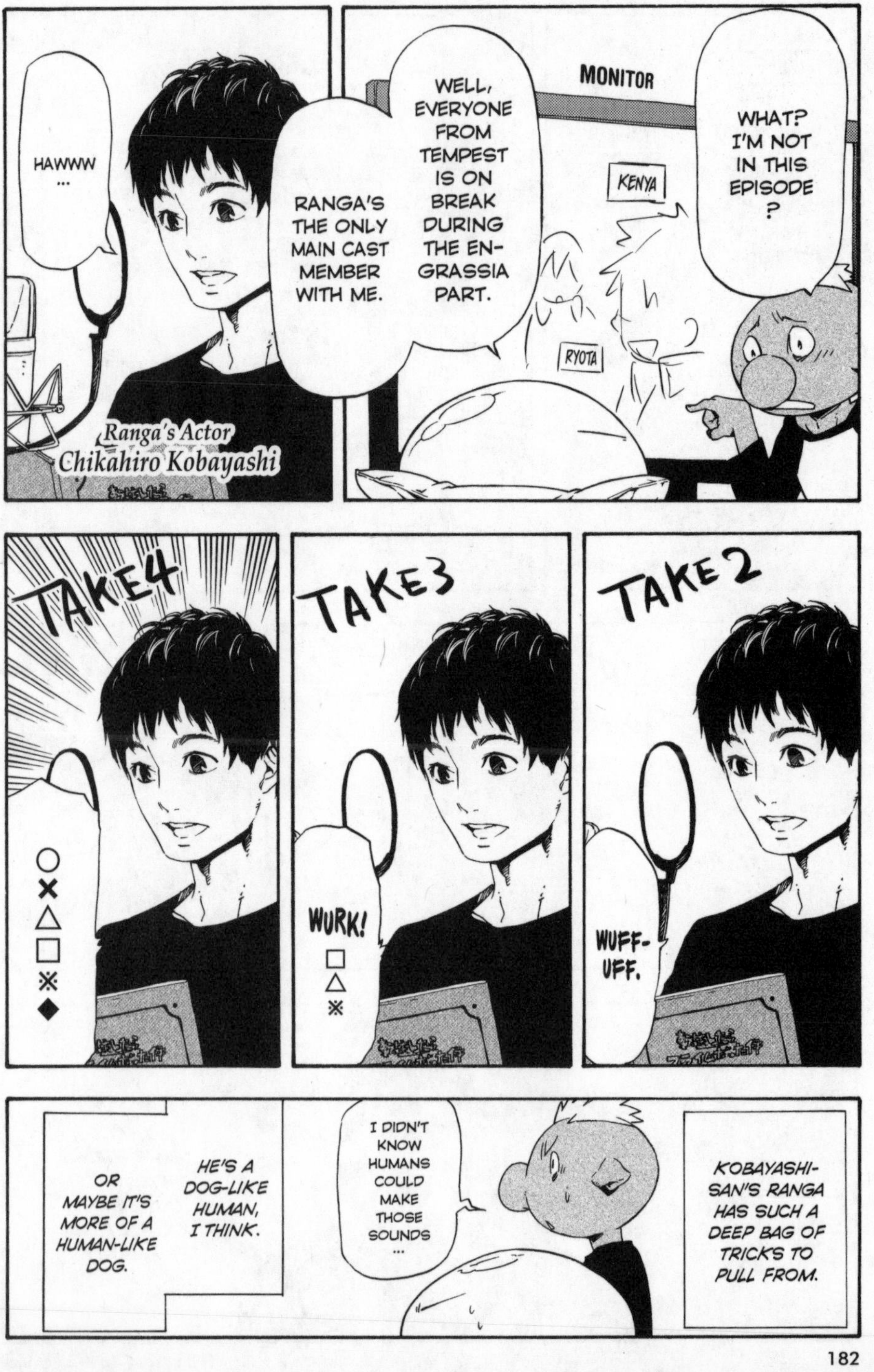
MONITOR
WHAT? I'M NOT IN THIS EPISODE?
KENYA
RYOTA
WELL, EVERYONE FROM TEMPEST IS ON BREAK DURING THE EN-GRASSIA PART.
RANGA'S THE ONLY MAIN CAST MEMBER WITH ME.
HAWWW...
Ranga's Actor Chikahiro Kobayashi
TAKE 2
WUFF-UFF.
TAKE3
WURK!
□△※
TAKE4
○×△□※◆
KOBAYASHI-SAN'S RANGA HAS SUCH A DEEP BAG OF TRICKS TO PULL FROM.
I DIDN'T KNOW HUMANS COULD MAKE THOSE SOUNDS...
HE'S A DOG-LIKE HUMAN, I THINK.
OR MAYBE IT'S MORE OF A HUMAN-LIKE DOG.

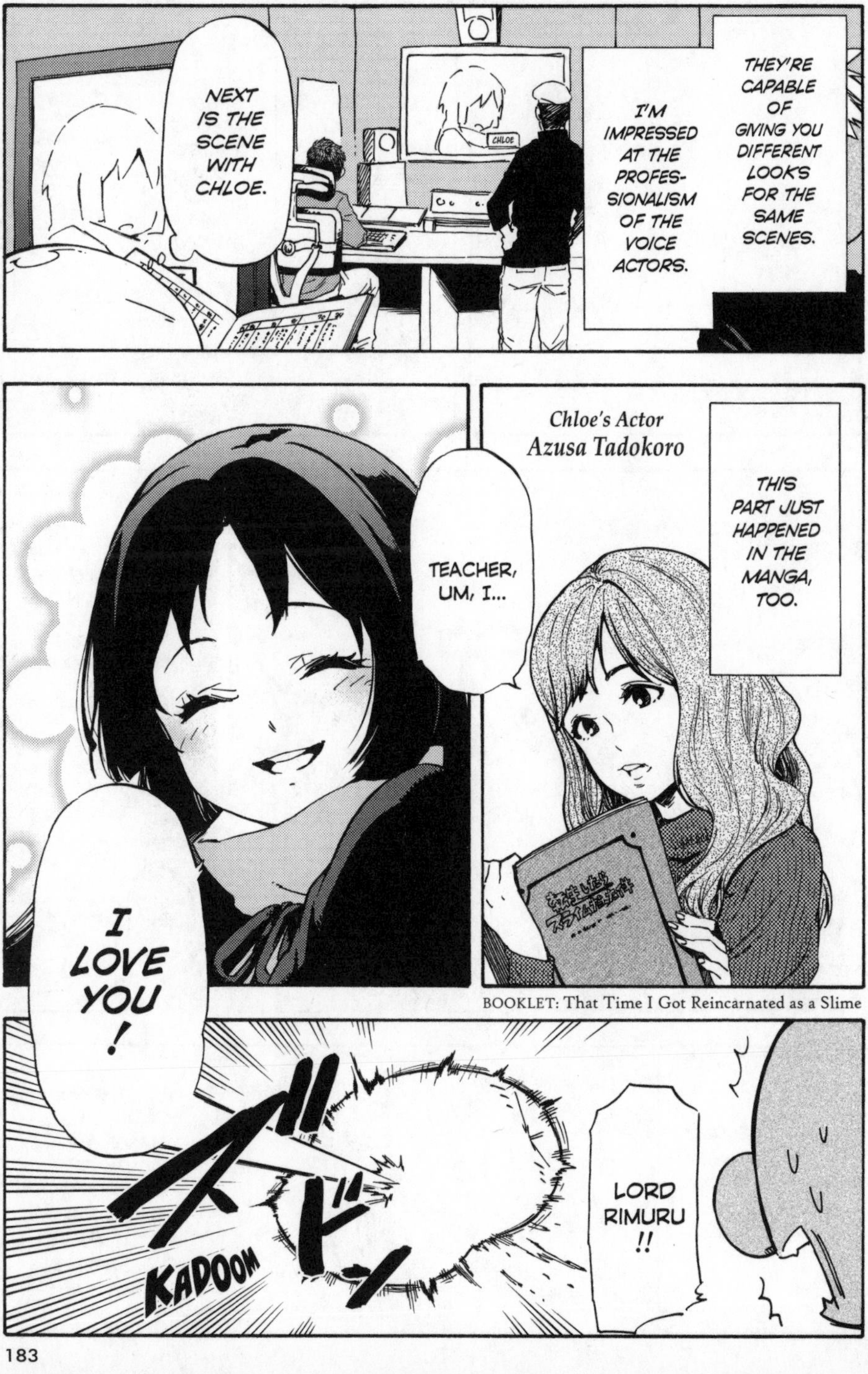
I'M IMPRESSED AT THE PROFESSIONALISM OF THE VOICE ACTORS. THEY'RE CAPABLE OF GIVING YOU DIFFERENT LOOKS FOR THE SAME SCENES.
NEXT IS THE SCENE WITH CHLOE.
THIS PART JUST HAPPENED IN THE MANGA, TOO.
Chloe's Actor
Azusa Tadokoro
BOOKLET: That Time I Got Reincarnated as a Slime
TEACHER, UM, I...
I LOVE YOU!
LORD RIMURU!!
KADOOM

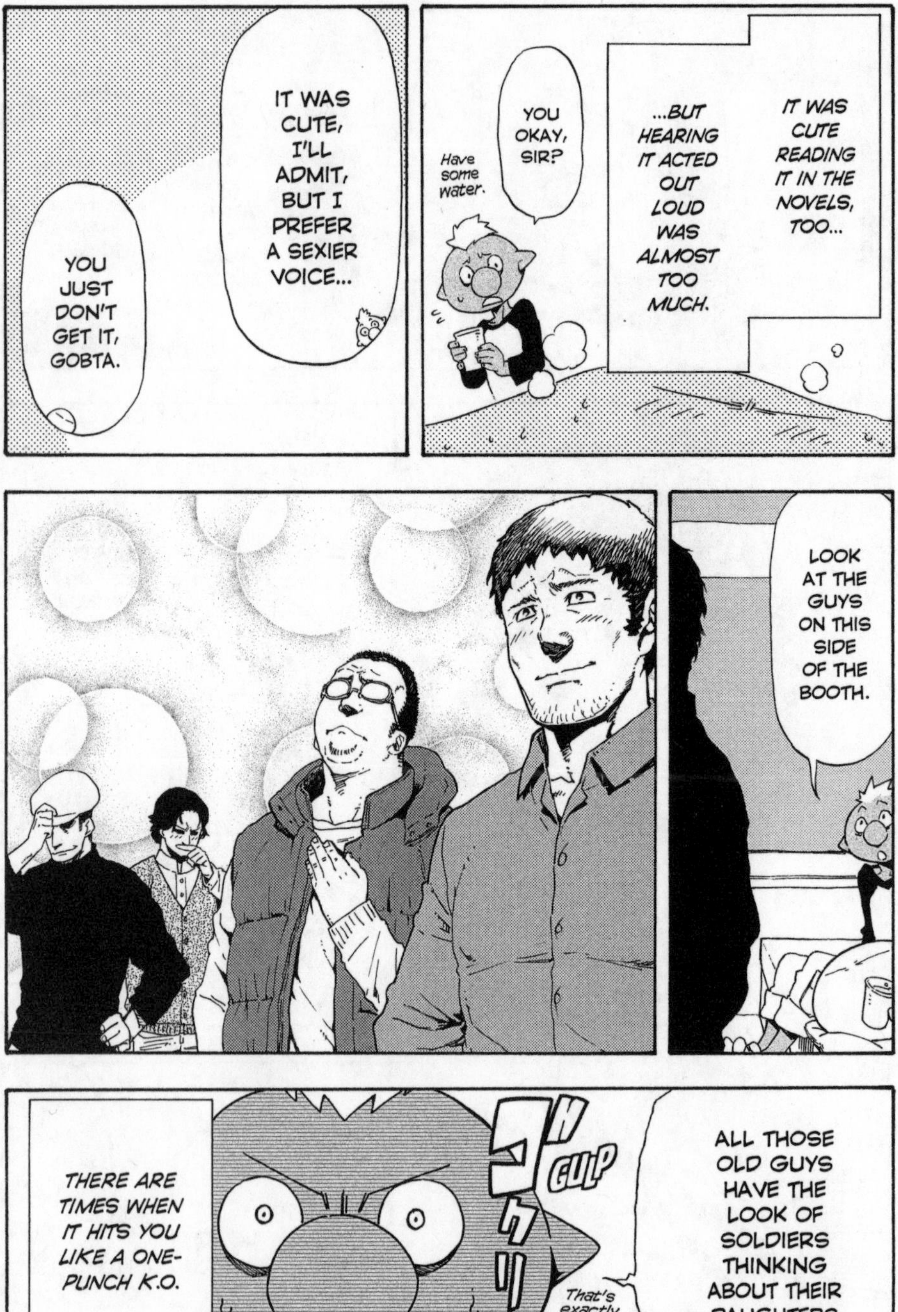
IT WAS CUTE READING IT IN THE NOVELS, TOO...
...BUT HEARING IT ACTED OUT LOUD WAS ALMOST TOO MUCH.
YOU OKAY, SIR?
Have some water.
IT WAS CUTE, I'LL ADMIT, BUT I PREFER A SEXIER VOICE...
YOU JUST DON'T GET IT, GOBTA.
LOOK AT THE GUYS ON THIS SIDE OF THE BOOTH.
ALL THOSE OLD GUYS HAVE THE LOOK OF SOLDIERS THINKING ABOUT THEIR DAUGHTERS BACK HOME!!
GULP
That's exactly the point.
THERE ARE TIMES WHEN IT HITS YOU LIKE A ONE-PUNCH K.O.

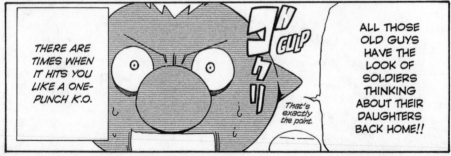

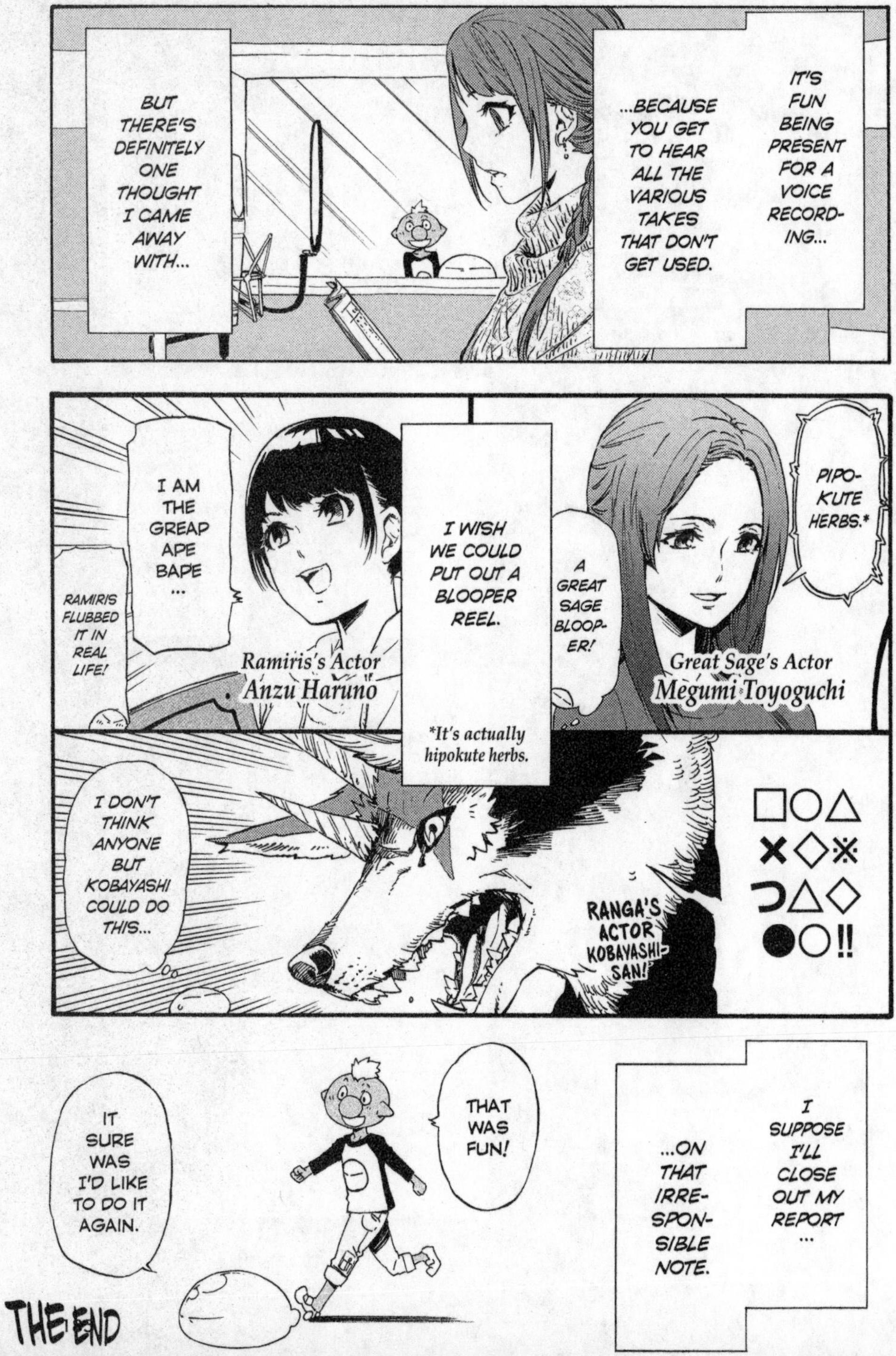
IT'S FUN BEING PRESENT FOR A VOICE RECORDING...
...BECAUSE YOU GET TO HEAR ALL THE VARIOUS TAKES THAT DON'T GET USED.
BUT THERE'S DEFINITELY ONE THOUGHT I CAME AWAY WITH...
PIPOKUTE HERBS.*
A GREAT SAGE BLOOPER!
Great Sage's Actor Megumi Toyoguchi
I WISH WE COULD PUT OUT A BLOOPER REEL.
I AM THE GREAP APE BAPE ...
RAMIRIS FLUBBED IT IN REAL LIFE!
Ramiris's Actor Anzu Haruno
*It's actually hipokute herbs.
□○△ ×◇※ つ△◇ ●○!!
RANGA'S ACTOR KOBAYASHI-SAN!
I DON'T THINK ANYONE BUT KOBAYASHI COULD DO THIS...
I SUPPOSE I'LL CLOSE OUT MY REPORT ...
...ON THAT IRRESPONSIBLE NOTE.
THAT WAS FUN!
IT SURE WAS I'D LIKE TO DO IT AGAIN.
THE END

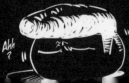

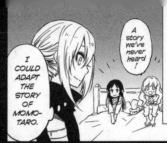

ONE SLEEPLESS NIGHT, THE KIDS ASKED FOR A FAIRY TALE.
A story we've never heard!
I COULD ADAPT THE STORY OF MOMOTARO.
IT'S EASIER TO TELL A BEDTIME STORY WHEN YOU TURN THE CHARACTERS INTO PEOPLE THE KIDS KNOW.
I'M GONNA VANQUISH THE OGRES!
OH? THE OGRES, YOU SAY?
THEN I WILL MAKE SOME MILLET DUMPLINGS FOR YOU TO TAKE ALONG!
NOOO!
WHAT'S WRONG, TEACHER?
Hmm...
I'M JUST HAVING A REALLY HARD TIME SEEING GOBOTARO SUCCESSFULLY VANQUISHING ANY OGRES...

LIST OF ACKNOWLEDGMENTS

AUTHOR:
Fuse-sensei

CHARACTER DESIGN:
Mitz Vah-sensei

TRAVEL GUIDE:
Sho Okagiri-sensei

REINCARNATED SLIME DIARY:
Shiba-sensei

TRINITY IN THE MONSTER KINGDOM:
Tae Tono-sensei

ASSISTANTS:
Muraichi-san
Daiki Haraguchi-san
Masashi Kiritani-sensei
Taku Arao-sensei
Takuya Nishida-sensei

Everyone at the editorial department

AND YOU!!

Pompadour Slime

Ahh?

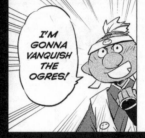

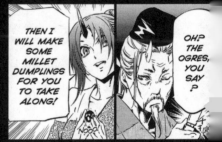

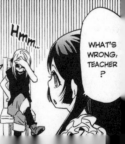

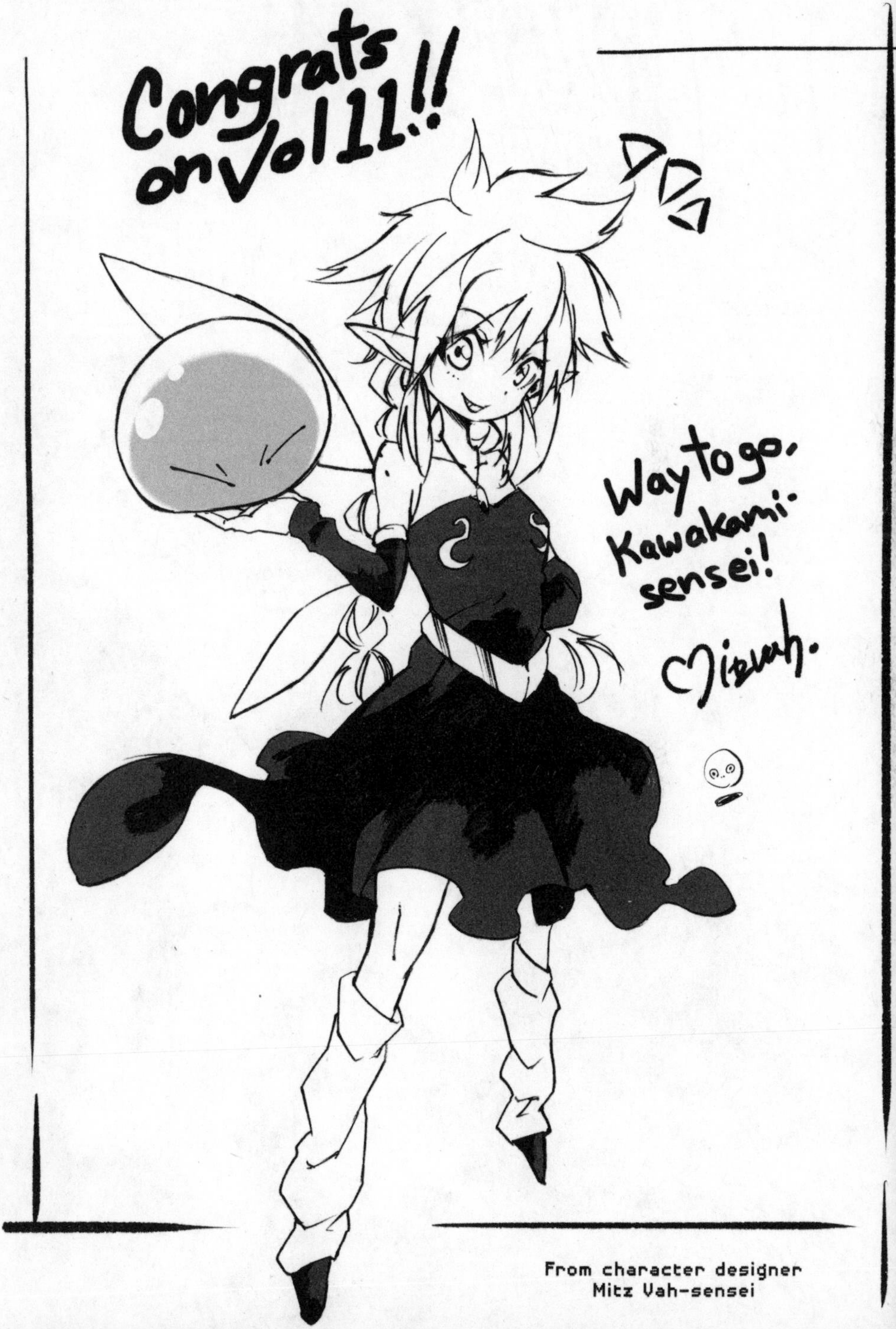
Congrats on Vol11!!
Way to go, Kawakami-sensei!

From character designer
Mitz Vah-sensei

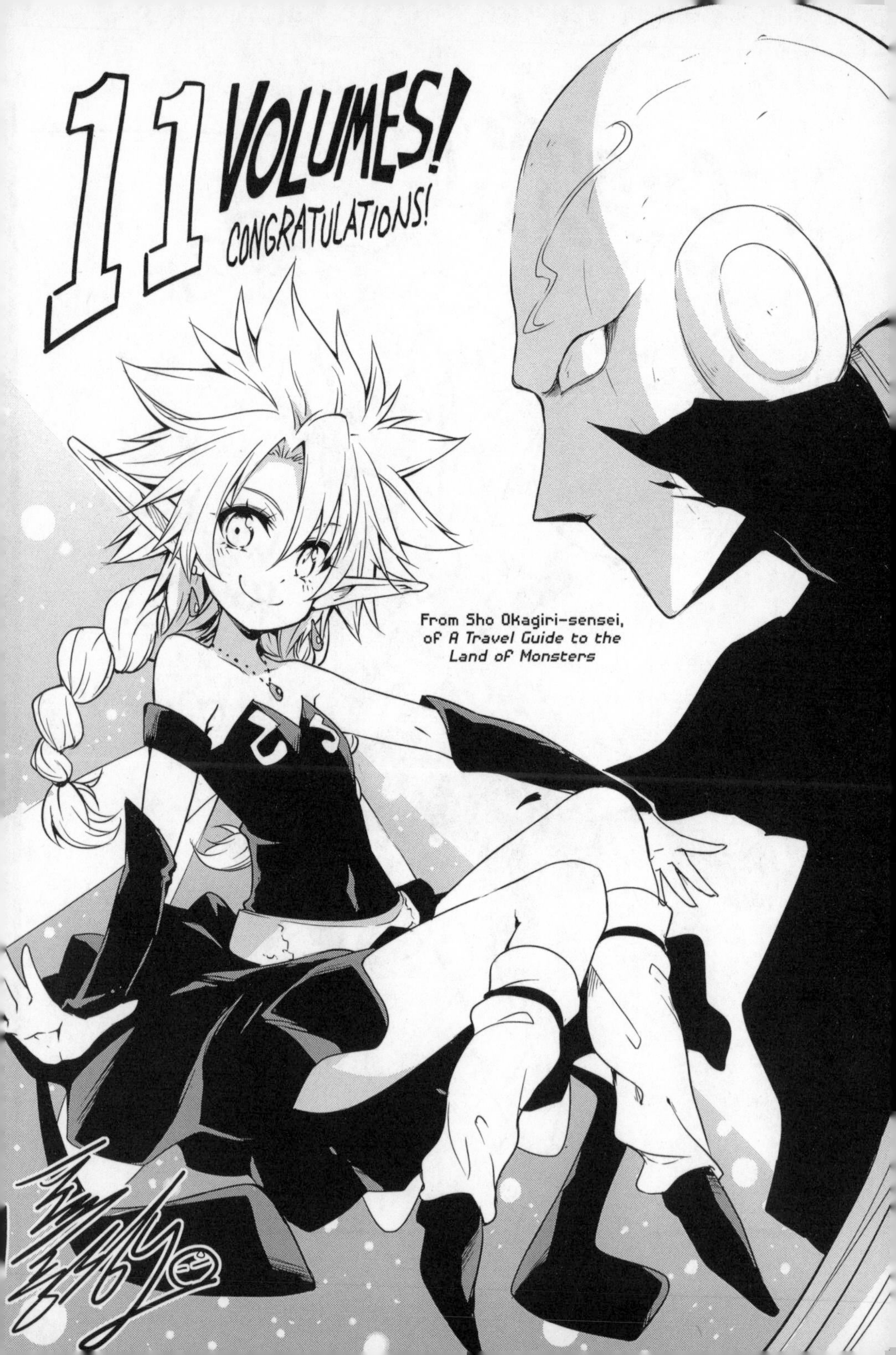
11 VOLUMES!
CONGRATULATIONS!
From Sho Okagiri-sensei,
of *A Travel Guide to the Land of Monsters*

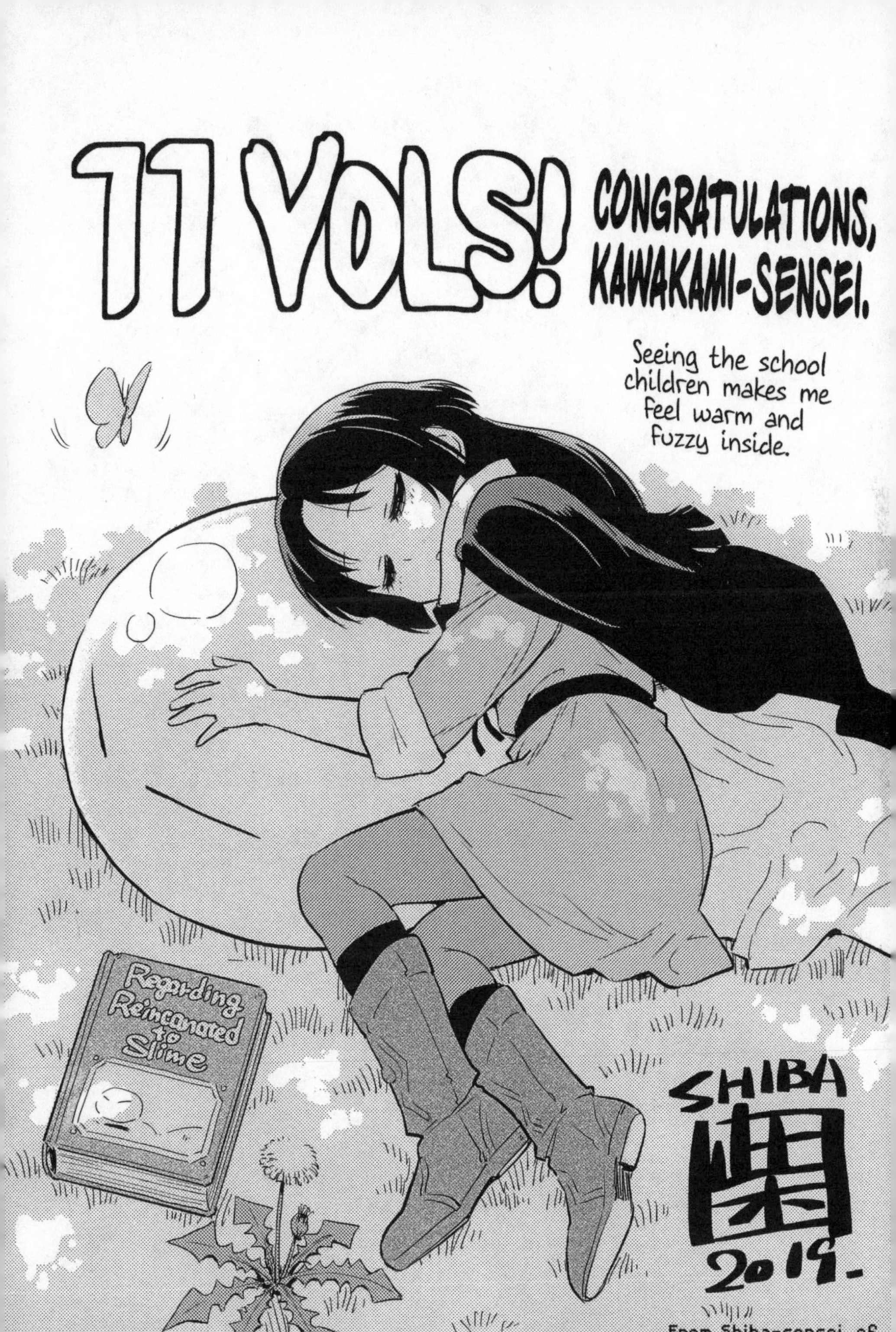
11 VOLS!
CONGRATULATIONS, KAWAKAMI-SENSEI.
Seeing the school children makes me feel warm and fuzzy inside.
Regarding Reincarnated to Slime
SHIBA
2019.

From Shiba-sensei, of *Reincarnated Slime Diary*

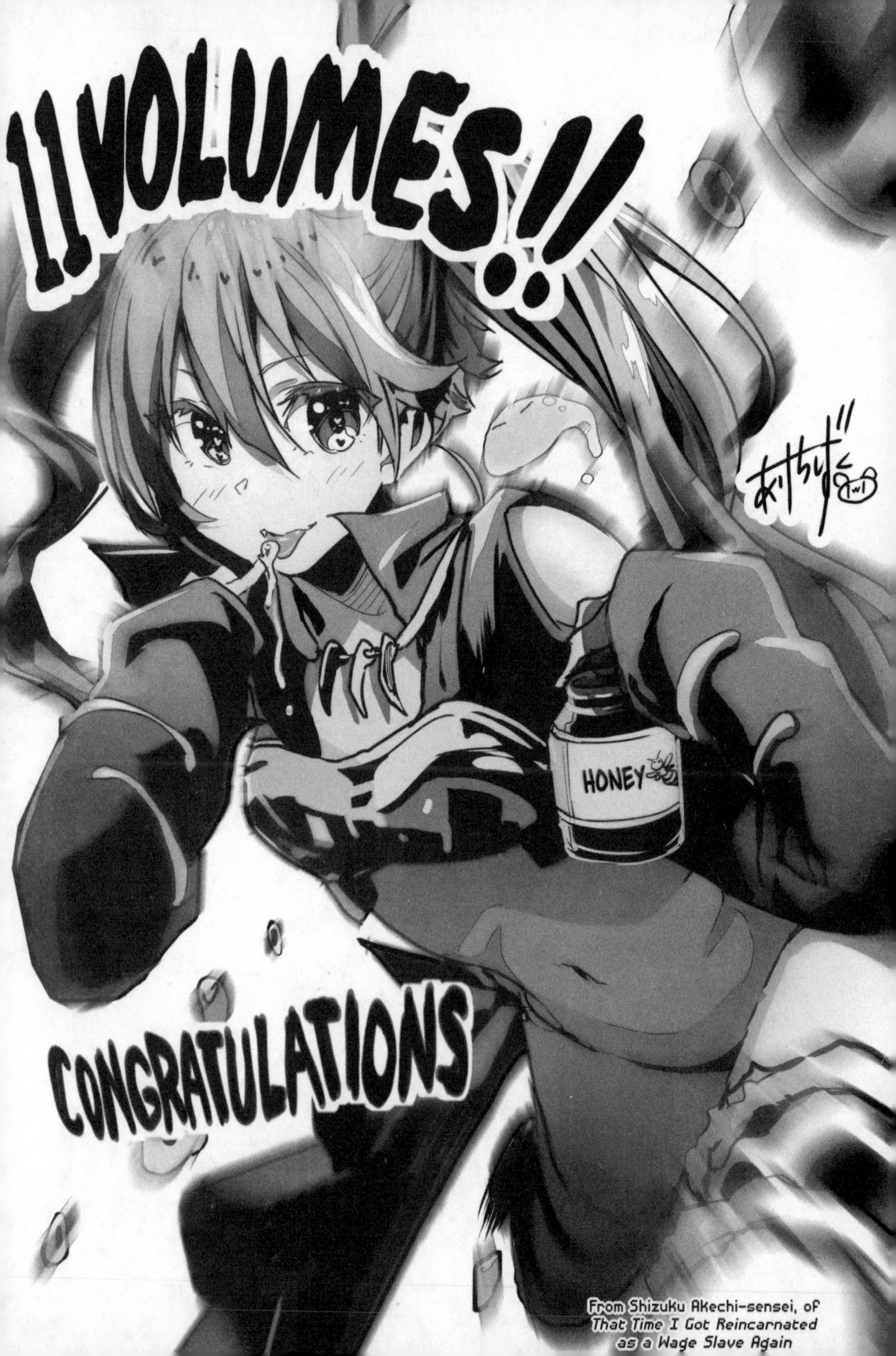
11 VOLUMES!!
HONEY
CONGRATULATIONS
From Shizuku Akechi-sensei, of *That Time I Got Reincarnated as a Wage Slave Again*

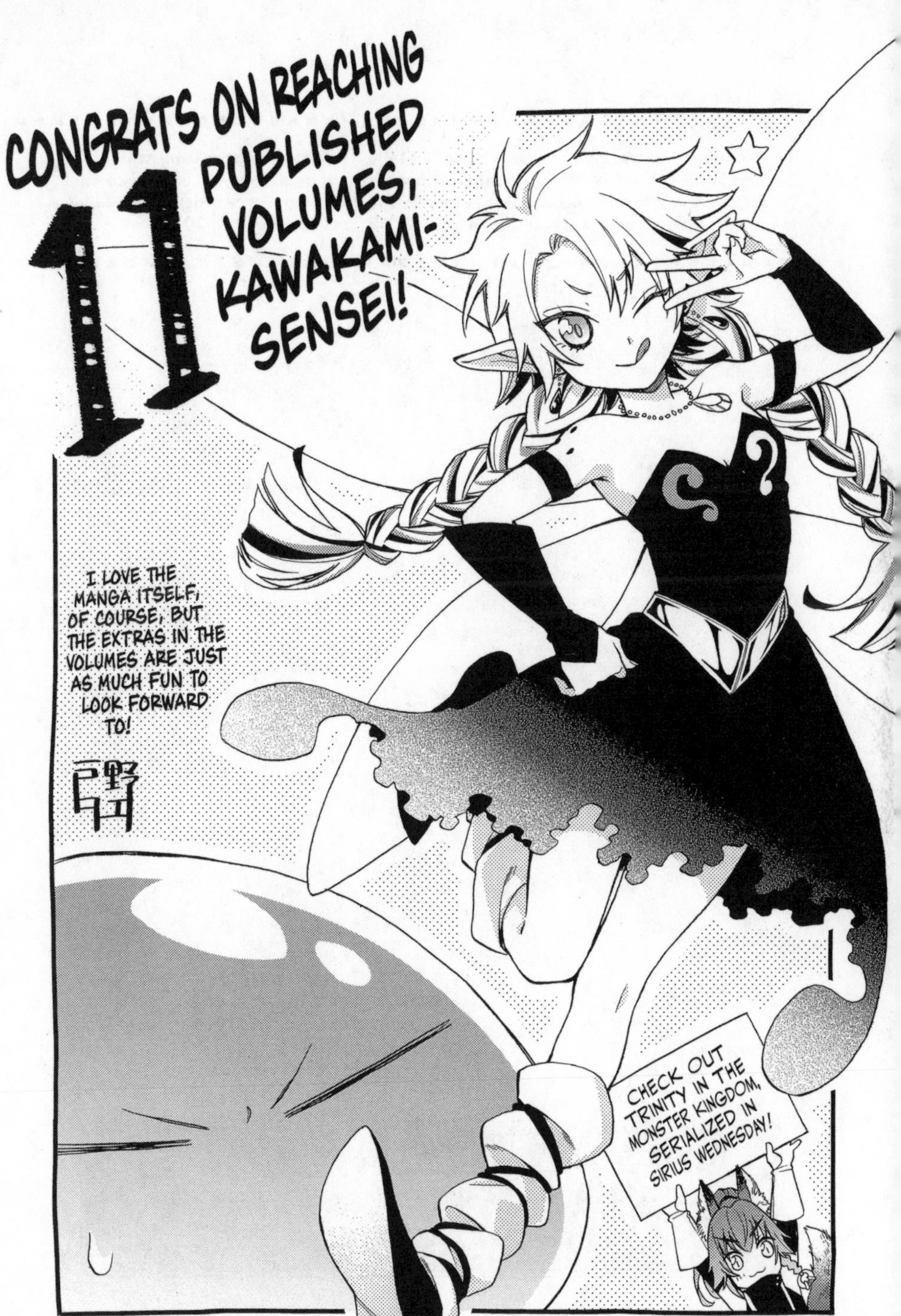
CONGRATS ON REACHING 11 PUBLISHED VOLUMES, KAWAKAMI-SENSEI!
I LOVE THE MANGA ITSELF, OF COURSE, BUT THE EXTRAS IN THE VOLUMES ARE JUST AS MUCH FUN TO LOOK FORWARD TO!
CHECK OUT TRINITY IN THE MONSTER KINGDOM, SERIALIZED IN SIRIUS WEDNESDAY!
From Tae Tono-sensei, of *Another Story: Trinity in the Monster Kingdom*

To commemorate the airing of each episode of the *Reincarnated as a Slime* anime, the *Shonen Sirius* official Twitter account (@shonen_sirius) made a series of promotional tweets. Here are the various congratulatory illustrations from other artists in the Sirius magazine, uploaded between December 3rd, 2018, and January 7th, 2019!

Konori Minosaki-sensei (@minosaki_konori)

Artist of Cursed by Akinashi-san?! in Palcy

刀坂
アキラ

Akira Tousaka-sensei (@tousakaaaa)

Artist of *The Handbook of Modern Witch-Hunting* in Magazine Pocket

▼

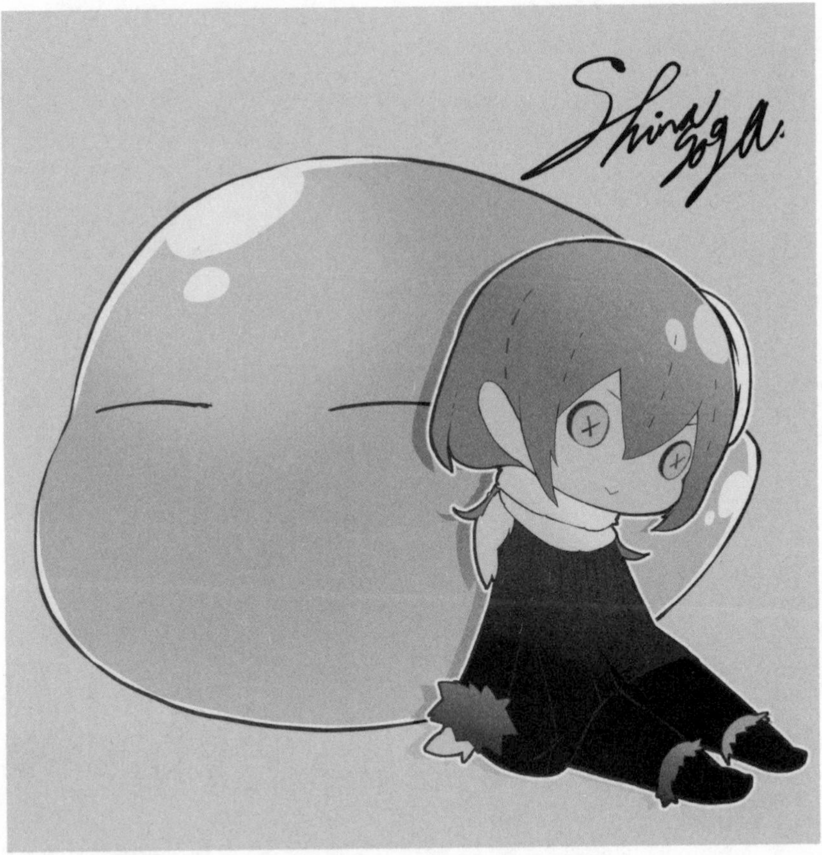
Shina Soga.

Shina Soga-sensei (@shinasoga)

Artist of *Old Testament Märchen* in *Monthly Shonen Sirius*

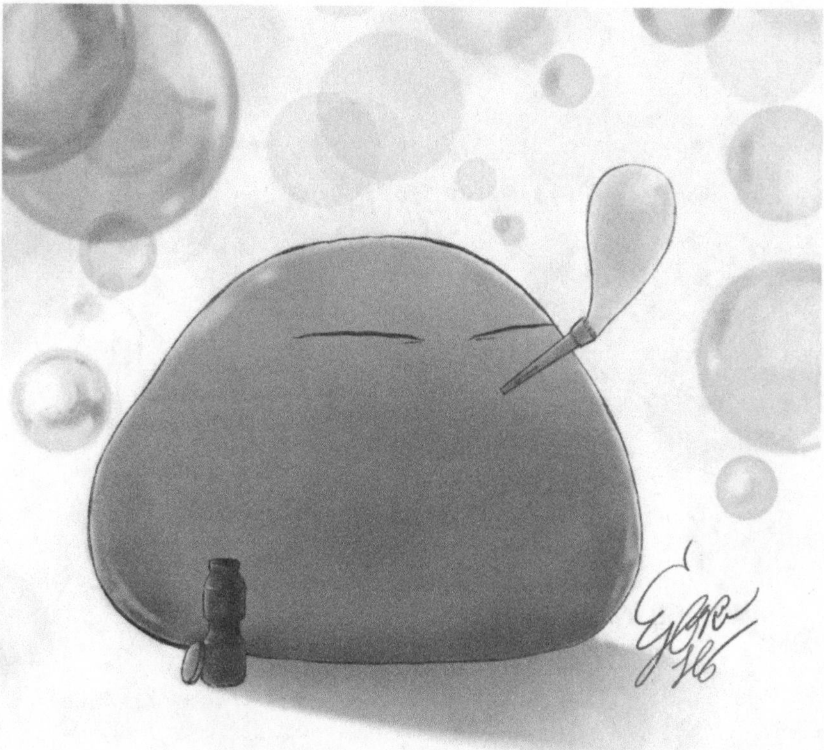

Takuto Igano-sensei (@iganotakuto)

Artist of *Student President Undoes It All on the Bed* in Nico Nico Seiga's *Sirius Wednesday*

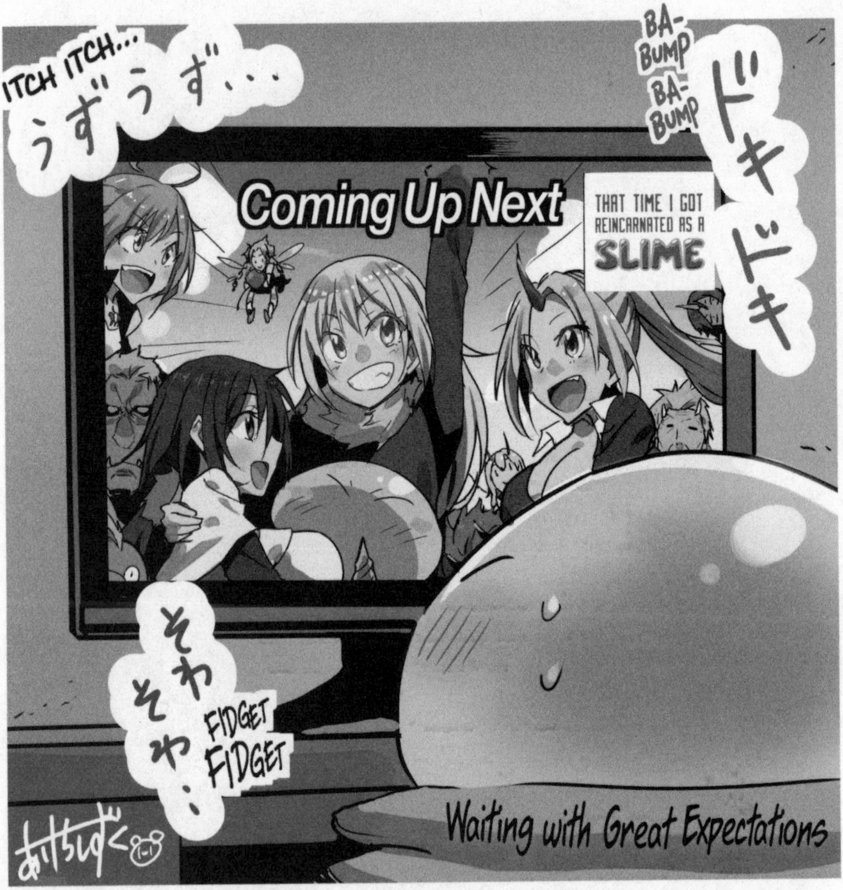
BA-BUMP BA-BUMP
ドキドキ
ITCH ITCH...
うずうず…
Coming Up Next
THAT TIME I GOT REINCARNATED AS A SLIME
そわそわ、
FIDGET FIDGET
Waiting with Great Expectations
ありちしずく

Shizuku Akechi-sensei (@sizuku0701)

Artist of *That Time I Got Reincarnated Again as a Wage Slave* in *Monthly Shonen Sirius* and *Nico Nico Seiga's Wednesday Sirius*

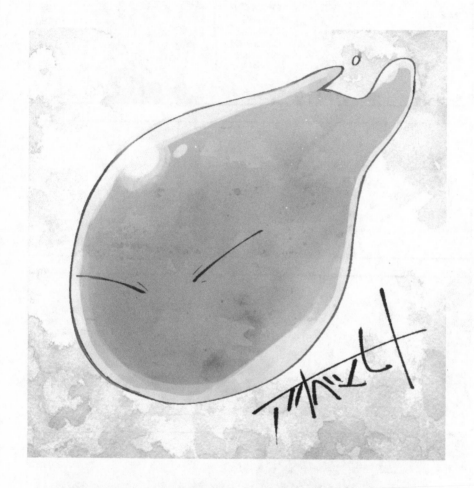

Mahito Aobe-sensei (@aobmht)

Artist of *Akushitsu no Morpho* in *Palcy*

Fate of the Backstagers

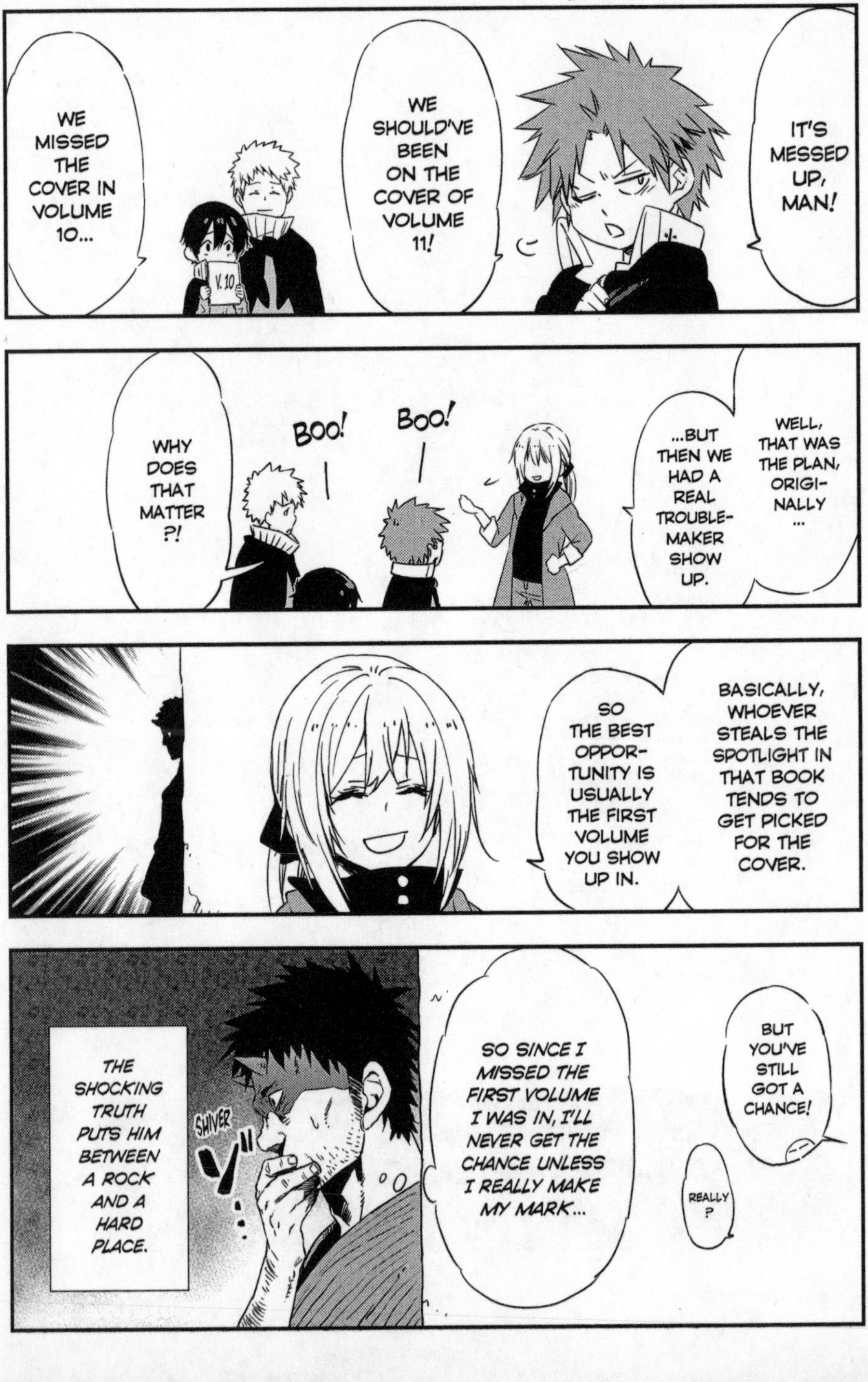
IT'S MESSED UP, MAN!
WE SHOULD'VE BEEN ON THE COVER OF VOLUME 11!
WE MISSED THE COVER IN VOLUME 10...
V. 10
WELL, THAT WAS THE PLAN, ORIGINALLY ...
...BUT THEN WE HAD A REAL TROUBLE-MAKER SHOW UP.
BOO!
BOO!
WHY DOES THAT MATTER?!
BASICALLY, WHOEVER STEALS THE SPOTLIGHT IN THAT BOOK TENDS TO GET PICKED FOR THE COVER.
SO THE BEST OPPORTUNITY IS USUALLY THE FIRST VOLUME YOU SHOW UP IN.
BUT YOU'VE STILL GOT A CHANCE!
REALLY?
SO SINCE I MISSED THE FIRST VOLUME I WAS IN, I'LL NEVER GET THE CHANCE UNLESS I REALLY MAKE MY MARK...
SHIVER
THE SHOCKING TRUTH PUTS HIM BETWEEN A ROCK AND A HARD PLACE.

Slimecakes

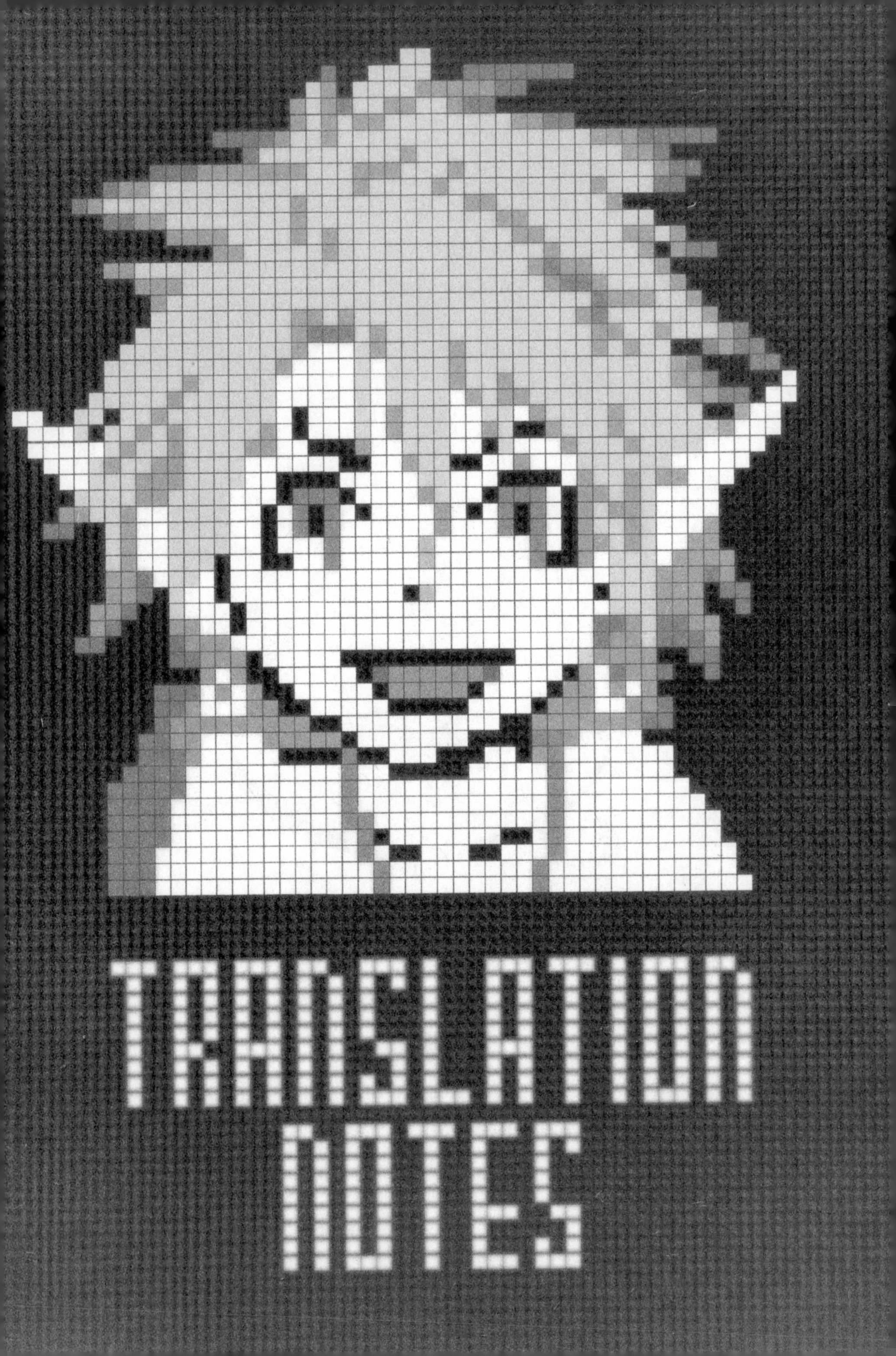

TRANSLATION NOTES

UNDER CHIN

page 53

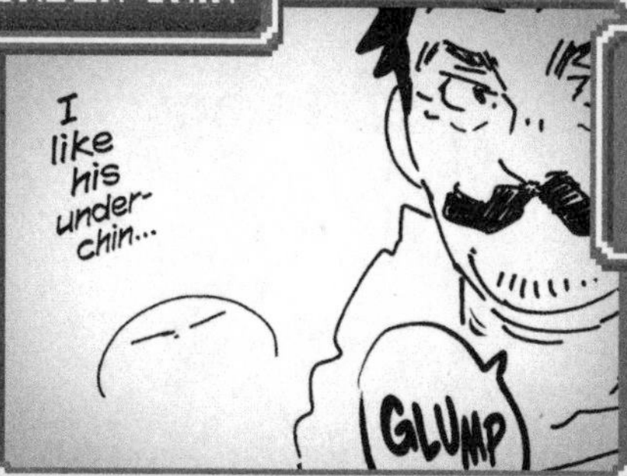
I like his under-chin...
GLUMP

An oblique reference to Coach Anzai from the basketball manga/anime *Slam Dunk*. The main character Sakuragi often enjoys paddling the portly coach's soft under-chin flesh because of the way it hangs down.

MOMOTARO

page 186

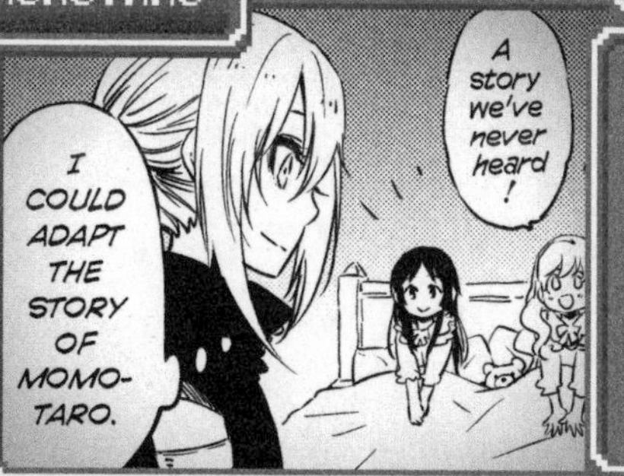
A story we've never heard!
I COULD ADAPT THE STORY OF MOMO-TARO.

A classic Japanese fairy tale about a boy born from a giant peach. Momotaro was found by an elderly couple who gave him millet dumplings to take on his quest to vanquish a band of oni (Japanese ogres). He recruits a dog, pheasant, and monkey by feeding them the dumplings, and his little army goes to the oni island (Onigashima) and defeats the evil oni. As the ogres/kijin from this manga are largely themed after oni, Rimuru has a hard time imagining his humble hero actually winning the battle.

◄ KAMOME ►
SHIRAHAMA

Witch Hat Atelier

A magical manga
adventure for
fans of Disney
and Studio
Ghibli!

Witch Hat Atelier © Kamome Shirahama/Kodansha Ltd.

The magical adventure that took Japan by storm is finally here, from acclaimed DC and Marvel cover artist Kamome Shirahama!

In a world where everyone takes wonders like magic spells and dragons for granted, Coco is a girl with a simple dream: She wants to be a witch. But everybody knows magicians are born, not made, and Coco was not born with a gift for magic. Resigned to her un-magical life, Coco is about to give up on her dream to become a witch…until the day she meets Qifrey, a mysterious, traveling magician. After secretly seeing Qifrey perform magic in a way she's never seen before, Coco soon learns what everybody "knows" might not be the truth, and discovers that her magical dream may not be as far away as it may seem…

KC
KODANSHA
COMICS

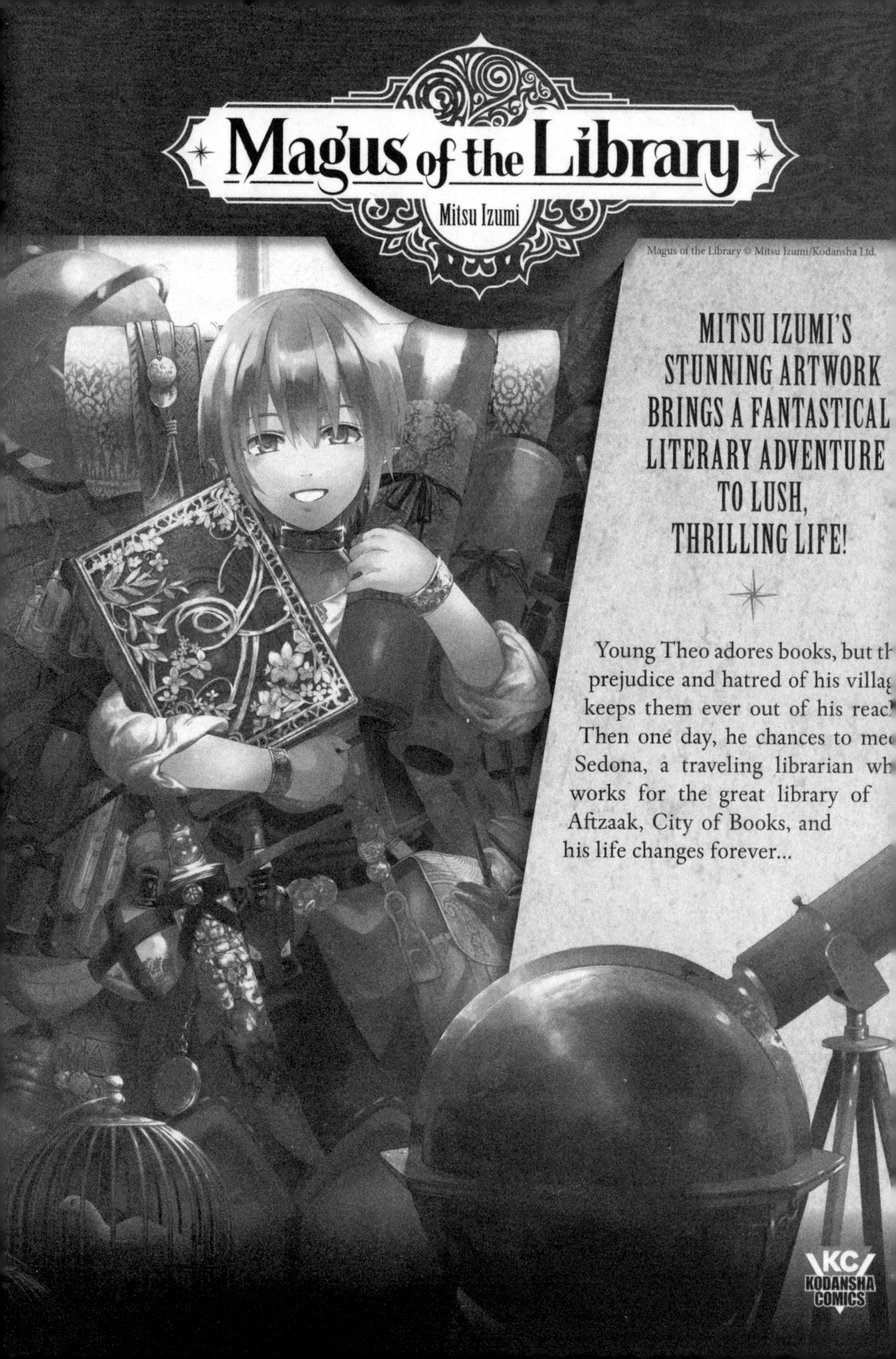

Magus of the Library
Mitsu Izumi
Magus of the Library © Mitsu Izumi/Kodansha Ltd.
MITSU IZUMI'S STUNNING ARTWORK BRINGS A FANTASTICAL LITERARY ADVENTURE TO LUSH, THRILLING LIFE!
Young Theo adores books, but th prejudice and hatred of his villag keeps them ever out of his reac Then one day, he chances to me Sedona, a traveling librarian wh works for the great library of Aftzaak, City of Books, and his life changes forever...
KC
KODANSHA COMICS

KC
KODANSHA COMICS

The award-winning manga about what happens inside you!

"Far more entertaining than it ought to be... what kid doesn't want to think that every time they sneeze a torpedo shoots out their nose?"
–Anime News Network

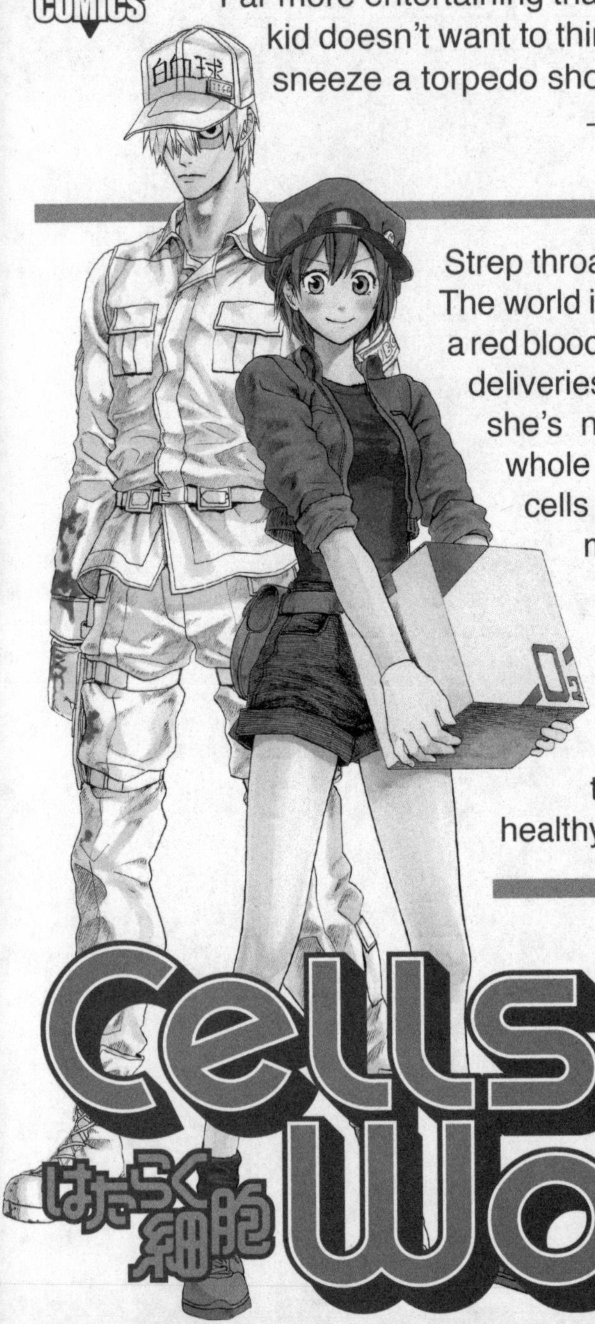

Strep throat! Hay fever! Influenza! The world is a dangerous place for a red blood cell just trying to get her deliveries finished. Fortunately, she's not alone...she's got a whole human body's worth of cells ready to help out! The mysterious white blood cells, the buff and brash killer T cells, even the cute little platelets—everyone's got to come together if they want to keep you healthy!

Cells at Work!

はたらく細胞

By Akane Shimizu

The Black Museum — The Ghost and the Lady

By Kazuhiro Fujita

Deep in Scotland Yard in London sits an evidence room dedicated to the greatest mysteries of British history. In this "Black Museum" sits a misshapen hunk of lead—two bullets fused together—the key to a wartime encounter between Florence Nightingale, the mother of modern nursing, and a supernatural Man in Grey. This story is unknown to most scholars of history, but a special guest of the museum will tell the tale of The Ghost and the Lady...

Praise for Kazuhiro Fujita's *Ushio and Tora*

"A charming revival that combines a classic look with modern depth and pacing... **Essential viewing both for curmudgeons and new fans alike.**" — Anime News Network

"**GREAT!** The first episode of Ushio and Tora captures the essence of '90s anime." — IGN

H·A·P·P·I·N·E·S·S

—ハピネス—

By **Shuzo Oshimi**

From the creator of *The Flowers of Evil*

Nothing interesting is happening in Makoto Ozaki's first year of high school. His life is a series of quiet humiliations: low-grade bullies, unreliable friends, and the constant frustration of his adolescent lust. But one night, a pale, thin girl knocks him to the ground in an alley and offers him a choice. Now everything is different. Daylight is searingly bright. Food tastes awful. And worse than anything is the terrible, consuming thirst...

Praise for Shuzo Oshimi's *The Flowers of Evil*

"A shockingly readable story that vividly—one might even say queasily—evokes the fear and confusion of discovering one's own sexuality. Recommended." —The Manga Critic

"A page-turning tale of sordid middle school blackmail." —Otaku USA Magazine

"A stunning new horror manga." —Third Eye Comics

KC KODANSHA COMICS

KC
KODANSHA
COMICS

Japan's most powerful spirit medium delves into the ghost world's greatest mysteries!

Story by Kyo Shirodaira, famed author of mystery fiction and creator of *Spiral*, *Blast of Tempest*, and *The Record of a Fallen Vampire*.

Both touched by spirits called yôkai, Kotoko and Kurô have gained unique superhuman powers. But to gain her powers Kotoko has given up an eye and a leg, and Kurô's personal life is in shambles. So when Kotoko suggests they team up to deal with renegades from the spirit world, Kurô doesn't have many other choices, but Kotoko might just have a few ulterior motives...

IN/SPECTRE

STORY BY KYO SHIRODAIRA
ART BY CHASHIBA KATASE

That Time I Got Reincarnated as a Slime volume 11 is a work of fiction. Names, characters, places, and incidents are the products of the author's imagination or are used fictitiously. Any resemblance to actual events, locales, or persons, living or dead, is entirely coincidental.

A Kodansha Comics Trade Paperback Original.

Published in the United States by Kodansha Comics,
an imprint of Kodansha USA Publishing, LLC, New York.

Publication rights for this English edition arranged through Kodansha Ltd., Tokyo.

First published in Japan in 2019 by Kodansha Ltd., Tokyo, as *Tensei Shitara Suraimu Datta Ken* volume 11.

ISBN 978-1-63236-749-5

Printed in the United States of America.

www.kodansha.us

9 8 7 6 5 4

Translation: Stephen Paul
Lettering: Evan Hayden
Editing: Ajani Oloye
Kodansha Comics edition cover design: Phil Balsman